God in the Classroom

God in the Classroom

Religion and America's
Public Schools

R. MURRAY THOMAS

Rowman & Littlefield Education
Lanham • New York • Toronto • Plymouth, UK
2008

Published in the United States of America
by Rowman & Littlefield Education
A Division of Rowman & Littlefield Publishers, Inc.
A wholly owned subsidiary of The Rowman & Littlefield Publishing Group, Inc.
4501 Forbes Boulevard, Suite 200, Lanham, Maryland 20706
www.rowmaneducation.com

Estover Road
Plymouth PL6 7PY
United Kingdom

British Library Cataloguing in Publication Information Available

Library of Congress Cataloging-in-Publication Data

Thomas, R. Murray (Robert Murray), 1921–
    God in the classroom : religion and America's public schools / by R. Murray Thomas.
        p. cm.
    Includes bibliographical references and index.
    1. Religion in the public schools—Law and legislation—United States. 2. Religion in the public schools—United States. I. Title.
    KF4162.T44   2007
    344.73'0796—dc22   2006028573

    ISBN-13: 978-0-275-99141-8 (cloth : alk. paper)
    ISBN-10: 0-275-99141-5 (cloth : alk. paper)
    ISBN-13: 978-1-57886-699-1 (pbk. : alk. paper)
    ISBN-10: 1-57886-699-5 (pbk. : alk. paper)

Contents

Chapter 1

Introduction: ~~As Seen from Here~~

The expression "as seen from here" refers to the intellectual vantage point from which religion-in-schools controversies are viewed. Throughout this book, that vantage point features four components:

- *The state*, a term meaning governments—federal, provincial, local (county, city, village).
- *The church,* meaning religious denominations.
- *Secularists* or *the concerned secular public*, meaning individuals who are neither (a) government employees, such as legislators, judges, school principals, teachers, nor (b) highly dedicated adherents of a religious body, such as ministers, priests, rabbis, imams, or doctrinaire parishioners. Instead, the secular public consists of nonreligious individuals and of ones who identify themselves with a religious faith—at least nominally—but assign secular considerations a higher priority than religious doctrine. Such people are called *concerned* because they are particularly interested in keeping public schools free of religious influence.
- *Public schools,* meaning institutions governed by publicly elected school boards and funded by tax moneys.

Thus, the book's interpretation of religion/school episodes focuses on the interaction of those four—on how they affect each other in determining the way state/church controversies develop and are resolved. The purpose of this opening chapter is to explain the nature of that interpretive scheme as preparation for its application in Chapters 3 through 11.

However, before the scheme is described, readers may find it useful to learn what kinds of school/religion confrontations are discussed in subsequent chapters. Therefore, the present chapter's detailed description of an "as-seen-from-here" viewpoint is preceded by a selection of episodes illustrating the types of issues that confront Americans with religion-in-schools dilemmas.

ILLUSTRATIVE CONFLICTS OVER RELIGION IN SCHOOLS

Chapter 2, which sketches historical roots of America's present-day dilemmas, is followed by nine chapters, each dedicated to the analysis of one sort of religion-in-schools issue. In the following paragraphs, the nature of each chapter's central issue is suggested by one or two sample episodes that involved the issue.

But first, as a foundation for understanding the significance of the episodes, it is important for readers to recognize the religion-in-schools implications of a passage from the first amendment to the U.S. Constitution that states:

Congress shall make no law respecting an establishment of religion.

Ever since that provision was added to the Constitution in 1791, jurists have generally interpreted it to mean that religion should be strictly separated from federal and local governments. And because schools supported by tax funds are considered a branch of local government, efforts have been made to exclude religious doctrine from public schools. However, over the decades, the propriety of such exclusion has been a matter of continual strife and debate.

Now to the illustrative episodes.

God and Darwin—Chapter 3

Charles Darwin's book *The Origin of Species*, published in 1859, proposed that humans were not originally created in their present-day form but, rather, they evolved over many thousands of years from simpler versions of animal life. Darwin's theory thus conflicted with the biblical account of human origins found in the opening book of the Jewish Torah and Christian Old Testament where an all-powerful being, called *Yaweh, Jehovah,* or *God,* created the first man (Adam) and first woman (Eve) in the same form as that of modern-day men and women. Since Darwin's day, his theory of evolution has become the accepted foundation of most biological sciences and has thus been taught in most schools' science classes. However, in recent years, proponents of the biblical story of creation have demanded that the Bible version—or a more recent variant called *intelligent design*—be substituted for, or taught along with, Darwinian theory. The U.S. scientific community has, in the main, objected to such proposals, contending that biblical creationism is not science but, instead, is a religious belief and thus should not be included in science programs.

An Episode

The governing board of the 3,500-student school district in Dover, Pennsylvania, passed a resolution ordering science teachers to identify the intelligent-design version of creationism as a reasonable alternative to Darwinian theory. The board's policy required that a statement be read to biology students asserting that evolution theory "is not a fact" so that students should "keep an open mind" and consider explanations of human beginnings other than Darwin's. Students were also urged to read a book that promoted intelligent design—*Of Pandas and People*. However, a group of parents filed a lawsuit charging that the board's action violated the U.S. Constitution's separation of church and state. Some of the board's critics suggested that intelligent-design theory should not be discussed in science classes but, rather, it could be treated as a religious concept in humanities courses (Dao, 2005).

The Issue

Should a version of creationism be taught in science classes—instead of, or along with, Darwinian theory?

Curricula and Text Materials—Chapter 4

The term *curriculum,* as intended in this book, refers to what students are expected to study. A school's curriculum is typically in the form of a publication specifying what instructors are to teach and, frequently, what methods to use. Often a curriculum is organized around teaching materials, such as a textbook, a series of pamphlets, videos, Internet sources, and the like. Controversies can arise whenever school personnel or members of the general public disagree about a curriculum's religious content or instructional methods.

An Episode

In 1997, the board of education in Lee County, Florida, authorized the establishment of a two-semester Bible-history course organized around an "Old Testament" curriculum developed by a local committee and a "New Testament" curriculum created by the National Council on Bible Curriculum in Public Schools (NCBCPS). The intent of the National Council, as expressed by its president in a 1995 radio interview, was "to expose kids to the biblical Christian worldview" (People for the American Way, 1998).

A group of Lee County parents filed a lawsuit to block the course offering, alleging that in its proposed form it would violate the U.S. Constitution's ban against advancing religion in public school classrooms. The court, in response to the suit, issued an injunction that prohibited the use of the "New Testament" curriculum and allowed the "Old Testament" curriculum to be taught only under strict monitoring. Following the court's ruling, the school board agreed to settle the case by withdrawing both the "Old Testament" and "New Testament" curricula, replacing them with a nonsectarian course based on a textbook titled *An Introduction to the Bible* (People for the American Way, 1998).

The Issue

Should students in public schools study about religion? If so, what should be the aim and content of that study?

Prayer and Scripture Reading—Chapter 5

Prayers are efforts to communicate with personages who dwell in an invisible spirit world—such personages as a supreme being, various gods, or shades of dead ancestors. The intent of prayer is typically to solicit the aid of the invisible spirits, to honor them, or to thank them for blessings they have conferred. Another ceremony intended to accomplish the same aims as prayer is scripture reading—reciting passages of a holy book in front of a classroom or assembly audience.

An Episode

As the result of a lawsuit brought by parents against the New Hyde Park (New York) school board, the U.S. Supreme Court in 1962 addressed the issue of prayer in public schools. In the lawsuit, parents objected to the New York State Board of Regents' regulation that required all public school students to begin each school day by reciting the following prayer:

Almighty God, we acknowledge our dependence upon Thee, and we beg Thy blessings upon us, our parents, our teachers, and our Country. (Robinson, 2002a)

Whereas two lower courts had declared the prayer permissible, the Supreme Court found in favor of the complaining parents, ruling that the "daily classroom invocation of God's blessings as prescribed in the Regents' prayer is a religious activity" and therefore violated the U.S. Constitution's separation of church and state. Public schools, as government agencies, "cannot compose official prayers for any group of the American people to recite as a part of a religious program carried on by government" (Robinson, 2002a,b).

The case represented the first important step toward ending a centuries-old public-school tradition—morning prayer and the reading of Bible passages.

The Issue

Can prayer and scripture reading legally be conducted in public schools? If so, under what conditions?

Holidays and Celebrations—Chapter 6

In modern times the meaning of a *holiday* has been extended beyond its original religious meaning of *holy day*. A holiday now is any period of time that students are permitted to be out of school and that workers are officially freed from their job responsibilities. Some of the most honored American holidays still represent key Christian beliefs and as such have become the subject of controversy.

An Episode

By mid-2005, Muslim parents in Baltimore County, Maryland, had lobbied for more than a year to get schools closed for two of the more important Islamic holidays: (a) Eid al-Fitr, which signals the close of the annual Ramadan month of fasting, and (b) Eid al-Adha, which celebrates, in Jewish–Christian–Muslim tradition, God's allowing Abraham to sacrifice a sheep instead of Abraham's son. The Muslims asked the school board why schools should not be closed on those two occasions, just as schools were traditionally closed for the Jewish Yom Kippur and the Christian Christmas (Muslim holidays, 2005).

The Issue

Should public schools close for religious holidays? If so, which religions' holidays should be so honored?

Financial Support—Chapter 7

In many nations—such as Britain, Indonesia, Italy, Saudi Arabia, and Sweden—public tax funds are used to support schools sponsored by religious orders or to pay for services that religious groups offer to public schools. However, in America the separation of church and state, as implied in the Constitution, has resulted in religious organizations being denied tax funds to finance their activities.

An Episode

For ten years, a nationwide Christian sex-education program known as the Silver Ring Thing was conducted to convince teenagers that they should abstain from sexual intercourse until after they were married. Thousands of youths who participated in the organization's training meetings were not only urged to forego premarital sex, but were also asked to buy silver rings to wear as symbols of their abstinence vow. However, in 2005 the American Civil Liberties Union (ACLU) in Pennsylvania filed a lawsuit against the U.S. Department of Human Health and Services, arguing that the department's contribution of more than 1 million dollars to the Silver Ring Thing violated the nation's constitutional separation of church and state. The ACLU offered evidence in support of the suit, including a Silver Ring Thing newsletter telling young people that "a personal relationship with Jesus Christ [is] the best way to live a sexually pure life" (Saltzman, 2005).

The Issue

Should any public funds be used to support religious groups' educational activities? If so, under what conditions?

The Pledge of Allegiance—Chapter 8

Traditionally, students in American public schools have been obligated on ceremonial occasions to recite a pledge of allegiance to the nation's flag and government. Over the past half century that oath has read:

I pledge allegiance to the flag of the United States of America and to the republic for which it stands: one nation under God, indivisible, with liberty and justice for all.

An Episode

In 2001, the father of a girl who attended a California public school objected to the word *God* in the pledge and filed a lawsuit to have *God* removed. The father charged that the notion of a supreme being—*God*—was a belief from a part.....
religious persuasion and therefore violated the U.S. Constitution's requi....
that religious beliefs and practices be excluded from government institu....,
including public schools (Greenhouse, 2004).

The Issue

Should the word *God* be eliminated from the pledge?

Released Time and Clubs—Chapter 9

American schools may provide time during the school day when pupils are released for religious instruction away from the campus. In addition, many schools make facilities available for meetings of extracurricular clubs in such fields as photography, chess, debating, leadership, international relations, mountain biking, skiing, and far more. Religious groups have often sought permission to use those facilities for faith-based clubs that promote the groups' belief systems. However, advocates of the separation of church and state have opposed such attempts.

An Episode

In 2001, a religious organization called the Child Evangelism Fellowship's Good News Clubs was the plaintiff in a 2001 Supreme Court case filed against a public school in New York State that had denied the group's application to include a Good News Club among the school's extracurricular offerings. The Supreme Court found in favor of the Child Evangelism plaintiffs on the grounds that their group deserved the same opportunity as that accorded other organizations, which were permitted to use the school building for after-school meetings. Over the three years following the court case, Child Evangelism quintupled its presence in public schools to 2,330 clubs (Vaznis, 2005).

The Issue

Should clubs advocating a particular religion be permitted in American public schools?

Symbols and Maxims—Chapter 10

Each religious tradition includes sacred symbols in the form of visual or auditory representations of the faith. Examples of visual symbols are the various Christian crosses, the Judaic six-pointed star and menorah, Islam's crescent moon and star, Sikhism's dagger, and the Hindu spot on the forehead. Visual symbols also include flags and banners of distinctive design and color. Auditory symbols can be the tolling of Christian church bells, Judaic chanting at the wall in Jerusalem, an Islamic call to prayer from a minaret, and Hindus' singing the Saraswati Vandana, hymn of praise to the goddess of learning and wisdom.

Religious maxims are sayings, adages, or proverbs that express significant beliefs of a religious sect.

An Episode

The most frequently cited Jewish and Christian guide to proper human behavior is the set of Ten Commandments (the Decalogue) in Chapter 20 of the book of Exodus in the Jewish Torah and Christian Old Testament. Those ten rules include three ways people should act and seven ways they should not act. Thus, people should (1) worship only the one true God, (2) respect one's parents, and (3) respect the Sabbath day by not working. People should not (4) use God's name in an insulting fashion, (5) worship idols, (6) kill, (7) steal, (8) commit adultery, (9) tell lies about others, or (10) yearn for anyone else's property or spouse.

An Episode

In 1980, the U.S. Supreme Court outlawed a Kentucky statute, which required that the Ten Commandments be posted in public-school classrooms. The Court ruled that the Commandments "are undeniably a sacred text" and "do not confine themselves to arguably secular matters, such as honoring one's parents, killing, or murder." Therefore, the posting would violate the constitutional tradition of keeping religious teachings out of public schools (Kentucky school district, 1999).

In 1999, officials of a school district in rural Jackson County, Kentucky, allowed volunteers to display the Ten Commandments in the district's five schools. The high-school principal described the posting as "an effort to start having good morals in school and making children aware of how they should act because of all the violent issues that have been showing up." But a spokesman for the Kentucky School Boards Association said his group urged districts to abide by the Supreme Court ruling and not display sectarian religious symbols, particularly because a lawsuit could cost the school district badly needed funds (Kentucky school district, 1999).

The Issue

Should the display of symbols or beliefs of a particular religion be permitted in schools? If so, under what conditions?

Sexual Matters—Chapter 11

Religious denominations usually subscribe to particular convictions about sexual behavior, including what sorts of sexual acts are permissible, what kinds of sex partners are proper (age, gender, ethnicity), what marital/nonmarital relationship between sex partners is suitable (premarriage, marriage, open marriage), where different sorts of sexual behavior can be properly pursued, and who should be responsible for instructing youths about sex and for monitoring their sexual behavior. With the passing decades, responsibility for sex education has increasingly been transferred from the family and the church to public schools. However, debate continues over the propriety of assigning such responsibility to the schools and over who should do the teaching, when, and how.

Episodes

In 1996 the U.S. Congress, at the urging of religious groups, authorized funds for sex-education programs that taught abstinence as the only way to prevent pregnancy and sexually transmitted diseases. Instruction about other birth-control techniques would not be permitted. By 2005, approximately $135 million per year, totaling nearly $1 billion, had been spent by the federal government on programs whose purpose was to teach the benefits that might be gained by abstaining from sexual activity. Also in response to pressure from religious groups, the Texas Board of Education endorsed the statewide purchase of health-education textbooks that exclusively promoted abstinence. In a similar move, the school board in Franklin County, North Carolina, ordered three chapters removed from a ninth-grade health textbook because the content went beyond the discussion of abstinence-only. The deleted chapters addressed AIDS and other sexually transmitted infections, marriage, partnering, and contraception (Planned Parenthood, 2005).

Health professionals critical of abstinence-only programs included members of the American Academy of Pediatrics who argued that teenagers need access to knowledge about birth-control and emergency-contraception methods besides abstinence (Tanner, 2005).

The Issue

Should schools' sex-education programs advocate sexual practices and beliefs that represent a religious group's views about sexual matters?

With the foregoing episodes in mind, we next describe the scheme used throughout this book for interpreting controversial relationships among schools, religion, and the state. The description begins with the three main components of the model, and then continues with the roles of belief constituencies, traditions, and critical events.

STATE, RELIGION, SECULAR PUBLIC, AND SCHOOLS

The contents of Chapters 3 through 11 focus on interactions among four sorts of institutions—the state, the church, the secular public, and public schools.

The State

In the context of this book, the expressions *the state* and *the government* are synonyms referring to the organization that holds the authority (official power) to control the behavior of the inhabitants of a defined territory. In such a sense, *the state* can be as large as an immense empire (the Roman Empire, the Chinese Empire, and the British Empire) or as small as a tiny village. The matters that fall within the state's authority are either specified in written documents (edicts, constitutions, laws, regulations) or passed from one generation to the next as unwritten customs. Throughout this book, *the state* means either the U.S. government, the fifty state governments, or a local government—city, county, town, and village. Public schools are *state* institutions.

Religions as Belief Systems (Churches)

A *belief system* or *worldview* is a collection of convictions a person uses for interpreting life's events. Such a system typically concerns matters of

The purpose of life (teleology);

The nature of existence and reality (ontology);

The nature of knowledge and how to distinguish fact from fantasy, truth from falsehood (epistemology);

The origin of the world and of life forms (cosmology);

Why things happen as they do (causality);

Rules governing people's treatment of other beings and the physical environment (morality, ethics); and

People's rights and obligations (privileges, responsibilities).

The word *church* is often used to identify an organized religious effort. For the purposes of this book, belief systems can be divided into two general types, *religious* and *secular.*

A religious system (a religion) typically includes faith in the reality of (a) invisible spirits (gods, angels, genies, ancestral shades, jinns, or the like) that influence events and affect people's destinies, (b) a continuation of spiritual life after physical death, and (c) rituals people can perform to influence the actions of spirits. Life in present-day America is definitely multireligious, distinguished by many varieties of Christianity, several forms of Judaism, at least two major versions of Islam, variations of Buddhism, Hinduism, Confucianism, Shinto, Voodoo, Wicca, Scientology, and far more.

Secular Belief Systems

Secular or nonreligious worldviews do not include a theology that recognizes such things as invisible spirits, life after death, and rituals intended to influence events. Five well-known nonreligious philosophical positions are *naturalism, materialism, humanism* (sometimes referred to as *secular humanism*), *agnosticism,* and *atheism.*

Naturalism is "the hypothesis that the physical universe is a 'closed system' in the sense that nothing that is neither a part nor a product of it can affect it. So naturalism entails the nonexistence of all supernatural beings, including the theistic God" (Draper, 2005).

In a similar vein, materialism asserts that there is only one substance in the universe and that substance is physical, empirical, or material. Everything that exists consists of matter and energy. Thus, the idea of spiritual substance is a delusion. There are no such things as supernatural, occult, or paranormal experiences or after-death existence. Those things are either delusions or can be explained in terms of physical forces.

Humanism proposes that people are responsible for fashioning their own destinies through their own efforts, limited only by their innate ability and the physical and social environments they inhabit. A typical humanist is convinced that people can lead fitting lives (a) without believing in God, in a soul that lives on after a person dies, or in the universe having been created by an intelligent being, and (b) believing that quite suitable lives and proper behavior can be based on reason, goodwill, and experience (Mason, 2004).

Agnostics believe that questions about invisible spirits or life after death are unanswerable—at least by any method presently available. In effect, agnostics say, "We just don't know." Atheists, on the other hand, reject outright the idea of invisible spirits and life after death, which are notions they regard as ridiculous.

Members of *a concerned secular public* are often people who subscribe to one of the nonreligious worldviews.

Schools as Sources of Education

The word *education* in these pages refers to intentional efforts to improve people's skills and knowledge. Such efforts can be made either by learners themselves (self-education) or by others (teachers, parents, ministers, mass-communication media) or by a combination of self and others. Schooling is one sort of education—the sort pursued is in a particular place (a school) with guides (teachers) who follow a prescribed set of goals and subject-matter (curricula, course of study). Schools can be public (state funded and controlled) or private (funded and controlled by nongovernmental groups or individuals). Private schools can be managed by either religious or secular sponsors.

The words *school* and *schools,* as used in this book, usually refer to public schools, ones financed by tax moneys and administered by a local government

Figure 1.1
Domain relationships in the United States.

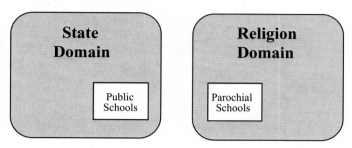

entity called a *school district.* Private schools—and especially ones conducted by religious orders—are mentioned only occasionally throughout the book.

With our definitions of *state*, *religion*, *secularists*, and *schools* now in mind, we next consider ways that interactions among the four can influence the place assigned to religion in public schools.

Patterns of Interactions

Although theoretically we can conceive of state, religion (the church), secularists, and schools as separate entities, in real life the four overlap and interact in ways that form diverse and often complex patterns. This point can be illustrated with the concepts of *domain*, *power*, and *authority.*

Domain

The term *domain* refers to the matters over which a state, religion, or school holds the right of decision. In the United States, the general relationship among state, religion, and school domains is portrayed in Figure 1.1. Schools fall in the two major domains of state and religion, with public schools located within the state's domain and parochial schools—those managed by religious orders—in religion's domain.

Frequently, religion/school controversies occur because one of the entities—state or church—has been accused of encroaching on, or lapping over, the other entity's domain. Such was the case in our earlier episode of the U.S. Federal Government furnishing public funds for the Silver Ring Thing program that limited sex education to a religious group's beliefs about acceptable sexual behavior. The funding in that instance produced a controversial overlap of state and religion domains (Figure 1.2).

A second example of the controversy about domain borderlines was the debate over including intelligent-design theory in public-school science classes. The conflict was not so much about whether intelligent-design should be taught at all in a public school (many evolutionists would accept the discussion of intelligent

Figure 1.2
Alleged domain encroachment—Silver Ring Thing.

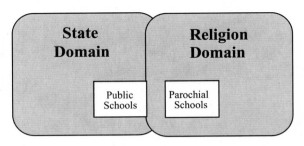

design in humanities or social-science classes) but, rather, about whether intelligent design qualified as science rather than as religious faith. Again, the conflict was about an alleged improper overlap of domains (Figure 1.3).

In summary, many religion/school controversies concern disputes over domains. Advocates of prayer in schools have argued that the government "has no business" telling students and teachers that they cannot communicate with God while on school property. Proponents of the Ten Commandments have charged the government with "overstepping its rights" in attempting to outlaw the long-existing practice of posting Judaic–Christian truths in schools as guides to moral virtue. Supporters of intelligent design have contended that the essence of scientific inquiry is free and open, non-prejudicial investigation, so that proposals about human beginnings, other than Darwin's, deserve a place in science classes.

Power and Authority

Power can be defined as the influence a person or group exerts over the beliefs and behavior of another person or group. If the presence of Group A changes the beliefs or actions of Group B in any way, then Group A has some measure of power over Group B. In confrontations between two groups, each group usually

Figure 1.3
Alleged encroachment by a religious theory.

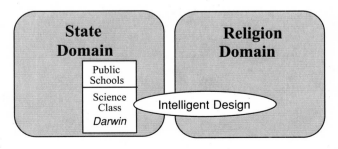

has some level of power, as shown by each one's behavior being affected by the presence of the opponent. The decision about which group "wins"—that is, which group's desires prevail—depends on which has the greater power. If the power ratio between the two is about equal, then they must negotiate a compromise if they want to avoid a stalemate.

Groups can vary in the tactics they employ to influence the outcome of a controversy. Such "power tools" include

- Publicity campaigns—Lauding a group's policies, revealing an opponent's faults.
- Facile arguments—Appealing to listeners' emotions, sense of fairness, and notions of convincing logic.
- Threats—Of bodily harm, of property damage, of unsavory rumors, of job demotion or job loss.
- Physical violence—Besting opponents by armed force, stealing, or destroying opponents' property.
- Bribery—Paying influential individuals or groups for their support.

Authority is the official power assigned to, or commanded by, an individual or group. There are various ways individuals or groups gain authority—by election to office, by appointment to office, by the violent ousting of existing authorities, by rules of succession, or by charismatic leadership. If authority is to serve as effective power, the members of the domain to which the authority applies must accept the authority as legitimate—or at least as power that prudent people would be wise to respect. The less the members of a group accept the titular authority, the less power those in authority have to influence the group's beliefs and behavior.

In estimating the role of authority in religion/school episodes, it is important to recognize that there can be different levels of authority, with the lower levels carrying less influence than the upper levels. This was illustrated in our earlier case of the New York State Regents' prayer in public schools. Three levels in the U.S. court system were involved in the case—a state court (with the least power), an appeals court (with more power), and the Supreme Court (with the most power). Both the district court and appeals court had ruled that the Regents' prayer did not violate the U.S. Constitution's separation of church and state. But the Supreme Court decided otherwise, so the prayer was outlawed.

Whenever people respect an authority and are thus willing to abide by its decisions, then authority serves as a very effective source of power. Hence, it usually is a considerable advantage for religion-in-school activists to hold office—and particularly high office—in state, religion, and school domains.

BELIEF CONSTITUENCIES

A *belief constituency* is a collection of people who subscribe to the same cluster of convictions. Controversies over religion-in-schools involve confrontations between two—or among several—belief constituencies. Thus, the task of understanding controversies profits from information about which constituencies are involved and about their beliefs, aims, membership, tactics, and sources of power.

By way of illustration, consider the constituencies involved in two of the cases described earlier: (a) Muslims asking the Baltimore school board to close the city's public schools in honor of two Islamic holidays and (b) Jackson County, Kentucky, school officials allowing volunteers in 1999 to post copies of the biblical Ten Commandments in the district's five public schools.

The two most obvious activists in the Baltimore episode were (a) a collection of the city's Muslims and (b) the public schools' board members. Additional constituencies that might engage in the debate through letters to newspapers and appeals to board members were (c) Christians who wished to limit religious holidays to the traditional ones, (d) secularists who would do away with any religious school holidays, and (e) members of other religions (Hindus, Buddhists, Scientologists) who would like to have their own holy days recognized by the closing of schools.

In the Ten-Commandments confrontation, the immediately involved constituencies included (a) the Christian group that had posted the commandments, (b) the school officials who had endorsed the posting, (c) the secularists who had filed a lawsuit to have the copies of the Decalogue removed, (d) the U.S. Supreme Court, which in 1980 had declared that the Kentucky statute requiring the posting of the commandments was unconstitutional, and (e) the Kentucky School Boards Association, which advised schools to abide by the court decision. Other constituents that might have participated in the controversy included (f) Christians and Jews who believed that the Decalogue was a universally valid guide to human behavior.

TRADITIONS AND CRITICAL EVENTS

Traditions are beliefs and practices so well established in a society that they not only become what people view as "the way things are" but frequently as "the way things should be." Members of a society who are referred to as *conservatives* are ones who seek to maintain traditions in the face of threats to the usual way things have been done.

Critical events are happenings that either alter traditions or serve to protect traditions from serious threats. Such events serve as decision junctures that can change the direction of affairs. Critical events are accompanied by conflicts between members of society who deem themselves *progressives*, willing to pursue the new tack that an event initiates, and other members who consider themselves *conservatives* attempting to protect the status quo.

Each of the controversies in our earlier description of religion/school episodes involved a conflict between a tradition and a critical event. The event that challenged the public schools' time-honored morning prayer and Bible readings was a secularist lawsuit questioning the constitutionality of the practice. In Dover, Pennsylvania, the school board's requiring that intelligent design be accorded attention in science classes was an event challenging the traditional status of Darwinian theory as the sole version of human beginnings that students studied. A California father's lawsuit was the event that brought into question the word *God* that had been inserted by Congress into the pledge of allegiance in 1954, an addition which at that time was a critical event altering the form of a pledge that traditionally had been free of any religious allusions.

CONCLUSION

The vantage point from which this book analyzes controversies about religion in American schools is provided by a scheme that focuses on interactions among four entities—the state, religion (the church), secularists, and schools. Aspects of those interactions that are accorded special attention are the entities' domains, the power of the entities' constituencies, societal traditions, and critical events.

From Then to Now

This chapter starts with a truism: *Nothing in our world arises entirely anew. Anything that seems new is just a novel variant of what already existed.* In other words, every innovation grows from historical roots. Thus, the task of understanding the how and why of today's patterns of religion in U.S. public schools can be aided by a review of several trends in American history. The purpose of this chapter is to offer such a review.

The chapter is divided into two major parts. Part one, titled "A Background Sketch," offers a four-century glance back at relationships among religion, state, and schooling from colonial times until the present day—relationships that help explain the origins of current controversies over religion in public schools.

Part two, titled "Trends of the Times," takes the form of an argument in support of four propositions, which assert that over the past four centuries:

- Religions in the United States became more *diverse.*
- Religious beliefs and practices were increasingly *removed from public schools.*
- The teaching/learning process grew more *institutionalized.*
- Sources of knowledge became more *secular* and *empirical.*

A BACKGROUND SKETCH

The following discussion is presented as a succession of eras entitled Colonial Times, The New Nation, The Evolving Nation, and The Present Era.

Colonial Times, 1600–1775

Exactly when and how human inhabitants first appeared in the Americas is a mystery not yet solved to everyone's satisfaction. Paleontologists, anthropologists, and linguists who study those matters continue to disagree. Most of them suggest that the western hemisphere's initial arrivals came from East Asia, traveling across the Bering Strait in the far-north Pacific when that region was a frozen land mass rather than a string of islands as it is today. However, the experts still argue about when the newcomers came, their mode of travel, and the routes they followed to populate the entire western hemisphere, from far-north Canada to the southern tip of South America.

During the opening decade of the twenty-first century, recent geological and genetic findings, along with their diverse interpretations, confronted scientists with an abundance of puzzles to ponder. Did the initial occupants of the Americas appear 10,000 years ago, as many scholars had thought, or did the first ones arrive even 10,000 or 20,000 years earlier? Had those travelers walked all the way from Northeast Asia to what is now Alaska and Northern Canada, then trudged south through valleys on the eastern side of the coastal mountains to eventually— after many millennia—disperse across North America, into Central America, and throughout South America? Or, instead of coming by land, had the migrants fashioned boats of stretched animal skins to sail along the coast of the Bering Sea and down the western shores of North America? Or might some have come by land and others by sea? And did the Asian travelers arrive during only a few time periods or were there many migrations? (Mann, 2005)

Although such matters are still unsettled, there is no question that millions of Native Americans occupied all parts of the western hemisphere and, in North America, spoke more than 250 languages by the time Europeans began colonizing eastern sectors of the continent. All Spanish attempts between 1513 and 1560 to establish a colony in Florida failed, so the successful efforts of Europeans to settle in North America came with the founding of the British colonies of Jamestown (Virginia) in 1607 and Plymouth (Massachusetts) in 1620. By 1770, a century-and-a-half later, more than 2 million people of European heritage lived in Great Britain's thirteen North American colonies.

Apparently most settlers came to America with two motives—one secular and the other religious. The secular motive was to earn a good living—to "get ahead in the world." The religious mission was not only to perpetuate Christianity among the colonists' own descendents but also to bring heathens into the Christian fold. In effect, religious leaders and much of the populace sought to obey Jesus' biblical command to "Go ye into all the world and preach the gospel to every creature" (St. Mark 16:15, 1611).[1] American Indians were seen as heathens. Then what was the nature of the colonists' missionary task? An answer can be suggested by our comparing the Christian belief system with Indian religions that were practiced at the time the colonists arrived.

Religions' Likenesses and Differences

All of the hundreds of Indian nations and tribes that were distributed throughout the Americas embraced religious convictions and practices that played a vital role in daily life. Even though each religion had certain unique characteristics, all of them had basic structural features in common. Those features were also typical of the Christian worldviews to which the colonists subscribed. In effect, Indians and colonists alike were convinced that

- Reality—in the sense of what actually exists—is not limited to what everyone who has intact sense organs can see, hear, or feel in this world. Reality also includes invisible beings, places, and events that are revealed only to special individuals and, perhaps, only when those individuals are in an altered state of mind.
- Invisible spirits, gods, or deities that created the universe continue to influence natural phenomena (crop yields, epidemics, floods, earthquakes) and affect individuals' lives (health, personal relationships, and occupational success).
- People must abide by the spirits' rules of conduct or else suffer unpleasant consequences. Not only is it important to know and obey the rules, but people are also wise to show that they honor and respect the spirits.
- When a personal or general disaster strikes, it is necessary to placate the spirits that have caused the catastrophe. Methods of mollifying the spirits include admitting one's wrongdoing, asking to be forgiven, performing acts of penance, promising to reform, and presenting offerings to the spirits.
- One's lifespan does not end with the death of the body. Rather, an essence of the individual's personality—often called the *soul*—can continue to exist in some form, perhaps as an invisible spirit.

Therefore, conflicts between religions were not over the existence of such structural features but, rather, were over the particular form the structural features assumed in different faiths.[2] This point can be illustrated with examples of (a) spirits' or gods' identities, (b) the creation of the universe and its inhabitants, (c) causality, (d) prayer and ceremonies, and (e) the human lifespan.

Spirits' and gods' identities. Each religion, Christian and Indian alike, had spirits that bore distinctive names, powers, and functions.

In the Christians' monotheistic system, the spirits were headed by a single all-knowing, all-powerful being called God, Jehovah, or Our Lord (Yaweh for Jews, Allah for Muslims). Christian doctrine held that God was represented as a trinity—three spirits in one: God the Father, Jesus the Son, and the Holy Ghost. God was assisted by aides in the form of angels who carried out assignments. One archangel, Satan, had turned bad, became God's enemy, and enticed people into evil behavior.

The typical Indian nation's religion included multiple spirits. Each spirit was thought to have special powers over aspects of the natural world, with the names of the spirits reflecting those aspects. For example, the religion of the Winnebago nation included spirits named Earthmaker, Earth, Sun, Moon, Water, Stars, and Night-spirits. Other Winnebago deities, such as Trickster, were thought to be the authors of special events. Still others in the Winnebago pantheon bore animal names and were credited with powers and functions associated with the animals' identities—Eagle, Black Hawk, Turtle, Hare, and Thunderbird (Radin, 1945).

Creation explanations. Religious doctrines typically include accounts of how the universe and its occupants began.

The Christian version is found in the Bible's opening paragraph, which explains, "In the beginning God created the heaven and the earth" (Genesis, 1:1, 1611). Heaven is located above a domed "firmament" that curves over the flat earth below. Subsequent paragraphs describe which of the universe's contents were produced on each of 6 days, until every type of inert matter (minerals, seas) and every type of living thing (plants, animals, humans) that would ever exist were now complete in form and function.

Indian lore contains many versions of creation and of the elements that compose the universe. The Navajos of the Southwest portray the dawn of life as beginning with three beings in a lower world—First Man, First Woman, and Coyote, who was a creator and trickster. The three climbed from the dark lower world up to a second world, where they would meet Sun Man and Moon Man, who governed day and night. Ultimately they climbed a ladder to the third world, where the Navajo people would be born and would multiply (Wherry, 1969).

A story from the Kwakiutl nation in the Northwest tells of Gyd'ee, a supernatural being in human form who went about creating the features of the world—mountains, rivers, plants, and even animals that could change into human forms and back again into animal shapes. One of Gyd'ee's creations was a man who had been a salmon and whom Gyd'ee ordered to don a beak and great wings covered with feathers. "Now you are Thunderbird," Gyd'ee told him. "When there is danger, you will make thunder by flapping your wings and flying. You will do the same thing when a man dies. By flashing your eyes, you will make lightning. With your wings folded, you will symbolize peace" (Wherry, 1969, pp. 63, 65).

In the Northeast, Algonquin tradition describes how the divine Gooskap created humans by shooting arrows at ash trees so that Indians came out of the bark. He next produced all of the animals, first making them very large and then readjusting their sizes or locations to suit the Indians' needs. Enormous Moose intended to pull trees down on the Indians, so Gooskap shrank Moose to a size that enabled Indians to kill him. Squirrel, who began the size of a wolf, said he would scratch trees down on the Indians, so Gooskap made him little. When White Bear said he would eat the Indians, Gooskap banished Bear to a region of ice and rocks that was devoid of Indians. In such a fashion, Gooskap devised a world in which the Algonquins could prosper (Leland, 1884, p. 19).

In the Sioux story of creation, the great Mysterious One is not brought directly upon the scene or conceived in anthropomorphic fashion, but remains sublimely in the background.

The Sun and the Earth, representing the male and female principles, are the main elements in his creation, the other planets being subsidiary. The enkindling warmth of the Sun entered into the bosom of our mother, the Earth, and forthwith she conceived and brought forth life, both vegetable and animal.

Finally there appeared mysteriously Ish-na-e-cha-ge, the "First-Born," a being in the likeness of man, yet more than man, who roamed solitary among the animal people and understood their ways and their language. They beheld him with wonder and awe, for they could do nothing without his knowledge. He had pitched his tent in the centre of the land, and there was no spot impossible for him to penetrate.

At last, the 'First-Born' of the Sioux became weary of living alone, and formed for himself a companion—not a mate, but a brother—from a splinter which he drew from his great toe. This was the Little Boy Man, who was not created full-grown, but as an innocent child, trusting and helpless. His Elder Brother was his teacher throughout every stage of human progress from infancy to manhood, and it is to the rules which he laid down, and his counsels to the Little Boy Man, that we trace many of our most deep-rooted beliefs and most sacred customs. (Eastman, 1911)

Causality. Religions offer explanations of why events happen as they do—why crops prosper or fail, why the rain needed for crops does or does not fall, why earthquakes occur, why individuals enjoy good health or become ill, why some people are rich and others poor, why some are beautiful to look at and others are ugly, why some are skilled and others inept, why some enjoy good fortune and others suffer bad luck, and so on.

Happenings whose causes are not directly apparent are explained by religions as mediated events. That is, (a) people behave in a certain way, (b) gods or spirits that are in control of the universe or of selected features of the universe are either pleased or displeased by people's behavior, and (c) the spirits then cause appropriate consequences for those people. If the behavior has pleased the spirits, good things happen to the people. If the behavior offends or annoys the spirits, bad things happen. So it is that spirits mediate between (a) people's actions or attitudes and (b) what happens in those people's lives. To promote their own welfare, people appeal to the deities by prayer and ceremonies.

Prayer and ceremonies. Prayer can be defined as actions addressed to a god or spirit as a means of (a) asking for favors or for aid in solving a problem or doing a task, (b) directing the spirit to perform services that further the supplicant's welfare or the well-being of people or missions that the supplicant considers worthy, (c) thanking the spirit for past or present blessings, (d) glorifying and honoring the spirit, or (e) commemorating a critical event. Prayers often assume the form of ceremonies passed from one generation to the next.

Types of Christian prayers offered by the colonists could differ from one denomination to another. A Protestant minister during the Sunday service would openly speak to God in the presence of the parishioners—giving thanks, asking for blessings, and suggesting matters to which God might give attention. The members of the congregation, at the close of the minister's delivery, displayed their endorsement of the prayer by intoning "Amen." During special prayer meetings, individuals could address their requests directly to the Lord. Catholics could accompany their solicitation with fingering prayer beads or lighting candles. And prayer was often expressed in song—psalms from the Bible, hymns of praise, and sacred anthems. Christian ceremonies designed to commemorate critical events and honor the Trinity include Christmas (Jesus' birth) and Easter (Jesus' death).

Indian religions have been replete with prayers and ceremonies in the form of oratory, dramatic dialogues, dances, chants, and offerings to the spirits—such offerings as tobacco and peyote. In the arid Southwest, winter dances among the Rio Grande Pueblos served as prayers to help hunters find abundant game and to apologize to the animals' guardian spirits for having killed the beasts. In the spring, Pueblo villagers not only danced for rain to water the crops, but also performed rites to drive out witches and rid the soil of destructive spirits, thereby enabling helpful deities to work in the fields unhampered. Among the Zuñi, a masked dancer would simulate the visage of Shalako, a sacred messenger who carried people's supplications to important deities. Navajo sand paintings were intended to promote the cure of illnesses. In the Great Plains, the Comanche war dance was expected to bring success in battle. Among the Hopi, masked Kachina dancers depicted spirits that brought seeds to plant, protected villages, and disciplined unruly children (Fergusson, 1931).

The human lifespan. As anyone—religious or not—can observe, the lifespan of the human physical self typically extends from around 70 years to nearly a century, unless cut short by accident or disease. However, there has always been a question about whether physical death entirely ends a person's life. Is there not also an essence of one's *self*—an essence often referred to as *the soul*—that lives on after the body is no longer animate? Religious doctrine typically says, "Yes, spiritual life does continue after physical death." But the conception of what that spiritual after-death existence is like can differ from one religion to another. In effect, both Christianity and Indian religions distinguish two life spans—the physical and the spiritual.

Christian doctrine generally holds that at some time during a woman's pregnancy, God inserts the essence of humanness—an immortal soul—into the unborn child. After birth, that soul not only will vivify its owner throughout the person's life on earth, but will also continue to live on in an invisible state after death. The soul may spend postmortem eternity in one of two places, a blissful and carefree heaven or an excruciatingly painful hell. Or some souls may end up in a rather indeterminate limbo or in purgatory where the individual is obliged to stay while being purged of remaining sins. God makes the decision about where each person's soul will go.

Most, if not all, Indian religions have also envisioned a soul and the soul's fate after death. Among the Winnebago in the Midwest, the soul not only continues to exist after the body has expired, but the soul can be reincarnated—inserted into another body "by having an individual born again into the very same family and reliving, in every detail, his previous existence" (Radin, 1945, p. 65).

For southwestern Indians, the original happy home was underground or below a lake where the gods still live, waiting to welcome the people back after death. . . . It is generally believed that before they emerged onto this earth, men and animals all lived together [underground] and spoke the same language. (Fergusson, 1931, p. xx)

Nearly all Indian traditions include the belief that the soul of the deceased is violated if the body is taken from the ground. Thus the removal of Native remains for study or display is felt by Indians to be an acute injury (Cockrell, 2005).

Summary. As illustrated earlier, the Christian colonists' objection to Indian religions was not because Indians failed to believe in prayer, invisible gods, or life after death. Rather, the colonists objected because Indians prayed in objectionable ways to the wrong gods and were mistaken about how the universe was created and what happened to the soul after death. The English-bred Puritans who took seriously Jesus' command to spread the gospel could not accept Indians' religions as tolerable belief systems that deserved at least grudging respect. Instead, the savages' flawed worldviews needed to be replaced by Christian doctrine. Colonial missionaries dutifully accepted that educational challenge.

State, Church, and School, 1600–1699

Throughout the seventeenth century, a variety of communities were established along the Atlantic coast of North America by groups from European countries— Britain, France, the Netherlands, Germany, Belgium, Sweden, Finland, and Spain. However, the largest number of immigrants were from England, principally members of the middle class—farmers, artisans, and tradesmen—along with unskilled laborers who came as indentured servants to settle in New England and Virginia. As the decades advanced, the immigrants spread west and south, gradually forming what would eventually become the thirteen colonies that created the United States of America near the end of the eighteenth century.

The Europeans peopled the New World with diverse Christian sects. The English included Anglicans, Independents, Puritans, and Quakers. There were French Catholics and Huguenots, Spanish Catholics, Swedish Lutherans, and Dutch Calvinists. Non-Christians included Spanish Jews, American Indians, and Africans (mainly slaves on southern plantations) who retained tribal practices (Cremin, 1970, p. 148).

As noted in Chapter 1, the term *state* refers to a government unit. A *state* can be a nation, a province, town, or village. In seventeenth-century America, the principal governing unit consisted of a village or town and its surrounding countryside. Although the New England colonies were officially under the jurisdiction of the British government, daily affairs were supervised by a village's or town's council or *board of selectmen* chosen by the citizens. As time passed, towns that comprised a colony elected legislatures that passed regulations promoting such Christian interests as teaching the Bible.

The colonial church cared for the inhabitants' spiritual needs and provided the moral foundation for towns' and villages' secular responsibilities—establishing laws governing people's personal behavior, maintaining civil order, settling property disputes, providing roads, directing commerce, and the like. Thus, any separation of church and state was only in the functions of the two institutions, not in their philosophies or goals. Both were dedicated to promoting a prosperous community of dedicated Christians.

Nor was education in colonial New England separate from religion. Quite the opposite. Education was designed primarily to further Christian goals and was conducted by the faithful in home, church, and school. The most fundamental educational unit was the home. Parents were expected to teach their offspring Christian precepts from the Bible and how to read and write. The ability to read was dictated by the Protestant conviction that people should be directly in touch with God and God's word rather than their requiring an intermediary, such as a priest, in order to understand and communicate with The Lord. The colonists' enthusiasm for reading would contribute not only to a lively business of importing books from "the old country" but also to the growth of print shops, publishers, and libraries over the seventeenth and eighteenth centuries.

At church on Sunday, the minister preached a sermon intended to inform the congregation of the contents of the Bible and how to apply scripture in everyday living. Before or after the sermon, the minister or a teacher could instruct the young in church doctrine, often by means of the official set of questions and answers about life and religion that formed the sect's catechism.

In Britain over previous centuries, schools had been founded at an increasing rate, usually by religious bodies. Thus, colonists brought to the Americas a tradition of schooling that focused on Christian doctrine and skills useful in vocations—reading, writing, and ciphering. Various colonial locations served as schools, including homes (kitchens or parlors), churches, ministers' dwellings (manses), meetinghouses, shops, barns, and schoolhouses. Frequently a mother in her home would not only instruct her own children but teach the children of neighbors as well, thereby creating the popular institution known as the *dame school.*

Pupils were taught by anyone and everyone, not only by schoolmasters, but by parents, tutors, clergymen, lay readers, precentors [choir directors], physicians, lawyers, artisans, and shopkeepers ... The content and sequence of learning remained fairly well defined, and each student progressed from textbook to textbook at his own pace. (Cremin, 1970, p. 193)

The materials of instruction in home and school typically included a *hornbook,* which was not a book in the usual sense but, rather, was a board (3-by-4-inches in size) on which was attached a sheet of paper covered with a transparent sheet of horn. The reading matter printed on the paper included the alphabet, a few common syllables, and a passage from the Bible, such as the Lord's Prayer or the Apostles' Creed.

The hornbook would typically be supplemented by a primer, which would prepare the young to read the Bible itself. For example, *The New England Primer*, a tiny volume hardly longer or broader than a young child's hand, is estimated to have sold 6 million copies, or an average of 40,000 a year, between 1687 and the mid-1800s in a sparsely settled America (Morison, 1936, p. 79). Two assumptions undergirded a Puritan view of child development: (a) children are born evil, bound to sin if not guided away from their natural state and (b) children are born with a capacity to learn. The first of these assumptions was founded on religious doctrine, the second apparently on common sense. Crucial to Puritan doctrine was the idea that the sin of disobedience to God that Adam and Eve committed when they ate the forbidden fruit in the Garden of Eden was a sin carried down through all generations. The newborn child was the recipient of this original sin and would be condemned to hell after death if not redeemed. *The New England Primer* (1836) introduced children to the first letter of the alphabet with a verse that made this premise clear (p. 11).

A = In Adam's fall we sinned all.

The letter *B* appeared beside a drawing of the Bible.

B = Thy life to mend, this Book attend.

The *Primer* explained at length that, because of innate sin, untutored children would naturally folic "and take delight among young folk who spend their days in joy and mirth," thereby passing their time in idleness, disobeying parents and others in authority, lying and cursing and stealing, ignoring their studies, playing truant from school, fighting with brothers and sisters and schoolmates, refusing to pray or attend church, failing to read the Bible, disobeying the Ten Commandments, and declining to accept or follow Christ (pp. 10–64). The verse accompanying letters *F* and *U* in the alphabet described the consequences of such waywardness (pp. 15–16).

F = The idle *F*ool is whipt at school.
U = *U*pon the wicked, God will rain a horrible tempest.

In effect, schooling in the colonies proceeded throughout the seventeenth century and beyond with a strong Christian bent.

A critical event in 1647 would significantly affect the course of public schooling in what would soon be the United States. The Massachusetts legislature issued a school act that compelled every community of fifty householders or more to establish a school that all students would attend, with the aim of foiling the scheme of "that old deluder, Satan, to keep men from the knowledge of the Scriptures." The school would be financed by "the parents or masters of such children or by the inhabitants in general" (Vaughn, 1972, p. 237). This step toward ensuring that all children and youths would become literate was soon taken by other colonies as well, so that publicly supported schooling for the general populace was on its way.

To summarize, in seventeenth-century North America—and especially in New England—state, church, and school were not institutions isolated from each other and pursuing separate goals. Instead, they were a trinity guided by, and dedicated to, promoting a combination of Christianity and worldly prosperity for the colonists. Christianity represented the Puritan part of colonial culture; worldly prosperity represented the Yankee part.

In contrast to the Europeans' educational methods were the Indians' traditional means of transmitting their culture to succeeding generations.

Native communities taught their children three dimensions of maturity: survival, spirituality, and ethics. Children's instruction came from multiple sources, including parents, elders, and spiritual leaders. On the Columbia River plateau boys learned to fish the rivers crowded with salmon each spring; in the fall they hunted for bear, deer, and elk. Girls smoked salmon, gathered roots and berries, wove baskets, and sewed clothing and moccasins. Both went on vision quests. In the high-desert Southwest, Anasazi boys learned to raise corn, beans, and squash in an arid land, to hunt and to weave cotton, and to understand the nature of their spiritual role. Girls cared for the home, ground corn and cooked, and participated in the seasonal ceremonies. Both learned that the village was of greater importance than the individual. Since native groups . . . relied exclusively on oral learning, storytelling was ubiquitous. (Szasz, 2006)

State, Church, and School, 1700–1775

A nascent philosophical movement known as *The Enlightenment*, which had sprouted in Europe, came to fruition in the eighteenth century and greatly impressed influential colonists, including the founders of the United States of America. The Enlightenment was grounded in the conviction that "human reason could be used to combat ignorance, superstition, and tyranny, and to build a better world" (Brians, 2000). Enlightenment thinkers' principal targets were religion and the domination of society by a hereditary aristocracy. Such French philosophical luminaries as Voltaire (1694–1778) pursued the movement's goals by attacking the fundamentals of Christian belief: that the Bible was the inspired word of God, that Jesus was an earthly version of God, and that nonbelievers in Christian doctrine were destined to roast in hell.

Rather than trusting holy books written by the ancients as the source of truth, Enlightenment's proponents trusted human reason—logical deductions based on careful observations of events. When conclusions found in holy scriptures clashed with conclusions drawn from empirical observations and logic, people should prefer the latter. Reason should win out over religious dogma.

This enlightenment worldview would become the foundation for both modern science and secular, democratic political structures. It would furnish a "framework for the American [1776] and French [1789] Revolutions, the [nineteenth-century] Latin American independence movement, the Polish Constitution [1791] [and would lead to] the rise of capitalism and the birth of socialism" (Age of enlightenment, 2005).

Thus, the 1700s generated the second of the two major belief systems that would participate in the twenty-first-century controversies over religion-in-public-schools that are described in this book's Chapters 3 through 12. That second system was Enlightenment's secularism which vied with the existing religious belief system for determining the place of religion in public schools.

Over the decades leading to the American Revolution, births in colonial families combined with immigration to increase the density and geographical spread of the population. From an estimated 50,400 colonists in 1650, the number of inhabitants rose to around 250,900 by 1700, to 629,400 by 1730, and to 2,148,100 by 1770 (*Colonial population estimates*, 2006). Such growth was accompanied by three developments that affected education in the colonies.

First, separate villages and towns became politically organized under overarching governing bodies, thereby forming provinces that would, in the final decades of the century, become the first thirteen united states. Decisions about education made by provincial legislatures would apply to all villages and towns within the province, thus encouraging greater uniformity among a colony's schools.

Second, population growth added diversity in educational opportunities as more types of schools and kinds of apprenticeship became available. The rate of increase in school enrollment exceeded the rate of general population growth as the citizenry saw formal education and training as increasingly important for getting ahead in the world. However, the expansion of schooling was limited mostly to whites. Indians and blacks who attended school were few in number. The most successful attempts to provide schooling for Indians appeared in New England, where missionaries not only made special efforts to enroll native youths in English-language schools but they translated the Bible into the Algonquin language so the word of God could be read by Indians in their own tongue (Cremin, 1970, pp. 194–195)

Third, immigration from abroad, along with travel within the colonies, added greater religious, ethnic, and cultural diversity to communities so that people were obliged to be more tolerant of neighbors whose life styles and belief systems differed from their own.

In summary, on the brink of the American Revolution the colonists' strong Christian tradition would be challenged by the Enlightenment's emphasis on using humans' reasoning powers to arrive at judgments about the universe and about proper relationships among people. That challenge was epitomized in Thomas Paine's (1737–1809) essay *Common Sense* (1776) that helped inspire the leaders of the Revolution. In his tract, Paine applied reason in assessing the colonies' relationship with Britain, portraying the colonists as victims of exploitation, evidenced by a recently imposed stamp tax on the colonists.

We have boasted the protection of Great Britain, without considering that her motive was *interest* not *attachment;* that she did not protect us from *our enemies* on *our account,* but from *her enemies* on *her own account,* from those who had no quarrel with us on any *other account,* and who will always be our enemies on the *same account.* (Paine, 1776)

Common Sense ended with a description of the ideal government, a description that closely resembled the government the colonists actually would create after their military victory over the British. In 1794 Paine wrote *The Age of Reason,* in which he reflected the convictions of a person who held to the tradition of believing in God and life after death but who was a secularist in founding conclusions about daily life on his ability to reason—on his skill at adducing a line of logic. This same kind of person would be later found among the twenty-first century participants in controversies over religion in American schools. Paine wrote:

I believe in one God, and no more; and I hope for happiness beyond this life. I believe in the equality of man; and I believe that religious duties consist in doing justice, loving mercy, and endeavoring to make our fellow-creatures happy....
    I do not believe in the creed professed by the Jewish church, by the Roman church, by the Greek church, by the Turkish church, by the Protestant church, nor by any church that I know of. My own mind is my own church. All national institutions of churches, whether Jewish, Christian, or Turkish, appear to me no other than human inventions, set up to terrify and enslave mankind, and monopolize power and profit.
    I do not mean by this declaration to condemn those who believe otherwise; they have the same right to their belief as I have to mine. But it is necessary to the happiness of man that he be mentally faithful to himself. Infidelity does not consist in believing, or in disbelieving; it consists in professing to believe what he does not believe. (Paine, 1794, part I)

The New Nation, 1776–1860

When the founders of the new republic composed the nation's constitution in 1789, they included two features vitally important for the future conduct of education. First, they did not assign responsibility for education to the federal government but left decisions about educational provisions to the individual states.

Second, in 1791 they added 10 amendments—a Bill of Rights—to the original constitution. The initial portion of the first amendment read:

Congress shall make no law respecting an establishment of religion, or prohibiting the free exercise thereof.

The first half of this passage is known as the *establishment clause* and the second half as the *free-exercise clause.* From 1791 until the present day there has been continual debate about what exactly such a church/state policy entails, particularly because in practice its two provisions can be in conflict. For example, what if a public school—on the basis of the establishment clause—denies a religious leader the chance to offer, in a public-school classroom, after-school religious instruction to children whose parents are of the leader's faith? Does that denial violate the children's right to the free-exercise of religion, and does it illegally prohibit the religious leader from freely exercising his or her faith?

In attempting to offer guidance about the specific intent of the establishment clause, jurists over the decades have tended to adopt a position suggested by the writings of such key framers of the Constitution as Thomas Jefferson and James Madison who urged separation between church and state. When he served as the U.S. president in 1802, Jefferson wrote,

Believing with you that religion is a matter which lies solely between man and his God, that he owes account to none other for his faith or his worship, ... I contemplate with sovereign reverence that act of the whole American people which declared that their legislature should "make no law respecting an establishment of religion, or prohibiting the free exercise thereof," thus building a wall of separation between church and state.

Fifteen years earlier, Madison had written,

In all cases where a majority are united by a common interest or passion, the rights of the minority are in danger. What motives are to restrain them? Religion itself may become a motive to persecution and oppression.

Since those early days, the Jefferson–Madison interpretation of the establishment clause has typically been applied in U.S. courts as they have declared unconstitutional any laws advocating religious influence in public schools. However, the vagueness of the clause as it appears in the Bill of Rights has left the door open for other interpretations of what sorts of religious matters can be included in publicly financed educational institutions. Such interpretations have been at the heart of the twenty-first-century controversies described in this book's Chapters 3 through 11. Thus, the insertion of the first amendment was a critical incident that altered the colonial tradition of a Christian state.

Another attachment to the Constitution—the fourteenth amendment—has also been important over the decades, for it stipulates that the provisions of the federal constitution are applicable in all of the nation's states. Therefore, constitutional decisions by the U.S. Supreme Court take precedence over laws of individual states. Specifically, the first section of the fourteenth amendment reads,

All persons born or naturalized in the United States and subject to the jurisdiction thereof, are citizens of the United States and of the State wherein they reside. No State shall make or enforce any law which shall abridge the privileges or immunities of citizens of the United States.

Lingering Religiosity

Despite claims by the builders of the new nation that they were creating a secular government in which church and state were separated, the Christian culture of the nation-planners' backgrounds invested government institutions with an obvious Judeo-Christian cast. Even with their recently acquired enlightened reasoning, the founders could not easily shuck off their religious upbringing, which included a belief in the Bible's Old Testament (especially the Jewish Torah).

When it came time to design a seal for the new nation, it is said that [Benjamin] Franklin wanted it to portray Moses bringing down the waters upon Pharoah, while Jefferson would have preferred a rendering of the children of Israel in the wilderness, with a cloud leading them by day and a pillar of fire by night. Neither of these prevailed, however, and the Great Seal that finally issued from the hands of Charles Thomson and William Barton showed the familiar eagle holding the olive branch and arrows, and on the obverse a pyramid watched over by the eye of Providence, with the mottoes *Annuit coeptis* (He [God] has favored our undertaking) and *Novus ordo seclorum* (A new order of the ages has begun). (Cremin, 1980, p. 17)

Deism of the sort Thomas Paine advocated—God represented in all of nature and humanity—competed with traditional sects' doctrines (Puritan, Quaker, Catholic, and more) for the allegiance of the new nation's citizens. And each sect had its own notion of what part religion should play in public education.

Contrasting Belief Systems

The twenty-first-century's religion-in-schools controversies that are depicted in this book's later chapters derived from incompatible characteristics of the new nation's dominant worldviews: (a) traditional Christianity and (b) the U.S. Constitution's version of the Enlightenment.

According to Christian doctrine (which was also essentially the same as Judaic and Islamic tradition), the properly organized society would be patriarchal, male-dominated, autocratic, and theocratic; it would promote the welfare of a chosen people—Christians—who were obliged to follow unalterable rules of conduct specified in ancient holy scriptures. An almighty God—referred to as *The Lord, Jehovah,* or *God the Father*—was the patriarchal, autocratic, theocratic authority, privileged to dictate the rules of human conduct and to punish those who failed to obey the rules. In the biblical book of Psalms (chapter 23, verse 1) God was portrayed as a shepherd in charge of humans who were obedient and grateful sheep. The patriarchal, male-dominated feature of the Christian worldview was reflected in the treatment of females in the Bible and in the traditional eighteenth-century Christian home and community.

In contrast to Christian tradition, the enlightened society envisioned by the framers of the Constitution deemed all people of equal worth (all "created equal"), with the society's changeable rules of conduct based on the decision of the majority of the citizens (democratic participation). Thus, the new nation's government would be "of the people, by the people, and for the people" rather than determined by an invisible supreme being whose dictates were to be found in a revered holy book. In practice, the intended government fell somewhat short of its "equality" ideal, as women, Indians, and black slaves could not vote or participate in public affairs in other important ways (membership in organizations, permission to engage in many occupations). Nevertheless, the main thrust of the Constitution was democratic, respectful of human reason, and nonreligious.

Those two worldviews—Christian and Enlightenment—were obviously incompatible. However, it was possible for people to adopt compromise positions that allowed them to combine parts of each perspective. For example, Christians could still believe in God, life after death, heaven, and hell without accepting the contents of the Bible as the literal truth. In effect, it was possible (a) to view the Bible as a record of ancient peoples' estimates of the nature of the universe, of their genealogical history, and of wise moral precepts rather than accepting the scriptures as God's revealed truth; and, at the same time, (b) to subscribe to the principles of a democratic society and the importance of human reason for deciding about what constitutes acceptable human behavior.

All three of these belief systems (Christian, Enlightenment, compromise) that appeared with the advent of the new American nation would play vital roles in the twenty-first-century controversies over religion in schools that are described in Chapters 3–12.

Limited Secularity

Evidence of the enduring Judeo-Christian tradition within an ostensibly secular society would appear in various forms between the years of the Revolution and the brink of the Civil War. Those forms included (1) new organizations designed to spread knowledge of Christian gospel throughout the entire American populace, (2) a burgeoning supply of reading matter for schools, and (3) the amalgamation of individual schools into school systems.

Sunday school et al. Important new purveyors of Christian doctrine included Sunday schools, evangelical revival meetings, Bible societies, and missionary societies.

The Sunday-school movement was imported from England, where it had been developed in the 1780s to furnish educational opportunities for people who were fully employed the other six days of the week. Originally intended as a one-day-a-week venture, Sunday schools in the American colonies would often extend their services throughout the week and thereby serve as regular "common" schools. The learning fare centered on reading, lectures, and discussions that featured Bible tales, church doctrine, and Christian morals.

Evangelical crusading consisted of dramatic, inspirational preaching by either ordained ministers or charismatic lay persons. During revival meetings, members of the audience, through prayer and the singing of hymns, were urged to publicly declare their conviction that Jesus died to atone for their sins. References to Bible verses were liberally distributed throughout sermons, and the faithful were exhorted to read and memorize passages of the Bible for themselves. These early efforts were the forerunners of the twenty-first century's evangelical megachurches that have been active in present-day controversies over religion in America's public schools.

Highly influential organizations that sprouted during the early nineteenth century included the American Education Society, American Tract Society, American Home Missionary Society, American Sunday-School Union, and American Bible Society. Such groups were sometimes supported by a coalition of denominations— Presbyterians, Baptists, Catholics, Episcopalians, and the Dutch Reformed working together. Their goals were to spread Christianity by providing free or low-cost Bibles and to inspire everyone to contribute to a Christian America. "In the struggle with Satan there could be no neutral ground; what was not already Christ's had to be won for Christ, or [America] remained in continuing danger of going to the Devil" (Cremin, 1980, p. 63).

Missionary efforts were intended to gather nonbelievers into the Christian fold, not only in America but overseas as well. The Home Missionary Society concentrated on colonists—those who moved westward to the Mississippi River and beyond—and on Indians. Missionaries who sought to proselytize among heathens abroad pursued their calling in such varied climes as the Pacific Islands (Hawaii, Samoa), India, China, Japan, Greece, Turkey, and Africa.

School books and tracts. The schools' emphasis on teaching reading was designed to equip Americans to study the Bible and become life-long learners, able to make informed decisions based on information found in newspapers, magazines, and books. The country's rapidly expanding publishing industry produced large quantities of textbooks, manuals, and tracts on diverse subjects. The American Sunday School Union by 1830 had issued 6 million copies of booklets teaching moral precepts to the young in the form of stories. By 1865 the American Tract Society had produced 20 million books and 250 million pamphlets (Cremin, 1980, p. 69).

Throughout much of the nineteenth century, the most popular textbooks for reading instruction in common (elementary) schools were the volumes of the McGuffey series. The purpose of the McGuffey readers was to furnish teachers a comprehensive reading program that advanced in difficulty from the initial primer through six more graded books, each more demanding than its predecessor. The subject matter of the readers included history, literature, natural science, and theology, with the contents chosen from writings "which extol, explain, and illustrate such virtues as honesty, charity, thrift, hard work, courage, patriotism, reverence for God, and respect for parents" (*McGuffey's readers*, 2006). The nature of the McGuffey stories is reflected in titles from the second, third, and fourth books in the series.

"The Greedy Girl"; *"The Kind Little Girl"*; *"The Honest Boy and the Thief"*; *"The Lord's Prayer"*; *"The Effects of Rashness"*; *"On Speaking the Truth"*; *"Consequences of Bad Spelling"*; *"Happy Consequences of American Independence"*; and *"Decisive Integrity."* (*McGuffey's readers*, 2006)

From 1836 into the twentieth century, more than 120 million sets of McGuffey's books were sold; during that era an estimated 80 percent of the nation's children learned reading from McGuffey's series.

School Systems

In colonial times, most schools had been individually independent units that followed their own rules about curricula, the hiring of teachers, and methods of funding. But under the new republic, efforts were gradually mounted to collect individual schools under a common set of regulations. In effect, systems of schools were created. In some cases, a state legislature issued laws that governed the conduct of the public schools across the state. In other cases, members of a religious denomination—Catholics, Presbyterians, Lutherans—devised their own coalitions of private schools.

Initially, the barrier between public and private schools was frequently vague and porous, with tax moneys used to finance both secular public schools and private religious institutions. However, the passing of time brought legislation that increasingly prevented the use of public funds to pay for schools sponsored by religious bodies. Thereby, the theoretical separation of church and state—at least in terms of school finance—became more of a reality. However, in schools' curriculum content, the tradition of including religious aims and lore continued in both public and private institutions, although a greater quantity of religious matter was usually found in faith-based schools than in public schools.

A significant outcome of merging schools into systems was that greater uniformity developed among individual schools because system-wide regulations applied to all members of such an alliance.

Indians and Negroes

The admirable educational progress that brought increasing numbers of Americans to school (over two million by 1840 and five-and-one-half million by 1860) was limited mostly to the nation's white settlers. In the main, Indians and Negroes were not welcome in schools.

The attitude of the U.S. Government toward the Indians—an attitude likely shared by most whites—was expressed by President Andrew Jackson in a speech to Congress on December 8, 1830. The government's actions at that time constituted a landgrab cloaked in self-righteous compassion, while bluntly denigrating Native Americans' lifestyles and religions.

It gives me pleasure to announce to Congress that the benevolent policy of the Government, steadily pursued for nearly thirty years, in relation to the removal of the Indians beyond the white settlements is approaching to a happy consummation. Two important tribes [Choctaw, Chickasaw] have accepted the provision made for their removal [to west of the Mississippi River . . . and it is believed that their example will induce the remaining tribes also to seek the same obvious advantages.

The consequences of a speedy removal will be important to the United States, to individual States, and to the Indians themselves . . . [The policy] puts an end to all possible danger of collision between the authorities of the General and State Governments on account of the Indians. It will place a dense and civilized population in large tracts of country now occupied by a few savage hunters. It will relieve the whole State of Mississippi and the western part of Alabama of Indian occupancy, and enable those States to advance rapidly in population, wealth, and power. It will separate the Indians from immediate contact with settlements of whites; . . . enable them to pursue happiness in their own way and under their own rude institutions; . . . and perhaps cause them gradually . . . to cast off their savage habits and become an interesting, civilized, and Christian community.

Toward the aborigines of the country no one can indulge a more friendly feeling than myself, or would go further in attempting to reclaim them from their wandering habits and make them a happy, prosperous people. The Choctaw and the Chickasaw tribes have with great unanimity determined to avail themselves of the liberal offers presented by the act of Congress, and have agreed to remove beyond the Mississippi River. (Jackson, 1830)

An estimated 100,000 Indians eventually relocated in the West as a result of the Indian-removal policy.

As for Indians' formal education, the Constitution's mandated separation of church and state was bypassed by Congress in 1819 when lawmakers endorsed a partnership between the federal government and church organizations through the Indian Civilization Fund Act, which provided federal dollars for "benevolent societies" to instruct Indians in reading, writing, arithmetic, and agriculture (Szasz, 2006). Thus, missionaries from various sects plied their trade in a number of tribal areas, endeavoring to Americanize Indians by teaching the English language, European culture, and Christian doctrine. However,

from the early seventeenth through the mid-nineteenth century, most Indian children had little contact with "white man's education." Those few who did learned in day or boarding schools from "Black Robes" or Protestant ministers or schoolmasters. In the Southwest, Franciscan padres taught Pueblo children; in the northeastern woodlands, Protestant schoolmasters, some of them American Indian, taught Algonquin or Iroquois youth. (Szasz, 2006)

Then there were the Negroes. Most of them (around two million) were plantation slaves in the South, generally viewed by the white population as inherently inferior beings—intellectually and morally—and undeserving of schooling. Efforts to Christianize them through informal religious instruction resulted in slaves merging Christian doctrine with traditional religious lore from Africa to form a syncretic belief system that was passed on to the young through the family and the singing of spirituals and telling of tales during secret meetings at night in fields adjacent to the slave quarters. Very few slaves were taught to read or write, so they were obliged to depend on an oral tradition for their education.

Although there were increasing numbers of free blacks (nearly a half million by 1860, mostly in Northern States), they were generally treated as inferiors and were discriminated against by the whites. As a result, they were seldom found in schools.

Summary

Schooling during the new-nation era (1776–1860) reflected tension between traditional Christian culture and an age-of-reason democratic secularism that was written into the U.S. Constitution. Most jurists interpreted the Constitution's first amendment to mean that church and state should be kept strictly separate. Hence, there should be no religious influence in schools funded by tax dollars. Nevertheless, a strong strain of Christianity continued to pervade public-school practice.

The new nation's whites were the chief recipients of formal education, both public and private. In the main, Indians and blacks were excluded from schools.

The Evolving Nation, 1861–1950

The 90-year period between the Civil War and the aftermath of World War II witnessed a variety of developments that significantly affected education in America. Those developments included the addition of new states, massive immigration with an emphasis on Americanization, a rural-to-urban trend, compulsory-education laws, new educational provisions for the nation's Indians and blacks, and no significant objection to traditional religious practices in public schools.

New States

The units that would comprise the United States began during the days of the American Revolution with the original thirteen colonies. Over the years 1776–1860, twenty more states were authorized. Then, during the five decades between 1861 and 1912, an additional fifteen were added, bringing the total to forty eight. Those added after 1860 were

Kansas 1861, West Virginia 1863, Nevada 1864, Nebraska 1867, Colorado 1876, North Dakota 1889, South Dakota 1889, Montana 1889, Washington 1889, Idaho 1890, Wyoming 1890, Utah 1896, Oklahoma 1907, New Mexico 1912, Arizona 1912. (Alaska and Hawaii would not win statehood until 1959.)

Educational opportunities in a region were significantly improved by a territory's becoming a state. First, in each new state, land was set aside to support public schools and colleges, as illustrated in the Kansas State Constitution.

Sections numbered sixteen and thirty-six in each township in the state, including Indian reservations and trust lands, shall be granted to the state for the exclusive use of common schools; and when either of said sections, or any part thereof, has been disposed of, other lands of equal value, as nearly contiguous thereto as possible, shall be substituted therefor. Five percentum of the proceeds of the public lands in Kansas, disposed of after the admission of the state into the union, shall be paid to the state for a fund, the income of which shall be used for the support of common schools. (*Constitution of the state of Kansas*, 1861)

In addition, provisions were often included in state constitutions to safeguard the source of funds for schooling, as in the state of Washington.

None of the permanent school fund of this state shall ever be loaned to private persons or corporations, but it may be invested in national, state, county, municipal, or school-district bonds. (*Washington State Constitution*, 1889)

In effect, statehood meant the responsibility for educating the young was not left to the initiative of individual communities but was formally assigned to the state legislature, as in the case of Texas.

A general diffusion of knowledge being essential to the preservation of the liberties and rights of the people, it shall be the duty of the Legislature of the State to establish and make suitable provision for the support and maintenance of an efficient system of public free schools. (*Texas Constitution*, 1845)

As states joined the union, they expressed their continued dedication to Christian culture. Thus, it should be no surprise that evidence of that culture would be found in public schools in the form of morning prayers, hymns, and Bible verses posted on classroom bulletin boards. Consider, for example, the fashion in which the preambles of state constitutions typically opened.

We, the people of New Mexico, grateful to Almighty God for the blessings of liberty, in order to secure the advantages of a state government, do ordain and establish this Constitution. (*Constitution of the state of New Mexico*, 1911)

We, the people of Colorado, with profound reverence for the Supreme Ruler of the Universe, in order to form a more independent and perfect government ... do ordain and establish this constitution. (*Colorado Constitution*, 1876)

The Massachusetts constitution, when the colony in 1788 had become the sixth one to join the new union, left no doubt that monotheistic religion was an essential qualification for citizenship.

It is the right as well as the duty of all men in society, publicly, and at stated seasons to worship the Supreme Being, the great Creator and Preserver of the universe. And no subject shall be hurt, molested, or restrained, in his person, liberty, or estate, for worshiping God in the manner and season most agreeable to the dictates of his own conscience; or for his religious profession or sentiments; provided he doth not disturb the public peace, or obstruct others in their religious worship. (*Constitution of the commonwealth*, 1788)

When Virginia in 1788 became the tenth state, the constitution's religious-freedom clause reflected a bent toward a Christian worldview but not in such a dogmatic fashion as the Massachusetts document.

Religion or the duty which we owe to our Creator, and the manner of discharging it, can be directed only by reason and conviction, not by force or violence; and, therefore, all men are equally entitled to the free exercise of religion, according to the dictates of conscience; and it is the mutual duty of all to practice Christian forbearance, love, and charity towards each other. No man shall be compelled to frequent or support any religious worship, place, or ministry whatsoever. (*Constitution of Virginia*, 1788)

However, the expectation that each citizen would necessarily embrace Christianity was not included in the constitutions of territories that achieved statehood after the mid-nineteenth century. Perhaps framers of state constitutions had become more tolerant of non-Christian belief systems by the second half of the century. Consequently, at the same time that authors of state constitutions expressed their devotion to God, they echoed the belief-system tolerance of the U.S. Constitution's first amendment.

The rights of conscience shall never be infringed. The State shall make no law respecting an establishment of religion or prohibiting the free exercise thereof ... There shall be no union of Church and State, nor shall any church dominate the State or interfere with its functions. (*Constitution of the state of Utah*, 1895)

In the twenty-first-century debates over proper state/church/school relationships, a key issue has been that of using tax money to support private religion-based schools or religious education in public schools. The creators of most state constitutions had avoided addressing the issue. But a few, such as Utah, made clear in their constitutions the state's official position.

No public money or property shall be appropriated for or applied to any religious worship, exercise, or instruction, or for the support of any ecclesiastical establishment. (*Constitution of the state of Utah*, 1895)

In summary, transforming federally administered territories into states would systematize and strengthen schooling by providing lands for erecting schools, by tax support, and by obligating legislatures to oversee the advance of education. A continuing dedication to monotheistic religion—essentially Christianity—was reflected in state constitutions, along with an endorsement of the religious-freedom amendment of the U.S. Constitution.

Compulsory-Schooling Laws

During the new American republic's first half century, the question of whether children attended school depended on their parents' decision. Especially in rural areas, parent's would often decide that the young could better spend their hours at home, helping with farming, herding, and housekeeping than by poring over books in a schoolroom. The practice of dismissing school for 3 months during the summer so that pupils could help during farmers' most intensive work season encouraged parents to allow youngsters to attend school. But such encouragement still did not ensure that all children and teenagers were enrolled. Furthermore, the distance traveled to a school was often long—and particularly arduous in wintertime—so children would stay home where a family member might tutor them in reading, writing, and ciphering.

However, because the new nation needed a universally literate polity, states began requiring that all children between about ages 7 and 16 attend school. Compulsory schooling legislation began with Massachusetts in 1852, followed by the District of Columbia in 1864, New Hampshire in 1871, Connecticut in 1872, Nevada in 1873, and New York, California, and Kansas in 1874. Over the next four decades additional states followed suit until the last of the compulsory-education laws were finally passed in Alabama, Florida, and Texas in 1915, Georgia in 1916, and Mississippi in 1918 (Compulsory, 2006).

Mandatory schooling not only promoted the development of a universally literate populace but it subjected all students—no matter what their parents' belief-systems might be—to the remnants of Christian habit found in virtually all public schools. Those remnants included (a) prayers, hymns, and passages of the Bible during the obligatory "opening exercises" with which the school day began, (b) such content as The Lord's Prayer in McGuffey's readers, (c) the Ten Commandments posted in hallways and classrooms, and (d) Christmas and Easter celebrations with their carols, pictures, and pageants depicting Jesus' birth and death.

Immigration

Immigration over the decades increased the variety of belief systems in the American population and greatly enlarged the membership of the dominant religious faiths.

Prior to the American Revolution, among the estimated 900,000 immigrant residents in the colonies, 46 percent were from Britain, of which 26 percent were English, 15 percent Northern Irish (from Protestant Ulster), 5 percent Scotch, and less than 1 percent Welsh. About 40 percent of the colonies' immigrants were from Africa (nearly all as slaves). The remaining 14 percent of the settler population came from Western Europe, including 11 percent Germans and less than 1 percent each of Southern Irish, Dutch, French, Swedes, and Jews (Szucs & Luebking, 1997).

Table 2.1
Patterns of U.S. Immigration

Years	Total immigrants	Europe (%)	Asia (%)	Americas (%)	Africa (%)	Oceania (%)
1861–70	2,314,824	89	3	7	0.1	0.9
1901–10	8,795,386	91.7	3.6	4.1	0.1	0.5

Source: Historical Immigrant Admission Data, 2006.

Over the 100 years leading to 1880, almost 86 percent of immigrants were from northwest Europe, mainly Great Britain, Ireland, Germany, and Scandinavia. Then, during the three decades leading to World War I, the proportion of immigrants from southern, central, and Eastern Europe increased to 69 percent (Cohn, 2001).

Consider the proportions of newcomers from different world regions during four decades between 1861 and 1910 (Table 2.1).

It is apparent that, from colonial times through 1950, the overwhelming majority of newcomers to the United States were Christians. From the earliest days until far into the nineteenth century, Protestants from Northern Europe—Presbyterians, Anglicans, Lutherans, Methodists, Baptists, Quakers—predominated. Then, as large numbers of Irish and Italians arrived in the late nineteenth and early twentieth centuries, Catholicism became a major force in the nation's religious life, a force that grew ever stronger as Latin Americans appeared in rapidly-increasing numbers throughout the 1900s and into the twenty-first century.

Such an immigration pattern served to add a measure of religious variety to America's belief-system mix. But, until the late twentieth century, most of that variety was within Christianity itself as different Christian denominations were appearing in increased numbers. True, the settlers from Europe would include some humanists, agnostics, and atheists, but they were rather rare. And such Asians as Chinese and Japanese would bring Confucianism, Taoism, Buddhism, and Shinto. But the overwhelming majority would be Christians of some sort. Thus, pupils in public schools might become acquainted with classmates of sects other than there own, but virtually all would be Christians, at least nominally. Therefore, it hardly seems surprising that the secular public schools would include Christian beliefs and practices without engendering complaints from the majority of the public. Morning prayer in the classroom, mottoes from the Bible on bulletin boards, and rules against using such words as *God, Jesus, damnation,* and *hell* in a disrespectful fashion were considered only proper. And viewing the rare Buddhist, Taoist, or Muslim classmate as a heathen to be avoided, or at least to be suspected, was normal. Thus, not until the last half of the twentieth century would a new attitude toward multiculturalism—including multifaith-ism—contribute significantly to debates over religion in public schools.

Americanization

Particularly during the early years of the twentieth century, a rising flood of immigrants from a greater variety of homelands confronted government officials with the problem of forming an American citizenry that was culturally united. Political leaders sought to cope with this problem by launching an official Americanization movement.

American presidents, Republicans and Democrats alike, agreed on two basic goals: teach the newcomers English and make them Americans. The clear aim was to strengthen our national identity—to reinforce the *unum* in *e pluribus unum*—by assimilating the new arrivals into American civilization. (Fonte, 2000)

Through the Americanization process, all citizens would assume the characteristics of such a genuine American. That process assumed its most intense form during Woodrow Wilson's presidency (1913–1921) when Wilson, in a "Message to Newly Naturalized Citizens," declared,

You cannot dedicate yourself to America unless you become in every respect and with every purpose of your will thorough Americans. You cannot become thorough Americans if you think of yourself in groups. America does not consist of groups. A man who thinks of himself as belonging to a particular national group in America has not yet become an American, and the man who goes among you to trade upon your nationality is no worthy son to live under the Stars and Stripes. (King 2000)

In 1919, Supreme Court Justice Louis Brandeis declared that newcomers to the United States would achieve "the national consciousness of an American" when they adopted "the clothes, the manners, and the customs generally prevailing here," substituted English for their native language, ensured that their "interests and affections have become deeply rooted here," and came "into complete harmony with our ideals and aspirations" (Huntington, 2004).

The Americanization program was pursued through a variety of institutions— churches, clubs, community organizations, and, above all, the nation's schools.

Indeed, public schools had been created in the nineteenth century and shaped in considerable part by the perceived need to Americanize and Protestantize immigrants . . . In 1921–22, as many as a thousand communities conducted special public school programs to Americanize the foreign-born. Between 1915 and 1922, more than 1 million immigrants enrolled in such programs. School systems saw public education as an instrument to create a unified society out of the multiplying diversity created by immigration. (Huntington, 2004)

From Farms to Cities

The 1861–1950 era saw America transformed from a predominantly rural, agricultural society into an increasingly industrialized nation of cities. In 1890 around 30 percent of Americans lived in cities. By 1920 city dwellers accounted for half of the population. In 1950 two-thirds of the nation's inhabitants were urbanites, and by 1980 that figure rose to 75 percent (Cremin, 1988, p. 4). As more people moved into cities, the cities' schools grew in size, so that the number of schoolmates a pupil encountered increased markedly.

In colonial times, public schools were organized within local school districts, with the governance of schooling in the hands of each community's elected school board. The size of a district was typically determined by the distance pupils would need to travel by foot, or perhaps by horseback, to reach school within a reasonable time. Consequently, school districts were geographically quite small. As settlers moved west and established communities, the number of the nation's school districts rapidly increased. Rural schools were often of the one-room or two-room variety. However, by the early decades of the twentieth century, motorized transportation—train, trolley car, and school bus—enabled pupils to attend schools that were farther from their homes. Thus, to profit from the economy of size, school boards found it feasible to combine several districts to form a single unified district that enrolled larger numbers of students in larger schools that could offer a greater variety of services at reasonable cost. As a result, the number of separate school districts across the nation diminished. In 1900 there were approximately 150,000. By 1960 that number had dropped to 45,000 and by the year 2004 to 14,752 districts that operated 105,105 public elementary and secondary schools (Good, 1962; School Matters, 2006).

An important effect of urbanization and district consolidation was that students daily met a greater diversity of schoolmates than ever before—schoolmates of ethnic origins and religious persuasions different from their own.

Indian Boarding Schools

The nation's leaders after the Civil War directed more attention to the education of the Indian population. By 1900, federal funds were being offered to public schools for enrolling Indian pupils, so that by 1928 the majority of Indian schoolchildren attended public school. However, more important for many Indians' educational experiences were the boarding schools financed by the federal government and Christian missions.

A limited number of Indians had attended boarding schools over the decades before the 1870s, with those institutions often operated as part of Christian missionary efforts. However, the truly significant growth of boarding schools began in 1879 when Richard Henry Pratt, an army officer and educator, founded the Carlisle Indian Industrial School in Pennsylvania with financial support from the federal government's Bureau of Indian Affairs. Within 10 years, twenty-four more versions of the Carlisle school were launched by the government in western states. Ultimately more than 100,000 Indian children attended nearly 500 such schools, some of which were on Indian reservations while others were located far from the students' homes. The boarding institutions were operated by either Christian missionaries or the U.S. Bureau of Indian Affairs.

The purpose of boarding schools was to Americanize Indians by removing them from their homes and immersing them full-time in "the white man's ways." This meant teaching Indian youths English and forbidding them to speak their native tongue, to wear tribal garb, or to engage in tribal religious practices. The schools' curriculum, moral climate, and strict discipline were heavy laden with Christian tradition. By 1930 most schools had been closed, but ones on reservations often continued to operate (Porterfield, 2006; Szasz, 2006).

Schooling for Blacks

Before the Civil War, most slave owners in the South had adopted strict measures designed to ensure that blacks did not become literate. In 1829, the Georgia legislature turned such a policy into a state law that decreed

If any slave, Negro or free person of color, or any white person shall teach any other slave, Negro, or free person of color to read or write, either written or printed characters, the same free person of color or slave shall be punished by fine and whipping, or fine or whipping, at the discretion of the court; and if a white person so offend, he, she, or they shall be punished with a fine not exceeding $500 and imprisonment in the common jail at the discretion of the court. (Jackson, 1953)

There were no such laws in the northern nonslavery states. Thus, long before the Civil War, freed blacks in the North had already founded churches that included Sunday schools in which parishioners might learn to read the Bible and to write about their experiences. Sometimes a Sunday school would evolve into a weekday school, but this was rather rare because many whites in the North had discouraged the establishment of schools for blacks.

Then, after the slaves were freed by Abraham Lincoln's Civil War emancipation proclamation, Negro leaders in both the South and North in 1863 joined white abolitionists from the North to provide schooling for the newly freed blacks. This effort included sending teachers—mostly from the North—to establish schools for blacks in the South. Records of the Freedmen's Bureau in the North reported substantial progress over the period 1866–1870 in the schools established under the Bureau (Table 2.2).

Swint (in Lewis, 2006) estimated that the expenditure for northern teachers in the South from 1862 to 1870 was between $5 million and $6 million. The principal benevolent organizations supporting this venture were the American Missionary Association and various Freedmen's Union Commissions. In effect, Christian organizations played a vital role in furnishing schooling for blacks in the South.

Illiteracy among Negroes, age 10 and above, was estimated to be 90 percent at the end of the Civil War. Over the following decades, illiteracy steadily declined from 80 percent in 1870, to 70 percent 1880, 57 percent in 1890, and 45 percent in 1900. By 1905–06, 55 percent of blacks, ages 5–18, were enrolled in school as more communities accepted the responsibility to provide education for their

Table 2.2
Schools for Negroes in the South

Year	Schools	Teachers	Pupils
1866	975	1,405	90,778
1867	1,839	2,087	111,442
1868	1,831	2,295	104,327
1869	2,118	2,445	114,522
1870	2,677	3,300	149,581

Source: Jackson, 1953, p. 101.

Negro residents (Jackson, 1953). However, the available opportunity for schooling, in the opinion of concerned blacks and civil-rights activists, was flawed. In many communities, black students were not permitted to attend the same schools as whites. The rationale adduced in support of such a policy was that blacks' chance to become educated was equal to that for whites if the two ethnic groups' school facilities were "equal." This issue of "separate but equal" would not be settled until the 1950s and beyond.

Summary

As proposed in the above discussion, schooling in America over the 90-year period between 1861 and 1950 was influenced by the addition of new states, massive immigration, the Americanization movement, a rural-to-urban trend, compulsory-education laws, and new educational provisions for the nation's Indians and blacks. During that era, there was no serious objection to including traditional elements of Christianity in public schools.

The Present Era, 1951–2007

Five social-political phenomena that coalesced to influence state/church/school relations over the 56-year period, 1951–2007, were colonialism's demise, America's immigration patterns, multiculturalism, scientific/technological progress, and political change.

Colonialism's Demise

Before World War II, a major portion of the world's regions were colonial possessions of several European nations, (Britain, France, Belgium, Italy, Spain, Portugal, the Netherlands), the United States, Japan, and—to a limited extent—Australia and New Zealand. The colonies held by Britain were so extensive that the British could rightfully brag, "The sun never sets on the British Empire."

Most of Africa, Southeast Asia, South Asia, and the Pacific Islands were colonial territories, as were parts of China and all of Korea.

In the decades before the war, cracks had already begun to appear in the structure of colonialism as a result of increasing unrest among the colonies' indigenous peoples who wanted control over their homelands. Yet despite the annoying cracks, the edifice of colonialism managed to stand. But after the war that changed. *Colonialism* became a bad word and its continued practice was widely condemned. As a result, through a combination of peaceful negotiations and armed conflict, most of the previously colonized regions won their independence. Freedom came to the Philippines in 1946, to India/Pakistan in 1947, Burma in 1948, Indonesia in 1950, the Sudan in 1956, Malaysia/Singapore in 1957, Ghana in 1957, Guinea in 1958, Chad and the Congo in 1960, Tanzania in 1962, Kenya in 1963, and Zambia in 1964. Others, such as Angola, did not win independence until the 1970s. Countries held by the Soviet Union—such as Latvia, Lithuania, and Estonia— gained the right to self-governance when the Soviet Union collapsed in 1991.

The newly created independent nations, upon the departure of their colonial masters, could now make their own decisions about (a) which belief systems to encourage or at least to tolerate and (b) how to conduct schooling. As a result, local church leaders often took over the direction of Christian religions that had been imported and managed by the colonial powers. Furthermore, indigenous folk religions and tribal beliefs that had been discouraged or suppressed by colonial authorities were now frequently accepted and revived by the newly installed native authorities. Thus, in at least some new nations, the diversity of belief constituencies increased. In all of those nations, immediate efforts were launched to extend schooling to the entire population, a policy that had not been practiced under most of the colonial powers.

Although colonialism did not entirely disappear after World War II, it did receive a near-fatal blow. France continued to govern several Pacific Islands, the United States still held American Samoa and Guam, and the Netherlands kept colonies in the Caribbean. However, those "vassal states" were accorded increasing degrees of self-rule.

The end of colonialism would affect religion in American schools through the influence it exerted on patterns of American immigration.

Immigration Patterns

The national origins of immigrants to the United States after 1971 were in sharp contrast to the origins of newcomers before World War II. That contrast is illustrated in Table 2.3, where Europe's domination as the source of immigrants during decades 1911–1920 and 1921–1930 disappeared in the final years of the twentieth century.

The change of immigrants' origins from Europe to Asia and the Americas (chiefly Latin America) resulted from several conditions that appeared following

Table 2.3
Patterns of U.S. Immigration

Years	Total immigrants	Europe (%)	Asia (%)	Americas (%)	Africa (%)	Oceania (%)
1911–20	5,735,811	75	0.4	19.5	0.1	5
1921–30	4,107,209	60	2.7	37	0.1	0.2
1971–80	4,493,314	17	36	45	1.8	0.2
1981–90	7,338,062	10	37	49	2.4	1.6
1991–2000	9,095,417	15	30.7	49.3	3.9	1.1

Source: Historical Immigrant Admission Data, 2006.

World War II. Those conditions were not independent of each other but, rather, interacted in ways that affected the nature of immigration.

A significant initial critical event was the creation of the United Nations in 1945, with member governments pledged to support principles of human rights and self-rule for peoples around the world. Another development was the series of attempts—through both peaceful negotiation and warfare—of colonized populations to achieve self-governance. Those efforts often produced refugees who suffered oppression because of the stand they had adopted in the anticolonialism struggles. Even more political refugees resulted after territories gained their independence and fighting broke out among the indigenous groups that competed for control of their new nation's government.

Many of the refugees sought asylum in the United States. For example, in America's ill-fated attempt to save France's Indochina colonies (Vietnam, Cambodia, Laos) between 1965 and 1973, the United States incurred an obligation to accept thousands of residents of those regions who found themselves in distress for having been—along with the United States—on the losing side of the conflict. Thus, the aftermath of the Vietnam War brought to America thousands of Southeast Asians.

Another factor accounting for the increase of Asians among America's immigrants was the change in American immigration policies. During the nineteenth century, U.S. immigration laws favored Europeans and discriminated against Asians. The 1882 Chinese Exclusion Act banned laborers from China. The 1885 and 1887 alien-contract-labor laws further prohibited certain workers from settling in the United States. But after World War II, a 1952 act established the modern-day immigration system which limits the number of immigrants on a per-country basis and gives priority to family members and people with special skills. Finally, 1968 legislation eliminated immigration discrimination based on race, place of birth, sex, or residence, and it officially abolished restrictions on immigration from Asia.

Two features of many Asian immigrants' worldviews influenced American culture and politics and affected the immigrants' success in their newly adopted country.

First, they brought to America their belief systems, including such religious persuasions as Buddhism, Confucianism, Taoism, Shinto, Hinduism, and a variety of Asian folk traditions. Atheists and nonbelievers were also included, as immigrants came from Communist China and other countries that officially promoted atheism. As a result, the diversity of religious and secular worldviews in American communities expanded along with the numbers of people subscribing to each view. That diversity was reflected in the public schools, so that many school systems now housed more students whose parents subscribed to a widening variety of belief systems.

Second, many of the Asians came from cultures in which schooling was highly valued so that parents emphasized the desirability—indeed, the necessity—of hard work at school. Thus, a high proportion of students of Asian heritage fared well in competition with students from other cultural traditions. For example, at the academically demanding University of California in Berkeley, 40.6 percent of the students in the 2004 freshman class were of Asian ancestry, yet Asians accounted for only 10.9 percent of California's general population (*California quick facts*, 2002; Look at UC Berkeley, 2004).

Asians' educational success contributed to their professional and economic success. Thus, as they grew in numbers, so did their ability to exert pressure on lawmakers and on the mass-communication media to ensure that their rights—including their belief-system freedoms—were respected in both the public schools and the general society.

Whereas Asians' greater opportunity to move to the United States came in the late twentieth century, massive immigration from Latin America began much earlier—chiefly after 1920. Two reasons for such an increase were (a) the need in the U.S. for low-cost laborers (especially for seasonal farm workers) and (b) the lengthy unguarded border between Mexico and the United States. In addition to Latin Americans who were granted official permission to immigrate, thousands more received temporary permission to work in the states. Frequently, after their work contracts expired, they failed to return to their homeland. Furthermore, the task of entering the United States from Mexico was relatively easy. Thousands of migrants secretly slipped across the border from Mexico into Texas, New Mexico, Arizona, or California, becoming illegal aliens who would merge undetected into the states' communities of Latin Americans.

By 2000, high rates of immigration from Latin America combined with high birthrates among Hispanics in the United States to raise the nation's Latin American inhabitants to 35.3 million, slightly larger than the African American population (34.7 million). The birth rate among Latin Americans exceeded that of whites and blacks. Births per 1,000 Hispanic women in 1997 were 107.7 (Mexicans 116.6, Puerto Ricans 71.7, Cubans 57.4, other Hispanics 87.6) compared to 57.0 for whites and 72.4 for blacks. There were 13 million more Hispanics in the

United States in 2000 than in 1990, a gain of 58 percent. At such a growth rate, the number of Hispanics would triple by 2025, thereby comprising 25 percent of the American population (National Center for Health Statistics, 1997; Population Resource Center, 2006).

The rising number of Hispanics who entered the country increased the Christian presence in both public and parochial schools. Although the majority of arrivals from Latin America were Catholics, a growing number were Evangelical Protestants, thus reflecting the marked success of the Evangelical and Pentecostal movements in Central and South America in recent decades.

Multiculturalism

As noted earlier, from the late nineteenth century through the 1940s, the U.S. government had supported an Americanization movement. The purpose of the effort was to meld immigrants' variegated personalities—French, Italian, German, Polish, Mexican, and more—into a common form, that of the authentic American citizen. American society would become a melting pot in which newcomers' disparate ethnic and religious traits would become homogenized. Immigrants would assume a new identify, renounce allegiance to "the old country," and pledge their loyalty to the United States. According to Huntington (2004),

America's core culture has primarily been the culture of the seventeenth- and eighteenth-century settlers who founded our nation. The central elements of that culture are the Christian religion; Protestant values, including individualism, the work ethic, and moralism; the English language; British traditions of law, justice, and limits on government power; and a legacy of European art, literature, and philosophy. Out of this culture the early settlers formulated the American Creed, with its principles of liberty, equality, human rights, representative government, and private property.

However, ultimately the *melting-pot* image, when confronted by the dramatic changes in global politics that accompanied World War II and its aftermath, would be replaced by a different image, the *mosaic*. A mosaic is created by arranging differently shaped forms in a pattern that results in a whole whose individual components retain their original profiles and are easily recognized. In effect, American society now became envisioned as a *multicultural mosaic*.

A group of nineteen scholars, asked in 1994 to identify the year that marked the "zenith of American national integration," chose 1950. In their opinions, after the mid-century "cultural and political fragmentation increased" and "conflict emanating from intensified ethnic and religious consciousness poses the main current challenge to the American nation" (Huntington, 2004).

Therefore, in a multicultural America, citizens of Chinese ancestry could retain elements of their mother culture—language, religion, customs—while still being Americans. So also could Mexicans, Iranians, Vietnamese, Pakistanis, Russians, and the rest hold onto familiar features of their ethnic and religious origins.

But the transition from Americanization to multiculturalism was fraught with problems. How can a nation remain unified and internally peaceful when citizens' loyalties, languages, worldviews, and customs are so diverse? In which ways should all citizens be alike and in which ways can they properly differ? Such questions as these are among the ones at the core of the conflicts over religion in public schools that are analyzed in this book's Chapters 3 through 12.

Scientific/Technological Progress

Probably no half century in the world's history ever witnessed as rapid and pervasive technological change as did the 1951–2007 era. The effects of the period's inventions were not limited to life in advanced industrialized nations but, instead, reached nearly everyone everywhere. The most dramatic and massively influential innovation was the electronic computer in its various guises, along with the Internet and its World Wide Web, which furnished billions of items of information that were accessed instantly from virtually any place on earth.

In addition to furthering computer technology, the science of the era equipped people to (a) map the human genome, (b) solve crimes by DNA analysis, (c) scrutinize the composition of distant stars and planets, (d) land people on the moon and house them in space ships that circled the earth for months at a time, (e) successfully combat a host of diseases, (f) clone animals, and far more.

Such advances in understanding the universe and in producing intentional changes in parts of that universe attested to the power of scientific methods founded on Enlightenment faith in human reason. Thus, people increasingly trusted science and technology to explain the nature of life around them. But empirical science has been unable to answer several perennial questions:

Are there invisible beings that control the universe and influence people's daily lives? If so, who are those beings and what powers do they command? Are there ways that people can influence those beings' actions? In addition, is there life after death? If so, what is the nature of post-mortem existence? Can people influence how and where they will spend everlasting life? If so, how can they exert that influence?

Because empirical science depends on observable phenomena for its data, science cannot furnish answers to queries about such invisible matters. Hence, people are obliged to depend on faith in tradition—on ancient scriptures and legends—to satisfy their yearning to understand such matters.

In the main, science/technology and religion address different questions, so people usually experience no conflict in their lives between science and religion. Among important questions that empirical science cannot answer are the following ones, so people are obliged to find answers in faith-based belief systems and philosophical ponderings.

- What is the purpose of life on earth?
- What should be the purpose or goal of my own life? What is the proper source of that goal; in other words, how and where do I find that purpose?

* What moral or ethnical precepts should guide people's lives, and what is the proper source of those precepts?

Yet there are many mundane questions that science can answer without affecting a person's religious of philosophical convictions. Thus, people can learn atomic theory, the structure of DNA, and how a gasoline engine works without abandoning a belief in God, heaven, or hell.

But in some cases, religion and science both seek to explain the same happenings, and those cases can be the source of controversy. Examples of such issues include (a) how the universe began, (b) the age of the universe, (c) how the earth's different life forms—plants, animals, humans—were created, (d) the causes of individuals' good fortune or ill fortune (financial gain, loss of loved ones, vocational failure), and (e) the causes of natural disasters (drought, fire, flood, earthquake). The influence of those conflicts on American public schools in the early twenty-first century is illustrated in Chapters 3 through 12.

Political Change

The words *politics* and *political*, as intended in this book, refer to the exercise of power. The expression *exercise of power* means the extent to which the behavior of one person (or group) influences the beliefs or behavior of another person (or group). As noted in Chapter 1, if Person A thinks or acts differently because of Person B's presence (bodily or symbolic), then Person B has power over Person A. But if Person A thinks or acts just the same, whether or not Person B is present, then B has no power over A. The amount of power B exerts over A is indicated by how drastically or inevitably A's belief or behavior is altered by the presence of B.

As also explained in Chapter 1, the word *authority* means the official power held by an individual or group. There are various ways by which authority is assigned to a person or group—(a) by the order of a conqueror who has bested foes in battle, (b) by rules written by persuasive leaders, with the rules published in a revered document (a religion's holy scripture, a nation's constitution), (c) by the majority of the populace that are qualified to vote in elections, or (d) by the population's chosen representatives. Since the creation of the American democratic republic, groups have gained their authority by means of the ballot box. Citizens have voted candidates into office. Being in office, rather than being an outsider, is a great advantage for having one's educational policies put into practice. At the federal-government level, the political party that controls the presidency and the houses of Congress can fairly well ensure that its preferences in educational matters will prevail in the nation's schools. Such is also the case at governmental levels below the national government, that is, at the state-legislature and district-school-board levels.

Although in U.S. elections various political parties compete for office, only two parties have enjoyed a reasonable chance to win—the Republicans and the Democrats. To a noticeable degree, Republicans and Democrats have expressed contrary views about certain state/church/school relationships. Whereas in recent times, Democrats have often hoped to increase the quality of students' learning by upgrading public schools, Republicans have tended to prefer aiding private schools as a means of improving the nation's education. The Republican initiatives, particularly during President George W. Bush's two terms in office (2001–2008), featured school-choice vouchers and special services to private schools that were funded by public tax moneys. Such proposals have contributed to the conflicts over state/church/school relationships described in Chapters 3 through 11.

Summary

In the above discussion, five conditions have been proposed as important influences on the nature of present-day state/church/school relationships in the United States. Those conditions, as they have developed over the past half century, have been colonialism's demise, America's immigration patterns, multiculturalism, scientific/technological progress, and political change.

To complete this chapter's sketch of the historical background of current religion-in-public-schools controversies, I next identify several recent developments in the educational experiences of American Indians and blacks.

Indians' Schooling

From the time European colonists first arrived in North America until the mid-twentieth century, the settlers' onslaught on American Indians' domains and cultures (through disease, warfare, land theft, religious conversion, and schooling) "persuaded some native survivors to adopt the Euro-American values of land ownership, individualism, and Christianity" (Szasz, 2006). Other Indians, however, vowed to fight back, using their European form of education to pursue legal means of reclaiming rights they felt had long been denied to them.

In the spirit of dissent and civil rights that pervaded the 1960s, educated Indians from both urban centers and reservations applied organized political pressure to state and federal governments in order to force improvement in the condition of the Native American population. Indian activists sought greater self-determination and recognition of treaties that the federal government had signed in the nineteenth and twentieth centuries. That political pressure resulted in Congress passing the Indian Education Act (1972) and the Indian Self-Determination and Education Assistance Act (1975).

The 1972 legislation focused on the educational needs of Indians from preschool through graduate school and reaffirmed the federal government's special responsibility for the education of American Indians and Alaska Natives. The act also offered educational services not available previously from the Bureau of Indian Affairs.

The 1975 act established "a meaningful Indian self-determination policy, which will permit an orderly transition from federal domination of programs for and services to Indians to effective and meaningful participation by the Indian people in the planning, conduct, and administration of these programs and services" (Council of Indian Nations, 2006). As a result, Indian nations gained a measure of control over programs for the 85 percent of their children who attended public schools. The nations could also contract directly for services in schools funded by the Bureau of Indian Affairs. Hence, Native Americans could finally bring their own languages, beliefs, and philosophies into their schools.

In 1978, the U.S. Congress passed a law to right another wrong from the past. The American Indian Religious Freedom Act declared that henceforth it would be

the policy of the United States to protect and preserve for American Indians their inherent right of freedom to believe, express, and exercise the traditional religions of the American Indian, Eskimo, Aleut, and Native Hawaiians, including but not limited to access to sites, use, and possession of sacred objects, and the freedom to worship through ceremonials and traditional rites. (*American Indian*, 1978)

Therefore, after two centuries under the United States government, the religions of native peoples would be accorded the same respect, rights, and privileges as those that Christian denominations had enjoyed since the founding of the republic. Indians were no longer to be viewed as heathen savages who subscribed to weird beliefs and engaged in bizarre pagan rites. By law, native peoples' worldviews and modes of worship would officially deserve protection and respect.

Blacks' Educational Rights

Abraham Lincoln's Emancipation Proclamation in 1863 launched a series of official acts designed to give black slaves their freedom and furnish them the full array of rights that all American citizens deserved. However, blacks' opportunity to enjoy those rights in daily life was constantly frustrated by tradition—by a long history of whites treating African Americans as inferiors, requiring blacks to ride in the rear of public buses, drink from special water fountains, occupy different hotels and restaurants than ones frequented by whites, and attend separate schools. Such prejudicial practices were most prominent and unyielding in former slave states where discrimination was bolstered by state and local laws. And prejudice against blacks was widespread in other parts of the nation as well.

African Americans' resentment over meager schooling opportunities reached a crisis in the early 1950s when blacks filed lawsuits in Kansas, South Carolina, Virginia, and Delaware, claiming prejudicial treatment in educational provisions. From those states, five similar cases were combined when they reached the U.S. Supreme Court in 1954 and were adjudicated under the title *Brown v. the Board of Education of Topeka, Kansas*.

In 1950 the Topeka National Association for the Advancement of Colored People set out to organize a legal challenge to an 1879 State law that permitted racially segregated elementary schools in certain cities based on population. For Kansas this would become the 12th case [focusing] on ending segregation in public schools. The local NAACP assembled a group of 13 parents who agreed to be plaintiffs on behalf of their 20 children. Following direction from legal counsel, they attempted to enroll their children in segregated white schools and all were denied. Topeka operated eighteen neighborhood schools for white children, while African-American children had access to only four schools. In February of 1951 the Topeka NAACP filed a case on their behalf. Although this was a class action, it was named for one of the plaintiffs, Oliver Brown. (*Brown v. Board of Education*, 2004)

At the 1954 U.S. Supreme Court hearing, lawyers defending communities' requirement that blacks attend different schools than those for whites claimed that blacks' rights were not being abridged if the facilities for the two ethnic groups were "equal." But lawyers for the black plaintiffs argued that even if facilities were alike—which they usually were not—the education received by the blacks would not be "equal." The Supreme Court found in favor of the plaintiffs on the grounds that

Segregation of white and Negro children in the public schools of a State solely on the basis of race, pursuant to state laws permitting or requiring such segregation, denies to Negro children the equal protection of the laws guaranteed by the [U.S. Constitution's] Fourteenth Amendment—even though the physical facilities and other 'tangible' factors of white and Negro schools may be equal. (*Brown v. Board of Education*, 1954)

The Court's school-desegregation decision was followed by two decades of turbulence as civil-rights activists were led by black Christian church leaders—such as Dr. Martin Luther King Jr.—to transform the decision into reality. Segregationists who sought to continue denying blacks and other non-whites access to certain public schools were ultimately defeated during ofttimes bloody struggles that involved state/church/school relationships. When local police arrested blacks who sought admission to white schools, the federal government sent troops to enforce the Supreme Court ruling. When local authorities repulsed blacks' attempts to claim equal rights (ride buses, use restrooms, eat at restaurants, attend schools), black church leaders responded by organizing mass public demonstrations and boycotts whose participants included white civil-rights activists.

By means of such activities, equal schooling opportunities for blacks continued to expand throughout the final decades of the twentieth century. By 2007, the average black youth still lagged behind the average white in educational accomplishment. However, blacks' opportunities for quality schooling had advanced remarkably over the 1951–2007 era and were in the process of receiving additional needed attention.

TRENDS OF THE TIMES, 1600–2007

As explained at the beginning of this chapter, a key purpose of our glance back into history was to illustrate state/religion/school trends in the form of four propositions. Thus, I suggest that over the 1600–2007 era,

Table 2.4
Religious Affiliation of U.S. Founding Fathers

Faith	Number (%)
Episcopalian/Anglican	88 (54.7)
Presbyterian	30 (18.6)
Congregationalist	27 (16.8)
Quaker	7 (4.3)
Dutch/German Reformed	6 (3.7)
Lutheran	5 (3.1)
Catholic	3 (1.9)
Huguenot	3 (1.9)
Unitarian	3 (1.9)
Methodist	2 (1.2)
Calvinist	1 (.06)
Total	204

Source: Adherents.com, 2005.

- religions in the United States became more *diverse*,
- religious beliefs and practices became increasingly *removed from public schools*,
- the teaching/learning process grew more *institutionalized*,
- sources of knowledge became more *secular* and *empirical*.

Each of these trends was accompanied by *transition lag*, meaning that whenever an innovation is introduced into a society, people differ in their willingness to embrace the new departure. Whereas some people adopt the innovation quite soon, others lag behind a bit, reluctant to accept the new until some time passes. Still others—perhaps many—cling to tradition, holding back in order to guard ways of life that have served them well in the past. Traditionalists may even attempt to reverse the trend, returning the society to policies and practices of yesteryear.

Religious Diversity

An impression of the religious composition of the United States at its beginning is suggested by the religious affiliation of the nation's founding fathers. The expression *founding fathers* refers to the men who either attended the Constitutional Convention of 1787 or served in the first Federal Congress (1789–1791) or signed one or more of three documents—Declaration of Independence, Articles of Confederation, or U.S. Constitution. As shown in Table 2.4, there were 204 such individuals, all members of a handful of Christian denominations; they were overwhelmingly Protestant (98%). Clearly, this listing fails to reflect the religious affiliation of the new nation's entire citizenry. For example, there was also a small percentage of Jews in the population. However, the table does convey a general sense of the religious composition of the country's non-Indian, nonslave populace.

Over the two-and-one-quarter centuries since the establishment of the American republic, the nation's religious pattern changed dramatically as the result of immigration, the creation of new faiths, and shifts in the proportions of people subscribing to different belief systems.

In 1900, the non-Christian portion of the U.S. population was 3.6 percent. By 1995, that portion had grown to 14.6 percent, which included atheists, Baha'is, Buddhists, Chinese-folk-religionists, Hindus, Jews, Muslims, Black Muslims, New-religionists, Non-religionists, Sikhs, and Tribal-religionists (*Non-Christian religious adherents*, 1995).

A survey in year 2000 of 14,301 religious congregations representing forty-one faith groups in the United States revealed rapid growth in Evangelical Protestant congregations and declining membership in Episcopalian, Lutheran, Methodist, and other mainline Protestant groups. The development of new churches for Roman Catholic and Eastern Orthodox populations declined at the same time that a rapid upsurge was observed in the growth of new congregations of Baha'is, Muslims, Jews, and Mormons (Broadway, 2001).

In three important ways, increases in America's religious diversity affected the role of religion in public schools. First, proponents of various non-Christian faiths sought to have their beliefs and practices accorded the same privileges as those traditionally available to Christians. For instance, they wanted the schools to recognize their denomination's holidays, celebrations, symbols, and holy scriptures. Second, they wanted certain services to be paid for by public funds—such as student transportation (school buses) and help for disabled and economically disadvantaged students. Third, political activists for various religions pressed textbook publishers and curriculum planners to portray their beliefs and histories in a positive light in the schools' teaching materials.

Removal of Religion from Public Schools

From the early days of the American republic, the first amendment to the U.S. Constitution had been generally interpreted to mean that public schools—as instruments of the secular government—should be free of religion. However, throughout the 1800s and the first half of the 1900s, rarely were objections raised about remnants of Christian belief and practice typically found in schools. Only in the closing decades of the twentieth century did advocates of the strict separation of church and state successfully argue in courts that elements of Christianity or Judaism should be banned from public schools. As explained in later chapters of this book, the U.S. Supreme Court outlawed such school traditions as prayer (1962), the teaching of a particular religion's doctrine (1963), and the permanent display of the biblical Ten Commandments (1980).

At the same time that vestiges of religion were being eliminated from public schools, religious activists were increasingly successful in convincing lawmakers and government administrators to furnish parochial schools public funds and services.

Learning Institutionalized

Although there were some schools in early colonial America, most children's and youths' education in those days came from outside the classroom. Parents taught the young at home to read the Bible, teenagers learned a trade by working alongside parents in the home or farm or shop, and youths were assigned to apprenticeships. However, over the advancing decades, compulsory-schooling legislation required all youngsters ages 6 through 16 to spend increasing amounts of time in school. Thus, as education became more institutionalized, children were obliged to spend time—both in class and out of class—with schoolmates from ethnic and religious groups other than their own. Such conditions could promote either of two contrasting outcomes: (a) greater religious tolerance among students who made friends with classmates from faiths different than their own or (b) greater interfaith suspicion and hatred when classmates from different sects accused and tormented each other.

Empirical Sources of Knowledge

With the rapid advance of science and technology over the centuries, schools increasingly taught ways of answering questions about life that depended on empirical evidence and scientific logic rather than depending on religion and folklore. Thus, rather than explaining good or poor health as the work of God or Satan, youths were urged to seek causes in their own behavior and in their environment. Instead of blaming hurricanes, tornadoes, floods, and earthquakes on angry spirits, the young were taught to seek for causes in barometric conditions, temperature changes, shifting sea currents, geologic formations, and the like.

Therefore, as schools focused more attention on scientific advances, the need for schools to teach religious explanations of life's events diminished. There was now more reason to eliminate religious explanations from public schools' curricula and customs.

SUMMARY

This chapter has been founded on the assumption that providing readers a historical sketch of state/church/school relationships in America over the four-century period 1600–2007 will help them understand the roots of the controversies over religion in public schools that are described in Chapters 3 through 11.

Each of the following chapters focuses on a particular set of controversies, with each chapter organized in the same pattern of three parts. Part one describes the nature of the controversial issue that is the subject of the chapter. Part two traces in detail the way the controversy developed. Part three offers guidelines that educators (teachers, administrators, school-board members) might follow when making decisions about the chapter's controversy in their own schools.

Chapter 3

God and Darwin

This chapter's controversial issue concerns the question of whether a religious version of human beginnings should be taught in public schools' science classes in addition to—or instead of—a secular Darwinian version.

HOW THE CONTROVERSY DEVELOPED

The doctrine of virtually every religion includes a proposal about the origin of the universe and of the earth's human inhabitants. Perhaps the world's best-known proposal is the one found in *Genesis*, which is the first book of the Jewish Torah and of the Old Testament of the Christian Bible. For many centuries that proposal has been accepted by faithful Jews, Christians, and Muslims as the true account of how the universe and humans began. The following version of that creation story is from the most widely used Protestant Christian Bible, the one authorized by King James I of England in 1611.

In the beginning God created the heaven and the earth. And the earth was without form and void; and the darkness was upon the face of the deep. And the Spirit of God moved upon the face of the waters. And God said, "Let there be light," and there was light . . . And God called the light Day, and the darkness he called Night. And the evening and the morning were the first day. (*Genesis, 1611, chapter 1, verses 1–4*)

On the second day God created a region—a dome-like firmament—that He called Heaven. On the third day, He created dry land below Heaven which He called Earth; and He produced waters that He called Seas, along with grass and fruit trees. On the fourth day He created the sun to light the day and the moon and stars to light the night and attached stars to the heavenly firmament. On the fifth day He created all sorts of fish for the seas and fowl for the earth. On the sixth day God said, "Let the earth bring forth every living creature after his kind—cattle, and creeping thing, and beast of the earth after his kind: and it was so."

And God said, "Let us make man in our image, after our likeness: and let them have dominion over the fish of the sea, and over the fowl of the air, and over the cattle, and over all the earth, and over every creeping thing that creepeth upon the earth." So God created man in His *own* image ... male and female created He them. And God blessed them and ... said unto them, "Be fruitful, and multiply, and replenish the earth, and subdue it: and have dominion over ... every living thing that moveth upon the earth." (*Genesis 1, verses 1–28*, 1611)

In a more detailed passage, the second chapter of Genesis explains that

The Lord God formed man of the dust of the ground, and breathed into his nostrils the breath of life; and man [named Adam] became a living soul ... And the Lord God caused a deep sleep to fall upon Adam ... and took one of his ribs ... [from which He] made a woman [Eve]. (*Genesis, 2, verses 7, 21–22*, 1611)

Across the centuries, this account had been accepted in Jewish, Christian, and Muslim societies as the true story of human beginnings. Then, in the mid-nineteenth century, Europeans and Americans alike were stunned by a proposal that men and women had not been created suddenly in their mature form by a supreme heavenly power. Instead, they had evolved gradually over eons of time from simpler forms of animal life through a process of mutation and natural selection by which varieties of animals that were well suited to survival as their environments changed would prosper, and those not well suited would die off. Therefore, humans were not unique beings, entirely separate from other animals. They were part of a complex pattern of linked life forms. The detailed version of that proposal appeared in the book *The Origin of Species* (1859) by Charles Darwin, an English naturalist; and the scheme became known as a theory of evolution.

Darwin's theory was not greeted with great joy in his day, nor is it universally accepted today. In the late nineteenth century, the theory was condemned from most pulpits; and the general public did not welcome the unattractive likelihood that their close biological relatives might have been apes and monkeys and that more distant ancestors could have been chickens, toads, and garden slugs. However, a massive accumulation of empirical evidence over the decades gradually convinced scientists of the theory's worth, so that today much of biological science as taught in schools is founded on an updated version of the theory of evolution called neo-Darwinism.

The Monkey Trial

The present-day public debate over which version of human origins should be taught in public-school science classes goes back to 1925. The most highly

Figure 3.1
Parallel traditions in teaching about human origins.

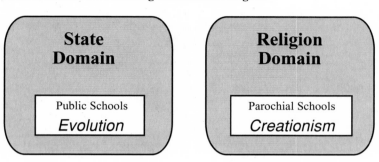

publicized early confrontation between *creationists* (advocates of the traditional biblical account of human beginnings) and *evolutionists* (proponents of Darwinism) would appear in Dayton, Tennessee. That critical event was a criminal court hearing known as *The Scopes Case* or *The Monkey Trial*. The question was whether evolution should be taught in schools in violation of Tennessee's antievolution statute that made it unlawful "to teach any theory that denies the story of divine creation as taught by the Bible and to teach instead that man was descended from a lower order of animals" (*State v. John Scopes*, 2004). John Scopes, a substitute biology teacher, was tried in court for teaching Charles Darwin's theory that humans were not created of a sudden in the Garden of Eden but, instead, they evolved over many thousands of years from gradual changes in animal species. The upshot of the case was that Scopes was declared guilty of breaking the law. However, the nationwide publicity that the trial attracted was instrumental in the defeat of antievolution-teaching laws in all but two (Arkansas, Mississippi) of the fifteen states that had such bills before legislatures in 1925.

By the middle of the twentieth century, Darwin's theory had become the version of human beginnings taught in most public-school science classes. At the same time, in the Bible classes taught in Christian and Judaic private schools, creationism continued to serve as the dominant account of how humans arrived on earth. Thus, there were now separate traditions advancing in parallel—the earlier centuries-old biblical creationism and the more recent century-old Darwinian theory (Figure 3.1).

In the decades approaching the twenty-first century, the debate about teaching evolution continued to surface periodically in various parts of the nation. The U.S. Supreme Court ruled in 1968 that a 1929 Arkansas statute prohibiting the teaching of evolution was unconstitutional. A federal court in 1982 rejected a newly passed Arkansas "balanced treatment" law mandating that *creation science* be taught alongside *evolution science*; the court declared that "creation science" was not science. In 1987, the U.S. Supreme Court ruled unconstitutional a similar 1981 Louisiana law on the grounds that teaching students that a supernatural being created humans was an improper endorsement of a religious doctrine.

Figure 3.2
Incursions of beliefs across domains.

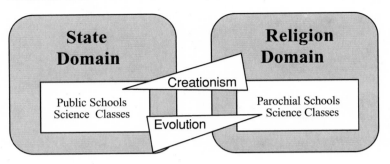

With the foregoing sketch of traditions and critical events in mind, we turn now to the condition of the creationism/evolution controversy in recent times.

The Present-Day Debate

The early years of the twenty-first century witnessed increasingly active incursions (a) of evolution into science classes in the religion domain and (b) of creationism into science classes in the public schools of the state domain (Figure 3.2).

Mainstream Catholic, Protestant, and Jewish schools welcomed the teaching of neo-Darwinism in science courses, reasoning that (a) the description of creation in Genesis was only ancient thinkers' estimate of how life began and thus should not be accepted as the literal truth and (b) God could easily have arranged for animate beings to evolve in the pattern Darwin proposed.

At the same time, more doctrinaire evangelical and pentecostal denominations rejected the teaching of Darwin's theory and, by accepting the story in Genesis as the literal truth, sought to have some form of creationism replace evolution, or at least be taught in addition to Darwinism in public schools. However, those attempts were rebuffed by the great majority of scientists and science educators as well as by advocates of the separation of church and state. Despite this resistance, there has been a rapid acceleration of attempts to teach creationism in state schools. In 2001, the Hawaii board of education struck down a proposal that would permit a biblical human-beginnings version in science classes along with Darwin's theory. In 2002, the Ohio board of education gave a form of creationism equal status with evolution in the public-school curriculum. In 2004, the Grantsburg (Wisconsin) school board issued a resolution allowing "various theories/models of origins" to be included among science studies.

To summarize, during the early years of the twenty-first century, the creationism/evolution debate became more widespread and contentious than at any time during the previous three quarters of a century. The nature of that confrontation is the matter to which we now turn. The discussion opens with (a) a description of present-day versions of the biblical creation story, then continues with (b) creation sciences, (c) evolutionists' responses, (d) public opinion, (e) the contending constituencies, (f) five illustrative cases, and (g) resolving the conflict.

Creationism

There are several versions of creationist doctrine. One is *young-earth creationism*, which proposes that (a) God produced the universe and everything within it during 6 days and (b) the Earth is only a few thousand years old—perhaps 4,000, maybe 6,000, or possibly 10,000. Another version accepts the notion that the Earth is millions of years old but holds that God originally created humans complete in their present form, distinctly different from all other manner of life. A third version rejects the notion of macroevolution (all species tracing their origins back to a common simple-celled organism) but accepts microevolution (changes within a given species as the result of selective breeding or adjustments to changed environments, as with humans in intense-sunlight tropical regions developing more protective dark skin pigment than humans in temperate zones).

The evidence on which creationists base their conviction is a holy book, respected as the source of authoritative truth.

In the somewhat distant past, supporters of teaching creationism in public schools openly stated that their proposal was founded on religious faith—on their conviction that the Bible version of human origins was the revealed word of God. However, in more recent times, an increasing number of creationism's proponents have labeled their proposal *scientific creationism* while others have called it *intelligent design*. The following examples illustrate these two versions of what has been termed *creation science*.

Scientific Creationism

Scientific creationism, as promoted by the Institute for Creation Research located in Southern California, is founded on nine tenets. The first two are

1. The physical universe of space, time, matter and energy has not always existed, but was supernaturally created by a transcendent personal Creator who alone has existed from eternity.
2. The phenomenon of biological life did not develop by natural processes from inanimate systems but was specially and supernaturally created by the Creator. (Tenets of scientific creationism, 1985, p. 12)

In a similar vein, the remaining seven principles assert that (3) all major types plants and animals were in complete form from the time the Creator produced them, (4) humans did not evolve from animal ancestors but were complete with moral consciousness, language, abstract thought, and religious nature from their very beginning, (5) the universe and earth were created in the rather recent past, (6) the natural laws by which the universe operates were originated and are daily maintained by their Creator, (7) imperfections (disease, catastrophe) in the way the originally perfect universe now operates show that the Creator has an ultimate purpose for the universe, (8) the world awaits the revelation of that purpose, and (9) "the human mind (if open to the possibility of creation) is able to explore the manifestations of that Creator rationally and scientifically, and to reach an intelligent decision regarding one's place in the Creator's plan" (Tenets of scientific creationism, 1985, pp. 12–13).

Two books among those offering scientific-creationism versions of the Earth's and humans' beginnings are *Grand Canyon: A Different View* (2003) and *Torah Views on Science and Its Problems* (1988). Authors of such volumes use several methods of lending their schemes a scientific cast. For example, the Grand Canyon book by Tom Vail asserts that 6,000 years ago God created the universe in 6 days, then subsequently produced a world-wide flood to wipe out "the wickedness of man." Vail's estimate differs dramatically from that of scientists who date the earth's age at 4.5 billion years, and the Grand Canyon's layers at some two billion years. In Vail's volume, photographs of the canyon on the Colorado River in Arizona are combined with verses from the Bible as ostensible evidence that the canyon was formed from the gigantic biblical deluge of Noah's time (Dean, 2004).

The *Torah-Views* volume offers a kind of timewarp explanation of how the universe and all its inhabitants were produced within 6 days. According to Rabbi Simon Schwab, author of one of the book's articles, time was extremely condensed during biblical creation's initial week, so that work which would require millions of years by our present calculation of the length of days was accomplished in 6 days at super-cosmic speed. After that first week, the passing of time immediately slowed to its current 24-hour-day rate and has continued at that deliberate pace ever since (Zindler, 1992).

Intelligent Design

Proponents of *intelligent design* or *divine design* have contended that the natural world is in the form of an extremely complex, integrated pattern that could not have occurred spontaneously. According to intelligent-design advocates, logic dictates that the universe's intricate pattern had to be devised by an extremely wise designer who not only created the universe but also continues to supervise its operation and the conduct of its inhabitants. Most intelligent-design adherents identify God as the designer and subscribe to a variation of biblical creationism, but others are unwilling, in a scientific context, to identify the source of the alleged intelligence.

The intelligent-design doctrine was introduced in the mid-1990s by a group of physicists, chemists, biologists, and philosophers as a challenge to Darwin's proposal that everything in the natural world arose by a spontaneous process of natural selection and random mutations. These skeptics doubted that natural processes had created life from chemicals, that all life had a common origin, and that humans and apes shared a common ancestor. Although proponents of intelligent design accept the notion of evolution within species—microevolution—they believe that such human equipment as brains and eyes, because of their highly ordered complexity, are best explained as a product of intelligent intent.

Three influential books issued in the 1990s to further the anti-Darwinian cause by touting intelligent design were (a) Davis and Kenyon's *Of Pandas and People: The Central Question of Biological Origins* (1989, 1993) (b) Johnson's *Darwin on Trial* (1993), and (c) Behe's *Darwin's Black Box: The Biochemical Challenge to Evolution* (1996).

The recent appearance of the intelligent-design explanation might imply that it is something new, but that is hardly the case. The notion comes from at least as far back as the nineteenth century when Darwin offered his opinion about its worth. In his autobiography, he observed,

Now that the law of natural selection has been discovered, we can no longer argue that, for instance, the beautiful hinge of a bivalve shell must have been made by an intelligent being, like the hinge of a door by man. There seems to be no more design in the variability of organic beings, and in the action of natural selection, than in the course which the wind blows. (Darwin, 1887)

And in a letter to a friend, Darwin wrote that the amount of pain in the world was not in keeping with the idea of a benevolent intelligent designer, so

the presence of much suffering agrees well with the view that all organic beings have been developed through variation and natural selection . . . I see a bird which I want for food, take my gun, and kill it. I do this *designedly*. An innocent and good man stands under a tree and is killed by a flash of lightning. Do you believe that a God *designedly* killed this man? Many or most persons do believe this; I can't and don't. (Darwin, 1887)

Although intelligent design today is less overtly religion-based than creation science, there is ample evidence of its support by fundamentalist Christians. For example, the publisher of *Darwin on Trial* is the InterVarsity Christian Fellowship. The copyright holder of *Pandas and People* is the Foundation for Thought and Ethics, a Texas-based Christian organization that identifies itself as having "produced major publishing breakthroughs on the subject of origins, helped to inspire the robust and exciting international movement of Intelligent Design, and launched an enriching series of high school textbooks now used in public and private schools" (Foundation for Thought and Ethics, 2006).

The nationwide leader in promoting intelligent design as an alternative to Darwinism has been the Center for Science and Culture within the Discovery Institute that was established in the 1990s in Seattle (Washington) with grants from a Southern California Catholic, billionaire Howard F. Ahmanson Jr. (founder of Dominos Pizza), and the Maclellan Foundation, which supports groups that are "committed to furthering the Kingdom of Christ."

Rather than offering specific explanations of how the universe and humans began, proponents of intelligent design (a) state that life arose through a purposeful plan by a divine being and (b) seek to expose flaws in specific applications of Darwinian theory. Thus, the Discovery Institute's position on teaching about human beginnings is that

examination of evidence and critical thinking are the hallmarks of good science educa- tion . . . It follows that students should learn about the scientific data that supports Darwin's theory of evolution, as well as the data that goes against the theory and which contin- ues to puzzle scientists . . . Our recommendation is that students receive a full and fair disclosure of the facts surrounding Darwin's theory and that the leading scientific criti- cisms of the theory not be censored from classroom discussion. (Discovery Institute staff, 2004)

Among the empirical findings that critics of evolution most often cite as evidence of the theory's flaws are the gaps in what should be—according to Darwinism—a consistent progression of evolutionary changes among fossil remains found in the successive layers of rock in the earth's crust. In other words, in the bone and petrified remnants of animal species from the distant past that are embedded in rock strata, why is there not an unbroken chain of gradual changes in species as the millennia progressed? Why are there such marked differences within one extinct species that supposedly—according to Darwin—had gradually evolved from another species over time? Such evidence, according to the critics, suggests that each sort of animal life did not result from gradual evolutionary changes but, instead, each had been created separately—all at the same time—by an intelligent designer.

A further charge against Darwin's theory has been that it offers no scientific explanation for the specific order of DNA bases, that is, for the components of the deoxyribonucleic acid that nearly all human cells contain as the genetic guide for growth and development.

Thus, the chief argument adduced by promoters of intelligent design is that Darwin's theory is irreparably defective, but they offer no empirical evidence suggesting that intelligent design would be a suitable replacement. According to Eugenie Scott, director of the National Center for Science Education in Oakland, California, "Creationists believe that all you have to do is disprove evolution, and creationism wins by default. Teach children that evolution is lousy science, and they will automatically default to God did it" (Hanna, 2005a).

In summary, rather than denouncing scientific approaches to questions about the origin of the universe and humans, opponents of Darwin's theory have in- creasingly furnished their own versions of *science*—versions they believe should be in public-school science curricula. The emphasis in promoting comparisons between Darwin's views and alternative versions of human beginnings has been on "the data that goes [sic] against [Darwin's] theory" as featured in such books as Sarfati's *Refuting Evolution* (1999).

Evolutionists' Responses

Four reactions of Darwin's supporters to the claims of creation-science advocates have concerned the meaning assigned to *science, theory, unexplained phenomena,* and *alternative explanations.*

Science Defined

The word *science,* in its commonly accepted version, refers to (a) collecting empirical observations of events, (b) organizing those observations, and (c) logically interpreting how the observations (facts) relate to each other. That three-step process is often referred to as *scientific method.* Actually, there is no single scientific method. Instead, scientific method consists of applying several operating principles that scientists share, such as the following trio.

- Science is concerned with understanding perceptible things—things seen, heard, touched, smelled. Increasingly, scientists depend on aids for extending and refining the impressions from their own senses, such aids as microscopes, telescopes, computers, radar, sonar, X-rays, magnetic resonance imaging, radiocarbon dating, cyclotrons, and more. Nonmaterial conceptions—invisible spirits, angels, jinns, gods, heaven, and the like—are thus outside the realm of science, although people's *reports* of believing in such things are within the purvey of scientists who study characteristics of people's beliefs.
- All observations (facts) and their interpretation are tentative, subject to revision and refinement on the basis of additional empirical observations. No observation or explanation is final.
- Interpreting cause-and-effect relationships among observations involves proposing hypotheses that can be tested to determine how likely they are true.

Evolutionists, who subscribe to such principles, claim that creationists are not being scientific when they accept an ancient holy book's rendition of human origins that fails to yield testable hypotheses. Ergo, creationism does not qualify as *science.*

Theory Defined

A typical charge that creationists aim at Darwinism is that it is "merely theory, not fact." In response, scientists argue that such critics misunderstand the meaning of *theory* in science. The board of directors of the Genetics Society of America wrote,

In common usage "theory" means "conjecture" or "speculation," whereas in scientific usage it means a systematically organized body of knowledge that explains a large set of observations and makes testable predictions. Science operates first by observation and then by developing a hypothesis as a preliminary explanation of the data. A theory is a hypothesis that has been subsequently confirmed by abundant, consistent data obtained from tests of the hypothesis. (Genetics Society of America, 2003)

Unexplained Phenomena

As noted earlier, proponents of creationism complained that Darwin's theory suffered from inconsistencies in its empirical support. Darwinism's supporters have responded to such complaints in three principal ways.

First, they have pointed out that are no final answers in scientific explanations. Theories are only estimates of reality, with those estimates always subject to testing and revision on the basis of new observations—new empirical discoveries. Thus, the modern-day revision of Darwin's proposal (neo-Darwinism) is like every other scientific explanation. It is considered to be the best explanation presently available, but it is still evolving as further examples of changes in species accumulate.

Second, it is unrealistic to expect to find all steps in the evolutionary sequence among fossils, because vestiges of many species from the past have long disappeared. Most animals that die will deteriorate completely, leaving investigators no remains to discover. Thus, it should hardly be surprising that not all of the links in the chains of evolving species have been found.

Third, apparent gaps in fossil sequences are continually being filled in as investigators unearth more remnants. For example, consider a segment of Brown University biologist Kenneth R. Miller's review of Michael J. Behe's book *Darwin's Black Box*. (Miller, the author of *Finding Darwin's God* and of widely used biology textbooks, is a Roman Catholic, as is Behe.) In *Darwin's Black Box*, Behe contended that certain characteristics of living beings were so "irreducibly complex" that those features could not have evolved gradually but, instead, must have been created of a sudden as an intact system. In support of this argument, Behe cited the case of the bones of the middle ear in mammals. Miller responded to that argument in the following fashion:

The three smallest bones in the human body, the malleus, incus, and stapes, carry sound vibrations across the middle ear, from the membrane-like tympanum (the eardrum) to the oval window. This five-component system fits Behe's test of irreducible complexity perfectly—if any one of its parts are taken away or modified, hearing would be lost. This is the kind of system that evolution supposedly cannot produce. Unfortunately for "intelligent design," the fossil record elegantly and precisely documents exactly how this system formed. During the evolution of mammals, bones that originally formed the rear portion of the reptilian lower jaw were gradually pushed backwards and reduced in size until they migrated into the middle ear, forming the bony connections that carry vibrations into the inner ears of present-day mammals. A system of perfectly-formed, interlocking components, specified by multiple genes, was gradually refashioned and adapted for another purpose altogether—something that [Behe's] book claims to be impossible. As the well-informed reader may know, creationist critics of this interpretation of fossils in the reptile to mammal transition once charged that this could not have taken place. What would happen, they joked, to the unfortunate reptile while he was waiting for two of his jaw bones to migrate into the middle ear? The poor creature could neither hear nor eat! As students of evolution may know, A. W. Crompton of Harvard University brought this laughter to a deafening halt when he unearthed a fossil with a double articulation of the jaw joint—an adaptation that would allow the animal to both eat and hear during the transition, enabling natural selection to favor each of the intermediate stages. (Miller, 1996)

As another example, researchers have found fossils of "ancient hippo-like animals that had begun to take on characteristics of today's whales: longer tails and skulls, shorter hind legs, and the movement of nostrils towards the top of the head. Those fossils were found in Pakistan, in an area once covered by shallow water, just where an animal would be if it were evolving from a land-dweller to a marine mammal" (Avril, 2005).

Furthermore, a recently invented scientific technique, DNA analysis, has equipped scientists with a valuable method for investigating the degree of genetic material common to different living species, thereby furnishing persuasive evidence of links among species.

Alternative Explanations

One argument critics of Darwinism offer for evolutionists' reluctance to include intelligent design in science classes has been that "The science establishment opposes intelligent design because it doesn't want challenges to the status quo." In response, supporters of Darwin's theory have declared that

scientific hypotheses are constantly challenged, revised, and even disproved. For every scientist invested in the prevailing "orthodoxy," there are probably at least 10 who would love nothing more than to revolutionize their field. But the status quo must be challenged through scientific inquiry, not wishful thinking. (Young, 2005)

As noted earlier, in recent times efforts to teach creationism in public schools have focused on including alternative versions of human beginnings that students can compare with Darwin's theory. Such a proposal would support teaching biblical creationism—perhaps in the form of intelligent design—and could avoid the appearance of privileging Jews, Christians, and Muslims over other religious groups if the proposals of various religious persuasions were included. However useful such an approach might be for fostering students' critical thinking, scientists have raised several questions about how practical the approach would be. Most, if not all, of the world's multitude of cultures have their own creation stories—Hindus, Shintoists, South African Zulus, Samoans, America's Navajos and Sioux, Haiti's Voodoo adherents, and on and on. So, which of these alternatives would students study? And how much time should be devoted to each version compared to the time dedicated to all of the other topics found in the science curriculum? In answering such queries, a University of Wisconsin botanist, Don Waller, argued that "insisting that teachers teach alternative theories of origin in biology classes takes time away from real learning, confuses some students, and is a misuse of limited class time and public funds" (Levy, 2004).

Brown University biologist Kenneth Miller suggested that the intelligent-design proposal was "what a philosopher might call the argument from ignorance. Because we don't understand something, we assume we never will and therefore we invoke . . . a supernatural creator" (Powell, 2005).

Ridicule

Finally, defenders of Darwin's theory have often added derision to their technical attacks on creation science.

Writing in *The New Yorker* magazine, a biologist labeled intelligent design "junk science." A spokesperson for the National Center for Science Education called intelligent design "creationism in a cheap tuxedo" and noted that rarely have any of the Discovery Institute's research articles been accepted for publication in scientific journals. Because intelligent design makes no mention of the Bible, some critics have labeled it *Neo-Creo*—just a new version of the Genesis account of creation. Others have called intelligent design "creationism lite" and "a theory in search of data."

Jerry Coyne, a professor of ecology and evolution at the University of Chicago, cited the great numbers of fossils of extinct species that have been found in the earth, and he then observed,

If this record does reflect the exertions of an intelligent designer, he was apparently dissatisfied with nearly all of his creations, repeatedly destroying them and creating a new set of species that just happened to resemble descendants of those that he had destroyed. (Boccella, 2005)

Public Opinion

Pollsters interested in learning how the creationism/evolution controversy was perceived by the American public conducted several personal-opinion surveys. Table 3.1 shows the percentages of respondents choosing among options posed in four such polls conducted in 2004–2005. Three of the surveys—Gallup, the Pew Forum on Religion in Public Life, and CBS—sampled people nationwide. The fourth was confined to Illinois. As the percentages show, opinions of a substantial portion of the public were at odds with the beliefs of most scientists and science teachers.

Public opinion on evolution has not changed so much over the years, but science teachers have in the past 10 years faced a more organized and vocal anti-evolutionism. In one [survey] of Minnesota teachers, nearly half reported in 2003 being pressured to avoid evolution. In 1995, 20 percent reported that experience. (Hirsch, 2005)

Attitudes toward teaching evolution differ somewhat by political party. In the Pew survey, nearly 60 percent of conservative Republicans held to a creationist view, while only 29 percent of liberal Democrats expressed such a belief

Table 3.1
Opinion Polls on Human Origins

People believe	Gallup (%)	Pew Illinois (%)	CBS (%)
Darwin's theory	28		13
Biblical or intelligent-design creationism	48		
Humans developed over time		48	
Humans were always in their present form		42	55
Evolution was guided by a supreme being		40	27
Schools should teach both evolution and creationism	64	57	65
Schools should teach only creationism	38		
Teaching creationism does not violate the constitutional separation of church and state	58		

Sources: Anderson, 2005a; Cavanagh 2005a,b; MacDonald, 2005; Stack, 2005.

(Cavanagh, 2005a,b). In February 2006, two Democratic lawmakers introduced a bill in the Wisconsin legislature that would ban public schools from teaching intelligent design as science. They said "pseudo-science" should have no place in the classroom (Foley, 2006a). In August 2005, Republican President George W. Bush said he believed intelligent design should be taught along with evolution. Senate Majority Leader Bill Frist, Tennessee Republican, agreed.

The president's brother Jeb Bush, a Catholic and the Republican governor of Florida, said, "My own personal belief is God created man and all life on earth" (Matus, 2005).

Of the candidates who want to succeed [Jeb] Bush [as governor] in 2006, the two Democrats, Sen. Rod Smith of Alachua and U.S. Rep. Jim Davis of Tampa, said intelligent design belongs in religion—not science—class. But Republican state Chief Financial Officer Tom Gallagher doesn't oppose it in science class, a spokesman said. Rep. Dennis Baxley, an Ocala Republican who chairs the state House Education Council, said he supports teaching intelligent design. (Caputo, 2005)

Summary

Across the eight decades since the 1925 "monkey trial," the controversy between creationists and evolutionists has gone through times of greater and lesser attention but has never entirely abated. The conflict continues active in the twenty-first century in the form of *creation science* and *intelligent design* jousting against neo-Darwinism in an atmosphere of dilemmas over the separation of church and state.

The Contending Constituencies

For convenience of analysis, people involved in the creationism/Darwinism controversy can be classified under four categories—(a) fundamentalist Christians, (b) nondoctrinaire Christians, (c) secularists, and (d) professional scientists and science teachers. These classes are not mutually exclusive, since scientists can be either Christians or secularists, and nondoctrinaire Christians can vary from those who almost qualify as fundamentalists to ones who are nearly secularists. However, even though the categories are not entirely separate, they are still useful for analyzing people's attitudes toward creationism and evolution.

Fundamentalist Christians versus Moderate Christians

The U.S. American population of 290 million at the end of the twentieth century—when divided into gross religious categories—was 85.3 percent Christian (Protestant 57.9%, Roman Catholic 21%, other Christian 6.4%), nonreligious 8.7 percent, Jewish 2.1 percent, Muslim 1.9 percent, and other beliefs 2 percent (Sparks, 2004, p. 723). In a 1998 survey, 53 percent of Americans considered religion very important in their lives, a figure far higher than the 16 percent reported in Britain, 14 percent in France, and 13 percent in Germany. However, only about 20 percent of Americans actually went to church one or more times a week (How many people, 2004).

For present purposes, the people designated as Christians can be divided into fundamentalist and moderate categories. Fundamentalists—often also identified as *conservatives, evangelicals,* or *pentecostals*—accept the words of the Bible as literal truth. They subscribe unquestionably to the account of creation offered in the first two chapters of Genesis. Jews and Muslims who also accept that account as the revealed truth belong with the group of fundamentalist Christians.

In contrast, moderate or nondoctrinaire Christians—along with non-doctrinaire Jews and Muslims—subscribe to certain beliefs of their religious tradition but not to the Genesis depiction of human beginnings. Instead, they accept a Darwinian explanation of species evolution.

Three characteristics that tend to distinguish fundamentalists from nondoctrinaire Christians are (a) the source of the evidence on which they base their beliefs, (b) their geographic location, and (c) their denominational affiliation.

Sources of evidence. As explained earlier, creationists base their convictions on holy writings from the ancient past, writings they regard as infallible. They also support their beliefs by identifying ostensible inconsistencies in Darwinian theory, thereby using a negative form of argument to bolster their own version of human beginnings. That is, if errors in Darwin's proposal render it unacceptable, then the other alternative—biblical creationism—must be right.

Nondoctrinaire Christians, Jews, and Muslims reject the biblical creation story by agreeing that the accumulation of empirical observations in support of Darwin's line of logic is highly persuasive. In effect, they can believe in an all-powerful God, heaven, hell, and life after death without having to accept the Bible's creation tale. They often interpret the Darwinian view as evidence that God's plan is marvelously more complex and awe-inspiring than (what they regard as) the simplistic tale in Genesis.

Geographic location. A geographic pattern appears to be formed by the states and communities most prominent in attempts to mandate the teaching of creationism and/or to block the teaching of Darwin's theory. Most evident in that pattern has been the sweep of states across the U.S. South—Georgia, Alabama, Kentucky, Tennessee, Mississippi, Louisiana, Arkansas, Oklahoma, and Texas—a region often referred to as "the Bible Belt." Of secondary importance have been states and communities in the Midwest. Ohio on the east and Kansas on the west have provided the most publicized recent statewide examples, with earlier individual-community cases appearing in Indiana, Illinois, Michigan, Pennsylvania, and Nebraska. Far less often and with less public attention, creationism/evolution controversies have appeared in New England, the Middle-Atlantic States, and the Far West.

Creationist/evolutionist confrontations reported in the public press also suggest that creationist efforts appeared more frequently in rural than in urban communities, as illustrated in the 2004 case of the school board in Grantsburg (Wisconsin)—population 4,494—authorizing the teaching of creationism in the public schools.

Denominational affiliation. Some Christian denominations are more prone than others to advocate teaching creationism in public schools. Consider the two types identified earlier in this chapter—doctrinaire-fundamentalists and nondoctrinaire-mainliners.

Doctrinaire Fundamentalists

The most prominent creationist efforts have come from the Southern Baptist Convention, which is a coalition of thousands of individual Baptist congregations that boast a total of 16 million church members, making the Convention the largest organization of Baptist churches in the world and the largest Protestant denomination in America. Although there are both fundamentalist and moderate members of the organization, the fundamentalists—past and present—have dominated the group's policies (Cline, 2004a). Numerous other types of pentecostal and evangelical churches also subscribe to creationism. So do Mormons, with the result that a biblical account of beginnings is informally included in both public and private schools in Utah, where the majority of students are from Mormon families. The following assessment of Darwinism is from a Jehovah Witnesses book titled *Life: How Did It Get Here? By Evolution or by Creation?*

We need to face the fact that the theory of evolution serves the purposes of Satan. He wants people to imitate his course, and that of Adam and Eve, in rebelling against God . . . Thus, believing in evolution would mean promoting [Satan's] interests and blinding oneself to the wonderful purposes of the Creator. (Quoted in Cline, 2004b)

While polls find that only 18 percent of Americans interpret the Bible as literal truth, about 45 percent reject evolution because they don't like the implication that humans are genetically related to animals (Filiatreau, 2000).

Efforts by fundamentalist groups to discredit Darwinism have been well funded. Slevin (2005a) reported that

in Seattle, the nonprofit Discovery Institute spends more than $1 million a year for research, polls, and media pieces supporting intelligent design. In Fort Lauderdale, Christian evangelist James Kennedy established a Creation Studies Institute. In Virginia, Liberty University is sponsoring the Creation Mega Conference with a Kentucky group called Answers in Genesis, which raised $9 million in 2003. He noted the recent hiring by the Southern Baptist Theological Seminary of Discovery Institute scholar and prominent intelligent design proponent William A. Dembski. The seminary said the move, along with the creation of a Center for Science and Theology, was central to developing a "comprehensive Christian worldview."

The Thomas More Law Center, whose announced mission is to defend the religious freedom of Christians, had a budget of $2.3 million in 2003. Anderson (2005b) reported that the Discovery Institute's $4 million annual budget "is heavily funded by conservative Christian donors."

Nondoctrinaire Mainliners

The attitude about teaching Darwinism expressed by several traditional mainline Christian faiths differs from that of evangelical denominations that oppose evolution theory. An example of mainstream attitude is the 1982 resolution adopted by the general assembly of the United Presbyterian Church of North America, a resolution that closed in the following manner:

[The General Assembly] affirms that, required teaching of a [biblical creationist] view constitutes an establishment of religion and a violation of the separation of church and state, as provided in the First Amendment to the Constitution and laws of the United States;
    Affirms that, exposure to the Genesis account is best sought through the teaching about religion, history, social studies, and literature, provinces other than the discipline of natural science, and
    Calls upon Presbyterians, and upon legislators and school board members, to resist all efforts to establish any requirements upon teachers and schools to teach "creationism" or "creation science." (Evolution and creationism, 1982)

In issuing similar statements, representatives of Methodist, Episcopal, Roman Catholic, Lutheran, Christian Science, and Unitarian churches have accepted the theory of evolution and have denounced the teaching of creationism in science classes. The spiritual leader of the worldwide Anglican Church, the Archbishop of Canterbury, spoke out against teaching creationism in schools (Anglican leader, 2006).

Secularists

The secularist category includes humanists, agnostics, atheists, realists, and people who simply consider themselves nonreligious. They typically support the teaching of evolution and either condemn or merely disregard proposals to teach creationism.

Scientists

The term *scientists* in the present context does not identify a group that is entirely separate from the religious and secularist categories but, rather, is a subgroup derived from portions of those categories. *Scientists* are people whose professional life consists of teaching science and/or conducting scientific research. They form a separate class in the creationism/evolution debate because they command detailed knowledge of the empirical evidence and logic supporting Darwin's theory and thus are specially equipped to marshal arguments in favor of the theory. With rare exceptions, scientists urge the teaching of evolution in the schools and reject the teaching of creationism in science classes. In support of such a position, a wide range of scientific societies have issued statements similar to the following declaration of the National Science Teachers Association.

Science curricula, state science standards, and teachers should emphasize evolution in a manner commensurate with its importance as a unifying concept in science and its overall explanatory power.

Science teachers should not advocate any religious interpretations of nature and should be nonjudgmental about the personal beliefs of students.

Policy makers and administrators should not mandate policies requiring the teaching of "creation science" or related concepts, such as so-called "intelligent design," "abrupt appearance," and "arguments against evolution." Administrators also should support teachers against pressure to promote nonscientific views or to diminish or eliminate the study of evolution. (The teaching of evolution, 2004)

In summary, the constituencies engaged in the creationism/evolution debate have included various combinations of religious and nonreligious groups that are concentrated in particular regions of the country and represent particular religious denominations (Figure 3.3).

Five Illustrative Cases

With the foregoing discussion as a background, we next turn to five series of events that illustrate several trends in religion/school conditions midway in the opening decade of the twenty-first century. Those trends appear in the Dover case, the Ohio case, the Kansas case, the Arizona case, and the Utah case.

The Dover Case

During the six-week period between September 26 and November 4, 2005, U.S. District Court Judge John E. Jones III presided over a case titled *Kitzmiller v. Dover Area School District*. The trial—held in Harrisburg (Pennsylvania)—concerned a lawsuit filed by eleven parents against the school board in nearby Dover, a small

Figure 3.3
Adversaries in the creationism/evolution controversy.

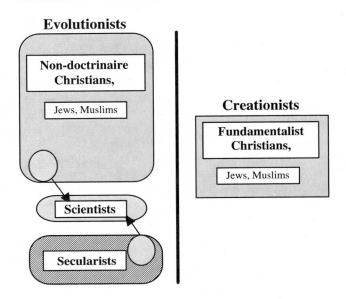

farming town (population 1,815 in 2000). The district's schools enrolled 3,600 students from the town and surrounding area.

In the suit, the plaintiffs charged that the school board had required that a statement casting doubt on the validity of Darwin's theory be read to students in each ninth-grade biology class before the theory was studied. The suit contended that the statement included support for an intelligent-design explanation of human beginnings and thus represented an expression of a religious belief, thereby violating the U.S. Constitution's separation of church and state.

The controversial statement, drafted by the Dover board of education on a 6-to-3 vote in October 2004, read as follows:

The Pennsylvania Academic Standards require students to learn about Darwin's theory of evolution and eventually to take a standardized test of which evolution is a part. Because Darwin's theory is a theory, it continues to be tested as new evidence is discovered. The theory is not a fact. Gaps in the theory exist for which there is no evidence. A theory is defined as a well-tested explanation that unifies a broad range of observations. Intelligent design is an explanation of the origin of life that differs from Darwin's view. The reference book *Of Pandas and People* is available in the library along with other resources for students who might be interested in gaining an understanding of what intelligent design actually involves. (Court rejects, 2005).

The eleven plaintiffs were represented by a team of attorneys assembled by the American Civil Liberties Union (ACLU) and by Americans United for Separation of Church and State. The Dover school board's defense was conducted by lawyers from the Thomas More Law Center, who declared that intelligent design was not religious and that the school board merely wanted to inform students of alternatives to evolution.

During the trial, the following events that had led to the lawsuit were revealed in testimony from witnesses.

At the end of the 2003–04 school year, science teachers had been summoned to a special meeting to watch "Icons of Evolution," a video that attacked evolution and supported intelligent design. The following summer, the school board delayed ordering new biology texts, charging that the ones under consideration were "laced with Darwinism." (Stephens, 2005)

When school opened in the fall of 2004, science teachers were told to read the board's "doubting-Darwin" statement to students and to recommend *Of Pandas and People*, "a book widely viewed by scientists as a creationist tome with language about intelligent design tacked on" (Stephens, 2005). The teachers refused to read the statement, and they issued an explanation of their refusal. School authorities then retreated a step from their original mandate by deciding that science teachers who objected to presenting their students the board's intelligent-design statement would not be required to do so. Instead, an administrator would read the statement to classes. Furthermore, students could be excused from having to listen if their parents objected (Morello, 2005; Teachers get choice, 2005). Again the teachers refused. Finally, a school assembly was held to tell students about *Of Pandas and People*—sixty copies of which had been donated to the school library by the church of board member William Cunningham. Several witnesses for the plaintiffs testified that they had heard Dover board members promote Christian views at public meetings and criticize evolution during the months before the intelligent-design statement to students was issued. An ACLU representative called intelligent design "a Trojan horse for bringing religious creationism back into the public school science classroom" (Worden, 2004).

Key witnesses other than teachers, parents, and school-board members were scientists and philosophers in the role of experts. The best-known scientist speaking on behalf of the defense was Michael J. Behe, a Lehigh University biochemistry professor and author of *Darwin's Black Box*. The most prominent scientist on the plaintiff's side was Brown University biologist Kenneth R. Miller, who had written the critique of Behe's book mentioned earlier in this chapter.

When the trial ended on November 4, Judge Jones (who had been appointed to the bench in 2002 by President George W. Bush) announced that his decision about the case would be released within a few weeks.

Coincidentally, the regular election of Dover school-board members was scheduled for the week following the end of the trial. Eight of the nine incumbents—all Republicans—were up for re-election. They were being challenged by a slate of Democrats that included a few Republicans who rejected the incumbents' intelligent-design convictions. In the election, voters ousted all eight of the board's incumbents, replacing them with the eight challengers. In one of the new board's early meetings, the previous board's doubting-Darwin statement was rescinded. Students would no longer be warned against evolution. *Of Pandas and People* would no longer be recommended as a proper replacement for the regular biology textbook.

Judge Jones's ruling was issued on December 20 in a 139-page document that found in favor of the eleven plaintiffs. Jones had decided that the Dover board members were motivated by religious convictions when they required that students be introduced to intelligent design as an alternative to Darwin's theory.

We have addressed the seminal question of whether ID [intelligent design] is science. We have concluded that it is not, and moreover, that ID cannot uncouple itself from its creationist, and thus religious, antecedents. (Cavanagh, 2005c)

News of the jurist's decision was applauded by most scientists and even enjoyed the support of an Italian Catholic, Fiorenzo Facchini, whose views were published in the Vatican's official newspaper, *L'Osservatore Romano*. Facchini, a professor of evolutional biology at the University of Bologna, stated that intelligent design was unscientific and that "it is not correct from a methodological point of view to stray from the field of science while pretending to do science" (Fisher & Dean, 2006). The judge's position was also defended by the Rev. George Coyne, director of the Vatican observatory, who called science and religion "totally separate pursuits" and said, "Science is completely neutral with regards to religious or atheistic views." Thus, he said, it was possible to believe in both God and evolution (Pittman, 2005).

However, it appeared that Vatican officials were not all of one mind about intelligent design, as Pope Benedict XVI at the time of the Dover trial said that the universe had been made by "an intelligent object" and that "the signs of God's love are seen in the marvels of creation and in the great gifts he has given to his people. The Fathers of the Church teach us to recognize in created things the greatness of God and his merciful love towards us" (More quotes, 2005)

The outcome of the Dover trial encouraged a group of parents in the small Tehachapi mountain community of Lebec, California (population 1,300), to file a lawsuit challenging the teaching of intelligent design in the local public school. The plaintiffs charged that school officials had defined a class in a way that would circumvent the objections to intelligent design that the judge cited in the Dover case (Weinstein, 2006).

In contrast to people who welcomed Judge Jones's ruling, supporters of intelligent design condemned his opinion and vowed to exert greater efforts to have intelligent design recognized as a scientific explanation of human beginnings. Defenders of intelligent design also contended that banning it from science classrooms was a violation of the U.S. Constitution's free-speech provision. John West, associate director of the Discover Institute in Seattle, announced that anyone who thinks a court ruling is going to kill off interest in intelligent design is living in another world. Americans don't like to be told there is some idea that they aren't permitted to learn about. It used to be said that banning a book in Boston guaranteed it would be a best seller. Banning intelligent design in Dover will likely only fan interest in the theory. (West, 2005)

West's prediction was supported in at least a minor way by a report that *Of Pandas and People* monthly sales had increased to 300 copies from the pretrial figure of 125, with the books bought mostly by parents who homeschooled their children. And in Cincinnati (Ohio) a fundamentalist Christian group was building a "science" museum depicting the seven-day biblical account of creation.

John Witte Jr., director of the center for the study of law and religion at Emory University, believed the Dover case would not likely settle the issue: "It's simply going to foment a great deal of new experimentation among districts. It's not the final word on this subject by any means. It's probably the first battle in what could be a decade or more of battles" (Cavanagh, 2005c).

In effect, contrasting trends illustrated in the Dover case were those of (a) the judiciary's increasing rejection of intelligent design as a scientific theory and (b) heightened efforts on the part of conservative Christians to promote intelligent design as a scientific alternative to Darwinism.

The Ohio Case

An important responsibility of the Ohio State Board of Education is that of setting standards for what students are expected to learn in the state's public schools. Those standards then become the foundation on which statewide tests are built. The board also publishes model lesson plans that teachers can use for implementing of the standards.

In 2002 board members deliberated at length about how the standards for science classes should be worded, with the issue of teaching about evolution as the main focus of their discussion. The matter was finally settled on December 11, 2002, when the eighteen board members unanimously agreed on (a) a definition of the term *science* and (b) a skill students would be expected to acquire.

In choosing a definition of *science*, the board rejected the proposal of the team assigned to write science-education standards—a definition that read: "Scientific knowledge is limited to natural explanations for natural phenomena based on evidence from our senses or technological extensions."

The board replaced that version with: "Science is a systematic method of continuing investigation, based on observation, hypothesis testing, measurement, experimentation, and theory building, which leads to more adequate explanations of natural phenomena."

A skill that students were expected to develop was that of "describing how scientists continue to investigate and critically analyze aspects of evolutionary theory."

John Calvert, managing director of the Intelligent Design Network, was among the commentators who applauded the elimination of the phrase "natural explanations for natural phenomena based on evidence from our senses" that the writing team had included in its definition. According to Calvert, the revised version that the board preferred implied that "the 'teaching or testing of intelligent design' is permitted" (Calvert, 2002). And the expression "critically analyze" in the proposed skill would emphasize finding fault with Darwin's theory.

To render the criticism of evolution more concrete, the state board on March 9, 2004, endorsed, by a 13-5 vote, a model lesson plan illustrating for teachers how the critical analysis of evolution might be presented to students. Members of an anti-Darwinism organization, Science Excellence for All Ohians, praised the lesson plan for "encouraging teachers to present evidence both supporting and challenging macroevolution (the theory of descent from a common ancestry) . . . The Ohio Board has [thereby] affirmed academic freedom for teachers and critical thinking for students" (Rudy & Lattimer, 2004).

The critical-analysis lesson plan was one out of nine bearing on evolution, with the other eight presenting Darwinian concepts and evidence without mention of such competing views as creationism or intelligent design. Although there was no state mandate for teachers to use model lessons, most school districts could be expected to follow them—at least to some extent—because state tests were based on the board's standards.

The Ohio board's definition of *science* and the critical-analysis lesson plan remained in effect throughout 2005, but came under fire after the announcement of Judge Jones's decision in the Dover case. Apparently frightened by Jones's ruling, members of the Ohio board on January 10, 2006, considered altering both the board's definition of science and dropping the critical-analysis lesson plan. After heated debate, a motion to make those changes was defeated in a 9-8 vote. But a month later, at the February 14 board meeting, the motion was reconsidered. As a result of persuasive arguments by the minority group, the members present voted, by an 11-4 margin, to remove the controversial lesson plan as well as the "critical-analysis-of-evolution" language from the state science standards.

The board's decision, hailed as a move in the right direction by most scientists and science teachers, was bitterly condemned by supporters of intelligent design. Representatives of Science Excellence for All Ohians called the board's February decision "outrageous" and declared that

the State Board of Education previously approved this lesson *three times* . . . Raising the issue again at the February board meeting was clearly unwarranted. The lesson does not include religion, creationism, or intelligent design. Although opponents claim the lesson contains "thinly veiled" ID [intelligent design] concepts, this is simply not true. The lesson calls upon students to critically study evidence that supports and evidence that challenges macroevolution (descent with modification from a common ancestry). The lesson is based on mainstream scientific criticisms of Darwin's theory of evolution. The references are taken from the scientific literature . . . The lesson adopts an approach overwhelmingly favored by citizens in Ohio. During the Standards adoption process in 2002, about 30,000 Ohioans contacted the State Board and/or Governor on this issue . . . At least three-fourths of these respondents favored the teaching of evidence both supporting and challenging macroevolution. Public opinion polls across the nation and in Ohio . . . have produced much the same results. (Science Excellence, 2006)

Finally, one trend illustrated by the Ohio case was the extension of influence of legal decisions beyond the jurisdictions in which those decisions applied. Although the ruling in the Dover case directly applied only in Dover, the likelihood that courts elsewhere might copy the Dover ruling caused educational decision makers—such as the Ohio board members—to modify their science-teaching policies.

A second trend was that of creationist and intelligent-design advocates mounting renewed efforts to influence public schools' science teaching after suffering a defeat at the hands of evolutionists and their allies.

The Kansas Case

Like the Ohio board, The Kansas State Board of Education sets the learning-achievement standards that are the basis for questions posed on mandatory state tests.

In August 1999, the Kansas board—in a 6-to-4 vote—changed science-curriculum standards prepared by a twenty-seven-member science committee. The change consisted of eliminating evolution from the standards. Prior to the vote, the presidents of Kansas' six public universities had sent the board a letter saying that eliminating evolution "will set Kansas back a century and give hard-to-find science teachers no choice but to pursue other career fields or assignments outside of Kansas. The argument that teaching evolution will destroy a student's faith in God is no more true today than it was during the Scopes trial in 1925." Kansas Governor Bill Graves, a Republican, warned board members not to adopt the antievolution curriculum, but they did it anyway (Gillam, 1999).

In the November 2000 election, three of the board members who had voted to oust Darwinism in 1999 were defeated by proevolution candidates, so that in the board's February 2001 meeting evolution was put back into the science standards by a 7-to-3 vote. The standards would remain in that form until they were due for reconsideration in 2005. The 2004 election again changed the board's composition, shifting the balance in favor of antievolution conservatives. Thus, throughout 2005 the Darwinism portion of the science standards was again a hot issue during board meetings.

During May 2005, a three-member panel of board members staged public hearings intended to pit antievolutionists against proevolutionists. The panel lined up a series of intelligent-design enthusiasts to endorse the board's intention to word science standards in a manner that questioned the validity of macroevolution. However, leaders of the state's science community boycotted the hearings, as did representatives of the American Association for the Advancement of Science, which is the world's largest general science organization and publisher of the journal *Science*. The head of the association, Alan I. Leshner, answered the invitation to join the debate by writing, "AAAS respectfully declines to participate in this hearing out of concern that rather than contribute to science education, it will most likely serve to confuse the public about the nature of the scientific enterprise" (American Association, 2005). The scientists argued that the forum would mislead the public into thinking that the proposals by supporters of the intelligent design concept had any real validity. As a result, the hearings consisted almost entirely of testimonials about flaws in Darwin's proposal.

On November 8, 2005—the same day that voters in Dover replaced eight school board members with proevolution candidates—the Kansas state board, by a 6-to-4 vote, adopted revised science standards that included strong criticism of evolution. In effect, the board's Republican majority overruled a twenty-six-member science committee and ignored the National Academy of Sciences and the National Science Teachers Association. Two Republicans and two Democrats voted against changing the standard (Slevin, 2005b).

Following the board's decision, the National Academy of Sciences and the National Science Teachers Association withdrew their permission to include materials from their publications in the Kansas curriculum, so the state's science-writing committee was obliged to begin creating new materials of its own.

The new standard could not dictate what would actually be taught about evolution, because such decisions were the province of Kansas' 300 local school boards. But the standard would determine what sorts of questions about human beginnings could appear on state tests.

In addition, the Thomas B. Fordham Institute in Washington, DC, awarded Kansas a grade of "F" and a rating of "worst in the nation" for its science standards. The Fordham report on the quality of science standards throughout the nation said that the Kansas board had "radically compromised" the concept of evolution. "The effect transcends evolution, however. It now makes a mockery of the very definition of science" (Education group, 2005).

During the state board's deliberations in October 2005, board members on a 6-to-4 vote selected Bob Corkins as state commissioner of education. Upon assuming his new post, Corkins voiced his support for the revised science standard that the board would soon officially endorse (Hanna, 2005a).

Finally, a trend revealed in the Kansas case was that of conservative religious forces rebounding strongly after a defeat of their agenda to once again take control of decisions about the place Darwinism is assigned in a state's science-education standards. Such a trend would appear in other regions of the nation as well. Kansas had now become the fifth state—along with Minnesota, New Mexico, Ohio, and Pennsylvania—to clear the way for teaching intelligent design and creationism.

The Arizona Case

When the Arizona State Board of Education in 2004 faced the task of setting curriculum standards for the schools, various organizations and individuals pressed their opinions on board members about how the science standards should be cast. A Christian group, the Center for Arizona Policy, urged the board to direct teachers to "test, modify, or refute the evolution theory" and engage students in a discussion of intelligent design. In opposition to that proposal, the president of Arizona State University, Michael Crow, in his role as a member of the state board, wrote to the state's superintendent of public instruction, expressing his belief that the standard should be limited to *science* as that concept is defined in the science community, because "strong, rigorous life-science standards are particularly critical in light of Arizona's efforts to build strength in the biosciences and related industries" (Tropiano, 2005).

The board's final decision appeared to represent a compromise that might accommodate the desires of religious groups and, at the same time, reflect an attitude acceptable to scientists. That is, the board's science standard stated that all science is theory, all scientific theories change as more is learned about the world, and theories should always be questioned and challenged so that knowledge might advance. The standard did not require that intelligent design be included.

An attorney for the Center for Arizona Policy interpreted the science standard to mean that schools could teach both evolution and such alternative explanations of human beginnings as intelligent design, because the standard included the "active process of investigation and the critical review of evidence related to the world around us, both visible and invisible" and students should be able to evaluate whether "investigational data support or do not support a proposed hypothesis." The Center's attorney judged that teaching intelligent design was compatible with the constitutional laws regarding the separation of church and state "as long as schools are not indoctrinating students in a specific religion" (Tropiano, 2005).

Although the wording of state board's science-standard statement might have been interpreted as allowing the study of theories based on "invisible" as well as "visible" evidence, the competencies students were expected to acquire as specified in the guidelines published for Arizona teachers' clearly promoted Darwinism and made no mention of such alternative views as intelligent design. For example, consider these two skills that were among those to be taught to biology students in Arizona high schools.

Describe how the continuing operation of natural selection underlies a population's ability to adapt to changes in the environment and leads to biodiversity and the origin of new species.
 Analyze how patterns in the fossil record, nuclear chemistry, geology, molecular biology, and geographical distribution give support to the theory of organic evolution through natural selection over billions of years and the resulting present day biodiversity. (*Science standards*, 2005)

Thus, the Arizona case illustrates a trend found also in other areas of the nation. The trend is for (a) politically influenced policy makers—such as boards of education—to describe science standards in broad and potentially ambiguous terminology which is then recast as specific directives for teachers by (b) curriculum specialists who limit the skills and knowledge students pursue to neo-Darwinism.

The Utah Case

In early 2006, Utah state legislators, in a 46-to-28 vote, defeated an origins-of-life bill that would have required science teachers to issue a disclaimer to their students, saying that not all scientists agreed about evolution. Although the bill did not mention alternative theories to Darwinism, some lawmakers believed the proposal was part of the drive to encourage the teaching of intelligent design.

The case drew national attention as Utah was seen to be a culturally conservative state in which most members of the House of Representatives' were both Republicans and members of the Church of Latter Day Saints. "Some Mormon legislators opposed the bill because they agreed that science and religion should remain separate, others because they thought intelligent design was not in keeping with traditional Mormon belief." A representative of Americans United for Separation of Church and State said, "If the creationists can't win in a state as conservative as Utah, they've got an uphill battle" (Johnson, 2006b).

The Utah incident reflected a trend in which dedicated Christians have chosen to keep religious faith separate from empirical science.

Resolving the Conflict

The creationism/evolution controversy addressed in this chapter has been limited to the question: "Should some form of creationism be taught in public-school science classes instead of, or in addition to, Darwin's theory of evolution."

Certainly the science-class question had not been resolved to anyone's satisfaction by the first decade of the twenty-first century. Nor would it likely be settled in the foreseeable future. The constituencies on both sides of the issue were too strong and too entrenched in their positions for anyone to expect a compromise that both sides might accept. The conflict of viewpoints about human beginnings has contributed to the *culture wars* that currently divide the American populace. People on the opposite sides of the debate differ particularly in the type of evidence they accept as the proper basis for belief. Creationists and intelligent-design enthusiasts base their conviction on holy scripture and "intuitive logic." Evolutionists base their belief on empirical studies of nature and on logical inference about the compiled evidence. Nussbaum (2005a) reported that

scientists tend to be much less religious than other Americans. About 40% of scientists, and only 7% of members of the National Academy of Sciences, said they believed in God, according to surveys published in the journal Nature in 1997 and 1998. Among the general public, polls show, more than 90% believe in God . . . Science has won most of the court battles. But it is making little headway in the wider culture, and now faces a new offensive from advocates of intelligent design.

According to such writings as a 1999 strategy document from the Discovery Institute in Seattle, the aim of opponents to Darwinism is to restore religious faith to a more central role in American life.

[Intelligent] design theory promises to reverse the stifling dominance of the materialist worldview, and to replace it with a science consonant with Christian and theistic convictions . . . [The aim is] nothing less than the overthrow of materialism and its cultural legacies. The social consequences of materialism have been devastating . . . We are convinced that in order to defeat materialism, we must cut it off at its source. That source is scientific materialism. This is precisely our strategy. If we view the predominant materialistic science as a giant tree, our strategy is intended to function as a wedge that, while relatively small, can split the trunk when applied at its weakest points. (Nussbaum, 2005b)

In April 2006, the Discovery Institute responded to the rejection of intelligent design in the Dover case by publishing a 123-page book titled *Traipsing into Evolution: Intelligent Design and the Kitzmiller v. Dover Decision*. The authors criticized Judge Jones' Dover decision and labeled him an "activist" jurist. When Jones had originally issued his opinion, he had foreseen such attacks and had written, "Those who disagree with our holding will likely mark it as the product of an activist judge. If so, they have erred as this is manifestly not an activist court" (Postman, 2006).

Members of the nation's scientific community continued to express alarm at what the dean of the medical school at Stanford University, Philip Pizzo, called "the rising tide of anti-science sentiment that seems to have its nucleus in Washington but which extends throughout the nation." The interim president of Cornell University, Hunter Rawlings, said that the dispute over intelligent design was widening political, social, religious, and philosophical rifts in U.S. society (Is US becoming, 2005).

The most obvious attempt to reach a rapprochement between pro- and antievolutionists has been the solution suggested by proponents of intelligent design. As noted earlier, their principal strategy has been to suggest that science curricula not only focus on the strengths of Darwinian theory but also on the theory's weaknesses—on potential rents in the theory's fabric. For the science community, such a proposal would seem most reasonable, since science progresses through the critical examination of any proposed explanation so as to identify possible weaknesses that can stimulate better data collection and more adequate explanation. However, the promoters of intelligent design have not stopped there but have contended that since Darwinism displayed shortcomings, the notion of an intelligent designer would be a proper scientific alternative. Ergo, intelligent design should be taught alongside evolution in public school science classes. But that is where scientists and science educators have balked. They have insisted that belief in an invisible all-powerful, all-knowing designer was a conviction founded solely on religious faith and thus did not qualify as scientific. Hence, intelligent design did not belong in science classes. And so the conflict continues unabated.

As for the peripheral question of whether creationism of any sort should be discussed at all in public schools, that matter is considered in Chapter 4—Curricula and Textbooks.

Conclusion

The creationism/evolution debate reflects the somewhat schizophrenic condition of an American society that is legally secular but culturally quite religious. In formal word (the U.S. Constitution), state and religion are separate. In daily life, state and religion meld together in ways that can differ from one person to another. The American citizenry's polyglot of beliefs was illustrated in the earlier-mentioned opinion survey conducted by telephone in mid-2005 with a sample of 2,000 adults by the Pew Forum on Religion and Public Life (Cavanagh, 2005b). When participants in the poll were asked about the teaching of creationism in public schools, the following were among the results:

- Teach creationism instead of evolution? 38 percent favor, 49 percent oppose.
- Teach both creationism and evolution? 64 percent favor, 26 percent oppose.
- Who should decide how evolution is taught? Scientists/science educators—28 percent; Parents—41 percent; School boards—27 percent.

The poll also showed that the more education a respondent had, the more likely the respondent would oppose teaching creationism instead of evolution. For example, 66 percent of college graduates would disagree with replacing creationism with evolution in science classes compared to only 29 percent of high-school dropouts. As for regional differences, 45 percent of respondents in the South would teach creationism instead of evolution compared to 30 percent in the East and 32 percent in the West. However, there were no significant regional differences over whether creationism should be taught along with evolution. Among evolution supporters, 26 percent believed the process occurred by means of Darwin's principle of natural selection while 18 percent thought a supreme being had guided the process.

Seventy percent of white evangelical Protestants [who were polled] ... believe humans have always existed in their present form, while only 31% of white Catholics share that view. Nearly 60% of conservative Republicans hold to that creationist view, while only 29% of liberal Democrats espouse that belief. (Cavanagh, 2005b).

The pollsters did, however, offer a caveat that could effect how the results of the study are interpreted. Not only was the sample of respondents rather small, but "We acknowledge there may be some confusion about the meaning of these terms [*creationism, evolution, intelligent design*] ... Many people take the default position—teach both sides and let people make up their own minds" (Lester, 2005).

Such survey results, coupled with President George W. Bush's 2005 endorsement of teaching both evolution and creationism in public-school science classes, suggests that the social pressure to include some variant of creationism in the nation's public-school science curricula is apt to increase in the years ahead.

A future for creationism?

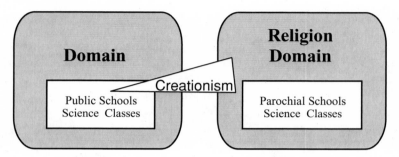

In 2005, legislators in at least twelve states voted on bills that either encouraged students to be skeptical about Darwinian theory as presented in public school science classes or to allow the teaching of alternative explanations for life's development. None of the bills passed. By mid-2006, the same sorts of legislation had been proposed in ten states, with much the same result. Thus, it appeared that state lawmakers would continue to face the task of deciding whether they would try to control the teaching about human beginnings in public schools (Cavanagh, 2006).

GUIDELINES FOR EDUCATORS

The purpose of these closing paragraphs is to summarize for school-board members, teachers, and administrators the legal status of teaching about human beginnings (Darwinism and/or religious beliefs) in America's public-school science classes. The summary is valid in the first decade of the twenty-first century, but subject to revision as the result of later court decisions.

The basic rule about teaching human beginnings in public-school science classes (or in science units-of-study in elementary-school classes) is as follows:

- Darwin's theory of evolution can be taught, and schools cannot restrict the teaching of that theory by issuing disclaimers, such as the teaching of evolution is "not intended to influence or dissuade the Biblical version of Creation or any other concept."
- Schools cannot avoid teaching evolution so as not to offend people's religious convictions.
- In science classes, schools cannot teach religious explanations of human beginnings that are not amenable to testing or verification by scientific methods. Thus, belief systems that attribute human origins to invisible beings or powers cannot legally be taught instead of, or in addition to, neo-Darwinism. Although supporters of intelligent design have

declared that their version of human origins is scientific and not religious, courts have judged otherwise, so intelligent design cannot lawfully be included in students' science studies (Anti-Defamation League, 2004a).

As noted earlier in this chapter, several states (Kansas, Minnesota, New Mexico, Ohio, and Pennsylvania) and local school systems have worded their science-education standards in a manner that could allow schools to teach religious versions of human origins in science classes. Such teaching can continue until some individual or group challenges the practice by filing a lawsuit and having the issue decided in court. That happened in the Dover case. It also happened in a 2005 Cobb County (Georgia) a case in which a school district pasted the disclaimer "Evolution is a theory, not a fact" in biology textbooks. But a district court's decision in a lawsuit applies only to schools within the jurisdiction of that court. Therefore, the decision in the Dover case applied only within the region of the U.S. Third Circuit Court, not throughout the entire nation. However, the ruling of a circuit court may also influence school policies in other areas of the country if boards of education fear that the same ruling would result in their own area if a similar lawsuit were filed there. Thus, a board may alter its standards in order to avoid the cost and bother of a potential lawsuit. Such occurred in the Ohio case where the state board of education reworded its science standard that bore on human origins and eliminated a lesson plan that included a veiled attack on Darwinism.

Whenever, by dint of the legal-appeal process, a suit advances from lower courts to the U.S. Supreme Court, the Supreme Court's ruling applies to all of the nation's public schools.

Chapter 4

Curricula and Text Materials

The controversial issue at stake in this chapter is the question of what place, if any, religion should have in the curricula of America's public schools.

At the outset it is important for readers to recognize that the word *curriculum* can mean different things to different people. Two popular meanings are *the published curriculum* and *the taught curriculum*. The published curriculum is a school system's printed description of what students are expected to learn—the subject matter they are to study and, often, the learning methods and materials that teachers are expected to use. In contrast, the taught curriculum consists of the information teachers actually offer students and the learning tasks teachers assign students to perform. A teacher constructs the taught curriculum from various sources, including the published curriculum, textbooks, the teacher's own experiences and creativity, other teachers' lesson plans, ideas that spontaneously come to the teacher's mind during a lesson, and more. Even though the published curriculum can be a useful guide to what may go on in a classroom, the published version is obviously not an accurate portrayal of what the students actually experience. The significance of this distinction between *published* and *taught* is illustrated throughout Chapter 4.

The term *text materials* refers to published reading matter that students are assigned to study. In most cases, text materials are in the form of a textbook. But throughout this chapter the term also refers to such things as assigned pamphlets, magazines, newspaper articles, and reading material in a computer file or on an Internet website.

HOW THE CONTROVERSY DEVELOPED

As described in Chapter 2, the culture imported to America by early settlers from Europe and by subsequent generations was predominantly Christian—more precisely, Protestant Christian. Over the centuries, American schools were important purveyors of that culture. But conflict over the propriety of including religious matter in schools' learning content became particularly frequent and contentious during the late decades of the twentieth century. Two factors contributing to the growing conflict were (a) the increased cultural diversity of the population due to high levels of immigration from non-Christian countries and (b) vigorous efforts of advocates of the separation of church and state to have religion excluded from public schools.

The nature of the controversy is described under the following sections: (a) main problem areas, (b) potential solutions to the conflict, and (c) a series of recent cases that illustrate difficulties faced in resolving the issue of religion in the curriculum.

Main Problem Areas

Although the subject-matter field of science was seen in Chapter 3 as the focus of vigorous debate, the conflict between science and religion has been limited mostly to the question of how humans originated. There has been no conflict over nearly all other matters in the vast domain of modern science and technology. But such is not the case with other subject areas, principally the social studies or social sciences in which religion has traditionally assumed a major role. In effect, issues bearing on people's belief systems—both religious and secular—have figured prominently in classes bearing such titles as world history, ancient history, American history, world civilizations, modern-world problems, nations of the world, cultural anthropology, social psychology, comparative religions, human geography, and more. Likewise, religious matters can be a concern in study units within the general social-studies curricula of elementary and middle schools. The focus of units can be suggested by typical labels, such as *Our Town's Churches, A Community of Immigrants, China's People, The Time of the Pharaohs, Life among the Pilgrims,* and *Plural Cultures.*

Within the schools' curricula, the language arts—particularly in the study of literature—have been second only to the social studies in introducing students to religious beliefs and practices. Stetson (in Talev, 2005) noted that "there are over 1,300 documented biblical allusions in Shakespeare. If kids don't understand the biblical allusions, they don't understand Shakespeare."

Potential Solutions

Four alternative solutions for conflicts about the place of religion in curricula involve (a) eliminating all material related to religion, (b) permitting only secular descriptions and appraisals of religion-related events, (c) focusing on the nation's predominant religious tradition as found in the Christian Bible, and (d) teaching about diverse religious persuasions.

In choosing among the four options, educators are obliged to recognize the constitutional confines that curriculum content must respect. According to the U.S. Office of Education, those confines include the following:

Teaching about religion: Public schools may not provide religious instruction, but they may teach about religion, including: the history of religion, comparative religion, the Bible (or other scripture)-as-literature, and the role of religion in the history of the United States and other countries. Similarly, it is permissible to consider religious influences on art, music, literature, and social studies.

Teaching values: Though schools must be neutral with respect to religion, they may play an active role with respect to teaching civic values and virtue, and the moral code that holds us together as a community. The fact that some of these values are held also by religions does not make it unlawful to teach them in school.

Student assignments: Students may express their beliefs about religion in the form of homework, artwork, and other written and oral assignments free of discrimination based on the religious content of their submissions. Such home and classroom work should be judged by ordinary academic standards of substance and relevance, and against other legitimate pedagogical concerns identified by the school. (Riley, 1995)

Eliminate All Material Related to Religion

The most extreme proponents of the separation of church and state would ban any mention of religion in both the published curriculum and the taught curriculum. Consider, then, the consequences of such a policy for classes or study-units in world history, current events, literature, and the arts.

In world history. Outlawing any mention of religion-related historical matters would mean that students would have no chance to learn about thousands of such places, people, and events as

- The Egyptian pyramids.
- Israelites escaping from Egypt under Moses' leadership.
- Gladiators in the Roman Coliseum.
- The birth and life-works of Sidhartha Gautama (Buddha, meaning the Enlightened One), of Jesus (Christ, meaning the Savior), of Mohammad (the Prophet), Gandhi (Mahatma, meaning Great Soul), the German Martin Luther, and the American Martin Luther King Jr.
- The Medieval Christian crusades.
- The Moor occupation of Spain.
- The marital problems of England's King Henry VIII.
- Joan of Arc's tragic end.
- Arabic numerals and mathematics.
- The Spanish Inquisition.

- Why Puritan colonists came to America.
- The Salem witch trials.
- The Nazi holocaust of World War II.

In Current Events. If, during the first decade of the twenty-first century, all religion-related matter were barred from curricula, students would never learn about

- Civil strife in Northern Ireland.
- Wars in Bosnia, Afghanistan, Iraq, and the Sudan.
- Abortion, the right-to-life, and stem-cell research.
- The head-scarf controversy in France.
- Groups that supported the election of President George W. Bush.

In Literature. If all literary works containing religious allusions were banned from the classroom, students would be denied the chance to learn

- Who, in Homer's epic *The Iliad*, promised the youthful Paris the most beautiful woman in the world.
- That Hamlet pled, "Oh ... that the Everlasting had not fix'd His canon 'gainst self-slaughter!'"
- That the title of John Steinbeck's novel *East of Eden* referred to the biblical *Book of Genesis* (chapter 4, verse 16) that tells of God's sending Cain to "the land of Nod on the East of Eden" for Cain's having slain his brother, Abel.
- The nature of the hero's fixation in Lloyd Douglas's novel *The Magnificent Obsession*.

In the Arts. Casting out religion-related drawings, paintings, and sculpture from the public-school curriculum would mean that students would never see

- Pictures of Michelangelo's ceiling in the Vatican's Sistine Chapel or his sculpture of David.
- Religious paintings of such artists as El Greco, Leonardo Da Vinci, Caravaggio, Peter Paul Rubens, Philippe de Champaigne, Gabriel De Sabato, Johan Moreelse, Jan Pynas, Hieronymus Bosch, Louis Testelin, Claude Simpol, Joseph Parrocel, and far more.

In summary, a policy of eliminating all mention to religion in the curriculum would so badly decimate the body of knowledge students have a chance to acquire that such a solution to the separation of church and state is widely recognized as pedagogically disastrous. Thus, the following three alternatives become the practical options from which educators could choose one—or a combination—as the religion-related curriculum pattern they would implement.

Require Secular Descriptions and Appraisals

One policy option that schools could adopt requires that only secular descriptions and appraisals of religious-linked events be allowed in public schools' curricula.

The expression *secular*, as intended here, means that

(1) Descriptions of what occurred in a historical event or recent happening would have to be "factual," in the sense of either (a) an account of events that is uncolored by the religious or belief-system bias of those who witnessed the events, so that if there are two sides in a disputed event both sides would agree on basic elements of what occurred, and (b), if the two sides disagreed, each side's perception of the event would be included in the description.

(2) The principles that guide any appraisal of events or people—as good or bad, desirable or undesirable, fair or unfair—should represent universal values rather than values unique to a particular religion. For instance, the biblical Ten Commandments include both unique and universal values (Exodus, 1611). Three of the commandments unique to Judeo-Christian tradition are those forbidding people to worship idols, to work on the Sabbath day, or to yearn for property belonging to other people. Among the commandments reflecting universal values—that is, values honored in many religions and belief systems—are those proscribing killing, stealing, and telling lies (bearing false witness) in such disputes as court cases. A modern-day example of universal values is the *United Nations Declaration of Human Rights* (1948), a document officially endorsed by most of the world's nations. The declaration's values include freedom

  • from being held in slavery or servitude.

  • from torture or cruel, inhuman, or degrading treatment or punishment.

  • from arbitrary arrest, detention, or exile.

  • to marry and to found a family. Marriage shall be entered into only with the free and full consent of the intending spouses.

  • to own property alone as well as in association with others.

  • of thought, conscience and religion; this right includes freedom to change one's religion or belief, and freedom, either alone or in community with others and in public or private, to manifest one's religion or belief in teaching, practice, worship and observance.

  • of opinion and expression; this right includes freedom to hold opinions without interference and to seek, receive, and impart information and ideas through any media and regardless of frontiers.

  • of peaceful assembly and association; no one may be compelled to belong to an association. (United Nations, 1948)

Within such a secular curriculum, all of the topics listed as unacceptable under the extreme church-separation policy described above would be proper subjects of study as long as students were not urged to accept one faith or belief system as superior to another. In effect, students would be free to make up their own minds about which system they would prefer.

Bible Class

A third possible choice among curriculum designs is that of teaching about a particular religion rather than about several. In the United States, that faith would be Christianity, because the majority of Americans identify themselves as Christians. Thus, it is not unusual for public schools to offer an entire semester-long class or a shorter unit of study focusing on the Christian Bible. An estimated 8 or 9 percent of American schools include the Bible in literature or social-studies classes, either as a separate elective course or as a study unit within a general English or history course. To do so legally, the curriculum must be designed to teach *about* the Bible without providing religious instruction aimed at recruiting students into the Christian faith or into a particular sect or denomination of that faith. Nor should the curriculum intend to portray the Bible as superior to the scriptures of other religions, such as the Islamic Quran or Hindu Vedas, because doing so could be interpreted as an effort to proselytize.

The legal guidelines for including study of the Bible in public schools were set by the U.S. Supreme Court's 8-to-1 ruling in the 1963 case of *School District of Abington Township v. Schempp* in which Justice Clark wrote,

It might be well said that one's education is not complete without a study of comparative religion or the history of religion and its relationship to the advancement of civilization. It certainly may be said that the Bible is worthy of study for its literacy and historic qualities. Nothing we have said here indicates that such study of the Bible or of religion, when presented objectively as part of a secular program of education, may not be effected consistently with the First Amendment. (Clark, 1963)

In deciding what to teach about the Bible, schools sometimes depend solely on the instructor assigned to the class. An example of a teacher-designed course of study is the plan devised by Wedge Crouch, an English teacher at Ozark High School in Missouri. As students' source of biblical literature in Crouch's class, they bring their own Bibles, whichever version they wish. Crouch explained that "Students must understand that the course is in no way a 'religion course'" and that its aim was to provoke students to think critically. For instance, when

he teaches the story of Noah, [he asks students] to imagine being notified that the rains are going to come and destroy everyone but them. What would they do? ... His syllabus for the class starts out with a sentence that reads, "Students must understand that his course is in no way a 'religion course.'"

To make sure he stays on the *about* side of teaching the Bible, Crouch said he prefaces any statements he makes about Biblical stories by using the phrase "according to the account," as in "According to the account, Noah and his ark survived rain for 40 days and nights." In 14 years of teaching the course, Crouch said, he's never had a complaint from a student or a parent about the content, structure, or teaching of the course. (Townsend, 2006)

In contrast to classes or units devised by individual instructors are those in which a commercially available course of study determines the curriculum content. The nature of such material is illustrated in the following section with two plans published in 2005. The first, titled *The Bible in History and Literature*, was a revision of an earlier curriculum. The second, called *The Bible and Its Influence*, was an entirely new plan. Each consisted of a textbook and an extensive instructor's manual.

The Bible in history and literature. This curriculum is a product of the National Council on Bible Curriculum in Public Schools, located in Greensboro, North Carolina. The only item to be purchased is the instructional 274-page paper-back guidebook, titled *The Bible in History and Literature,* which directs teachers in how to use the eighteen instructional units that comprise the course of study. The main textbook for the class is the Bible, which students can bring from home, or they may study Bibles provided by the school. A supplementary two-volume textbook—*The Bible Reader: An Interfaith Interpretation*—is included with the guidebook in the form of a compact disc that can be read on a computer screen. In defending the use of the Bible as the textbook, a member of the Council's board of directors has written:

The law prohibits only the mandatory reading of the Bible on a daily basis as a devotional exercise; it does not bar an elective course that permits students to read the Bible voluntarily as part of their normal school work . . . Any Bible curriculum that does not allow students to read [the Bible] for themselves and draw their own conclusions insults the intelligence of the students and short changes them from getting a well-rounded education. In the final analysis, refusal to allow students to use their own Bibles in a Bible class is the ultimate in arrogance and arbitrary censorship. (Crampton, 2005)

The units focus on such diverse topics as (a) the first twenty-five chapters of the book of Genesis, (b) Isaac, Jacob, and Joseph, (c) Moses in Egypt, (d) the Passover, (e) Hebrew law, (f) Old Testament literature highlights, (g) the Dead Sea scrolls and other archeological finds, (h) the four gospels of the New Testament, (i) biblical influence on America's founding fathers and their view on human rights, and (j) biblical art. Eleven of the eighteen units concern the Old Testament, three concern the New Testament, and the remaining four address more general matters.

A typical unit, as described in the instructor's manual, consists of the unit's objective, the expected learning outcomes, and sample lesson plans in which students are directed to read selected Bible passages. The structure of a typical lesson can be illustrated with a segment of a lesson plan that focuses on the function of questions in works of poetry. This lesson is only one of a series in Unit 9. The unit is labeled "Literature Highlights—Job and Psalms."

Lesson title: **Characteristics of Hebrew Poetry: The Question**

(Lesson Plan Segment)
Objectives: To see the frequent use of questions, and simplicity of diction and construction, as a means of securing added rhythm and stress to sentences, variety of style, and suggestions of both pathos and mystery in Hebrew poetry. To examine figurative language as a powerful means of expression.
Readings: Psalms 137, 139, 8, 13; Job 38–41

Activities:
1. Read Psalms 137 and 139 as illustrations of pathos and mystery in a question. Have students select at random other examples from the Psalms as illustrations of the use of the question.
2. Read at least Chapter 38 in Job to show the power of the question in obtaining stress and rhythm. Point out melody and rhythm and the pictorial value of single words.
3. Explain the use of figurative language in Hebrew poetry. Review terms such as metaphor, simile, personification, hyperbole, etc Explain that the two most common types used by the Hebrews are metaphor and simile, with the simile being the most frequent. Ask the class to find examples of figurative language in the Psalms, Job, and the Song of Solomon and to write them down. They should also designate each figure of speech.
4. Add to the student's vocabulary: personification, metaphor, hyperbole, simile, under-statement, iteration.

Source: The bible in history and literature. (2005). Greensboro, NC: National Council on Bible Curriculum in Public Schools, p. 130.

As evidence that schools have found the National Council curriculum satisfactory, Council officials reported that their materials had been adopted by 346 school districts in thirty-seven states.

What, then, are strengths and limitations of the National Council's curriculum? Among assessments offered by independent reviewers of the curriculum is a comparison of the Bible as a literary work and as a historical record. Some reviewers have concluded that the Council's literary units are more easily defended and more convincing than are those concerning history.

Programs that focus on literary features of the Bible usually address one or both of two questions. (a) How can the Bible be understood *as* a work of literature? (b) How does knowledge of the Bible contribute to readers' understanding allusions to the Bible that appear *in* other literary works, such as Shakespeare's plays or Dante's *Inferno*? As shown above in the lesson-plan segment about Hebrew poetry, the Council's Unit 9 concerns the "understood-as-literature" goal by addressing questions of "How can the Bible's contents by analyzed as types of literature and literary styles?" I imagine that there is little, if any, disagreement among critics that *The Bible in History and Literature* successfully accomplishes that task.

As in the case of literature, the Bible can be viewed both *as* history and *in* its influence on historical events. It is here that a goodly amount of controversy has occurred. Viewing the Bible *as* an accurate historical record is continually being questioned. Many chapters of the Old Testament purport to trace ancient family lineages (such as the descendants of Adam, Noah, Moses, or David) and to chronicle wars waged by the people of Israel and Judah. If those accounts are to be accepted as persuasive descriptions of what actually occurred, they may call for support from sources outside the Bible. But even more questionable are reports of events that are so unusual that they beg for verification. Such reports include

- The description in Genesis of the creation of the universe and its contents.
- Adam, Seth, Enos, Cainan, Jared, and Methuselah each living for more than 900 years.
- Noah's building an ark 300 cubits long (about 450 feet) that housed pairs of all living species during a 40-day rainstorm.
- The Red Sea parting to allow the Israelites to escape from Egypt.
- Joshua's followers shouting loud enough to shatter the walls surrounding the city of Jericho.
- Satan and God wagering on how religiously faithful Job would be if Job lost his wealth, family, and good health.
- Jonah living in a whale's belly for 3 days.
- Jesus walking on water, changing water to wine, multiplying a few fish and loaves enough to feed a multitude, and rising from the dead after being crucified.

Now, to explain why individuals might differ in their opinions about the historical accuracy of the Bible's descriptions of those events, consider two questions about people's judgments of such matters:

- How should the term *historical account* be defined?
- How are people's worldviews influenced by the kinds of evidence on which they base their beliefs?

Defining "historical account." One way to define *history* or *a historical account* is to call it "a description of what actually happened in the past." Or, as an alternative, *historical account* can be defined as "someone's estimate of what likely happened in the past." This second option takes into account the perspective or viewpoint of the person who wrote the description. That viewpoint could be influenced by the writer's religion, gender, ethnic affiliation, social-class status, academic training, access to evidence, language skills, and more. As a result, different writers will view an event through different mental lenses. So, defining history as "what actually happened" assumes that the resulting account will be "the objective truth," but defining history as a person's "estimate" admits that all accounts will involve a measure of subjectivity and are thus a combination of both an event and the perspective from which the particular historian views that event.

Some Christians—particularly ones of an evangelical or pentecostal persuasion—consider history as depicted in the Bible to be an accurate version of what really transpired. Other Christians—including ones in traditional mainstream denominations—consider the Bible's historical reports to be writers' estimates of what likely occurred or might have happened. In like manner, some Jews regard their holy scriptures—the Christians' Old Testament—as literal historical fact, whereas others consider the account to be writers' suppositions about the past.

In brief, people's definitions of *historical account* will affect how convincing they find the Bible as history.

Acceptable evidence. People can differ regarding the sources of evidence on which they base their beliefs, including their beliefs about biblical accounts of historical events. Two sources of evidence in which individuals may place their confidence are "an authority" and "empirical data."

Trusting an authority means accepting someone's word as unerring truth. The authority usually is a person (parent, minister, priest, rabbi, imam, professor, senator, or others) or a document (*Bible, Torah, Quran, Vedas, Book of Mormon,* Scientology's *Fundamentals of Thought,* or others). If a person believes absolutely in the Christian God and invests indubitable faith in the Bible as God's true word, then the Bible's historical narratives are, without question, literally true. And such miraculous happenings as the parting of the Red Sea, Joshua's shouting down the walls of Jericho, and Jesus' resurrection are not problems to be explained but, instead, merely confirm God's omnipotence. Those amazing happenings are simply proof of the Lord's unlimited power.

People may offer several reasons for accepting the word of an authority as convincing evidence. They may say the Bible has stood the test of time, revered by many millions of people across two millennia, so the Bible must be true. They may point out that thousands of prestigious scholars across the centuries have attested to the Bible's accuracy. Or they say they were taught the Bible from early childhood and now, in their adult life, it still offers invaluable comfort and guidance.

In contrast to trusting an authority, people may place their faith in *empirical data* or *empirical evidence* that has been collected and is critically analyzed. Three of the techniques that such a process often involves are those of (a) gathering multiple independent reports, (b) using archeological findings, and (c) comparing an event to other similar events.

The assumption underlying the practice of collecting various reports of an incident is that the greater the consensus among independent witnesses about what happened, the greater the confidence warranted in the accuracy of the historical account. For example, scholars have sought to assess the accuracy of reports about Jesus' life and works by comparing the first four books of the New Testament—the gospels of Matthew, Mark, Luke, and John—to determine the degree of consistency among the four. Some scholars have also included a fifth gospel in their comparisons, a Coptic document attributed to the disciple Thomas, found in a cave in the Egyptian desert in 1946 (Reluctant Messenger, 2006). However, there remains an unresolved question about whether the four New Testament versions are actually independent reports. For instance, the first three—Matthew, Mark, and Luke—are often referred to as *synoptic* (Greek *syn* = together and *opsis* = appearance) because they have many parables in common and a general consensus on the order of events, thereby suggesting a common source for all three.

A second kind of empirical evidence is archeological, that is, using scientists' digs which yield artifacts from biblical times. The age of objects from the past can be accurately determined today by carbon-dating techniques, and genetic relationships between unearthed bones and people living at different times can be measured by such forensic techniques as DNA analysis. Those findings can help confirm or disconfirm events depicted in the Bible.

A third approach to estimating the accuracy of biblical accounts involves comparing a described episode to similar episodes with which an investigator is acquainted. An example is the Bible tale of teenage David pitted against an over-nine-foot-tall (6 cubits and a span) giant, Goliath (Samuel I, 1611). How likely could David launch a stone into Goliath's forehead with a slingshot? We might answer by reasoning that there are people today who can cast spears, darts, arrows, knives, baseballs, and other objects with great accuracy. Thus, it seems plausible that David, as a practiced slinger of stones, could have struck Goliath in the forehead. Therefore, we might conclude that the David/Goliath account was probably true—surely more so than the story of Jonah surviving unharmed after 3 days inside a whale.

Now, keeping in mind the foregoing discussion of defining *historical account* and *acceptable evidence*, we return to the National Council's curriculum in order to consider how it treats the Bible as history. Whereas the title of the Council's guidebook is *The Bible in History and Literature,* the book's contents show that much of the guidebook presents the Bible *as* history and literature. What position, then, does the book take on the definition of *historical account*— "the Bible chronicles exactly what occurred" or "the Bible is historians' estimate of what might have occurred"? The guidebook does not directly address this matter, but only mentions that different people might interpret the Bible's historical accounts as either factual or allegorical (symbolic but not literally true). Thus, judging the factual accuracy of the historical accounts is left up to each teacher who uses the curriculum or to the students enrolled in the class.

The Bible and its influence. This curriculum consists of a 387-page student textbook, *The Bible and Its Influence,* and a 450-page teacher's edition that consists of the basic textbook enhanced with notes and resources for the instructor. The student text was published in late 2005, followed in June 2006 by the teacher's edition. *The Bible and Its Influence* is the result of a long-term project of the Bible Literacy Project, under the general editorship of Cullen Schippe and Chuck Stetson, with headquarters at Front Royal, Virginia.

The student textbook is a 9-by-12-inch hardback volume elaborately illustrated with full-color photographs of religious paintings, portraits of significant persons, maps, and drawings on high-gloss paper. Nearly every pair of pages contains one or more illustrations that accompany the text content.

The students' book is divided into fourteen study units, with each unit composed of two or more chapters to make a total of forty chapters. The first unit addresses the question "Why study the Bible?" and also introduces students to the Hebrew Bible. Other units focus on such biblical books as Genesis and Exodus, on Hebrew kingdoms and prophets, on the four gospels of the New Testament, on Paul's letters to church groups, and on the book of revelation. A large portion of these chapters consists of easily understood overviews of happenings that are more detailed and difficult to follow in such Bibles as the King James Authorized Version. A study unit on writings and wisdom includes chapters on songs and poetry, wise sayings, problems of suffering, women of valor, and visions of the future. Each unit closes with a "feature." Four of the features illustrate biblical influences on the writings of John Milton, St. Augustine, Shakespeare, and Dante's *Purgatoria*. Still other features speak of literary genres in the Bible, meanings of death, and "freedom and faith in America." Frequent sidebars throughout the textbook highlight "The Bible in Literature" and "Cultural Connections" to American history, the theater, music, art, science, religious communities, and more. Each chapter also suggests projects that students can carry out. Here are three examples:

Chapter 3: In the Beginning—Genesis.—Look up some other ancient literature and mythology of the origins of the world (such as *Enuma Elish, Gilgamesh,* or *Praise of the Pickax*). Compare what you have read there with the first two chapters of Genesis. Share your comparisons.

Chapter 5: Abraham and Sarah. Write a short story or develop a short dramatization using a contemporary setting and characters to explore one or more themes from the stories of Jacob and Joseph:

a. Sibling rivalry

b. Trickery or deceit

c. The power of dreams

d. Overcoming temptation

Find a commentary on Genesis on the Internet that will help you with your creative task.

Chapter 34: Social Order—1 and 2 Timothy and Philemon. Research the abolitionist movements in Great Britain and in the United States. How did the Bible influence the activists on both sides of the movement? How was the Bible used in the movements to abolish slavery? Report on your findings. (Schippe & Stetson, 2005)[1]

A typical page of the teacher's manual that accompanies *The Bible and Its Influence* consists of a small reproduction of a page from the students' textbook surrounded by suggestions relating to the content of that page in the students' text. The suggestions for how a teacher might treat the content of the students' page are offered under such titles as (a) lesson objectives, (b) working with the text, (c) visual learning (such as interpreting the meaning of famous paintings that appear in the students' book), (d) vocabulary meanings, (e) cultural connections,

(f) the Bible in literature, (g) the Bible and science, and (h) discussion questions. Suggestions are also added about what students might write as their own reactions in personal journals they keep about their study of the Bible. The following pair of quotations illustrate the nature of typical passages in the teacher's manual. Both segments focus on the creation story at the beginning of the book of Genesis.

Working with the Text: "Ask students to share their impressions of and reactions to [the first six days] of the creation narrative. Be sure to keep the discussion focused on the text itself. Remind students to show respect for one another even when they disagree on the interpretation of this passage, and note that the purpose of this class is not to resolve such disputes. The text shows a God creating order where there was chaos, making light and darkness, night and day, heaven above and watery earth below, dry land and seas, plants and animals, and finally male and female—and judging his work good." (Bible Literacy Project, 2006)

Literature Extension: "Locate and distribute copies of: The Creation: A Negro Sermon" by James Weldon Johnson. Have students work in small groups to prepare a choral reading of this poem. Encourage students to echo the poem's tone of creative exuberance in their presentation. Johnson (1871–1938) was a lyricist, poet, diplomat, and teacher who collected and made available anthologies of African American poetry and spirituals. 'The Creation' is a part of a longer work entitled *God's Trombones*." (Bible Literacy Project, 2006)[2]

The programs compared. So, in 2005, two well-publicized curricula were published for teaching a public-school course on the Bible. They were *The Bible in History and Literature* (*Bible Hist-Lit*) and *The Bible and Its Influence* (*Bible Inf*). How, then, do the two compare in terms of focus, resources for students, teachers' instructional burden, varied interpretations, examples of influence, and student projects?

Focus. Although both urge students to read the Bible, *Bible Hist-Lit* concentrates more heavily on assigned Bible reading than does *Bible Inf*, which places primary emphasis on reading the textbook and then refers students to appropriate selections in the Bible itself.

Resources for Students. The learning sources that students have at hand are far greater and more convenient with *Bible Inf* than with *Bible Hist-Lit*. The *Bible Inf* student textbook provides learners with a great host of information about the history of biblical literature over the centuries and about its influences in literature and culture. In contrast, the *Bible Hist-Lit* program depends on the teacher to furnish such information, aided by a much smaller body of material in the instructor's manual than is found in the *Bible Inf* student textbook and instructor's guidebook. Although the *Bible Hist-Lit* manual does suggest an extensive list of other books as supplementary resources, it is necessary for teachers to purchase those resources separately in order to make them available to students.

Teachers' Instructional Burden. A teacher's task in creating and delivering lessons appears far more demanding with the *Bible Hist-Lit* curriculum than with the *Bible Inf* course of study, principally because of the *Bible Inf* student textbook.

Many lessons in the *Bible Inf* plan will consist of the teacher assigning class members to read sections of the textbook; the reading is then followed up with class discussions or projects that oblige students to ponder and apply what they have learned from the textbook. However, in the *Bible Hist-Lit* approach, the teacher apparently must create lectures that equip learners with the sort of background information found in the *Bible Inf* student book. The help the *Bible Hist-Lit* program offers teachers toward developing lectures seems quite meager.

Varied Interpretations. As noted earlier, the *Bible Hist-Lit* curriculum rarely, if ever, suggests that the Bible can be interpreted in different ways. That is, the program avoids such issues of history-as-what-really-happened versus history-as-peoples'-estimates. Any interpretations that might be drawn are apparently left up to the classroom teacher's initiative. In contrast, the *Bible-Inf* plan confronts that matter of interpretations quite directly. Consider, for example, the following passage that identifies four alternative ways that Jews may read the Bible.

- A *plain-sense* reading (in Hebrew, *peshat*) looks to the surface, though not necessarily literal, meaning of the text, [and draws] on knowledge of word meanings, grammar, syntax, and context.

- An *inquiring* reading (in Hebrew, *derash*) looks for further layers of meaning. This kind of interpretive reading is what a rabbi or minister does when giving a sermon or homily on a biblical text, using story and example to add understanding. *Midrash*, the Jewish tradition of interpreting the Scriptures through creative storytelling, derives from this way of reading.

- An *allegorical* reading (in Hebrew, *remez*) looks for parallels between the scriptural text and more abstract concepts. This kind of reading sees biblical characters, events, and literary compositions as standing for other truths.

- "A *mystical* reading (in Hebrew, *sod*) looks at the biblical text as a symbolic code, which with piety and effort will yield hidden wisdom and personal connection with the divine. The Jewish mystical tradition known as *Kabbalah* relies on complex symbolic interpretation of each individual letter of the biblical text." (Schippe & Stetson, 2005, p. 9)

This multiple-interpretations viewpoint is then expressed periodically through the student textbook in such observations as

whether the reader sees the Bible as divinely inspired or as the work of human ingenuity (or both), the power of [the Book of Genesis] is undeniable. (Schippe & Stetson, 2005, p. 29)

Educators who accept the content of the Bible as literal truth—telling what really happened and how it happened—can be expected to disapprove of the *Bible Inf* curriculum with its multiple interpretations and will much prefer the *Bible Hist-Lit* plan that does not address the matter of multiple understandings. That point is illustrated later in this chapter under the description of *The Odessa Case.*

Examples of Influence. Far more examples of how the Bible has influenced history, culture, and literature are offered in the *Bible Inf* program than in the *Bible Hist-Lit* curriculum—by virtue of the *Bible Inf* student textbook and teacher's guidebook—than in the *Bible Inf* curriculum.

Student Projects. The two curricula are quite similar in the kinds of projects students pursue in applying what they have learned from their study of the Bible.

In late 2005 and throughout 2006, controversy erupted over which of the two curriculum programs was better. A bill introduced in the Alabama legislature would have required the use of *Bible Inf* as the textbook for an elective Bible class in Alabama schools, but the bill was defeated by supporters of the *Bible Hist-Lit* program. A typical criticism of the *Bible Inf* was offered by Dr. D. James Kennedy of Coral Ridge Ministries when asked by a legislator to review the textbook in February 2006. Kenndy replied,

I have examined the [*Bible and Its Influence*] text and other material and I believe this would be a tremendous mistake to impose such very anti-Biblical material upon our children in public schools. Holding a Ph.D. in Bible and Theology, I can tell you the approach of this material is extremely radical and should not be chosen to represent the approved views of the Alabama legislature. (Problems with, 2006)

In contrast to Kennedy's opinion was that of Dr. Peter Lillback, Ph.D., president of Westminster Theological Seminary, who wrote about the *Bible and Its Influence*: "The informational content, accuracy, exposition, illustrations, and tone are all extremely well done" (Group defends, 2006).

Comparative Religion

The fourth alternative for teaching about religion in public schools involves offering a class or unit in which various religions are compared. Such a class is more frequently taught in colleges than in high schools. However, as interest in teaching about religion increases throughout the country, comparative religion as an elective course or study unit may become more common.

Sometimes such a class is organized around one or more textbooks. An example of a pair of texts suitable for advanced high-school students is the combination of Huston Smith's *The World's Religions: Our Great Wisdom Traditions* (1991) and Philip Novak's *The World's Wisdom: Sacred Texts of the World's Religions* (1991). Smith's book introduces students to Hinduism, Buddhism, Confucianism, Taoism, Judaism, Christianity, Islam, and such "primal religions" as Native American and African faiths. Novak's volume serves as a companion to Smith's text, offering segments of scriptures from the Hebrew Bible, the Christian New Testament, Chinese Taoism's Tao Te Ching, Islam's Quran, and others.

Rather than building a comparative-education course around a textbook or two, some instructors devise their own plan that uses selected readings to supplement lectures. Such is the case with the following two examples of typical introductory courses at the college level—classes that could also be suitable for those high school students capable of succeeding in advanced-placement courses.

Introduction to religious studies. The principal objectives of a course taught by Professor Kristin Johnston Largen at the University of South Carolina are that students will

1. Learn about the academic study of religion, including how religion is defined, and how religion functions in the lives of human beings.
2. Gain an overview of the history of Hinduism, Judaism, Buddhism, and Christianity, and a familiarity with the main beliefs and practices of each.
3. Gain an understanding and appreciation of some of the sacred texts from each religion.
4. Learn how to compare religions in an academic setting, and apply this knowledge in a constructive paper on a topic of the student's choice. (Largen, 2006)

To explain the experiences that class members can expect, Largen has written:

This course introduces students to the academic study of religion, focusing on the history and classical texts of four major world religions: Hinduism, Judaism, Buddhism, and Christianity, studied in that order. In addition, there is also a comparative component, so students will be expected not only to learn about each religion individually, but also gain an understanding of the discipline of comparative religions and put that knowledge into practice.

We will spend the first few weeks talking about religion in general: what defines a religion, the major characteristics of a religion, and some of the ways religion functions in the lives of human individuals and societies. Also included in this beginning section will be a discussion of the discipline of comparative religion, including some of the history and major figures, as well as current trends in the field. After this general orientation, we will begin the study of each religion in order. We will start with an historical overview of the religion, including the origins of the religion, major influences, foundational ideas, and key figures. The students also will learn the geography of the religion—where it developed and how it traveled, for example, as well as a timeline of major events. We then will discuss how the main characteristics of the religion were formed and eventually codified, and then how they were modified by different communities in different places. Finally, we will look at the practice of the religion today, and how it has evolved in modern times. At the appropriate places in the course we will discuss our texts, and examine how they promulgate the central tenets of the religion. (Largen, 2006)

The main content of Largen's course is offered in a sequence of lectures, with the lectures supplemented by students reading selected sections of three books: *The Ramayana* by R. K. Narayan, *The Diamond Sutra & The Sutra of Hui-Neng* by A. F. Price, and *The Bible* (new revised standard version).

Comparative religion. Professor Jim Ford's class at Rogers State University in Oklahoma is similar to Largen's course, except that in Ford's class the second half of the semester is dedicated to considering how three religions cope with the problem of how an omnipotent, omniscient God could permit so much pain and tribulation in today's world.

The course begins with an introduction to the academic study of religion, an overview of what religion involves and how to approach religious traditions in a classroom context. After that introduction to studying religion, most of the first half of the course is a comparative study of several of the world's major religious traditions, including Hinduism, Buddhism, Judaism, Christianity, and Islam. The second half of the course is devoted to analyzing how individual believers in three of those traditions (Judaism, Christianity, and Islam, the "People of the Book") deal with a single problem, [which is] belief in a single, all-good, all-powerful, and all-knowing God given the existence and prevalence of human suffering. Given the kinds of suffering we see every day in the world, from the ravages of AIDS and cancer to the horrors of 9/11, how can believers make sense of this problem? Are those approaches rational? (Ford, 2006)

The textbooks in Ford's version of comparative religion differ from those in Largen's version. Ford requires more books, and they are not limited to the basic scriptures of different faiths.

Greene, Graham. *The Power and the Glory*. Viking Penguin, 1991.

Lewis, C. S. *A Grief Observed*. Bantam Doubleday Dell, 1976.

Molloy, Michael. *Experiencing the World's Religions*. Mayfield/McGraw-Hill, 2004..

Scriptures of the World's Religions. Editors: James Feiser and John Powers. McGraw-Hill.

Wiesel, Elie. *Night*. Bantam Doubleday Dell, 1982.

Wolterstorff, Nicholas. *Lament for a Son*. Eerdmans, 1987.

Summary. In their two most popular forms, comparative-religion courses or units are (a) organized around one or more textbooks, with the textbooks determining which religions are compared and in what order they are studied or (b) organized around the instructor's own plan for lectures and discussion sessions that are supplemented with assigned readings. Comparative religion can legally be taught in public schools as long as the several faiths are objectively described and none is either favored or denigrated in comparison to the others.

Published Curriculum versus Taught Curriculum

Early in this chapter a distinction was drawn between an official, printed curriculum and the way that curriculum is implemented in classrooms (the taught curriculum). The reason such a distinction is important is that the intent of a legally acceptable published course of study—to teach *about* religion without seeking to convert students to a particular faith—may break down in practice if teachers favor one religion over another during their classroom presentations. It seems apparent that the task of presenting different religions in a strictly neutral, objective fashion can be difficult for teachers who are thoroughly convinced that their own faith is the true one. In effect, by stressing ostensible weaknesses of religions other than their own faith and by highlighting desirable characteristics of the faith they prefer, teachers can bias the impression students receive about competing belief systems. Thus, the final judgment of whether schools are proselytizing rather than only teaching *about* religion must be made at the classroom level. Ultimately, the taught curriculum is the one that really matters. And the fact that a teacher has violated the ban against proselytizing will not come to the public's attention unless students or their parents complain to authorities or file a lawsuit.

Illustrative Cases

Diverse forms that controversies over curricula can assume are reflected in the following six episodes that concerned teaching about religion in public schools.

The Odessa Choice

During 2005, the school board in Odessa (Texas)—population 94,000— was involved in a heated dispute over which of two curriculum plans to adopt for an elective, nonsectarian high-school Bible class that the school district intended to offer. The plans were *The Bible in History and Literature* (from the National Council on Bible Curriculum in Public Schools) and *The Bible and Its Influence* (from the Bible Literacy Project).

Before an overflow crowd at the board meeting of December 20, advocates for each of the plans argued in favor of their choice. Then the issue, which the community had debated for months, seemed finally settled by the board's adopting the *Bible in History and Literature* in a split vote, 4-to-2. During the board's deliberations, three dozen members of the Life Challenge United Pentecostal Church had demonstrated outside the school district's administration building with posters demanding "Give us the Bible" and "Bible as Text Book." After the vote was announced, the group chanted "victory."

But the possibility that the settlement was only temporary was suggested by comments from observers who believed the wrong plan had been chosen. The two board members who had voted against the *Bible in History and Literature* thought that a course focusing exclusively on a Protestant Bible could offend students who held other worldviews. The two agreed that Odessa's schools had "an obligation to protect the minority—the Jews, the Muslims, the Hindus and any other religious faith. We're a public school. We have to remember that. Each student should feel comfortable in this course" (Lee, 2005).

An Odessa College professor said he would bring a lawsuit against the board, contending that the *Bible in History and Literature* violated the constitutional separation of church and state. In rebuttal, an attorney for the publishers of the curriculum told the school board,

A lot of talk about a lawsuit has been bandied about. Let me say this as unequivocally as I can: We stand behind this curriculum 100 percent—academically, legally and, yes, financially. In the unlikely event you are sued, this district will not spend a dime. I'm here tonight to guarantee that. (Lee, 2005)

Although several speakers during the board meeting had claimed that the *Bible in History and Literature* had never been challenged in court, a representative of the Texas Freedom Network said that the plan had been taken to court in Florida where parents successfully sued their school board over the adoption of an earlier version of the National Council's course materials.

Therefore, in spite of the board's vote, it seemed clear that the controversy in Odessa over the Bible class was still far from resolved.

Portraying Hinduism in California Textbooks

The notion that curriculum planning in multifaith societies can be a political activity was demonstrated in a 2005–2006 controversy over the contents of history books in California. That event also demonstrated how religious events in other nations may affect how religions are depicted in text materials that students study in America's public schools.

In 1987, California education officials rewrote the state's guidelines for social studies to include the study of religion and its effect on history, with an emphasis on multiculturalism. Because California is one of the states whose board of education determines which textbooks are to be adopted in public schools, the new guidelines influenced decisions about textbook contents. Every 6 years, the board reviews the books submitted by publishers and suggests changes that would be needed in those texts if they are to receive the board's approval.

Over the period 2005–2006, the board faced the task of deciding whether to alter the accounts of Hinduism in sixth-grade history books that publishers were offering for adoption. The task was complicated by the contradictory appeals of two competing groups of Hindus living in the United States. The antagonism that separated the contending groups had its roots in India's national election of 1998 when the Bharatiya Janata Party (BJP) defeated the Congress Party that had ruled the nation over several decades. Among the steps the BJP leadership then took to promote its Hindu-nationalism agenda was to revise the officially authorized school history books. Much to the distress of the Congress party and history scholars, the new texts depicted Aryans as the original people of India— "indigenous geniuses who created the Indus Valley civilization"—rather than accepting evidence that Aryan nomads had entered India from the Russian steppes (Ramesh, 2004). In addition, the texts minimized the pernicious effects of the caste system, entirely omitted such "awkward facts" as a Hindu nationalist's assassinating Mahatma Gandhi, and changed traditional historical accounts in a variety of other ways (Panikkar, 2005).

In assessing the significance of the BJP textbook program, K. N. Panikkar proposed that the revisions were

inspired by the political project of Hindu fundamentalism, to transform the multicultural and multireligious Indian nation into an exclusively Hindu state. What the textbooks have attempted is to reshape the Indian past to derive legitimacy for this political project and to communally reconstruct the historical consciousness of the coming generations. In the process, the generally accepted norms and methods of historical discipline have irreparably suffered. (Panikkar, 2005)

When the BJP was ousted from office by the Congress Party in India's 2004 election, the new leaders assigned a team of historians to cleanse the textbooks of changes the BJP had made.

Subsequently, rumblings from the book battle in India reverberated in California during the state board's deliberations. In September 2005 several religious groups suggested hundreds of changes to history textbooks the board was considering adopting. The vast majority of the proposals came from a pair of U.S.-based Hindu organizations with long ties to Hindu nationalist parties in India—the Vedic Foundation and the Hindu Education Foundation.

Most of the proposed changes would erase or alter passages dealing with caste and gender discrimination in ancient South Asia. The changes also were aimed to dispute the notion that Aryan peoples from outside India played a key role in the formation of Hinduism . . . Michael Witzel, a professor of Sanskrit at Harvard University, entered the process with a letter signed by nearly 50 other professors [that labeled] the Hindu groups' proposals "unscholarly" [and said that adopting such suggestions] would "trigger an immediate international scandal." (Ranganathan, 2006)

Among the notions that the nationalists sought to insert in California textbooks were assertions that

Indian civilization is 1,900 million years old, the Ramayana and Mahabharata [epic poems] are historical texts to be understood literally, and ancient Hindu scriptures contain precise calculations of the speed of light and exact distances between planets in the solar system . . . [In the nationalists' suggestions], women's history was reduced to "different" rights while the caste system, which subjugated millions of Indians as virtual slaves in the untouchable caste, was simply a division of labor. By spelling God with a capital letter they are trying to position Hinduism as monotheistic, making it look more "modern." (Thapar & Witzel, 2006)

Opponents of the Hindu nationalists included not only American university professors but also modernist Indians living in the United States who charged that the proposed changes not only distorted history but also served to conceal caste discrimination that persists today.

When the state board issued its final decision in March 2006, around 20 percent of the Hindu nationalists' 500 requests were accepted, but 80 percent—including those that glossed over the caste system—were rejected in an 8-to-0 vote, with two abstentions. A spokesman for Friends of South Asia—a group that had fought the Hindu nationalists' proposed corrections—thanked the board for "rejecting the ideologically motivated edits." University of California-Berkeley Professor Gautam Premnath said, "On the whole, we are pleased . . . The process worked out the way we hoped for. It is an important positive step" (Krieger, 2006). However, one nationalist group, the Hindu American Foundation, filed a lawsuit on March 16, 2006, seeking to block the printing of the sixth-grade textbooks on the grounds that state law forbade instructional materials from reflecting adversely on any race, color, creed, national origin, or ancestry (Burress, 2006).

Other changes, less controversial, were proposed and accepted by members of the Jewish, Christian, and Islamic communities. Language was deleted because it promoted anti-Semitism. For instance, students will now learn that Romans, not Jews, crucified Christ. A sentence was deleted that suggested that God punished the Jews due to their evil ways. Also dropped was a section that asked students to bring a Bible to class, as well as an assignment to write a short essay about current attempts to end the violence between Israelis and Palestinians. (Krieger, 2006)

When the term *political* is defined as "the exercise of power," then curriculum planning in a multifaith society can be recognized as a political activity in which proponents of each faith seek to have their belief system represented favorably in what students learn at school. The word *favorably* refers to curriculum content that accords (a) more frequent reference to the group's beliefs, (b) greater appreciation of that faith's admirable qualities, (c) greater recognition of contributions the faith has made to individuals' lives and the society at large, and (d) greater acknowledgment of ill treatment that members of the faith have suffered at the hands of nonbelievers. The Hindu-nationalist activists in the California-textbook squabble were clearly engaged in such political activity. Baldauf (2006) interpreted the nationalists' efforts to mean "that this seemingly arcane Indian debate has spilled over into California's board of education is a sign of the growing political muscle of Indian immigrants and the rising American interest in Asia."

Religious Role Playing

Teachers sometimes use *role-playing, sociodrama,* or *creative dramatics* to help pupils better understand other people's actions, feelings, motives, and perspectives toward life. A typical role-playing session consists of pupils imagining themselves in the position of someone else, such as a historical figure, an inhabitant of a foreign country, or an adherent of a religion different from their own. In their adopted guise, pupils then act out events the way they envision their model character would behave. However, whenever it is a religious role that students are assigned to adopt, a question arises about whether such a learning activity violates the constitutional separation of church and state. The issue can become particularly contentious if the religious faith students are expected to depict is different from that of their parents. Such an issue was at the center of a lawsuit that a pair of parents filed against a school district in California's Contra Costa County.

The parents' complained that a role-playing activity used by a teacher at Excelsior Middle School in Byron (California) violated the constitutional separation of church and state. When the parents' lawsuit was rejected by a lower court, they took their case to the U.S. Ninth Circuit Court of Appeal in San Francisco.

The suit accused the teacher of assigning seventh graders to imagine, through role playing, what their lives might be like if they were Muslims. She had followed directions in an instructional guidebook, telling the class that they would "adopt roles as Muslims for three weeks to help them learn what Muslims believe" (Egelko, 2005). She encouraged them to use Muslim names, she recited prayers in class, and she urged them to give up something for a day, such as viewing television or eating candy, so as to simulate the sacrifice Muslims were obliged to make by fasting during the month of Ramadan. In addition, students were to wear nametags with religious symbols, to create a student-made banner that praised Allah, and to memorize a passage from the Islamic holy book, the Quran. At the end of the 3-week study unit, students were to critique aspects of Muslim culture.

In the court case, the parents were represented by an attorney from the Thomas More Law Center, a Christian defense organization, who said that teaching youngsters about Islam was not objectionable. But he charged that the role-playing techniques used at Excelsior Middle School "crossed the line into an unconstitutional endorsement of religion" (Egelko, 2005).

The attorney representing the Byron school district disagreed, arguing that the teacher was merely helping students learn history and culture in an enjoyable fashion. "There was nothing sacred or worshipful about any of the activities" because "students who were asked to recite a line from a religious text did not kneel on prayer rugs or do anything else to suggest a solemn occasion" (Egelko, 2005).

The Ninth Court's three-judge panel found in favor of the seventh-grade teacher and the Byron school district by declaring that "the Islam program activities were not overt religious exercises that raise (constitutional) Establishment Clause concerns" (Egelko, 2006).

The court's decision was greeted with derision by conservative Christian organizations. Typical of such responses was an article in the *California Conservative* that asked,

Does anyone believe the court would've voted this way in favor of teaching Christianity? But maybe we should be thankful. The most notoriously liberal court in the land has just set precedent by dismissing the recitation of prayers as a not an "overt religious exercise." This should open the doors to other lawsuits and maybe Christians will finally get their day in court. As for Byron Union [School District], the ruling comes just in time for Christmas, so perhaps these same schools will have the children dress up and role-play the nativity scene. The law should now allow it. (Egelko, 2006)

An educational researcher, writing about desirable and undesirable teaching techniques, contended that

role-playing should NOT be used as a method of teaching about religion. Such activities, no matter how well-intentioned, may lead to stereotyping and oversimplification. They also may violate the conscience of students asked to play roles in a group with different religious traditions than their own. Instead, primary documents [a religion's holy scriptures], audio-visual sources, or classroom guests can provide students with first hand knowledge about religious beliefs and practices. (Risinger, 1993)

When the complainants appealed the ruling to the U.S. Supreme Court in 2006, the justices allowed the Ninth District Court's decision to stand, contending that the middle-school teacher had not engaged in unconstitutional religious indoctrination when she taught students about Islam by having them recite language from prayers (Egelko, 2006).

Scientology Influence

Critics of a Narconon antidrug program for schools have charged that concepts at the core of the program are doctrinal beliefs of the Church of Scientology and that the medical theories underlying the program are irresponsible "pseudoscience." For years, the Narconon program has been offered free to schools throughout America, conducted by lecturers from the Scientology movement. According to Narconon records, the antidrug sessions reached more than 1.7 million of the nation's students over the period 1995–2004 (Azimov, 2004).

Among the program's Scientology concepts are the beliefs that (a) the body stores drugs indefinitely in fat, causing drug cravings and flashbacks, and (b) sweating that is generated by exercise or sauna baths rids the body of those "poisons." Sometimes Narconon speakers tell students that drug residues produce a colored ooze when exiting the body. Thus, critics say, students attending Narconon sessions are introduced to principles and methods of Scientology without realizing it (Azimov, 2004).

The Scientology movement, founded in 1954 by science-fiction author L. Ron Hubbard (1911–1986), is a rapidly growing religion that claims to improve the well-being of followers through courses aimed at self-improvement and global serenity. Narconon officials deny any connection between the organization's drug-prevention program and Church of Scientology doctrine. However, members of the nation's drug-education profession often cite such a connection and express skepticism about Narconon's theory and treatment methods. The director of substance abuse programs at the Veterans Administration Medical Center in San Francisco labeled Narconon's principles "pseudoscience, right up there with colonic irrigation." A professor of psychiatry in the Center for Medicinal Cannabis Research at the University of California in San Diego said, "I'm not aware of any data that show that going into a sauna detoxifies you from toxins of any kind" (Azimov, 2004).

Despite such criticisms, teachers and students who have participated in Narconon programs often enthusiastically praise Narconon speakers' spirited presentations. School health officials in San Francisco, where the program had been used with more than 30,000 students since 1991, said they saw no church-state problem with Narconon or with any pseudoscience that might be taught.

However, the Rev. Barry Lynn, executive director of Americans United for the Separation of Church and State, called the connections between Narconon and the Scientology Church "very disturbing."

Any time you have a religion which preaches something that shows up in nearly parallel form in public schools, it sounds to me like you have a church-state problem that is real and should be examined by school officials. (Azimov, 2004)

Until the Narconon program is successfully challenged in court, it will continue operating in schools throughout the country.

New-Age Religion

A Christian group entitled Call2Action in Raleigh (North Carolina) protested to the school board that a class in stress reduction at Partnership Elementary School violated the constitutional ban on imposing religious beliefs on pupils in public schools. The Call2Action complaint contended that the class required pupils to practice "conscious breathing," meditation, chanting, and "using their life forces" as part of New-Age spiritual activities associated with Hindu religious faiths. The teacher who was the target of the complaint denied that she was doing "anybody's religion." However, supporters of Call2Action pointed out that she was the founder of the Rites of Passage Youth Empowerment Foundation and had recently returned from a spiritual pilgrimage in the Himalayas of Tibet and Nepal, where she had written her newest book, *A Rite of Passage to Spiritual Enlightenment: Living with Compassion.*

The chairman of Call2Action said, "If a person had been taught to pray to Jesus Christ to reduce stress, that would have been stopped."

School officials then faced the task of deciding whether to eliminate the stress-reduction program (Christian group, 2005).

The Georgia Bill

In March 2006, the Georgia legislature passed a bill requiring the state department of education to adopt curricula for two high-school electives—"History and Literature of the Old Testament Era" and "History and Literature of the New Testament Era"—by the middle of the 2006–2007 school year. In April, Governor Sonny Perdue signed the bill into law. The bill was in the form of "enabling legislation," since it permitted rather than forced schools to offer such classes, and students would not be required to enroll in them. However, the law did stipulate that the Old Testament and New Testament would be the compulsory textbooks

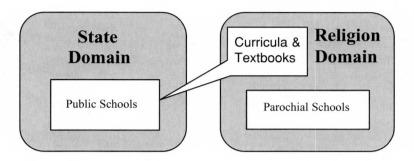

for the courses. The legislators' enthusiasm for Bible classes was reflected in the House of Representatives' 151-to-7 vote in favor of the bill. Although classes focusing on the Bible were offered in other states, this apparently was the first time that a state legislature had passed a law mandating the preparation of curricula for such classes (Badertscher & Gutierrez, 2006).

Conclusion

The two-fold purpose of this chapter has been (a) to explain ways in which public schools can legally teach about religion and (b) to describe cases that illustrate several problems that can arise in the treatment of religion in schools.

The chapter has also revealed the status of the state/church/school relationships in matters of curriculum content during the early years of the twenty-first century. The state, through its legal system, has allowed religion an important role in the content of what public schools teach, but only if one worldview is not favored over others and if students are not urged—even subtly—to prefer one belief system over another. In contrast to public schools, private schools are legally permitted to advocate the faith they favor and to denigrate competing belief systems.

The main areas of the curriculum in which religion has assumed a strong presence have been the language arts (particularly the study of literature), the social studies (history, cultures), and the arts (painting, sculpture, drama, music). As noted earlier, an important distinction has been drawn between religion *in* and religion *as*. The expression *religion in* refers to ways a particular religion's traditions are portrayed *in*—or have influenced—the world's literature, history, or art. The term *religion as* refers to how well a particular religion qualifies as literature, history, or art. The most controversial use of religion in curricula has been that of portraying scripture *as history,* when "history" is defined as "what really happened in the past." Thus, doubts have often been voiced about the historical accuracy of such scriptural writings as the Christian *Bible*, the Hebrew *Torah*, the Islamic *Quran*, the Hindu *Ramayana*, the Buddhist Theravada canon, the Sikh *Guru Granth Sahib,* the Shinto *Nihongi*, the Church of Latter Day Saints *Book of Mormon*, and others.

GUIDELINES FOR EDUCATORS

In 1989, a coalition of seventeen religious and educational organizations issued a set of principles for distinguishing between *teaching about religion* in public schools and *religious indoctrination*. Teaching about religion means that

- The school's approach to religion is academic, not devotional.
- The school strives for student awareness of religions, but does not press for student acceptance of any one religion.
- The school sponsors study about religion, not the practice of religion.
- The school exposes students to a diversity of religious views; it does not impose any particular view.
- The school educates about all religions; it does not promote or denigrate any religion.
- The school informs students about various beliefs; it does not seek to conform students to any particular belief. (Risinger, 1993)

Chapter 5

Prayer and Scripture Reading

This chapter concerns two sets of questions:

Is it legal for people to pray and read holy scripture in public schools? If so, under what conditions?

What problems do schools face in relation to prayer and scripture reading? What efforts have been made to solve those problems, and with what success?

The words *praying* and *prayer*, as used in this book, refer to remarks or silent thoughts or actions that people address to one or more invisible deities. Prayers can be intended to serve diverse purposes, such as,

- Giving thanks for one's good fortune and for blessings received.
  We gratefully thank Thee, Lord, for this bountiful meal Thou hast provided.
- Exalting and paying tribute to a deity.
  Allah be praised.
- Appealing for a deity's help.
  We beseech Thee to give us the strength to endure the hardships ahead.
- Drawing a deity's attention to a problem that should be solved.
  Dear God, the Smith family is in dire need of your support.
- Issuing advice, suggestions, or orders for a deity to perform particular tasks.
  Stop the hurricanes that are destroying the lives of so many good folks.
  Lead us not into temptation, and deliver us from evil.
  Bless our missionaries who labor in foreign lands.
- Asking forgiveness and mercy for having done wrong.
  Forgive us our sins, as we forgive those who sin against us.

- Doing penance for having behaved badly.
  To compensate for what I did wrong, I will give baskets of food to the needy this holiday season.
- Appealing to be transported to a place of eternal bliss.
  Now I lay me down to sleep; I pray the Lord my soul to keep.
  If I should die before I wake, take me to heaven for Jesus' sake.
- Bargaining with a deity.
  If You fix it so our side wins, I'll faithfully attend all the weekly religious services the rest of this year.

To add strength and conviction to a prayer, supplicants may close their plea with "good words"—a *benediction*. A typical Christian benediction reads, "In the name of the Father, the Son, and the Holy Ghost," in reference to the trinity of God, Jesus, and the Holy Spirit.

Prayers can be cast in various forms. The most common are oral remarks and silent thoughts. However, prayers can also assume the form of actions—fingering Catholic prayer beads, twirling a Buddhist prayer wheel, sacrificing a sheep or goat in Judaic tradition, preparing a Navajo sand painting, carving a Hopi kachina doll, performing an Ojibway jingle-dress dance, singing an Anglican anthem, and more.

Closely allied to prayers are scriptural readings or recitations. For instance, a school assembly program might begin with a teacher or student reading verses from the Bible in addition to offering a prayer. Consequently, this chapter's focus is not limited to prayers but also concerns scriptural recitations as controversial activities in public schools.

HOW THE CONTROVERSY DEVELOPED

The way present-day conflicts over prayer in public schools have evolved is described in the following pages in a sequence of topics that starts with (a) the late eighteenth century, then continues with (b) acts of the state, (c) acts of religious groups, (d) acts of nonreligious groups, and (e) illustrative cases.

In the Beginning

From the nation's earliest days, it was apparent that offering a Christian prayer during public gatherings was considered quite appropriate in the sort of a secular democracy that the founding fathers had created. During the Constitutional Convention that the American colonists convened in 1787, squabbling among the participants inspired an exasperated 81-year-old Benjamin Franklin to speak out:

In the beginning of the contest with Britain, when we were sensible of danger, we had daily prayers in this room for Divine protection. Our prayers were heard, and they were graciously answered. All of us who were engaged in the struggle must have observed frequent instances of a superintending providence in our favor, and have we now forgotten this powerful Friend? Or do we imagine we no longer need His assistance?

I have lived a long time, and the longer I live, the more convincing proofs I see of this truth: "that God governs in the affairs of man." And if a sparrow cannot fall to the ground without His notice, is it probable that an empire can rise without His aid?

I therefore beg leave to move that, henceforth, prayers imploring the assistance of Heaven and its blessings on our deliberations be held in this assembly every morning before we proceed to business. (MacLeod, 2000)

Even though public education for the masses, as promoted in the nineteenth century, was supposed to be nonsectarian, school practice typically reflected the forms of Protestantism to which the majority of Americans subscribed. It was common for each school day to open with devotional readings from the King James version of the Bible and with pupils reciting a Protestant form of the Lord's Prayer. Students were expected to participate whether or not they shared such religious views. However, near the middle of the century, Catholics were objecting to children of their faith being forced to listen to the Protestant Bible rather than a Catholic edition. The conflict became so bitter in Philadelphia in 1844 that several Catholic churches and a convent were set fire. The "Bible War" in Cincinnati caused the board of education to discontinue mandatory Bible instruction in 1868 (Americans United, 2006).

Tensions like this led to the first round of legal challenges to school-sponsored religious activity in the late 19th century. Several states ruled against the practices. Compelling children to recite prayers or read devotionals from certain versions of the Bible, these courts said, was not the job of public schools. They declared government-imposed religion a violation of state constitutions and the fundamental rights of conscience. Eventually, the U.S. Supreme Court adopted this view as well, applying the church-state separation provisions of the First Amendment of the U.S. Constitution. (Americans United, 2006).

Acts of the State

As explained in Chapter 1, the expression *the state* refers to the secular government at national, provincial, and local levels. A useful way to view the state's participation in school-prayer controversies is to consider the role of each of the principal branches of government—judicial, legislative, and executive. The judicial—by dint of court decisions—has been the most important of these bodies for determining the status of prayer in schools. The legislative and executive branches have assumed only subsidiary roles.

Judicial Decisions

The present-day status of prayer in public schools is the result of a series of U.S. Supreme Court rulings which, over the last four decades of the twentieth century, gradually refined judicial interpretations of the U.S. Constitution's separation of church and state. The following chronology of court cases reveals how that process advanced.

Engel v. Vitale, 1962. This case was not the first to address the issue of religion in public schools, but it is noteworthy for having yielded a decision about prayer that critically influenced subsequent court judgments. The issue at stake in *Engel v. Vitale* was a generic, nonsectarian, twenty-two-word prayer that the New York State Board of Regents in the late 1950s required students and teachers to repeat each morning in all of the state's public schools.

Almighty God, we acknowledge our dependence upon Thee, and we beg Thy blessings upon us, our parents, our teachers and our country.

The Regents—when including the prayer as part of a "Statement on Moral and Spiritual Training in the Schools"—expressed the hope that the prayer would be "subscribed to by all men and women of good will, and we call upon all of them to aid in giving life to our program" (Black, 1962).

In the 1962 court case, Engel was one of ten parents who filed a lawsuit against the school board of the Hyde Park (New York) Unified Free School District No. 9. Vitale was the president of the school board. The plaintiffs' suit charged that the prayer obligated students to express a belief in a particular deity, and thereby violated the U.S. Constitution's first amendment clause that prohibited the establishment of a government-sponsored religion. A lower court had ruled that the Regents were warranted in requiring such a prayer. When the parents then appealed the case to the U.S. Supreme Court, friend-of-the-court briefs were filed by the attorneys general of twenty-two states, urging the justices to declare the prayer constitutionally acceptable. But most of the justices disagreed with the briefs and, in a 5-to-2 vote, reversed the lower court's decision.

In defense of the Supreme Court's ruling, Justice Hugo Black wrote,

The petitioners contend ... that the state laws requiring or permitting use of the Regents' prayer must be struck down as a violation of the Establishment Clause ... We agree with this contention since we think that, in this country, it is no part of the business of government to compose official prayers for any group of the American people to recite as a part of a religious program carried on by government. (Black, 1962)

Opponents of the outcome were appalled and referred to the case as "the day God was kicked out of the public schools." Billboards funded by religious groups called for the impeachment of Chief Justice Earl Warren, and such prestigious religious leaders as Billy Graham, Norman Vincent Peale, and Cardinal Spellman condemned the decision.

Abington township school district v. Schempp, 1963. A Pennsylvania law, passed in 1949, mandated daily devotional Bible reading in public schools throughout the state, with at least ten verses to be read aloud by teachers or students in each public classroom, followed by class members reciting the Lord's Prayer.

Any teacher who refused to abide by the law would be dismissed. By the 1960s, four other states had similar laws. Another twenty-five allowed "optional" Bible reading, while the remaining states had no laws either supporting or prohibiting Bible reading (Corbett, 1995).

Whereas *Engel v. Vitale* banned state-mandated prayer in public-school class-room, it said nothing about scripture-reading and the recitation of scripture passages. That issue would be the focus in the next significant case of the 1960s.

In Pennsylvania's Abington Township, a Unitarian parent, Edward Schempp, in 1958 sued the local school district in federal district court, charging that the Bible-reading law was unconstitutional because it promoted Christianity at state expense. After the court ruled in favor of Schempp, the Pennsylvania legislature altered the law to allow students to skip the Bible and prayer sessions if their parents so requested. Schempp deemed that solution unacceptable because it would make his children appear to be "odd balls" as they left the classroom during scripture reading, so he took the matter back to the court, which again supported him. The Abington Township School District then appealed the decision to the U.S. Supreme Court. At the same time, a similar case arrived from Maryland, where the nation's best-known atheist, Madalyn Murray O'Hair, had challenged a Baltimore school-board rule requiring the "reading, without comment, of a chapter in the Holy Bible and/or the use of the Lord's Prayer" (School prayer decision, 1988).

The Supreme Court heard arguments in the two cases during February 1963 and in June rendered a judgment covering both lawsuits. In an 8-to-1 decision, the justices found in favor of Schempp and O'Hair. Writing the majority opinion, Justice Thomas Clark stated,

It is true that religion has been closely identified with our history and government . . . Indeed, only last year an official survey of the country indicated that 64% of our people have church membership . . . while less than 3% profess no religion whatever . . . therefore, . . . as in the beginning [of our republic], our national life reflects a religious people . . . In addition, it might be well said that one's education is not complete without a study of comparative religion or the history of religion and its relationship to the advance-ment of civilization. This is not to say, however, that religion has been so identified with out history and government that religious freedom is not likewise as strongly embedded in our public and private [lives]. This freedom to worship [as we please, or not at all, is] indispensable in a country whose people come from the four quarters of the earth and brought with them a diversity of religious opinion. Today authorities list 83 separate religious bodies, each with membership exceeding 50,000, existing among our people, as well as innumerable smaller groups. (Clark, 1963)

Thus, the ruling in *Abington v. Schempp* outlawed both official prayer and scripture-reading in public schools. The judgment also established that decisions about matters of prayer were not the province of individual states but, rather, were subject to the fourteenth amendment of the U.S. Constitution and thus within the control of the federal government. The disposition of *Abington v. Schempp* would henceforth serve as a critical incident setting a precedent for similar cases over the following decades.

Wallace v. Jaffree, 1985. In 1978, the Alabama legislature enacted a law that required students and teachers to begin each public school day with a moment of silence "for meditation." The law was deemed constitutionally acceptable because it did not designate the period of silence as a religious activity. However, in 1981 the legislature authorized Statute 16-1-20.1 that expanded the 1978 provision to a 1-minute period of silence "for meditation or voluntary prayer." When Ishmael Jaffree, the father of three public-school pupils, objected to the statute and filed a lawsuit, the district court ruled that 16-1-20.1 did encourage a religious activity, but the court also contended that the establishment clause of the U.S. Constitution's first amendment did not prohibit a state from establishing a religion. The Wallace of *Wallace v. Jaffree* was the Alabama governor, who declared, "I don't care what they say in Washington, we are going to keep right on praying and reading the Bible in the public schools of Alabama" (Herndon, 2004). The district court's ruling was subsequently reversed by a court of appeals, whose decision was then endorsed in a 6-to-3 vote by the U.S. Supreme Court on the ground that the purpose of the legislation was religious rather than secular. As such, the statute was an effort to "return voluntary prayer to schools." Further evidence of such a purpose was provided by the 1982 Alabama statute that had authorized teachers to lead "willing students" in a prescribed prayer. The Supreme Court justices explained that a genuinely neutral moment of silence was appropriate, so long as the legislation had a secular purpose. Such a nonreligious period of silence was legally being observed in many other states and municipalities (FindLaw, 1985).

Lee v. Weisman, 1992. In preparing for the June 1989 graduation ceremony at Nathan Bishop Middle School in Providence (Rhode Island), the school principal, Robert E. Lee, invited Rabbi Leslie Gutterman of the Temple Beth El in Providence to open the ceremony with an invocation prayer and close it with a benediction. Prior to the event, Lee advised the rabbi that the prayers should be nonsectarian, and he furnished Gutterman a pamphlet titled "Guidelines for Civic Occasions" from the National Conference of Christians and Jews. The Guidelines recommended that public prayers at nonsectarian civic ceremonies be composed with "inclusiveness and sensitivity" (Kennedy, 1992).

Daniel Weisman, the father of one of the graduates, learned of the plan to have a clergyman pray at the graduation service, and he appealed to a court to have a restraining order placed on the plan. His appeal was denied, so the event took place as intended, with the rabbi's invocation spoken as follows:

God of the Free, Hope of the Brave:

For the legacy of America where diversity is celebrated and the rights of minorities are protected, we thank You. May these young men and women grow up to enrich it. For the liberty of America, we thank You. May these new graduates grow up to guard it. For the political process of America in which all its citizens may participate, for its court system where all may seek justice, we thank You. May those we honor this morning always turn to it in trust. For the destiny of America, we thank You. May the graduates of Nathan Bishop Middle School so live that they might help to share it. May our aspirations for our country and for these young people, who are our hope for the future, be richly fulfilled. Amen. (Kennedy, 1992)

Weisman then sought a permanent injunction to prevent Lee and other Providence public school officials from inviting clergy to deliver invocations and benedictions at future graduations. The district court granted the injunction and instructed school officials to cease having official prayers at graduation services on the ground that prayer violated the establishment clause of the Constitution's first amendment. When the school district challenged the judgment in the court of appeals, the judges there supported the circuit-court decision. The school district then carried its case to the U.S. Supreme Court, where the justices by a 5-to-4 margin sustained the ban on school-sponsored prayers at graduation ceremonies (Kennedy, 1992). Thus, the nation's public schools were enjoined from having administrators, teachers, or invited clergy offer a public prayer. Nor could school officials grant religious speakers preferential access to public audiences or otherwise select public speakers on a basis that favors religious speech.

However, the ruling in *Lee v. Weisman* did not address the question of whether students—such as valedictorians—or guests who spoke at graduation time would be prohibited from offering a prayer or religious remarks. In other words, would such speakers' freedom of speech be subject to the Court's interpretation of the first amendment? Several lawsuits addressing this issue were tried in lower courts and resulted in somewhat conflicting rulings. For example, consider the following three cases.

Idaho district prayer policy, 1999. The Madison (Idaho) School District policy governing graduation speeches read: "The school administration may invite graduating students to participate in high school graduation exercises according to academic class standing . . . Students selected to participate may choose to deliver an address, poem, reading, song, musical presentation, prayer, or any other pronouncement of their choosing." The family of a graduating senior objected to the prayer aspect of the policy and filed a lawsuit that reached the Ninth Circuit Court of Appeals which ruled that the school's policy did not violate the U.S. Constitution's separation of church and state, because no tax money was being used to implement the policy (Robinson, 2003a).

Graduation address about Jesus, 2001. Officials at a California high school prevented the graduation ceremonies' valedictorian from giving an address in which he planned to ask the audience to "accept God's love" and live by "Jesus' example." In response to the ban, the student sued the school district. When lower courts ruled that the school was within its rights to censure such a speech, the student appealed to the U.S. Supreme Court, where the justices refused to hear the case, thereby leaving the lower courts' ruling intact (Robinson, 2003a).

Adler v. Duval County School Board, 2002. Schools in Duval County (Florida) routinely had a member of the clergy offer a prayer during the graduation service.

After the U.S. Supreme Court outlawed that practice in 1992, school officials let high-school seniors choose a fellow student to give a "brief opening and/or closing message" at graduation. That selected student would decide the message's content with no review by school officials.

In 1998, a group of students and their parents sued the school district, charging that the policy violated the constitutional separation of church and state by allowing student speakers to insert religious matter into their orations. When the case reached the Eleventh Circuit Court of Appeals, the court ruled that the policy was constitutionally acceptable because "students make the choice about what to hear at graduation, and prayer is not the only choice they can make." The plaintiffs' attorneys complained that the "clear purpose of the challenged policy is to preserve a tradition of prayer at graduation." But lawyers for the school board said the policy "neither establishes nor prohibits religious speech. It merely permits graduating senior classes to decide whether or not to include an unrestricted message as part of their ceremonies." Because the Supreme Court declined to hear the case, the appeals-court decision remained in force (Robinson, 2003a; Supreme Court, 2002).

In an effort to help school officials decide what policies to adopt regarding prayer, the federal Department of Education in 2003 issued a statement summarizing the conditions under which prayer is allowed. The section on graduation ceremonies advised officials that

where students or other private graduation speakers are selected on the basis of genuinely neutral, evenhanded criteria and retain primary control over the content of their expression, that expression is not attributable to the school and therefore may not be restricted because of its religious (or anti-religious) content. To avoid any mistaken perception that a school endorses student or other private speech that is not in fact attributable to the school, school officials may make appropriate, neutral disclaimers to clarify that such speech (whether religious or nonreligious) is the speaker's and not the school's. (U.S. Department of Education, 2003)

The ban on formal prayer at graduation exercises applied only to public schools. Private schools were free to sponsor whatever prayers they chose. The forms that such appeals to a deity may assume are sometimes suggested by religious groups. Here is an example of a proposed prayer for use by individual students in parochial schools.

Father, I have knowledge, so will You show me now how to use it wisely and find a way somehow to make the world I live in a little better place and make life with its problems a little bit easier to face. Grant me faith and courage and put purpose in my days, and show me how to serve Thee in effective ways so my education, my knowledge, and my skill may find their true fulfillment as I learn to do Thy will. And may I ever be aware in everything I do, that knowledge comes from learning, and wisdom comes from You. Amen. (Steinmetz, 2004)

Santa Fe independent school district v. Doe, 2000. In Santa Fe (Texas) two families—one Mormon, the other Catholic—did not want their names on a lawsuit they filed against the local school district, so the case was listed as the *School District v. Doe*. The families claimed that issuing a prayer over the public address system before high-school football games violated the Constitution's establishment clause and thus should be banned. After both a district court and an appellate court found in favor of the families, the school district appealed the judgment to the U.S. Supreme Court, where the justices, in a 6-to-3 vote, upheld the lower courts' ruling. Such prayers at school athletic events did violate the establishment clause.

The Supreme Court's majority opinion contended that the prayer was public speech—not private speech—and was officially endorsed by the school.

The message is broadcast over the school's public address system, which remains subject to the control of school officials. It is fair to assume that the pregame ceremony is clothed in the traditional indicia of school sporting events, which generally include not just the team, but also cheerleaders and band members dressed in uniforms sporting the school name and mascot. The school's name is likely written in large print across the field and on banners and flags. The crowd will certainly include many who display the school colors and insignia on their school T-shirts, jackets, or hats and who may also be waving signs displaying the school name. It is in a setting such as this that "[t]he board has chosen to permit" the elected student to rise and give the "statement or invocation." In this context the members of the listening audience must perceive the pregame message as a public expression of the views of the majority of the student body delivered with the approval of the school administration. (Stevens, 2000)

Like the restrictions on graduation prayers, limitations on praying at sports events apply only to public schools. Official prayers at private schools' games are legal. The form that parochial-school supplications may assume can be illustrated with the authorized football-players' prayer at Joliet Catholic High School (JCHS) in Illinois.

We are JC. We are Hillmen. We are motivated. We are dedicated. We will give our all. We will do our best. We will never quit. We will hit every play. We will hit every player. We will hit the whole game. We believe in God. We believe in JC. We believe in ourselves. We believe in each other. Yea, though we walk through the valley of death, we will fear no opponent, for we are the best team on the field. Gung Ho, Gung Ho, Gung Ho, Amen. (Joliet Catholic High, 2004)

Legislative Action

As far as schools are concerned, legislative bodies form a hierarchy of four types extending from the local level to the national level:

- School-district boards of education that issue regulations, such as the daily Bible-reading mandate of the Baltimore board in *Abington v. Schempp*.

- State boards of education that set rules, as in the New York Regents' required prayer in *Engel v. Vitale.*
- State legislatures that pass laws, such as the Alabama statute mandating a moment of silent prayer in *Wallace v. Jaffree.*
- The U.S. Congress that passes laws, such as the 2001 *No Child Left Behind* legislation.

Members of these four types of legislative bodies can typically perform several functions:

- Express their opinions to the general public via speeches, press releases, comments to news reporters, and letters to constituents.
- Suggest actions that an agency, such as a court or school district, should take.
- Propose and pass rules, regulations, or laws.
- Launch inquiries and investigations.

Consider, then, the following reactions from members of Congress to three of the Court's rulings.

Engel v. Vitale. When the Court's decision in *Engel v. Vitale* was announced, Congressman Frank Becker called the ban on prayer "the most tragic in the history of the United States." Senator Sam Ervin said, "I should like to ask whether we would be far wrong in saying that in this decision the Supreme Court has held that God is unconstitutional and for that reason the public school must be segregated against Him?" Hearings were held into school prayer by the House Judiciary Committee in 1964. They were published in three volumes, totaling 2,774 pages.

Abington v. Schempp. Congress immediately responded to the court's outlawing required Bible reading in schools by proposing bills that would amend the U.S. Constitution. By April 1964, more than 150 amendments had been submitted. Over the following decades, more calls for changing the Constitution continued, in most instances sponsored by conservative Republicans and by Religious Right activists. The intent was to allow students to pray or read the Bible.

As evidence that such action was needed, proponents of an amendment claimed that there was a dramatic rise in campus crime, unwanted pregnancies, suicides, and murder, accompanied by lower aptitude test scores, since the "banning of prayer and Bible reading" in the 1960s. But critics called that claim "simplistic and ignorant of complex socio-economic realities" that surfaced since the early 1960s (Corbett, 1995).

One of the most vigorous attempts to change the Constitution was led by Newt Gingrich, who served as speaker of the House of Representatives from 1995 to 1999. He proposed to alter the nation's most basic legal document by adding the proviso that

nothing in this Constitution shall be construed to prohibit individual or group prayer in public schools or other public institutions. No person shall be required by the United States or by any State to participate in prayer. Neither the United States nor any State shall compose the words of any prayer to be said in public schools. (Constitutional amendment, 2002)

The first sentence of the Gingrich change would allow public officials, including teachers, to dictate how, when, and where school children and others should pray. Critics of the proposal charged that the U.S. Supreme Court had repeatedly decided that officially organized prayer was coercive in a school environment, even when designated as "voluntary." Like other similar bills before it, the Gingrich proposal failed to attract enough support to launch a serious amendment drive. Amending the Constitution is a daunting task, since it requires the approval of two-thirds majorities in both houses of Congress and in the legislatures of three quarters of the states.

Santa Fe independent school district v. Doe. When the Supreme Court was about to hear attorneys' arguments regarding prayers at athletic events, two Texas congressmen—one a Republican, the other a Democrat—were jointed by twenty-eight other members of the House of Representatives in sponsoring a resolution urging the Court to allow official prayers at such events. The nonbinding resolution was passed on a voice vote.

The Reverend Barry W. Lynn, executive director of Americans United for Separation of Church and State, expressed his dismay at the resolution by saying,

America has education problems that need to be dealt with seriously. If prayer at football games is all the House has to offer, heaven help us! Maybe we should send the House leadership back to the locker room until they come with up a better game plan. This is shameless political posturing. The Supreme Court, not Congress, decides constitutional issues such as school prayer. The House ought to find something better to do with its time. (Lynn, 1999)

A humorist used the occasion to remind critics of the resolution that high-school football in Texas held the status of a sacred ritual worthy of the time and attention of the nation's highest legislative body. "The Court clearly misunderstood the importance of high school football in the State of Texas. It is not a life-or-death matter, it is more important than that" (American Civil Liberties Union, 2000).

Summary. As the overview of court cases has demonstrated, the last four decades of the twentieth century and the early years of the twenty-first century witnessed the gradual refinement of legislation defining the conditions under which praying can legally take place in public schools. The fact that such issues have been highly contentious is reflected in the close votes—often 5-to-4 or 6-to-3—in Supreme Court decisions.

Executive-Branch Participation

The federal government's executive branch is headed by the U.S. president and his or her staff. At the state level, the executive branch operates under the aegis of each governor and the governor's staff.

Rarely has the executive arm of government, at either the federal or state level, introduced regulations or sponsored legislation regarding school prayer. Participation of members of the executive in such matters has usually been limited to their endorsing the position of one side or the other in the debate.

When George W. Bush was governor of Texas, he actively supported the Santa Fe School District in its fight to foster prayer at football games. After the U.S. Supreme Court banned such prayer, Bush said, "I support the constitutionally guaranteed right of all students to express their faith freely and participate in voluntary student-led prayer" (Mauro, 2000).

During the presidency of the governor's father, George H. W. Bush (1989–1992), the administration had argued that the rabbi's graduation prayer in *Lee v. Weisman* had not demonstrated a religious endorsement. Thus, the elder Bush's administration called for the Court to overturn the criteria that had led to its ruling (Religious Freedom, 1992).

The Gingrich proposal to amend the constitution to permit school prayer came during the Bill Clinton presidency (1993–2000). When Clinton was asked his opinion of such an amendment, he "apparently concluded from the election results that he must appease the new Republican majority, [and therefore] caved in almost immediately. First, he announced that he was open to working with Congressional Republicans on a school prayer amendment. The next day, the administration said the President had been misunderstood, and that what he had in mind was a federal statute permitting 'moments of silence' in the schools" (American Civil Liberties Union, 2002).

Acts of Religious Groups

Some religious groups strongly favor public prayer in schools; they would support a constitutional amendment permitting prayer. But other religious denominations oppose school prayer.

Proponents of school-endorsed prayer have adopted several lines of logic in support of their cause. For example, we may recall that the first amendment to the U.S. Constitution contains two parts—the establishment clause and the free-exercise clause: "Congress shall make no law respecting an establishment of religion, or prohibiting the free exercise thereof." Whereas opponents of school prayer consider official prayer in public schools to be a violation of the establishment clause, advocates of prayer argue that banning prayer violates the free-exercise provision by preventing teachers and students from exercising their constitutional right to pray.

A second reason in support of school prayer is based on the majority-rule principle. As Evangelist Billy Graham argued, "Eighty percent of the American people want Bible readings and Prayer in the schools . . . Why should the majority be so severely penalized by the protests of a handful?"

A third argument offered by some prayer advocates holds that the nation's record of social disorder and moral deterioration since 1962 is due, at least in part, to "kicking God out of the classroom"—as shown by "a strong correlation between the expulsion of prayer from our schools and the decline in morality ... Former Secretary of Education William Bennett revealed in his cultural indexes that between 1960 and 1990 divorce doubled, teenage pregnancy went up 200%, teen suicide increased 300%, child abuse reached an all-time high, violent crime went up 500%, and abortion increased 1000%" (Should schools, 2003).

The types of organizations that urged the reinstatement of prayer in schools was suggested by the list of religious groups supporting a proposed constitutional amendment that would permit official praying. The following is a sample of such bodies (*Religious freedom amendment*, 1995).

- American Conference of Jews and Blacks
- Americans For Voluntary School Prayer
- American Muslim Council
- Christian Action Network
- Christian Coalition
- Christian Voice
- General Council of the Assemblies of God
- International Pentecostal Church of Christ
- National Association of Evangelicals
- Southern Baptist Convention
- Christian Life Commission

In contrast to proponents of school prayer are members of other denominations who object to the practice. For example, Kirk Jowers, a professor of political science at the University of Utah, explained that Mormons do not want prayer in public schools because "if you push to have prayer in school, then outside of Utah the prayer would not typically be a Mormon's prayer. So is that road you want go down?" (Johnson, 2006a). In like manner, U.S. Senator Phillip A. Hart (Michigan) said, "I'm a Catholic and I hope a devout one, but I think that the public school classroom is no place for me to try and impose my world formula for prayer on children who don't share it, and for that very reason, I don't want my children in a public school classroom to be exposed to someone else's religion or formula" (Robinson, 2002b).

A brochure on prayer in public schools, issued by Americans United for Separation of Church and State in 2002, listed the following organizations as faith groups supporting the First Amendment in its original form and opposing government-sponsored prayer in public schools (Americans United, 2006).

- American Baptist Churches, USA
- American Jewish Congress
- Christian Church (Disciples of Christ)

- Evangelical Lutheran Church in America
- Friends Committee on National Legislation (Quakers)
- General Conference of Seventh-Day Adventists
- Mennonite Central Committee
- National Council of Churches
- North American Council for Muslim Women
- Presbyterian Church (USA)
- Soka Gakkai International—USA
- The Church of Christ, Scientist
- The Episcopal Church, USA
- Union of American Hebrew Congregations
- Unitarian Universalist Association
- United Church of Christ
- United Methodist Church

As the above lists suggest, people advocating sanctioned prayer in school are dominantly of evangelical and pentecostal persuasions, whereas those opposing school-endorsed prayer are more often from mainstream denominations and sects that fear the intrusion into schools of beliefs contrary to their own.

Acts of Nonreligious Groups

A variety of organizations with no obvious ties to a religious denomination have also participated actively in controversies over prayer in schools. Supporters of the proposed constitutional amendment that would allow schools to institute prayer included

- American Family Association
- Concerned Women for America
- Family Research Council
- Focus on the Family
- Religious Freedom Party
- Toward Tradition
- Traditional Values Coalition

Organizations that have actively opposed prayer in schools include

- American Civil Liberties Union
- American Ethical Union
- Americans United for Separation of Church and State

- Interfaith Alliance
- People for the American Way

In summary, numerous religious and secular groups have been—and continue to be—actively engaged in the school-prayer debate. In the national political arena, Republicans have more often endorsed school-sponsored prayer than have Democrats. The greatest strength of the Republican school-prayer effort has come from the most conservative wing of the party referred to as the Religious Right. However, the school-prayer issue does not divide cleanly along party lines. Members of both parties are found on each side of the debate.

Illustrative Cases

Regardless of what the Supreme Court has ruled about school prayer, there are always school districts—and even states—that continue to introduce prayer regulations that would appear to violate the Court's decisions. Such a condition persists because schools and states can do whatever they wish about prayer so long as no one challenges them in court. Whereas there are agencies—police departments, sheriffs, the Federal Bureau of Investigation—ready to arrest any person or organization that violates criminal laws, there are no agencies responsible for monitoring how diligently schools abide by court rulings about prayer. Therefore, if schools' or states' prayer policies and practices are to be effectively challenged, someone must file a lawsuit. In effect, school or state officials must be taken to court, which is a very expensive venture, particularly because of the exorbitantly high fees that attorneys typically charge and the length of time cases can take as they plod through the legal system. Because of the expense, time, and tribulation that plaintiffs must endure to challenge prayer policies in court, individuals who disagree with the policies often lack the resolve or funds to pursue the task. As a result, questionable practices can continue unchecked.

As a further constraint on rectifying questionable prayer practices is the nature of a given court's jurisdiction. A district court's ruling in a school-prayer case directly affects only the schools within that court's authority. Schools outside the court's bailiwick are not obligated to abide by the ruling. Hence, what is declared unlawful in one part of the nation is not unlawful in another part that is outside that court's authority. Only when the U.S. Supreme Court issues a judgment are public schools throughout the nation obligated to obey the decision.

So there are always new instances of prayer regulations and practices that will continue in effect unless contested in court. Several forms that such instances can assume are illustrated in the following four cases.

The Pontotoc County Case

In 1993, Lisa Herdahl moved from Wisconsin to Pontotoc County (Mississippi) where she was distressed by the county's 80-year history of prayer in the public schools. As the mother of six school children, she filed a lawsuit in the U.S. District Court aimed at ending the school's practice of conducting daily devotionals over schools' intercom systems, teaching a class with the Bible as the sole textbook, and holding teacher/student prayer sessions in the school gym. On June 3, 1996, Federal Judge Neil B. Biggers Jr. found in Mrs. Herdahl's favor. One month later, school authorities voted unanimously not to appeal the decision. Instead, they organized prayer in a manner that they felt would circumvent the court ruling—they held mandated prayers 10 minutes prior to the official start of the school day.

In 1997, Mrs. Herdahl filed a second suit, this time to recover $144,000 in legal expenses incurred in the earlier case. When Judge Biggers approved that amount, members of the Pontotoc community were outraged, claiming that such a judgment would bankrupt the county. "On 6 May 1997, school officials, including superintendent Jerry Horton, led prayers at a 'school pride day' assembly at which students were required to be present, in apparent violation of the judge's order" (Steel, 1996–1997).

Muslims at Berkner High

In late 2005, a law firm retained by Muslim students' parents complained to officials at Berkner High School in Richardson (Texas) that the students were prevented from leaving classrooms to abide by Islam's requirement that Muslims pray five times each day. Initially, Berkner's acting principal had ruled that the students could not leave class, since that would constitute a special privilege not available to students of other faiths. In response to the lawyers' complaint, the school announced new guidelines that read,

Students may pray in the empty hallway next to the cafeteria after lunch, but if the group becomes too large, the cafeteria monitor may stagger the times students gather. October through March, when a prayer falls during fifth-period class, students may pray outside the classroom in the nearest alcove just after the tardy bell. Prayers should be completed as quickly as possible to minimize lost class time. (Hughes, 2005)

A representative of the law firm praised the new policy:

Now the students have some certainty. All students win when the school district recognizes its obligation to accommodate private student prayer. The First Amendment's [free-exercise clause] is alive and well again at Berkner High. (Hughes, 2005)

An Arkansas Teacher-Training Course

Steve Warnock, an art teacher in De Valls Bluff School District (Arkansas), was required by district officials to attend an inservice-training course at a college sponsored by a religious denomination. Each session of the course included a prayer by the district superintendent. Warnock objected to the prayers and asked that they be eliminated from future sessions. The superintendent refused the request, so Warnock filed a lawsuit in the federal district court to obtain an injunction against including prayers in the class. The district court found in Warnock's favor on the ground that the praying had offended him. When the superintendent took the case to the Eighth District U.S. Court of Appeal, the justices ruled that the district court had been right in issuing an injunction against prayers, but the appeal judges gave a different reason for their decision. Instead of basing the ban on Warnock's having been offended, they supported the ruling because the prayers had inserted religion into mandated training sessions conducted by a public-school district (Adkins, 2004).

De Valls Bluff officials found themselves again in the appeal court in April 2006 when a panel of justices issued a unanimous order for the school system to stop sponsoring prayer at school events. This time the infraction involved a 2005 high-school baccalaureate ceremony, which district officials claimed was organized entirely by students but actually involved two school employees supervising the planning of the event, producing the program for the service using school resources, and handing out copies of the program at the service (Federal appeals court, 2006).

Praying Continues after Court Ruling

In February 2005, a district-court judge ordered Tangipahoa Parish School District near Baton Rouge (Louisiana) to cease praying at school events. The court case was the result of the American Civil Liberties Union (ACLU) filing a lawsuit to end the Tangipahoa school board's 30-year tradition of praying at each school-board meeting. However, the cease-and-desist order was intended to apply also to any variety of school-sponsored praying in the district.

In June, the state's ACLU executive director, Joe Cook, charged that praying had continued in the schools in violation of the court order. Cook complained, "They've tried to promote creationism in the classroom. They had a preacher coming in, giving away free pizza at lunchtime, preaching and proselytizing students. And then we've had prayers at football games after the Supreme Court ruled against that."

Cook cited four instances of prayer since the school district had lost the February court case: (a) a teacher's aide led the Lord's Prayer for students during a school-board meeting; (b) a man prayed over the public address system before a baseball game between two parish schools; (c) at a school banquet, a Loranger High School student recited a prayer to Jesus that a teacher had given him; and (d) a student teacher was denied her teaching certificate after she reported that the master teacher to whose class she had been assigned at D.C. Reeves Elementary School had forced the fourth-graders to pray to Jesus at lunchtime and "would bring her Bible to class and recite Bible verses in the classroom."

One supporter of the school board's position said, "We're a parish that's really unified with God and with prayer and we believe that's the foundation of our moral values." The school board intended to contest the February ruling by taking the case to the Fifth Circuit Court of Appeals, aided by the Alliance Defense Fund, a Christian legal group started by such evangelical leaders as Dr. James Dobson of *Focus on the Family* (Tapper & Sandell, 2005).

To summarize, we can note the interaction of state, church, and secular institutions in determining the place of prayer in public schools.

The state—at both the federal and provincial levels—has been very active over recent decades in determining the role of prayer in public schools. The most influential of the state's three divisions (judicial, legislative, and executive) has been the judicial with its district courts, appeal courts, and the U.S. Supreme Court.

The church as a social institution has been divided in its attitude about school prayer. Evangelical Protestant denominations have been the most vigorous advocates of prayer, with their efforts to defend the longtime American custom of prayer and Bible recitation growing more vehement in recent decades. In contrast to faiths that advocate prayer, most traditional mainline churches have urged that such religious practices as prayer be kept out of public schools.

In addition to the representatives of the state (judicial, legislative, executive) and of religious faiths who have engaged in the school-prayer debate, activists from nongovernmental and nonreligious groups have also participated. The most notable of those groups have been (a) Americans United for the Separation of Church and State and (b) The American Civil Liberties Union.

Conclusion

The main trend in court decisions has been toward curtailing prayer in school settings by banning school-sponsored prayer. But prayer is permitted in the form of students praying individually on their own initiative or small groups using their free time to pray together.

Prayer intrudes into state domain.

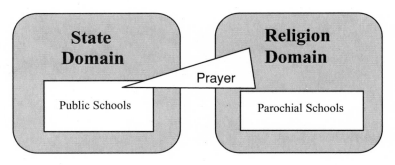

GUIDELINES FOR EDUCATORS

In view of the complex issues related to prayer in public schools, under what circumstances can people legally pray and under what circumstances are they forbidden to do so?

The basic rule is that organized, school-endorsed prayer in public-school settings—classrooms, athletic events, lunchrooms, faculty meetings, school-board meetings, graduation ceremonies—is unconstitutional. The only kind of prayer the Constitution allows is private, voluntary prayer that does not disturb the school's educational function.

Students have the right to engage in voluntary individual prayer that is not coercive and does not substantially disrupt the school's educational mission and activities. For example, all students have the right to say a blessing before eating a meal. However, school officials must not promote or encourage a student's personal prayer. Students may engage with other students in religious activity during non-curricular periods as long as the activity is not coercive or disruptive. In addition, while students may speak about religious topics with their peers, school officials should intercede if such discussions become religious harassment . . . Personal religious activity may not interfere with the rights or well-being of other students, and the threat of student harassment and pressure must be carefully monitored. It is also critical to ensure that the religious activity is actually student-initiated, and that no school employee supervises or participates in the activity. Any school promotion or endorsement of a student's private religious activity is unconstitutional. (Anti-Defamation League, 2004b)

A portion of the school day—usually a few moments—can be dedicated to a period of silence if that portion is not designated as an opportunity for students to pray.

Prayer can be discussed as a social phenomenon during the comparative study of religions, and such study can include examples of prayers of different faiths so long as the contents of prayers are not taught as truth that students are expected to believe. In comparative studies, one faith or secular philosophy is not to be favored over another (Robinson, 2004).

Chapter 6

Holidays and Celebrations

As in Chapter 5, this chapter offers answers for two sets of questions:

Can students be absent from school on religious holidays without exposing themselves to punitive sanctions? If so, under what conditions?

Can students, school personnel, or invited guests engage in activities at the school in celebration of religious holidays? If so, what sorts of activities are permitted and under what circumstances?

HOW THE CONTROVERSY DEVELOPED

The Christian practices that colonists from Europe brought to the Americas included their venerating holy days by taking time off from customary work and dedicating that time to worshipful activities. Thus, in keeping with the Judeo-Christian God's command in the book of Genesis, believers set aside the seventh day of each week for religious observances. In addition, other days in Judeo-Christian custom were also honored by freeing people from mundane activities. The most important occasions were Christmas (Jesus' birthday), Good Friday (Jesus' crucifixion), and Easter (Jesus' resurrection). Some Christian denominations also identified additional times as holy days, such as All Saints' Day (November 1, worship for all of God's saints), All Souls' Day (November 2, prayers offered for the souls of the departed who still suffer in purgatory), and Pentecost (commemorating the descent of the Holy Spirit upon the Apostles 50 days after Easter).

From the earliest years of the American colonies, schools were closed on the holidays that were formally observed by the schools' sponsors who, in the main, were dedicated Christians. And as faith-linked schools gradually evolved into public schools supported by tax dollars, the holiday practices remained; they still continue today in a large percentage of the nation's public institutions. From early times, the week that schools closed between Palm Sunday and Easter was called "Easter Vacation." But in recent years, the March or April week during which students are freed from studies has been referred to as "spring break" and no longer is scheduled the week before Easter.

Furthermore, in the days leading up to an important holiday, colonial schools celebrated the coming event with appropriate religious songs, dramatizations, recitations, and exhibits. After the American Revolution, those customs continued to be practiced in the new nation's schools and have lasted into modern times. However, in the twentieth century—and particularly during the latter decades as changing immigration patterns increased the nation's religious diversity—public schools faced growing criticism about activities relating to religious holidays. Controversies over such matters would become increasingly common during the opening decade of the twenty-first century. The nature of such conflicts is described in the following two sections that concern (a) allowing students to be absent from school on religious occasions and (b) celebrating religious holy days with pageants, dramatizations, displays, and musical activities.

Absent from School on Holidays

There are two main ways that public schools excuse students from attending school on religious holy days. One way is by closing the school, so that students of all faiths—and those having none—are not obliged to attend. The other way is by permitting students to be absent on a holy day of their particular faith. Sometimes these two systems are combined, with the school closed on certain holidays—such as the Christian Good Friday or the Jewish Yom Kippur (a day of fasting and prayer for the atonement of sins) and with individual students permitted to be absent on other days that are important for their particular faith.

School Closings

School districts differ significantly in their choice of which religious holidays to honor by closing school. For example, in Florida a review of school calendars showed that most counties (forty-three of the sixty-seven) had no school on Good Friday in 2005. In thirteen cases, spring break included that day. At least ten school districts in the Tampa area gave students Monday off after Easter. Schools rarely closed for Jewish Yom Kippur or the Muslim Eid al-Fitr (the end of the Ramadan month of fasting). Pinellas County was the only district that gave no time off on any religious holiday other than Christmas (Varian & Ave, 2005).

Thanksgiving Day is a special case. The first Thanksgiving in the New England colonies was a three-day affair celebrated in 1621, a year after Pilgrims from England had settled in their adopted land. The new arrivals owed much of their survival to the local Indians who had taught them to plant corn and trap game, so both Pilgrims and Indians joined in the celebration. The event appears to have been a continuation of autumn festivals in Europe that involved giving thanks for a bountiful harvest. Throughout the eighteenth century and well into the nineteenth, one-day thanksgiving celebrations were held on different dates in various parts of the nation, until in 1863 President Abraham Lincoln proclaimed a national day of thanks to be held on the last Thursday of November. Since that time, Thanksgiving has been a nationwide holiday, which, though originated by Protestants, has become a nondenominational occasion for expressing gratitude. Because the day is officially a national holiday declared by the president, students are dismissed for Thursday and Friday. Thus, school officials are spared the need to decide whether to open or close their schools.

The appeals of non-Christian faiths to have schools close on one or more of their holidays pose a difficult decision for school boards. By state law, schools are required to hold sessions for a particular number of days during the year—typically 180. For each additional religious holiday that a school district closes, another non-religious holiday—such as Presidents Day or Martin Luther King Day—would have to be eliminated, or else the school year would need to be lengthened. Then if one religious denomination is permitted to have school closed for its holiday, would it not be fair to allow other faiths the same privilege? And if there is to be true separation of church and state, why should any religious holidays be observed by closing schools? These questions have confronted officials in recent years as they have tried to balance the Constitution's establishment clause against its free-exercise-of-religion clause.

Provisions for Individuals to Be Absent

Many states and school districts allow students to miss school on one or more occasions that are holy days in the students' particular faith. However, the manner in which this provision is carried out can differ from one state or district to another. For example, the education code for the state of Pennsylvania provides that

upon written parental request, and in accordance with the policies of the district's board of school directors, students may be excused from school for religious holidays observed by bona fide religious groups. A student's absence from school for religious holidays or for religious instruction shall be recorded as an excused absence. A penalty may not be attached to an absence for religious holidays or instruction. (Pennsylvania Code, 2006)

State law in New Jersey requires the state commissioner of education to submit a list of "religious holidays permitting pupil absence from school." The list in 2005 identified sixty-four different days on which one or more faiths celebrated a holy event. In some cases, an event lasted more than one day so a pupil would be excused for several days. In addition, more than one denomination might have a revered event on the same day. As a result, the list contained a total of seventy-four different sacred occasions. The diversity of holidays can be suggested by the following sample of fifteen items from the New Jersey list (Davy, 2005).

- September 7 (Buddhist) His Holiness the 17th Gyalawa Karmapa's birthdate
- September 14 (Eastern, Greek, Russian Orthodox) The Exaltation of the Holy Cross
- October 3 (Islamic) First Day of Ramadan
- October 4–5 (World Wide Church of God, United Church of God, Global Church of God) Feast of Trumpets
- October 4–5 (Judeo) Rosh Hashanah (Jewish New Year)
- October 10–12 (Hindu) Dussera
- October 20 (Baha'i) Birth of the Bab
- October 31 (Protestant, Lutheran) Reformation Day
- November 15 (Sikh) Guru Nanak's Birth
- December 8 (Roman Catholic) Feast of the Immaculate Conception
- December 26–January 2, Kwanzaa
- January 6 (Armenian) Christmas
- January 29 (Chinese, Korean, and Vietnamese) New Year
- March 1 (Roman Catholic, Protestant) Ash Wednesday
- March 6 (Eastern Orthodox) Lent

The New Jersey list was accompanied by directions on how the pupil-absence provision should be implemented:

[Any school district's] board of education has the right to add any bona fide religious holiday to the list for its own schools. Some parents might ask for an excused absence for their child on every day listed as a religious holiday for members of their faith, while others might request an excuse for only part or some of the days listed.

1. Any pupil absent from school because of a religious holiday may not be deprived of any award or of eligibility or opportunity to compete for any award because of such absence;
2. Pupils who miss a test or examination because of absence on a religious holiday must be given the right to take an alternate test or examination;
3. To be entitled to the privileges set forth above, the pupil must present a written excuse signed by a parent or person standing in place of a parent;
4. Any absence because of a religious holiday must be recorded in the school register or in any group or class attendance record as an excused absence;
5. Such absence must NOT be recorded on any transcript or application or employment form or on any similar form. (Davy, 2005)

The question of whether and how students can be absent from school on their religion's holy days has become a more controversial issue as the nation's religious diversity has increased through immigration and as the followers of non-Christian sects have been emboldened to challenge long-established tradition. That tradition has favored Christians by closing schools on such days as Christmas and Good Friday. In recent decades, states and school districts have adopted policies that accommodate the requests of students' from all faiths to be absent from school on their denomination's sacred days.

Religious Holiday Activities

Public schools have a long history of celebrating religious holidays with parades, dramatizations, displays, and music. In the past, the most prominent events were related to such Christian holidays as Christmas, Easter, and Thanksgiving. As long as the great majority of parents were Christians—at least nominally—complaints about such festivities in public schools were rare. Seldom did anyone challenge a chorus rendering *Silent Night* and *Hark, the Herald Angels Sing.* A Christmas tree in the school foyer with a star or angel at its peak was an accepted sight. Nor did folks object to pupils, in an assembly program, depicting Pilgrims and Indians at the first Thanksgiving. While it would be unusual prior to Easter to have an exhibit of student art that featured Jesus on the cross, the secular accoutrements of the Easter season—egg hunts, pet bunnies, and pet chicks—would be common in primary-grade classrooms.

However, in recent decades such celebrations in public schools have become the target of censure and lawsuits. Controversy focuses on such questions as: Can students, school personnel, or invited guests engage in activities at the school in celebration of religious holidays? And if so, what sorts of activities are permitted and under what conditions?

Answers to these questions, and a discussion of the complexities they involve, are offered in the following pages under the headings *dress-up parades and parties, dramatizations, displays,* and *musical events.*

Dress-Up Parades and Parties

On or before a holiday, pupils—particularly those in elementary schools—come to school in costumes to parade around the corridors and enjoy a classroom party with games and refreshments. The holidays usually celebrated have been Thanksgiving, Christmas, Easter, and Valentine's Day. And then there is Halloween, the most popular of all. But is Halloween a religious holiday? Some say yes; others say no.

Complaints about Halloween have come mostly from critics who refer to the origins of the Wicca religion nearly 3,000 years ago. Wicca began as a Celtic autumnal rite "appropriated in the 600s by the Roman Catholic Church as All Saints Day. Halloween came to America with the Irish, whose traditional harvest rituals involved dressing up and chasing restless 'spirits' away as winter's dark nights crawled into villages" (Moon, 2005).

Critics of Halloween in schools have included Christians, Muslims, and present-day adherents of Wicca. Certain Christian and Muslim sects dub Halloween "paganism," charging that Wicca features the glorification of Satan and is thus to be avoided. On the other hand, Wiccans object to Halloween celebrations as distortions of the sect's beliefs and practices. (There are an estimated 750,000 Wiccans in the United States, including many who keep their membership secret for fear of suffering attacks from other religious groups [Robinson, 2001].)

At Halloween time in recent years, a variety of schools around the nation altered their traditional practices in several ways. Some simply cancelled the costume parades and parties. Others created "Fall-o-ween" events that focused on the harvest season but excluded the controversial ghosts and goblins. Still others moved Halloween parties to out-of-school hours. One elementary-school principal reported that pupils decorated pumpkins and teachers dressed up, but the only costumes that were allowed were ones of literary figures for a "curriculum-driven" literary parade; and teachers avoided using the word Halloween (Jonsson, 2005). A school district in Missouri allowed students to dress in costumes "provided they follow district guidelines. Costumes can be as varied as the students who wear them. But the garb cannot be gory or promote violence and weaponry" (Moon, 2005).

Dramatizations

The term *dramatizations* in the present context refers to plays and programs presented by pupils, teachers, or invited guests. The question that school boards, administrators, and teachers face is: What conditions affect whether a drama or program involving religious content can be presented in schools without violating the U.S. Constitution's establishment clause that forbids the government's undue entanglement with, or endorsement of, a particular faith? The court case most often cited as a guide to answering that question is one involving the Sioux Falls School District in South Dakota.

Florey v. Sioux Falls School District, 1980. The 1977 Christmas-season program at an elementary school in Sioux Falls resulted in a parent filing a lawsuit against the school district on the ground that the program was replete with religious material that violated the establishment clause of the Constitution's first amendment. Typical of the program's objectionable content was the following segment of a discourse between a kindergarten teacher and her pupils entitled "The Beginners' Christmas Quiz."

Teacher: Of whom did heav'nly angels sing, and news about His birthday bring?

Class: Jesus.

Teacher: Now, can you name the little town where they the Baby Jesus found?

Class: Bethlehem.

Teacher: Where had they made a little bed for Christ, the blessed Saviour's head?

    Class: In a manger in a cattle stall.

Teacher: What is the day we celebrate as birthday of this One so great?

    Class: Christmas.

In response to complaints that such material put the school in the position of promoting a particular religion, the school board appointed a citizens' committee to prepare rules designed to permit Christmas programs that would be legally acceptable. The rules submitted by the committee were prefaced by a policy statement:

It is accepted that no religious belief or non-belief should be promoted by the school district or its employees, and none should be disparaged. The Sioux Falls School District recognizes that one of its educational goals is to advance the students' knowledge and appreciation of the role that our religious heritage has played in the social, cultural, and historical development of civilization. (Heaney, 1980).

The rules stipulated that

- The only holidays that could be observed were ones that had both a religious *and* secular purpose, so holidays with only a religious purpose could not be celebrated in schools.
- Music, art, literature, and drama having a religious theme or basis could be included in the school curriculum only if "presented in a prudent and objective manner and as a traditional part of the cultural and religious heritage of the particular holiday."
- Religious symbols could be included as teaching aids or resources and only if "such symbols are displayed as an example of the cultural and religious heritage of the holiday and are temporary in nature." (Heaney, 1980)

When the case was argued in a federal district court, the judge declared that the 1977 Christmas program had, indeed, breached the first amendment's separation of church and state. In addition, the court stated that the new rules adopted by the Sioux Falls board of education were reasonable and, if diligently followed, would be in keeping with the first amendment's intent. Thus, the court found in favor of the school district.

However, the plaintiff was dissatisfied with the decision, claiming that the rules still fostered "an excessive government entanglement with religion," so he took that case to the U.S. Eighth District Appeal Court where the two judges who heard the case sustained the district court's judgment.

Although the rules permit the schools to observe holidays that have both a secular and a religious basis, we need not conclude that the School Board acted with unconstitutional motives. (Heaney, 1980)

In effect, holiday celebrations whose *principal* or *primary* effect neither advanced nor inhibited religion were deemed constitutionally acceptable. Christmas programs could legally be conducted in the future if they met the test of the school district's rules.

The appeal-court judges did not consider their ruling in *Florey v. Sioux Falls* to be a definitive judgment that would settle the "entanglement" issue in all such cases. Rather, the judges, Haeney and McMillian, wrote that the unique quality of different cases required that each be adjudicated on its own merits.

We recognize that this opinion affirming the district court will not resolve for all times, places, or circumstances the question of when Christmas carols, or other music or drama having religious themes, can be sung or performed by students in elementary and secondary public schools without offending the First Amendment. The constitutionality of any particular school activity conducted pursuant to the rules, in association with any particular holiday, cannot be determined unless and until there is a specific challenge, supported by evidence, to the school district's implementation of the rules. We simply hold—on the basis of the record before us—that the policy and rules adopted by the Sioux Falls Board of Education, when read in the light of the district court's holding that segments of the 1977 Christmas program at one of the elementary schools were impermissible—[do not violate] the First Amendment. (Heaney, 1980)

Although the U.S Supreme Court has not issued a definitive ruling on matters of religious holidays in schools, the Court did let stand the *Foley v. Sioux Falls* decision that recognition of holidays may be constitutional if the purpose is to provide secular instruction about religious traditions rather than to foster a particular religion. Thus, *Foley v. Sioux Falls* continues to serve as the primary guide in such matters.

Displays

Models, pictures, and symbolic objects are the most common types of school displays with religious themes.

Models are often dioramas or other three-dimensional depictions of religious scenes. The most common model at Christmas time has been a crèche—Mother Mary and her husband Joseph in a stable, watching over the infant Jesus in a manger, with animals, angels, shepherds, and wise men witnessing the event. The dominant Christian model at Easter time has been a crucifix—Jesus nailed to the cross. Models can also portray famous religious personalities, such as a carved bust of Buddha or Confucius. Models may also be in the form of dried-leather shadow puppets from the Hindu tradition in Java.

More frequent than models are pictures of religious events, places, and personages in drawings, paintings, or photographs—Jorg Breu's oil portrait of Mary holding Jesus, Leonardo da Vinci's *Last Supper* painting, a photo of the wailing wall in Jerusalem, a Hindu water color of Radha welcoming Krishna, Haida

Blackfish's Native American painting of a bear transformed into a human, a fifteenth-century Islamic painting of *The Journey of the Prophet Muhammad,* and Kailash Raj's water color of the Sikh patriarch, Guru Nanak.

Symbolic objects are designs associated with particular religions—the Celtic Christian cross, the Hebrew six-pointed Star of David, the Islamic crescent moon and star, and the American-Indian thunderbird.

The key question schools face about religious displays is: Under what conditions can religious symbols be exhibited in public schools? A policy statement endorsed by a wide range of educational and religious organizations offers the following answer.

The use of religious symbols, provided they are used only a example of cultural and religious heritage, is permissible as a teaching aid or resource. Religious symbols may be displayed only on a temporary basis as part of the academic program. Students may choose to create artwork with religious symbols, but teachers should not encourage or discourage such creations. (Christian Legal Society, 2006)

Musical Events

The U.S. Supreme Court has issued no opinions about the propriety of religious music in public schools. However, advice about the role music can legally assume in schools can be inferred from the Court's decisions about such related matters as dramatizations, displays, and religious symbols and from lower-court rulings regarding music.

For instance, consider the line of argument offered by the Tenth District Court of Appeal in *Bauchman v. West High School* (Brorby, 1997). When Rachel Bauchman was enrolled as a student at West High School in Salt Lake City, she joined an a-capella choir directed by Richard Torgerson. However, Rachel, as a Jew, was offended when the preponderance of the choir's musical selections were Christian religious songs, and the places in which the choir performed included such Christian venues as the Church of the Madeleine, the First Presbyterian Church, and the Mormon Temple Square. When Torgerson rejected Rachel's pleas to have religious music dropped from the choir's repertoire, Rachel's mother filed a lawsuit in federal district court, charging that the U.S. Constitution's establishment clause was being violated because Torgerson "selected songs for the religious messages they conveyed . . . [and] selected religious sites for Choir performances with the purpose and effect of publicly identifying the Choir with religious institutions" (Brorby, 1997).

However, the district court rejected the Bauchmans' claim and found in favor of Togerson and the school district. When the Bauchmans took the case to the Tenth U.S. Circuit Court of Appeal, the three justices who heard the arguments supported the district court's ruling. They decided that the school system, through its choir director, had not violated the Constitution's prohibition against the government's endorsing a religion. How such a ruling could be defended is illustrated in the line of reasoning adduced by the appellate judges to arrive at their decision. The essence of their logic was as follows.

To begin, the jurists cited law precedents which held that "the Constitution does not require that the purpose of every government-sanctioned activity be unrelated to religion . . . Courts have long recognized the historical, social, and cultural significance of religion in our lives and in the world, generally" (Brorby, 1997). Thus, under proper circumstances, religion could have a place in public schooling.

Next, the judges reasoned that music could have a secular intent as well as a religious aspect or intent. For the purpose of distinguishing between the *secular* and *religious*, it is useful digress a few moments from *Bauchman v. West* to view vocal music from three perspectives—form, content, and presentation. *Form* refers to structural features of a musical composition. *Content* refers to the meaning of the words of a song, that is, to the lyrics. *Presentation* concerns the manner in which a composition is performed.

The following are examples of form components:

Melody—the sequences of tones, often referred to as *the tune*

Harmony—chords and the pattern of transition from one chord to another

Rhythm—the pattern of the duration of a musical composition's sounds

Orchestration or arrangement—the parts of a musical selection that are assigned to different instruments or voices

Scale—the set of tones that a composer has available for creating a musical selection. The most familiar major scale in European musical heritage consists of seven basic tones and five "half tones." The traditional Chinese scale consists of five tones. Javanese gamelan music has two scales—the five-tone *slendro* and the seven-tone *pelog*.

Now to *content*—the meaning of the lyrics. Content can be of various sorts representing religious themes, country-western themes, romantic-love themes, comic themes, blues themes, rap themes, jail-house themes, and more.

Presentation can include how a song is paced, the singers' intonation, changes in emphasis throughout the selection, rhythm and volume variations, timbre, and the physical positioning of the singers.

Even though certain musical forms may often be associated with certain kinds of content (some forms more commonly used with country-western songs, blues, or rap), forms and content are actually separate entities. The melodies, harmonies, rhythms, and scales used in religious music are not inherently religious, so both form and presentation can be properly regarded as neutral or secular because they can be used with any kind of content.

Next, consider the matters of *intent* and *effect*. One critical factor in determining whether music violates the Constitution's establishment clause is the intent of those who plan or perform the music. If the intent is to promote a religion's doctrine and attract recruits to the faith, then the music should not be played in a public school. But if the intent is to feature or teach form (secular) aspects of a musical selection (melody, harmony, and the like) or to teach presentation skills (intonation, phrasing, breath control, timing), then the music is permissible in a public school, regardless of the content.

Not only is the intent of those who offer music significant, but the effect of the performance on listeners is important as well. If the effect is undeniably that of convincing an audience to adopt or favor a given religion, then the music is not acceptable in public schools. But if the effect may differ from one listener to another, as a result of each person's way of perceiving a musical selection, then the music does not have the effect of proselytizing in favor of a given religion and thus can be used in schools.

Now to the appellate court's estimate of intent and effect in *Bauchman v. West*. Because it was difficult—if not impossible—to know the choir director's true motive in selecting of songs and venues, the judges gave Torgerson the benefit of any doubt by estimating that his intent could very well have been secular, that of emphasizing musical form and presentation, with the Christian religious content being no more than incidental. Furthermore, the jurists speculated that the choir director's choice of Christian-related venues had been to take advantage of the acoustic and visual qualities of those sites and not because the sites were associated with Christianity. Furthermore, the judges suggested that the probable effect of singing such songs in such places would vary from one person to another, depending on their individual attitudes, and would not necessarily attract audiences to Christianity.

Here is the way the court phased the ruling:

We believe a reasonable observer aware of the purpose, context, and history of public education in Salt Lake City, including the historical tension between the government and the Mormon Church, and the traditional and ubiquitous presence of religious themes in vocal music, would perceive the following with respect to Ms. Bauchman's factual allegations concerning the Choir curriculum and performance venues: the Choir represents one of Salt Lake City's public high schools and is comprised of a diverse group of students; many of the Choir's songs have religious content—content predominately representative of Judeo-Christian beliefs; in contrast to a church choir, this Choir also performs a variety of secular songs; the Choir's talent is displayed in the diverse array of songs performed and in a number of different public (religious and nonreligious) settings, all of which reflect the community's culture and heritage. Certainly, any given observer will give more or less meaning to the lyrics of a particular song sung in a particular venue based on that observer's individual experiences and spiritual beliefs. However, the natural consequences of the Choir's alleged activities, viewed in context and in their entirety by a reasonable observer, would not be the advancement or endorsement of religion. Ms. Bauchman's complaint therefore fails to support a claim that the Choir curriculum or Choir activities have a principal or primary effect of endorsing religion. (Brorby, 1997)

When the court's ruling was announced, cries of "unfair" and "ridiculous" came from a variety of organizations, including other religious denominations. Those who disagreed with the decision cited not only Torgerson's behavior in the

Bachman incident but also past years during which he promoted the Mormon faith through the choir's performances.

A typical dissenting opinion is the following appraisal of the case from the Agnoticism/Atheism website:

[The appellate court's judgment,] if used as precedent by other courts, drastically narrows the ability of public school students to get legal relief when school officials use their positions to endorse one religion or disparage another. Based upon this decision, even a school official with a long and disturbing history of misusing his office to advance his religious beliefs could still be found not in violation of the Constitution, at least so long as the court in question can think up some vaguely plausible reasons for the immediately challenged actions.

This decision is often cited as precedent for the idea that public schools are permitted to include religious compositions in various choral or orchestral music programs, [on the ground that] "there is a legitimate time, manner and place for the discussion of religion in the public classroom." [Granted, that statement is] entirely valid and expresses an important principle—the mere fact that something religious has gotten mixed in with a government activity does not, by itself, mean that this activity is necessarily and automatically unconstitutional. However, the Court seems to err by going too far in the other direction when it argues that the mere existence of a possible secular motive is sufficient to validate such activities—especially when abundant evidence of past religious motivation is dismissed. (Brorby, 1977; *Bauchman v. West High School*, 1997)

In summary, the outcome of *Bauchman v. West High School* bore important implications beyond the Salt Lake School District, because the ruling has been used as the basis for school officials' decisions in other areas of the nation as well. Whether a different appeal court or the U.S. Supreme Court would issue a different ruling will not be known until someone outside the jurisdiction of the Tenth U.S. Circuit Court brings a similar case to trial.

The dilemma school officials face in choosing how to cope with music during the Christmas season was demonstrated in the policies different Arizona school districts followed. Some schools avoided religious songs and celebrated the season by sticking with such selections as *Frosty the Snowman* and *Jingle Bells*. Other schools added tunes unrelated to Christmas. For instance, Yavapai Elementary in Scottsdale avoided religious Christmas music by presenting a holiday concert consisting of *It's Beginning To Look a Lot Like Christmas, Santa Claus—You Are Much Too Fat*, a Hanukkah song, a Spanish song, and an African song. The school principal explained that "We don't do *Silent Night*, [because] you have to be real sensitive not to infringe" (Ryman, 2005).

Schools that offered a combination of religious and nonreligious selections were careful to balance the number of religious and secular songs. At Las Sendas Elementary in Mesa, *O Come, All Ye Faithful* was followed by an Israeli folk song, *Driedel*, and such nonreligious tunes as *Rudolph, the Red-nosed Reindeer* and *Santa Is Coming to Town* (Ryman, 2005).

ILLUSTRATIVE CASES

As the foregoing discussion has shown, decisions about public schools' treatment of religious holidays have been fraught with complexities and inconsistencies. Further examples of how such events have played out in different school systems are provided by the following cases from Florida, Wisconsin, California, and New York.

The Hillsborough Dilemma

The continuing struggle in American society over two conflicting traditions—one religious, the other secular—was demonstrated in the Hillsborough (Florida) County School District's response to Muslims' request to have public schools close on a Muslim holy day, such as Eid al-Fitr.

Hillsborough public schools traditionally closed for the Jewish Yom Kipper holiday and for the Christian Good Friday and the day after Easter. Schools were also out on Christmas Day, but that did not count as a special school holiday because Christmas came during the year-end vacation week. In 2005, Muslims pressed the Hillsborough school board to recognize an Islamic holiday by dismissing school, as was done for Christians and Jews. Two proposals before the board for solving the problem of equal treatment of faiths were (a) to add an Islamic holiday or (b) to eliminate all religion-linked holidays. The Muslim member of the district's calendar-committee objected to eliminating all religion-related holidays because "Muslims don't need any more negative attention than we're getting. We were just trying to get equal treatment" (Ave, 2005a).

In late October 2005, the school board, in a 5-to-1 vote, eliminated all religion-related holidays, an action that the majority of board members said was fair because it clearly separated church and state. However, the director of the Council on American-Islamic Relations objected to the decision: "We feel like this is an extreme measure. We can't say it enough, especially to Christian and Jewish folks, our brothers and sisters in faith. This was not our doing, and we didn't ask for it" (Ave, 2005b).

The board's actions brought an immediate retort from County Commissioner Brian Blair, who voiced his opposition on national television, blaming the political "far left" for trying to erode America's Judeo-Christian tradition: "Why are so (few) affecting so many in an adverse way?" His television appearance was followed by more than 3,500 e-mails from around the country, faulting the school board for eliminating Christian and Jewish holidays rather than adding a Muslim holiday. Two weeks later, the board, in a 5-to-2 vote, reversed its earlier decision and restored Yom Kippur and Good Friday as school holidays. In effect, religious tradition ultimately trumped secularism.

The board's reversal was then assailed in a *St. Petersburg Times* editorial as a cowardly "cop-out."

There was no reason for the School Board to indulge Christian conservatives, who bullied the board over what was mostly a symbolic issue. What was worse than seeing board members fail to uphold the American principles that their own employees teach was the self-serving rationale officials gave for mingling church and state. Board chair Candy Olson blamed—what else—a communication problem. Member Carolyn Bricklemyer said: "I never wanted to be a part of anything this divisive." Superintendent Mary Ellen Elia, who crafted the cop-out, had the gall to frame the reversal as an act of gallantry that would get the board back to the business of education. (School board, 2005)

Thus, the Hillsborough case exposed once again the conflict in American society between a long religious tradition and a secular belief system that had been adopted by the nation's founders when they created the U.S. Constitution and its first amendment.

A Wisconsin Incident

Two elementary schools in Wisconsin faced potential court action at the end of 2005 over questions of how much traditional Christmas music should be included in schools' year-end holiday programs in comparison to secular tunes and music from other faiths.

The conflict arose when a school in Dodgeville and one in Glen-River Hills were charged with anti-Christian discrimination by Mat Staver, president of Liberty Council, a Florida-based conservative Christian group endorsed by fundamentalist Baptist minister Jerry Falwell.

Staver's complaint against the Glen-River Hills "Holiday Sing" program was that Christian songs were excluded while Hanukkah and Kwanzaa songs were retained. However, Glen-River Hills officials noted that the program included the Christmas carol *Angels We Have Heard On High* and the song *Let There Be Peace on Earth*. In response to Staver's accusation, a school-district administrator defended the choice of songs by saying, "We have a very diverse community . . . We produce a balanced program to honor and recognize as many of the cultures as we can" (Fly, 2005).

The Liberty Council's criticism of the Dodgeville school's presentation of the copyrighted playlet "The Little Tree's Christmas Gift" was that one of its songs, titled *Cold in the Night*, consisted of newly composed words set to the tune of *Silent Night*. Staver protested, "They're discriminating based upon a religious viewpoint. It sends a tremendous disconnect to a young person when you're familiar with the song *Silent Night* and all of sudden you learn the same tune with totally secular words . . . We are, after all, celebrating a national holiday—Christmas." (Fly, 2005).

Scientology at a Human-Rights Conference

The question of a religious group's participation in holiday celebrations is similar to the question of such groups' activities in schools' special-event days. For

example, Los Angeles school officials were surprised to discover that representatives of the Church of Scientology were the leaders of an upcoming three-day
conference on human rights at Jordon High School in the Watts district. The conference would involve teenagers from two-dozen countries meeting with Jordan
students to discuss human rights under various forms of government. Not until
a press release from the Church of Scientology advertised the conference as a
church-sponsored activity a few days before the event did Jordan administrators
realize that the group, which had originally suggested such a forum, Youth for
Human Rights International, was linked to the church.

A school-district official said she might have canceled the event if she had been
alerted to it earlier, because of the appearance that the church was so closely
associated with the conference. But she said she was confident that the gathering
would remain focused on human rights—"It is a good thing for young people
around the world to meet and get a world view. But we made it very clear what
the limitations of this event will be" (Rubin, 2005).

A Debatable Decision in New York

In early 2006, the Second U.S. Circuit Court of Appeal, in a 2-to-1 vote, upheld
a lower court's decision that the New York City School District could ban Christian
nativity scenes in schools and, at the same time, could allow the display of Judaic
and Islamic symbols. Only the nativity scene would be prohibited. Such ostensibly
secular objects as Santa Claus, reindeer, and pine trees would be permitted.

The rationale in support of the decision was that

allowing secular symbols neither advanced nor inhibited religion. The appeals court said no
objective observer would believe the city wanted to communicate to its students "any official
endorsement of Judaism and Islam or any dismissal of Christianity." Instead, the court
said, the purpose was to use holidays to encourage respect for diverse cultural traditions.
(American Civil Liberties Union of Florida, 2006)

However, the dissenting judge who voted against the ruling objected that Judaic
and Islamic symbols were not secular, so the school system's policy "utilizes
religious symbols of certain religions, but bans the religious symbols of another"
(American Civil Liberties Union of Florida, 2006). As a result, the court's ruling
appeared to muddle more than clarify the conditions under which religious symbols
could appear in New York's public schools.

Conclusion

As demonstrated throughout this chapter, the long-established tradition of recognizing Christian holidays in public schools by dismissing classes and presenting
holiday pageants and displays has changed in recent decades. Challenges to the tradition by advocates of other faiths and by secularists have pressed school officials
to deemphasize religious aspects of holidays and to adopt a comparative-religions

approach to the study of various faiths' holidays. However, issues of religious holidays have not yet been definitively clarified. Inconsistent court decisions have left such matters in a somewhat confused state.

Religious celebrations intrude into the state domain

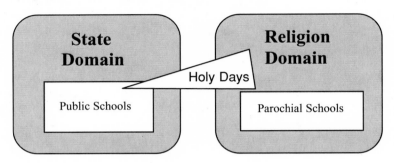

GUIDELINES FOR EDUCATORS

There are several valuable sources of suggestions for teachers, administrators, and other school personnel who seek help in coping with questions about the proper handling of religious holidays in schools.

First, consider a suggested set of policies regarding religious holidays issued by sixteen educational and religious organizations, including the

- American Association of School Administrators
- American Federation of Teachers
- American Jewish Congress
- Islamic Society of North America
- National Association of Evangelicals
- National Conference of Christians and Jews
- National Education Association

This coalition of organizations proposed that,

in a pluralistic society, public schools are places for persons of all faiths or none. Schools may neither promote nor denigrate any religion. In order to respect religious liberty and advance education, we recommend that each school district take the following steps:

- Develop policies about the treatment of religious holidays in the curricula and inform parents of those policies.
- Offer preservice and inservice workshops to assist teachers and administrators in understanding the appropriate place of religious holidays in the schools.

- Become familiar with the nature and needs of the religious groups in the school community.
- Provide resources for teaching about religions and religious holidays in ways that are constitutionally permissible and educationally sound. (Christian Legal Society, 2006)

A second source of guidance is a document issued by the U.S. Office of Education advising school personnel that, "generally, public schools may teach about religious holidays, and may celebrate the secular aspects of the holidays and objectively teach about their religious aspects. They may not observe the holidays as religious events. Schools should generally excuse students who do not wish to participate in holiday events" (U.S. Department of Education, 1995).

A third valuable source of advice is a publication titled "Teaching about Religious Holidays."

Teachers must be careful not to cross the line between teaching about religious holidays (which is permitted) and celebrating religious holidays (which is not). Celebrating religious holidays in the form of religious worship or other practices is unconstitutional. Teaching about a holiday will be constitutional if it furthers a genuine secular program of education, is presented objectively, and does not have the effect of advancing or inhibiting religion. Religious symbols such as crosses, crèches and menorahs may be used as teaching aids in the classroom provided that the symbols are displayed as examples of the cultural and religious heritage of the holiday, and are temporary in nature.

Music, art, literature, and drama with religious themes may be included in teaching about holidays, provided that their overall effect is not to endorse religion . . . and relate to sound, secular educational goals. Thus, a school's choral group can sing songs that are religious in nature but may only do so if the song is part of a larger program of music which is secular.

School-sponsored activities should also focus on more than one religion and religious holiday.

If the religious beliefs of students or their parents conflict with the content of classroom activity, students may be excused. However, in excusing a student, care should be taken to avoid stigmatizing or appearing to punish the student (for example, a student who is not permitted to take part in a holiday party should not be required to sit in the hall and do math problems). (Anti-Defamation League, 2004c)

It is apparent that the Anti-Defamation League's advice represents a cautious approach to religious holidays. Following such advice should be a safe way for school officials to avoid the problems faced in the New York City religious-symbols incident, the Wisconsin Christian-discrimination charge, and such cases as *Bauchman v. West High* and *Florey v. Sioux Falls.*

Chapter 7

Financial Support

The financial-support debate over church/state/school relationships concerns two questions:

Should public tax funds ever be used to support schools operated by religious organizations? If so, under what circumstances?

HOW THE CONTROVERSY DEVELOPED

The historical setting of court cases that bear on the public finance of religious schools was reviewed by U.S. Supreme Court Justice Hugo Black when he wrote the Court's majority decision in the 1947 case of *Everson v. Ewing Township*. In his historical sketch, Black explained that

A large proportion of the early settlers of this country came here from Europe to escape the bondage of laws which compelled them to support and attend government-favored churches. The centuries immediately before and contemporaneous with the colonization of America had been filled with turmoil, civil strife, and persecutions, generated in large part by established sects determined to maintain their absolute political and religious supremacy. With the power of government supporting them, at various times and places, Catholics had persecuted Protestants, Protestants had persecuted Catholics, Protestant sects had persecuted other Protestant sects, Catholics of one shade of belief had persecuted Catholics of another shade of belief, and all of these had from time to time persecuted Jews. In efforts to force loyalty to whatever religious group happened to be on top and in league with the government of a particular time and place, men and women had been fined, cast in jail, cruelly tortured, and killed. Among the offenses for which these punishments had been inflicted were such things as speaking disrespectfully of the views of ministers of government-established churches, nonattendance at those churches, expressions of non-belief in their doctrines, and failure to pay taxes and tithes to support them.

These practices of the old world were transplanted to and began to thrive in the soil of the new America. The very charters granted by the English Crown to the individuals and companies designated to make the laws which would control the destinies of the colonials authorized these individuals and companies to erect religious establishments which all, whether believers or non-believers, would be required to support and attend. An exercise of this authority was accompanied by a repetition of many of the old world practices and persecutions. Catholics found themselves hounded and proscribed because of their faith; Quakers who followed their conscience went to jail; Baptists were peculiarly obnoxious to certain dominant Protestant sects; men and women of varied faiths who happened to be in a minority in a particular locality were persecuted because they steadfastly persisted in worshipping God only as their own consciences dictated. And all of these dissenters were compelled to pay tithes and taxes to support government-sponsored churches whose ministers preached inflammatory sermons designed to strengthen and consolidate the established faith by generating a burning hatred against dissenters. These practices became so commonplace as to shock the freedom-loving colonials into a feeling of abhorrence. The imposition of taxes to pay ministers' salaries and to build and maintain churches and church property aroused their indignation. It was these feelings which found expression in the First Amendment. No one locality and no one group throughout the Colonies can rightly be given entire credit for having aroused the sentiment that culminated in adoption of the Bill of Rights' provisions embracing religious liberty. But Virginia, where the established [Anglican] church had achieved a dominant influence in political affairs and where many excesses attracted wide public attention, provided a great stimulus and able leadership for the movement. The people there, as elsewhere, reached the conviction that individual religious liberty could be achieved best under a government which was stripped of all power to tax, to support, or otherwise to assist any or all religions, or to interfere with the beliefs of any religious individual or group.

The movement toward this end reached its dramatic climax in Virginia in 1785–86 when the Virginia legislative body was about to renew Virginia's tax levy for the support of the established church. Thomas Jefferson and James Madison led the fight against this tax. Madison wrote his great Memorial and Remonstrance against the law. In it, he eloquently argued that a true religion did not need the support of law; that no person, either believer or non-believer, should be taxed to support a religious institution of any kind; that the best interest of a society required that the minds of men always be wholly free; and that cruel persecutions were the inevitable result of government-established religions. Madison's Remonstrance received strong support throughout Virginia, and the Assembly postponed consideration of the proposed tax measure until its next session. When the proposal came up for consideration at that session, it not only died in committee, but the Assembly enacted the famous "Virginia Bill for Religious Liberty" originally written by Thomas Jefferson. The preamble to that Bill stated among other things that:

Almighty God hath created the mind free; that all attempts to influence it by temporal punishments, or burthens, or by civil incapacitations, tend only to beget habits of hypocrisy and meanness, and are a departure from the plan of the Holy author of our religion who being Lord both of body and mind, yet chose not to propagate it by coercions on either . . . ; that to compel a man to furnish contributions of money for the propagation of opinions which he disbelieves, is sinful and tyrannical; that even the forcing him to support this or that teacher of his own religious persuasion, is depriving him of the comfortable liberty of giving his contributions to the particular pastor, whose morals he would make his pattern. (Black, 1947)

In effect, the U.S. Constitution's prohibition against using public funds to finance religious institutions was the American colonists' reaction against church/state policies under which so many immigrants had suffered in Europe—in "the old country."

Although the Constitution's establishment clause challenged past church/state financial relationships, it failed to end conflicts over tax money for religious activities. For example, consider the arguments advanced by parents who want to send their offspring to parochial schools. They complain that they pay taxes, which are used to support public education, yet they are also obliged to pay the fees charged by private schools for educating their children. Isn't that a form of double taxation? Why shouldn't a family's school-tax money be available to pay the costs of private schooling for their children?

In contrast, consider the reasoning of people who object to using tax funds for religious schools. They maintain that all American adults—whether or not they have children in school—are obliged to pay property and income taxes from which public schools receive their funds. And the purpose of those taxes is not simply to pay for educating one's own children but, rather, it is to help ensure that the nation has the kind of literate, well-informed citizenry necessary for a democratic government to operate properly and for the economic system to function efficiently. All families are entitled to send their children to public schools. But if families choose, instead, to patronize parochial schools that teach religious doctrine, they should be willing to pay for that privilege by bearing the cost of private schooling.

Over the past half century, the general trend in church/school relationships has been toward increasing restrictions on the traditional role of religion in public schools, as in matters of prayer, scripture reading, and holidays. But the trend in providing public funds for religious schools has been quite the reverse, with tax moneys being granted to parochial schools at an accelerating pace. How that trend developed can be traced through cases of legislation and judicial decisions concerning (a) transporting students to parochial schools, (b) furnishing textbooks to religious schools, (c) paying the salaries of teachers in religious schools, (d) funding school repairs, (e) reimbursing parents for private-school tuition costs, (f) furnishing testing services, (g) offering tax credits to parents of private-school students, and (h) providing tax-funded vouchers for children to attend sectarian schools.

As the examples illustrate, a variety of questions about using tax funds to pay costs incurred by parochial schools have been addressed in judicial proceedings. The U.S. Supreme Court cases have been especially notable for the slim margins by which rulings have been passed by the nine justices—often by only a 5-to-4 or 6-to-3 vote. Thus, most cases have been highly contentious, with majority opinions sharply challenged by dissenters.

Busing Students

One of the earliest court cases over the use of public funds for religious schools' activities was *Everson v. Ewing Township* in 1947.

Under a New Jersey statute that authorized school districts to transport children to and from schools (except private schools operated for profit), the board of education of Ewing Township reimbursed parents for fares paid by children who rode city buses to either public schools or Catholic schools. A taxpayer named Everson complained that Catholic schools provided religious instruction in the Catholic faith in addition to teaching secular subjects. Thus, he filed a lawsuit challenging the statute's reimbursing parents for transporting children to sectarian schools. He contended that such a practice violated the constitutional separation of church and state.

The New Jersey Supreme Court ruled that the state legislature lacked the authority under the state constitution to authorize reimbursement to parents of bus fares paid for transporting their children to any schools other than public schools. However, when the case was taken to the New Jersey Court of Appeals, the judges there reversed the ruling, stating that the statute did not breach either the state constitution or U.S. Constitution. Everson then appealed the case to the U.S. Supreme Court where the justices, in a 5-to-4 vote, upheld the appeals court decision by declaring that the bus-fare payments to parents of children in parochial schools did not violate the Federal Constitution's establishment clause.

Justice Hugo Black, who wrote the majority opinion, defended the payment of students' bus fares by reasoning that the practice was no different than the state's providing other services (such as police and fire protection) to church-related institutions on a religiously neutral basis. In paying bus fares, he argued, "The State contributes no money to the schools. It does not support them. Its legislation, as applied, does no more than provide a general program to help parents get their children, regardless of their religion, safely and expeditiously to and from accredited schools" (Black, 1947).

However, the majority opinion was assailed by Justice Robert H. Jackson, one of the four dissenters in the case. In his minority statement, Jackson noted that under the New Jersey statute "children are classified according to the schools they attend and are to be aided if they attend the public schools or private Catholic schools, but they are not allowed to be aided if they attend private secular schools or private religious schools of other faiths. [Therefore], if we are to decide this case on the facts before us, our question is simply this: Is it constitutional to tax this complainant [Everson] to pay the cost of carrying pupils to Church schools of one specified denomination?" Jackson answered his own question with:

The state cannot maintain a Church and it can no more tax its citizens to furnish free carriage to those who attend a Church. The prohibition against establishment of religion cannot be circumvented by a subsidy, bonus, or reimbursement of expense to individuals for receiving religious instruction and indoctrination. (Black, 1947)

Hence, in Jackson's view, the New Jersey statute did violate the Constitution's establishment clause by favoring Catholic schools. The three other justices who concurred with Jackson's dissent were Burton, Frankfurter, and Rutledge.

Two features of the *Everson v. Ewing Township* ruling are noteworthy. First, the payment of bus fares was declared constitutionally valid by only one vote. If a single justice who had voted with the majority had decided that the New Jersey statute was constitutionally invalid, the reimbursement of bus fares would have been banned. Second, although *Everson v. Ewing Township* concerned special conditions under which transportation to religious schools could be paid from tax moneys, the general impression left by the case was that spending public funds for carrying children to parochial schools was proper, no matter what the conditions in a given case might be.

Despite the general message sent by the ruling in *Everson v. Ewing Township*, the decision did not settle the transportation-payment issue for all time. Over the 60 years since *Everson*, the nuances in specific instances have brought additional cases to the courts and have resulted in various outcomes. For example, until 2002, students attending the private Bethesda Lutheran School in Hot Springs (South Dakota) had been transported to school free-of-charge on public-school buses. But when the school district's insurance carrier said covering the private-school students was beyond the district's insurance policy, the district invoked a long-established Blaine amendment[1] to the North Dakota state constitution that read "No money or property of the state shall be given or appropriated for the benefit of any sectarian or religious society or institution" (Becket Fund, 2006). Bethesda pupils could no longer ride public-school buses. In response to the district's action, the Puckets (parents of two Bethesda students) filed a lawsuit (*Pucket v. Rounds*) to reinstate the transportation arrangement. As a result of a vigorous appeal to North Dakota authorities by the Becket Fund for Religious Liberty, the state in 2006 changed its position on busing sectarian-school students and, ignoring the Blaine amendment, "stated under oath that it cannot and will not prohibit the busing of Bethesda students." Bethesda pupils were again bused to school (Becket Fund, 2006).

Textbooks

A New York State law required public-school districts to lend textbooks free-of-charge to parochial schools in grades 7 through 12. When several local school boards failed to lend texts, state officials threatened to remove board members from office for not obeying the law. The school boards, in response, filed a lawsuit, charging that the state law offended the Constitution's first and fourteenth amendments. Although the trial court found in favor of the school boards, that judgment was reversed by the New York Court of Appeals which ruled that the law did not violate the constitutions of either New York or the United States. In reaching their judgment, appeals-court jurists declared that the expressed purpose of the law was "to benefit all school children, without regard to the type of school attended [and] that only textbooks approved by school authorities [such as local school-board members] could be loaned, and therefore the statute was completely neutral with respect to religion" (White, 1968). When the case reached the U.S.

Supreme Court, the majority of the justices, in a 5-to-3 decision, supported the appeals court by concluding that the law should continue in force. A key issue in the case was the proviso that local school officials were responsible for deciding whether textbooks requested by church-operated schools included content that would further the schools' religious mission. Justice Byron White foresaw that critics might complain about some school-board members bringing a religious bias to the task of evaluating textbooks. Hence, White wrote,

We cannot assume that school authorities, who constantly face the same problem in selecting textbooks for use in the public schools, are unable to distinguish between secular and religious books or that they will not honestly discharge their duties under the law. In judging the validity of the statute on this record we must proceed on the assumption that books loaned to students are books that are not unsuitable for use in the public schools because of religious content. (White, 1968)

However, Justice William O. Douglas—one of the three judges who voted against the majority opinion—objected to the New York statute's providing texts for parochial schools. He noted that sectarian-school officials were not obliged to choose from among textbooks already being used in public schools. Instead, the officials were authorized to ask for the particular books they wanted. Marshal then asked, "Can there be the slightest doubt that the head of the parochial school will select the book or books that best promote its sectarian creed?" (White, 1968). In support of Douglas' suspicion, Justice Abe Fortas wrote,

Despite the transparent camouflage that the books are furnished to students, the reality is that they are selected and their use is prescribed by the sectarian authorities. The child must use the prescribed book. He cannot use a different book prescribed for use in the public schools. The State cannot choose the book to be used. It is true that the public school boards must "approve" the book selected by the sectarian authorities; but this has no real significance. The purpose of these provisions is to hold out promise that the books will be "secular," but the fact remains that the books are chosen by and for the sectarian schools. (White, 1968)

So it was that the *Board of Education v. Allen* decision interpreted parochial schools' missions as twofold and separate—with the secular and religious partitioned. The decision suggested that public-funded textbooks could help with the secular assignment without the religious assignment also benefiting. But the Court's three dissenters speculated that parochial-school authorities would use the plan as a way of teaching religious convictions.

The Lemon Test

The 1971 case of *Lemon v. Kurtzman* is of particular importance for judging the proper relationship between church and state in schooling matters, because the three criteria proposed by the justices in that case have since been applied in adjudicating numerous other lawsuits bearing on the Constitution's establishment clause. The three criteria are typically referred to as *the Lemon test*. As explained by Chief Justice Warren Burger, the test has three parts: any law or statute under consideration must (a) have a secular (religion-free) purpose, (b) neither advance nor inhibit religion, and (c) not foster "an excessive government entanglement with religion" (Burger, 1971).

The case of *Lemon v. Kurtzman* was heard by the U.S. Supreme Court at the same time as *Early v. DiCenso* and *Robinson v. DiCenso* because the three cases involved the same issue—the legality of the government paying the salaries of teachers in private schools that were operated by religious organizations. *Lemon v. Kurtzman* concerned a 1968 Pennsylvania statute that provided for public funds to be paid to church-sponsored schools for teachers' salaries, textbooks, and instructional materials. Most of the concerned schools were affiliated with the Roman Catholic Church. A lower court had declared the practice unconstitutional, and the case was appealed to the U.S. Supreme Court for final judgment.

The two cases that involved DiCenso challenged Rhode Island's 1969 Salary Supplement Act that paid a 15 percent salary supplement to teachers in non-public schools in which the average per-pupil expenditure on secular education was below the average in public schools. Education officials reported that about 25 percent of the state's elementary students attended nonpublic schools, with 95 percent of those students in Roman-Catholic affiliated schools. Up to the time that the case came to trial, 250 teachers at Roman Catholic schools had been the sole beneficiaries under the act. The DiCenso cases were appealed to the U.S. Supreme Court from a lower-court where a three-judge panel had ruled that the salary-supplement law did not violate the U.S. Constitution's establishment clause and therefore could remain in effect.

However, the Supreme Court, by a 7-to-1 vote, declared that both the Pennsylvania and Rhode Island statutes breached the establishment clause because the parochial schools were "an integral part of the religious mission of the Catholic Church," and the statutes fostered "excessive entanglement" between government and religion (Burger, 1971). Thus, the two laws failed to meet the "excessive entanglement" portion of the three-part Lemon test that had been created for adjudicating *Lemon v. Kurtzman*.

In sum, *Lemon v. Kurtzman* set the precedent for banning the use of public funds to directly pay salaries of personnel in any of the nation's parochial schools.

Facilities Repair and Tax Benefits

In 1973 the U.S. Supreme court decided the case of *Committee for Public Education v. Nyquist* which concerned amendments to New York's Education and Tax Laws that established three financial-aid programs for nonpublic elementary and secondary schools:

1. Direct money grants to "qualifying" nonpublic schools for "maintenance and repair" of facilities to protect students' "health, welfare and safety." A "qualifying" school was a

nonpublic, nonprofit elementary or secondary school that served a high concentration of pupils from low-income families.

2. Tuition reimbursement for parents of children in nonpublic elementary or secondary schools.

3. Tax relief to parents failing to qualify for tuition reimbursement. Each eligible taxpayer-parent was entitled to deduct a stipulated sum from his adjusted gross income for each child attending a nonpublic school. (Powell, 1973)

By a 6-to-3 vote, the Court declared the three amendments unacceptable because they breached the U.S. Constitution's separation of church and state. Specifically (a) the maintenance-and-repair features of the New York statute violated the establishment clause "because its inevitable effect is to subsidize and advance the religious mission of sectarian schools" and (b) the tuition reimbursement and tax-benefit provisions were "not sufficiently restricted to assure that [they would] not have the impermissible effect of advancing the sectarian activities of religious schools" (Powell, 1973)

In explaining the majority ruling about the maintenance-and-repair amendment, Justice Lewis F. Powell wrote that the provision authorized "direct payments to nonpublic schools, virtually all of which are Roman Catholic schools in low-income areas . . . No attempt is made to restrict payments to expenditures related to the upkeep of facilities used exclusively for secular purposes. Nothing in the statute, for instance, bars a qualifying school from paying out of state funds the salaries of employees who maintain the school chapel or the cost of renovating classrooms in which religion is taught" (Powell, 1973).

Testing Services

The 1973 U.S. Supreme Court case of *Levitt v. Committee* pitted the New York State comptroller—Levitt—against the Committee for Public Education & Religious Liberty. The issue at hand was whether the New York state legislature had erred in authorizing $28 million to reimburse nonpublic schools (secular and religious) for services mandated by the state. The most prominent of those services was the administration of tests (both standardized and teacher-made) and the reporting of results. The Committee for Public Education filed a lawsuit charging that such a use of public funds was a violation of the Constitution's separation of church and state. A three-judge district court agreed with the Committee's charge and rejected the defendants' claim that that a state may reimburse church-related schools for costs incurred in performing any service mandated by state law. When the case was appealed to the U.S. Supreme Court, the justices—in a 7-to-1 vote—supported the district court's judgment. In explaining why the legislature's funding bill was unconstitutional, Justice Warren Burger wrote,

The statute constitutes an impermissible aid to religion contravening the Establishment Clause, since no attempt is made and no means are available to assure that internally prepared tests, which are "an integral part of the teaching process," are free of religious instruction and avoid inculcating students in the religious precepts of the sponsoring church. (Burger, 1973)

In response to the Court's rejection, New York legislators revised the statute, prompting a new lawsuit which, like its predecessor, ended up at the U.S. Supreme Court in 1979, this time as *Regan v. Committee for Public Education* (with Regan as the new state comptroller). The revised version of the law placed all test construction in the state's hands. No teacher-made tests or ones constructed by a private school would be involved. This time the funding of testing in religious schools was approved by the Court in a 5-4 decision that the jurists reached by applying the three-part Lemon test. As Justice Byron White wrote in the majority statement:

A legislative enactment does not contravene the Establishment Clause if it has a secular legislative purpose, if its principal or primary effect neither advances nor inhibits religion, and if it does not foster an excessive government entanglement with religion.

The New York statute has the secular purpose of providing educational opportunity of a quality that will prepare New York citizens for the challenges of American life. The statutory plan calls for tests that are prepared by the State and administered on the premises by personnel of the nonpublic schools, which, however, have no control over the contents of the tests. Although some of the tests are graded by nonpublic school personnel, in view of the nature of the tests, which deal only with secular academic matters, the grading by nonpublic school employees affords no control to the school over the outcome of any of the tests, and there is no substantial risk that the examinations can be used for religious educational purposes.... Thus, reimbursement for the costs of so complying with state law has primarily a secular, rather than a religious purpose and effect. (White, 1980)

But as the 5-to-4 vote attests, four justices disagreed with the majority opinion. Justice Harry Blackmun (supported by Brennen, Marshall, and Stevens) charged that the majority ruling "takes a long step backwards in the inevitable controversy that emerges when a state legislature continues to insist on providing public aid to parochial schools." He cited two earlier Court judgments (*Meek v. Pittenger* 1975 and *Wolman v. Walter* 1977) in which the majority had ruled that "substantial direct financial aid to a religious school, even though ostensibly for secular purposes, runs the great risk of furthering the religious mission of the school as a whole because that religious mission so pervades the functioning of the school." Thus, in the four dissenters' view, the New York statute failed the second part of the Lemon test (White, 1980). Blackman contended that the statute also failed the Lemon test's third part by unduly entangling the state in the affairs of religious schools, since New York officials would continually need to evaluate newly created examinations "to ensure that reimbursement for expenses incurred in connection with their administration and grading will not offend the First Amendment" (White, 1980).

In short, the Court was badly split over giving money directly to parochial schools for state-mandated testing services, with the decision seemingly at odds with the rulings in two similar cases within the past five years.

Tax Credit

A Minnesota law entitled parents to a state income-tax reduction for tuition, textbooks, and transportation costs that their children incurred while attending elementary or secondary schools, including church-sponsored schools. In reaction to the law, a group of taxpayers filed a suit in district court, claiming that such tax write-offs breached the U.S. Constitution's establishment clause. At the time—1982—about 11 percent of Minnesota's elementary and secondary students attended private schools, with 95 percent of those students enrolled in church-sponsored schools.

The district-court judges—focusing on the second part of the Lemon test—ruled in favor of the state, asserting that the tax-relief statute was "neutral on its face and in its application and does not have a primary effect of either advancing or inhibiting religion" (Rehnquist, 1983). When the taxpayers then took their case to an appeals court, the result was the same, so they went to the U.S. Supreme Court where, in a 5-to-4 vote, the majority agreed with the two lower courts' judgments. Hence, the tax-deduction statute could remain in effect.

Justice William H. Rehnquist, who wrote the majority opinion, stated that the Minnesota statute passed the Lemon test because the tax write-off

(a) Has the secular purpose of ensuring that the State's citizenry is well educated, as well as of assuring the continued financial health of private schools, both sectarian and nonsectarian.

(b) Does not have the primary effect of advancing the sectarian aims of nonpublic schools. It is only one of many deductions—such as those for medical expenses and charitable contributions—available under the Minnesota tax laws; is available for educational expenses incurred by all parents, whether their children attend public schools or private sectarian or nonsectarian private schools; and provides aid to parochial schools only as a result of decisions of individual parents rather than directly from the State to the schools themselves.

(c) Does not "excessively entangle" the State in religion. The fact that state officials must determine whether particular textbooks qualify for the tax deduction and must disallow deductions for textbooks used in teaching religious doctrines is an insufficient basis for finding such entanglement. (Rehnquist, 1983)

The crucial point that distinguished this ruling from the Court's decisions in earlier cases (such as *Nyquist*) was the fact that state funds were not being paid directly to parochial schools. Instead, parents received dollars (in the form of tax relief), which they then could use to pay pupils' expenses in church-related schools.

On behalf of the four jurists who disagreed with the majority opinion, Justice Thurgood Marshall wrote,

The Establishment Clause of the First Amendment prohibits a State from subsidizing religious education, whether it does so directly or indirectly. In my view, this principle of neutrality forbids ... any tax benefit, including the tax deduction at issue here, which subsidizes tuition payments to sectarian schools. I also believe that the Establishment Clause prohibits the tax deductions that Minnesota authorizes for the cost of books and other instructional materials used for sectarian purposes. (Rehnquist, 1983)

Once again, as a result of a 5-to-4 vote, a critical decision about funding parochial schools was decided by a single Supreme Court justice. If any one of the five judges who voted to uphold the Minnesota statute had, instead, joined the four dissenters, not only would the Minnesota law have fallen but other states that contemplated similar legislation would have been deterred from acting.

During the 1980s and 1990s, voters in four states faced ballot initiatives that would give parents tax credits, including parents who sent their children to parochial schools. In each of those elections, voters rejected the tax-relief provision. In the District of Columbia (1981), 89 percent of the electorate voted against tax credit, in Utah (1988) 70 percent rejected credits, in Oregon (1990) tax reduction was turned down by two-thirds of the voters, and in Colorado (1998) tax write-off were rejected by 60 percent of those who went to the polls (People for the American Way, 2000). In effect, tax-credit proposals have not succeeded with the voting public. As a result, states in which such statutes have been adopted are ones in which legislatures have passed the measures, partly as the result of pressure from religious groups.

Vouchers

A school voucher is a monetary grant that enables a student to pay the cost of attending a school that is not part of the public-school district in which the student resides. The school the student chooses can be (a) a privately operated institution that is either within or outside the student's public-school district, or (b) a public school outside that district. The private schools can be ones conducted by either secular or religious sponsors.

Voucher funds can come from either private or public sources. Private sources are usually philanthropic foundations, business organizations, or wealthy individuals. Public sources are local, state, or federal governments, including school districts.

The intention behind vouchers is nothing new. From colonial times onward, there have always been individuals or agencies willing to pay for pupils to enroll in schools other than the local public school. However, the present-day voucher movement is a new phenomenon—new not only in its use of the word *voucher* but new in the extent of government participation and in the rapidity with which the movement has spread. New, also, is the controversy over using public funds to finance vouchers and, particularly, over paying for students to attend church-sponsored schools.

The Pros and Cons

Government-financed school vouchers have become a highly contentious public issue, vociferously argued by adherents on both sides of the debate. By way of illustration, consider the claims of constituencies that advocate tax-funded vouchers as compared to claims of voucher critics.

Kennedy (2001) estimated that three kinds of groups are the main advocates of voucher programs: (a) political/economic libertarians who want the market place (customer demands) to determine which schools might best prepare students to compete in the business world, (b) the Christian Right that is concerned about moral education, and (c) the Catholic Church, which is the primary private-school sponsor that benefits financially from government-funded voucher plans.

In contrast, Kennedy's analysis suggests that the chief opponents of vouchers are (a) members of public-school systems (school boards, administrators, and teachers whose welfare is at stake), (b) civil libertarians and people who stress the need to maintain the separation of church and state, and (c) African American organizations that believe vouchers will set back the school-integration movement.

What, then, are the advantages and disadvantages of vouchers? According to proponents of using tax dollars to pay the expenses of children attending schools of parents' choice (including church-sponsored schools), voucher programs are desirable because

1. Rich parents have a choice of schools for their kids; poor parents should have the same choice.
2. Competition between schools is increased, leading to greater efficiency and results in all schools.
3. Private schools have a better history of getting results in teaching information and values than public schools.
4. Those parents who send their kids to private schools must in effect pay twice; i.e. their taxes pay for public schools that their children don't even attend.
5. Providing private school access to everyone will increase diversity.
6. The parent makes the choice between religious or non-religious schooling; thus, the government isn't imposing religion. (Messerli, 2006)

In contrast, critics of voucher plans charge that

1. Most of the private schools in the program are religious, so government funding violates the First Amendment separation of church and state.
2. Vouchers take funds away from already underfunded public schools.
3. Private schools aren't accountable to any oversight organization; thus, they may not act responsibly.
4. Public schools must accept everyone regardless of disabilities, test scores, religion, or other characteristics; private schools can show favoritism or discrimination in selecting students. (Messerli, 2006)

The American Association of University Women (AAUW), in the belief that a "strong, free public education system is the foundation of a democratic society," opposed vouchers for the following reasons:

Private and religious schools are not required to observe federal nondiscrimination laws. In fact, voucher proposals often contain language specifically intended to avoid application of civil rights laws, and many proponents insist voucher funding does not flow to the school but instead to the parent or student. This specificity in language allows private institutions to discriminate on the basis of religion, gender, disability, and language proficiency. Further, private and religious schools can reject a student based on the school's own admissions criteria and discriminate against a student in access to classes, guidance counseling, extracurricular activities, and other aspects of education.

Private and religious schools are not held to the same accountability and testing standards established in the No Child Left Behind Act.

Vouchers are taxpayers' dollars spent according to the policies of a private school board—not the decisions of a democratically elected and publicly accessible school board.

Vouchers disproportionately help families with children already in private schools. In fact, in Cleveland, 61% of students already in private or religious schools when the program began used Cleveland Scholarship and Tutoring Program vouchers to continue their attendance at those schools. (AAUW, 2004)

Among the most controversial claims in favor of vouchers has been that pupils in private schools receive a better education than those in public schools. Investigations focusing on this claim have produced inconclusive results. In 2000, Kober reported that research studies by independent firms in three current voucher programs produced "mixed conclusions about whether students who use vouchers improve their achievement compared with students who remain in public school . . . Some researchers have found no significant improvement in the achievement of students who use vouchers; others have found gains in one or two areas, such as mathematics or vocabulary; and others have found significant gains across more than one subject" (Kober, 2000). It appears that some private schools achieve better test results than their neighboring public schools, but in other communities the opposite result obtains—public-school students do better on the average than their private-school counterparts. And in still other locations, no significant achievement differences have been found between public and private schools.

An example of the uncertain success of vouchers is found in the oldest of the state plans, the Minnesota program.

Vouchers in Minnesota

The Minnesota plan began in 1990 in Milwaukee where the state provided funds that allowed poor families to send their children to private or parochial schools at a rate of up to $6,351 per student. In 2006, the plan's seventeenth year of operation, the program was slated to cost nearly $94 million. In Minnesota, as in other states, voucher supporters averred that the plan allowed pupils to escape bad schools and, in the process, to force public schools to improve by having to compete for students. Teacher unions and church/state separationists complained that the voucher program drained money and talent from inner-city schools and violated the principle of free, universal public education.

Assessments of the effect of the Minnesota plan on student achievement have proven inconclusive. "Researchers have done dozens of studies on Milwaukee and programs in Cleveland and Washington, DC. For every study that shows school-choice students perform better than their public school counterparts, another study contradicts it" (Fredrix, 2006).

Despite the lack of clear evidence that the voucher plan had produced its intended results, Minnesota's Governor Jim Doyle signed a measure in 2006 to increase the number of participants in Milwaukee from 15,000 students to 22,500 in 2007. Reacting to that news, a representative of the American Teachers Federation said, "You've got to wonder about the wisdom of increasing the program by 50 percent when there's no evidence from Milwaukee and no evidence from places like Cleveland that vouchers have succeeded in raising student achievement" (Fredrix, 2006). Funding the Milwaukee plan resulted in a huge budget shortfall, leaving the public schools desperate for funds.

A question about whether the Milwaukee program fostered religious doctrine at state expense was answered when Terry Brown, president of St. Anthony's School, said his 800 students thrived because the school focused on instruction that included Catholicism in daily routines (Fredrix, 2006).

How, then, have voucher programs fared in lawsuits filed by voucher opponents? For an answer, we can turn to three key court cases. The first (*Zelman v. Simmons-Harris*) reached the U.S. Supreme Court. The second and third (Colorado's *Owens v. Colorado Congress of PTS* and Florida's *Bush v. Holmes*) ran afoul the two states' constitutions.

Vouchers in Cleveland

The Ohio state legislature in 1995 authorized a Pilot Project Scholarship Program, which was implemented in the city of Cleveland, with the program designed for families below the poverty level. Enrollment began in 1996. By the 2005–2006 school year, 5,700 students were participating, with their vouchers worth up to $3,450 per student. Children's eligibility for the program was determined during their primary-school years (kindergarten through grade three), but once pupils qualified, they could continue using vouchers through the tenth grade. The plan was paid for by diverting up to $19-million a year from a Cleveland public school fund aimed at educating disadvantaged students (National School Boards Association, 2006). By 2002, over 99 percent of the pupils receiving vouchers attended religious schools, with 61 percent of them already enrolled in church-sponsored schools at the time the voucher bill went into effect (AAUW, 2004).

When a group of Ohio taxpayers filled a lawsuit challenging the state's voucher law for ostensibly offending the establishment clause of the U.S. Constitution, the district court judge who heard the case found in favor of the taxpayers and declared the law invalid. After the Sixth Circuit Appeals Court upheld the lower-court verdict, state officials in 2002 took *Zelman v. Simmons-Harris* to the U.S. Supreme Court where the justices, in a 5-to-4 vote, reversed the appeals-court judgment by declaring that the Ohio voucher statute did not violate the Constitution's separation of church and state. Thus, the Cleveland voucher program could continue.

The rationale adduced by the five majority justices in support of their decision included the assertion that, by giving money to parents rather than to schools, the Ohio statute did not use public funds to support schools sponsored by religious bodies. As explained by Justice William H. Rehnquist,

[The voucher program] is neutral in all respects towards religion, and is part of Ohio's general and multifaceted undertaking to provide educational opportunities to children in a failed school district. It confers educational assistance directly to a broad class of individuals defined without reference to religion and permits participation of all district schools— religious or nonreligious—and adjacent public schools . . . The constitutionality of a neutral educational aid program simply does not turn on whether and why, in a particular area, at a particular time, most private schools are religious, or most recipients choose to use the aid at a religious school. (Rehnquist, 2002)

However, Justice David H. Souter, representing the four judges who disagreed with the majority opinion, contended that the Ohio statute did, indeed, promote religious doctrine at government expense. He wrote,

In the city of Cleveland the overwhelming proportion of large appropriations for voucher money must be spent on religious schools if it is to be spent at all, and will be spent in amounts that cover almost all of tuition. The money will thus pay for eligible students' instruction not only in secular subjects but in religion as well, in schools that can fairly be characterized as founded to teach religious doctrine and to imbue teaching in all subjects with a religious dimension. Public tax money will pay at a systemic level for teaching the covenant with Israel and Mosaic law in Jewish schools, the primacy of the Apostle Peter and the Papacy in Catholic schools, the truth of reformed Christianity in Protestant schools, and the revelation to the Prophet in Muslim schools, to speak only of major religious groupings in the Republic. (Rehnquist, 2002)

A journalist in the *Village Voice* sought to illustrate the soundness of Souter's argument by quoting passages from several Cleveland religious schools' policy statements that revealed the schools' religious missions.

The Saint Rocco School handbook says that education there is designed "to make . . . faith become living, conscious, and active through the light of instruction' and that 'religious truths and values permeate the whole atmosphere of the school."

The Saint John Nottingham Lutheran School handbook states that "the one cardinal objective of education to which all others point is to develop devotion to God about our Creator, Redeemer, and Sanctifier."

The Calvary Center Academy handbook requires students to "pledge allegiance to the Christian flag and to the Savior for whose Kingdom it stands. One Savior crucified, risen and coming again with life and liberty for all who believe." (Hentoff, 2002)

The outcome of *Zelman v. Simmons-Harris* was hailed by President George W. Bush as a "landmark ruling and a victory for the American family" (Frieden, 2002). The Bush administration had contributed to the victory by having Solicitor General Charles Olson defend the Ohio law before the Supreme Court.

In summary, the Cleveland case provided a welcoming atmosphere for similar voucher plans to be initiated in other cities and states.

Vouchers in Colorado

The first state to introduce a voucher plan following the *Zelman v. Simmons-Harris* decision was Colorado in April 2003. The state's voters had already rejected previous fund-transfer schemes. In 1992 they had turned down a voucher proposal and in 1996 had defeated a tuition tax credit plan which, like vouchers, would have diverted public funds to private schools, including religious schools. So, in April 2003, rather than trusting the state's electorate to decide whether a voucher plan would be adopted, the legislature—with strong support from Republican Governor Bill Owens—passed a Colorado Opportunity Contract Pilot Program.

Initially the number of children eligible for vouchers would be limited to 1 percent of the students in eleven low-performing school districts, for a total of about 3,400 voucher recipients. By the program's fourth year, a permanent cap of 6 percent would be applied, meaning that as many as 21,000 students statewide could be using state-funded vouchers to attend private and religious schools (Fusarelli, 2004).

One month after Owens signed the Pilot Program into law, voucher opponents filed a lawsuit—*Owens v. Colorado Congress of Parents, Teachers, and Students*—claiming that the statute violated the state constitution. When the case arrived in the Colorado Supreme Court, the majority of the justices agreed with the plaintiffs that the plan was, indeed, unconstitutional. In the judgment issued June 28, 2004, Justice Michael L. Bender explained the Court majority's rationale:

The Pilot Program directs local school districts to allocate a statutorily prescribed portion of their funds, including funds derived from locally-raised tax revenues, to participating nonpublic schools. This aspect of the program violates the long-standing constitutional requirement that local school districts maintain control over locally-raised funds. Because the Pilot Program conflicts irreconcilably with article IX, section 15 of the Colorado Constitution, the program cannot stand as currently enacted. To achieve the goals of the legislation, the General Assembly must either seek to amend the constitution or enact legislation that comports with the requirements of the Colorado Constitution. (Bender, 2004)

Following the defeat of the Pilot Program, legislators began working on a revised voucher plan that might pass constitutional review.

Vouchers in Florida

In June 1999, Florida Governor John Ellis "Jeb" Bush endorsed the legislature's statewide voucher bill titled the *Opportunity Scholarship Program* (OSP). The plan gave vouchers of up to $3,389 a year to families whose children attended what state officials called "failing schools." Parents could use the voucher funds to enroll pupils in any schools of their choice, including ones operated by religious bodies. However, a coalition of opposing groups (including the Florida Parent/Teachers Association, League of Women Voters, teachers unions, and the National Association for the Advancement of Colored People) challenged the law in court. The opponents contended that while the voucher plan did not give tax dollars directly to religious schools, it indirectly accomplished that aim through parents as intermediaries.

Both a district court and an appellate court found in favor of the opponents to the *Opportunity Scholarship* legislation by declaring it unconstitutional. When the case—labeled *Bush v. Holmes*—reached the Florida Supreme Court, the justices supported the lower courts' ruling. The reasoning behind the decision was included in Chief Justice Barbara J. Pariente's explanation that the state constitution stipulated that

it is ... a paramount duty of the state to make adequate provision for the education of all children residing within its borders. Adequate provision shall be made by law for "a uniform, efficient, safe, secure, and high quality system of free public schools." We [the Court] find that the OSP violates this language. It diverts public dollars into separate private systems parallel to and in competition with the free public schools that are the sole means set out in the Constitution for the state to provide for the education of Florida's children. This diversion not only reduces money available to the free schools, but also funds private schools that are not "uniform" when compared with each other or the public system. Many standards imposed by law on the public schools are inapplicable to the private schools receiving public moneys. In sum, through the OSP the state is fostering plural, nonuniform systems of education in direct violation of the constitutional mandate for a uniform system of free public schools. (Pariente, 2006)

Although the Court did not address the question of whether the OSP also violated the church/state separation clause of the state constitution, the justices did let stand an earlier appellate court judgment that the voucher plan offended the section of the constitution that read,

[N]o revenue of the state or any political subdivision or agency thereof shall ever be taken from the public treasury directly or indirectly in aid of any church, sect, or religious denomination or in aid of any sectarian institution.

As in Colorado, the governor and legislators in Florida responded to the courts' rejection by searching for ways to avoid the constitutional arguments against their voucher plan. In April 2006, voucher proponents in the state legislature offered a proposal (SJR 2170) that would ask voters to amend the state constitution so as to exempt all voucher programs from the constitution's impeding passages so that students in "pre-kindergarten through college who have disabilities, or are economically disadvantaged, or meet other legislatively specified criteria could receive taxpayer-financed vouchers to attend private and religious schools" (Miller & Dáte, 2006).

Although the state court decisions in Colorado and Florida served temporarily to slow the expansion of the school-voucher movement, the federal government in 2004 hastened the expansion by means of the next event we inspect.

Vouchers in Washington, DC

The District of Columbia is not administered by a state government but, rather, by the federal government. As a result, the legislative and executive branches of the United States government are responsible for the policies and practices of Washington's public schools. In January 2004, the U.S. Congress responded to reports of the unsatisfactory academic progress of the city's public-school students by authorizing a $14-million, 5-year voucher program for the nation's capital. Although the George W. Bush administration had earlier urged the establishment of a national voucher system, the plan for the city of Washington was the first direct federal expenditure of funds to cover the costs of pupils attending religious schools. A similar bill passed by Congress in the late 1990s had been vetoed by President Bill Clinton.

The new program, under the title Washington Scholarship Fund, began in the fall of 2004 with 1,000 participants from low-income families. By 2006, the number had risen to 1,700 enrolled in fifty-nine private schools, with each student receiving up to $7,500 for tuition, fees, and transportation (Lively, 2006). Among the fifty-nine private schools, 51 percent were part of the Roman Catholic Archdiocese of Washington, 21 percent were non-Catholic religious schools, and the remaining 28 percent were independent and nonsectarian. Seven additional schools signed up for the 2006–2007 academic year (Clyne, 2005).

Thus, the practice of the federal government funneling tax funds through parents into religious schools was now officially established.

Conclusion

Many court rulings in recent decades that concern religion in public schools have served to strengthen the wall that Thomas Jefferson said should separate church from state. This has been true with jurists' decisions about the teaching of creationism, religious curricula, the content of public-school textbooks, prayer, and holidays. In contrast, most decisions about furnishing tax moneys to church-operated schools have served to weaken Jefferson's wall. At an increasing rate, court judgments have opened ways for states and the federal government to channel public funds to parochial schools in the form of transportation, special-education services, state-financed textbooks, tax credits, and vouchers.

Tax moneys funneled to religious schools

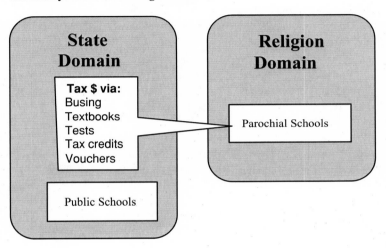

There have been conflicting reactions from different segments of American society to such judgments as the one supporting the Ohio voucher law. Enthusiastic approval of the U.S. Supreme Court's action has been voiced by social and religious conservatives who favor penetrating the wall by strengthening parental control over education and reducing the public schools' ostensible "monopoly."

However, other commentators have deplored the trend toward providing more tax money for religious schools. U.S. Supreme Court Justice David H. Souter, in his dissent from the majority opinion in the Ohio case, wrote: "Whenever we remove a brick from the wall that was designed to separate religion and government, we increase the risk of religious strife and weaken the foundation of our democracy" (Rehnquist, 2002). Rev. Barry Lynn, head of Americans United for the Separation of Church and State, said of the ruling about the Ohio voucher law: "This is probably the worst church-state case in the last 50 years. It really brings a wrecking ball to a part of the wall separating church and state" (Frieden, 2002).

The likely effect on private schools of such court decisions may be estimated by our recognizing that in 2003–2004 there were 28,384 private schools across the nation—either secular or church-sponsored—that enrolled 5,122,772 students. Private-school students represented approximately 10 percent of the nation's total elementary and secondary population, with the percentage expected to rise if voucher programs are substantially expanded (NCES, 2006).

By 2006, millions of tax dollars were annually flowing into the coffers of parochial schools as a result of vouchers, tax credits, textbooks, special-education services, and busing arrangements. The greatest beneficiary of these funds was the Roman Catholic Church, which operated the largest network of private schools in the country. In 2003, over 2.6 million students—half of the nation's private-school enrollment—attended the church's 7,142 elementary schools and 1,376 high schools (USCCB, 2003). The fear that religious groups' political efforts could promote those groups' welfare at public expense was expressed by Justice Hugo Black in the U.S. Supreme Court case *Board of Education v. Allen*:

To authorize a State to tax its residents for . . . church purposes is to put the State squarely in the religious activities of certain religious groups that happen to be strong enough politically to write their own religious preferences and prejudices into the laws. (White, 1968)

However, supporters of greater parental choice in the selection of where children will be educated have often dismissed such complaints as the carping of secular idealists who refused to accept the reality of a nation in which the majority of taxpaying citizens held religious convictions that deserve to be honored through the schooling alternatives available for their children.

GUIDELINES FOR EDUCATORS

Rulings in court cases—and particularly decisions of the U.S. Supreme Court—can serve as the source of inferences about the legality of using tax money to pay the expenses of students enrolled in church-sponsored elementary and secondary schools.

First, the practice of giving public funds directly to private schools to pay for salaries or building construction and repair violates the U.S. Constitution's establishment clause. However, tax money can legally be accepted by private schools—including ones operated by religious groups—if parents become the intermediaries between a public school district and a private school. In effect, parents can receive public funds in the form of vouchers or tax credits to pay for their children's tuition, transportation, and learning supplies at church schools.

Second, students who attend church-sponsored schools have a right to ride public-school buses to and from school.

Third, parochial schools can be reimbursed for costs they incur while carrying out such state-mandated services as administering and scoring tests, so long as the tests have been constructed by state personnel and not by church/school staff members.

Fourth, parochial schools are entitled to receive free textbooks from public-school districts, with the religious-school officials deciding which books they want and with school-district personnel responsible for verifying that the chosen texts do not promote a religious mission.

Finally, a word of caution is warranted in applying these guidelines in particular school districts. Although these four rules-of-thumb derive from U.S. Supreme Court decisions and should therefore be applicable throughout the nation, any given case of church/state/school relationships is affected not only by the federal constitution but also by the constitution of the particular state in which the case is set. Thus, as shown in our earlier examples of vouchers in Colorado and Florida, the application of such guidelines is constrained by courts' interpretations of both federal and state constitutions.

Chapter 8

The Pledge of Allegiance

The issue addressed in this chapter concerns the question:

Should the word "God" be removed from the official pledge of allegiance to the flag of the United States of America?

HOW THE CONTROVERSY DEVELOPED

The September 8, 1892, issue of the Boston-based *Youth's Companion* magazine offered a pledge of fealty to the United States that children could recite on October 11 during the nationwide 400th anniversary celebration of Columbus's arrival in America. This initial version of "The Pledge to the Flag" read,

I pledge allegiance to my Flag, and to the Republic for which it stands: one Nation indivisible, with Liberty and Justice for all.

Because the pledge was published anonymously, the name of the exact author is a bit of a mystery. Perhaps the credit should be shared by Francis Bellamy (1855–1931) and James Upham. Bellamy had been a Baptist minister before he abandoned the pulpit because members of his congregation disliked his Christian-Socialist political convictions. In his sermons and lectures, he had advocated the creation of a socialist form of government that would include a planned economy with universal political, social, and economic equality. Upon leaving the ministry, he was hired in 1891 as an assistant to Daniel Ford, editor of *The Youth's Companion*.

Francis Bellamy also held another position that contributed to the first publication of the pledge. He was chairman of the national committee of state superintendents of education within the National Education Association, responsible for planning the nationwide Columbus Day activities. Bellamy intended the celebration to feature a flag-raising and flag-salute ceremony that included children reciting the newly created pledge.

James Upham was a member of *The Youth's Companion* staff, helping Bellamy plan the Columbus Day activities. So it is possible that Upham, rather than Bellamy, prepared the exact wording of the pledge as it first appeared in print.

Baer (1992) reports that Bellamy originally "considered placing the word, 'equality,' in his Pledge, but he knew that the state superintendents of education on his committee were against equality for women and African Americans," so he omitted "equality" in order to render the pledge acceptable to the committee members.

On Columbus Day, 1892, an estimated 12,000 pupils in the forty-four U.S. states repeated the pledge, thereby establishing a tradition in which the nation's school children declared their devotion to the flag and to the U.S. government, usually at the start of each school day.

The widespread willing adoption of the pledge was in keeping with the current unification period in American nation-building. The Civil War had settled the question of whether the United States would survive as one nation. As a next step, with the recent dramatic increase of immigration from Europe, officials sought to ensure the development of a unified citizenry by means of an Americanization process. Over the two decades 1880–1900, more than nine million immigrants entered the country, the largest number of any previous 20-year period. The newcomers contributed significantly to the 50 percent increase in the nation's population that rose from 50 million in 1880 to 76 million in 1900 (Growth of the nation, 2004). In the year 1890, 87 percent of immigrants were Europeans, mainly from northern and western Europe. Another 10 percent were from Canada and the remaining 3 percent from elsewhere.

The aim of the Americanization movement was to have the motley crowds of foreign immigrants abandon allegiance to "the old country" and be homogenized in the American "melting pot." The new arrivals would be obliged to speak the nation's dominant language (an emerging variety of English), to don the accouterments of an evolving American culture, and to place the welfare of the United States above that of all other nations. The pledge of allegiance was designed to foster that transformation.

Thus, the tradition of school children reciting the pledge was successfully carried from the 1890s to the present day, but not without changes occasioned by a succession of critical events.

During a National Flag Conference sponsored by the American Legion and the Daughters of the American Revolution in 1923/1924, the pledge's expression *my Flag* was expanded to *the Flag of the United States of America*. Bellamy objected to the revision, but his opinion was ignored (Baer, 1992).

The pledge remained an unofficial declaration of loyalty until the U.S. Congress on June 22, 1942, added it to the United States Flag Code. The following year the issue of whether students could be compelled to recite the pledge was settled when the U.S. Supreme Court ruled that children could not be forced to repeat the pledge as part of a school routine (Hall of Heroes, 2005).

The years 1950–1954 are sometimes referred to as "The McCarthy Era" in the history of the United States. During that period, a committee of the U.S. House of Representatives (the House Un-American Activities Committee) reached the height of its effort to expose a suspected Communist threat to the U.S. government and to the nation's general welfare. The chief architect of the committee's method of rooting communists out of the U.S. government and the nation's entertainment industry (primarily in Hollywood) was Joseph McCarthy, elected to the U.S. Senate by the citizens of Minnesota and appointed chairman of the Senate's equivalent of the House committee. In a 1950 speech, McCarthy told a West Virginia audience that "I have in my hand a list of 205 cases of individuals who appear to be either card-carrying members or certainly loyal to the Communist Party" (HUAC, 2005). He then spent the next four years in a widely publicized campaign to discover and prosecute communists.

To his supporters, he appeared as a dedicated patriot and guardian of genuine Americanism; to his detractors, as an irresponsible, self-seeking witch-hunter who was undermining the nation's traditions of civil liberties. (HUAC, 2005)

At the end of 1954, after McCarthy's tactics had far exceeded what fellow senators regarded as proper behavior, his colleagues voted 67-to-22 to censure him for "conduct contrary to Senatorial tradition." It was only the third time in the Senate's history that such an admonishment had been issued.

Although McCarthyism had now passed away, its residue would carry over to the pledge of allegiance. During the four years of "The Communist scare," the Catholic laymen's society, Knights of Columbus, had sponsored a successful campaign to insert the word *God* into the pledge of allegiance as a means of emphasizing the contrast between a religion-based America and an atheistic Soviet Union. On June 14 (Flag Day), 1954 U.S. President Dwight Eisenhower sanctioned the addition of the words "under God" to the pledge of allegiance. Consequently, the revised version of the oath would thenceforth read,

I pledge allegiance to the flag of the United States of America, and to the republic for which it stands: one nation under God, indivisible, with Liberty and Justice for all.

To make clear his purpose in ordering the change, the president explained,

In this way we are reaffirming the transcendence of religious faith in America's heritage and future; in this way we shall constantly strengthen those spiritual weapons which forever will be our country's most powerful resource in peace and war... From this day forward, the millions of our school children will daily proclaim in every city and town, every village and rural schoolhouse, the dedication of our Nation and our people to the Almighty. (Hall of Heroes, 2005; Lawmakers blast, 2002)

The Present-Day Debate

In the early years of the twenty-first century, public debate about the pledge was chiefly over the words "under God." The nature of the conflict was epitomized in a lawsuit that wended its way through the nation's court system.

The suit was filed in the U.S. District Court in Sacramento (California) in 2002 by a 50-year-old emergency-room physician, Michael A. Newdow. At the time, his daughter was enrolled as a kindergartener in the nearby Elk Grove Unified School District. Newdow charged in the complaint that the school district violated the U.S. Constitution by having the kindergarten teacher lead children each morning in reciting the version of the pledge of allegiance that included the words "under God." The charge was not directed solely at two school districts (Elk Gove, Sacramento) but also cited at the United States, the U.S. president, Congress, the State of California, and their officials. The reason the suit included both California and Elk Grove was that the kindergarten teacher, in conducting the oath recitation, was abiding by a California law that obliged public schools to conduct daily "patriotic exercises." Elk Grove complied with that law by requiring "Each elementary school class [to] recite the pledge of allegiance to the flag each day." The U.S. Congress became a defendant because Congress had voted "under God" into the pledge in 1954 and the U.S. president had endorsed that law.

When asked his purpose in filing such a suit, Newdow explained,

I brought this case because I am an atheist and this offends me, and I have the right to bring up my daughter without God being imposed into her life by her school teachers . . . I believe in the Constitution. The Constitution says that government isn't supposed to be infusing religion into our society, and so I asked to have that upheld. (Litigant explains, 2002)

Three facts that would significantly affect the final disposition of the case were

- Newdow had both a medical degree (University of California, Los Angeles, 1978) and a law degree (University of Michigan, 1988). Therefore, as a lawyer who had passed the California bar, he did not need to hire an attorney to prepare his briefs nor to present his arguments in court.
- Newdow and his daughter's mother, Sandra Banning, had never been married nor did they live together at the time the suit was filed.
- Under California law, Ms. Banning had the final say about their daughter's education. As a Christian, she did not object to including "under God" in the pledge.

Newdow's suit at the district-court level did not fare well. The judge threw the case out on the grounds that "the ceremonial reference to God in the pledge does not convey endorsement of particular religious beliefs."

In response, Newdow took his suit to the Ninth-Circuit Federal Court of Appeals in San Francisco, where a panel of three judges heard his arguments on June 25, 2002, and rendered a 2-to-1 split decision in his favor. The majority report held that the pledge of allegiance was unconstitutional because the oath could not legally be recited in schools since it included the words "under God." In support of that position, the majority justices—Alfred Goodwin and Stephen Reinhardt—cited an earlier U.S. Supreme Court ban on prayer in schools. They contended that a school district's policy directing students to utter the words "under God" as part of teacher-led daily recitals of an oath of allegiance to their country is a "religious act" and, consequently, an unlawful establishment of religion in violation of the U.S. Constitution's first amendment. Their ruling declared,

When school teachers lead a recitation of the Pledge of Allegiance according to school district policy, they present a message by the state endorsing not just religion generally, but a monotheistic religion organized "under God." While Newdow cannot expect the entire community surrounding his daughter to participate in, let alone agree with, his choice of atheism and his daughter's exposure to his views, he can expect to be free from the government's endorsing a particular view of religion and unconstitutionally indoctrinating his impressionable young daughter on a daily basis in that official view. The pledge to a nation "under God," with its imprimatur of governmental sanction, provides the message to Newdow's young daughter not only that non-believers, or believers in non-Judeo-Christian religions, are outsiders, but more specifically that her father's beliefs are those of an outsider, and necessarily inferior to what she is exposed to in the classroom. Just as the foundational principle of the Freedom of Speech Clause in the First Amendment [of the U.S. Constitution] tolerates unpopular and even despised ideas, see Cohen v. California, 403 U.S. 15 (1971), so does the principle underlying the Establishment Clause protect unpopular and despised minorities from government sponsored religious orthodoxy tied to government services. (Goodwin, 2002)

Whereas the third judge in the case, Ferdinand Fernandez, agreed with some parts of the decision, he disagreed with the overall sense of the ruling. He wrote that "under God" and the "In God We Trust" that appear on U.S. coins have "no tendency to establish religion in this country," except among people who "most fervently would like to drive all tincture of religion out of the public life of our polity." He added that under

Newdow's theory of our Constitution, accepted by my colleagues today, we will soon find ourselves prohibited from using our album of patriotic songs in many public settings. "God Bless America" and "America the Beautiful" will be gone for sure, and while use of the first and second stanzas of the Star Spangled Banner will still be permissible, we will be precluded from straying into the third. (Lawmakers blast, 2002)

The Ninth Circuit Court's decision was met in the nation's capital with a high level of outrage and blistering oratory from Republicans and Democrats alike. The Senate voted 99-0 and the House of Representatives 416–3 to reaffirm the words "under God" in the pledge. President George W. Bush called the court ruling "ridiculous," and an irate Senator Kit Bond (Missouri Republican) imagined that "Our Founding Fathers must be spinning in their graves. This is the worst kind of political correctness run amok. What's next? Will the courts now strip 'so help me God' from the pledge taken by new presidents?" An estimated 150 members of the House of Representatives gathered on the Capitol steps to repeat the pledge and sing "God Bless America" (Lawmakers blast, 2002; Reaves, 2002).

While the American Center for Law and Justice was calling the Ninth Circuit Court's ruling flagrantly wrong, the American Civil Liberties Union lauded the decision as "consistent with recent Supreme Court rulings invalidating prayer at school events" (Pew Forum, 2004).

As the next major step in the controversy, Elk Grove school officials appealed the Ninth-Circuit Court decision to the U.S. Supreme Court where the justices gave Newdow permission to personally present his own side of the conflict.

The charge against the atheist father in this new *Elk Grove v. Newdow* case was twofold:

(a) Michael Newdow lacked *standing*, meaning that he lacked the legal requirement for representing his daughter's interests in court—he did not have primary custody of the girl. Her mother, Sandra Banning, had such custody and had filed a brief with the Supreme Court expressing her desire that the daughter, now age 10, continue to recite the pledge in its "under God" form.

(b) The school district policy of having willing students recite the pledge with the words "one nation under God" is a patriotic exercise that is part of an unbroken history of official government acknowledgment of the role of religion in American life (Cassidy, 2004).

A variety of constituencies that were vitally concerned with the issues at hand lined up on each side of the conflict. The nature of the supporters is reflected in the following list compiled by The Pew Forum on Religion and Public Life (2004).

Constituencies that presented briefs in favor of the Elk Grove position included

American Jewish Congress

American Legion

Bipartisan Legal Advisory Group of the U.S. House of Representatives

Catholic League for Religious and Civil Rights; Thomas More Law Center

Center for Individual Freedom

Christian Legal Society et al.

Citizens United Foundation

Claremont Institute Center for Constitutional Jurisprudence

Common Good Foundation et al.

Focus on the Family, Family Research Council and Alliance Defense Fund

Grassfire.Net and Hundreds of Thousands of Americans

Institute in Basic Life Principles, Faith and Action, et al.

Liberty Counsel, WallBuilders, and William J. Federer

Knights of Columbus

National Education Association

National Jewish Commission on Law & Public Affairs

National Lawyers Association Foundation

National School Boards Association

Pacific Justice Institute

Pacific Research Institute and Pacific Legal Foundation

Rutherford Institute

United States Senate

Constituencies that submitted briefs in support of Michael Newdow's position were

American Atheists

American Humanist Association et al.

Americans United for Separation of Church and State

Anti-Defamation League

Associated Pantheist Groups

Atheist Law Center

Atheists and Other Freethinkers

Atheists for Human Rights

Buddhist Temples et al.

Church of Freethought

Council for Secular Humanism

Freedom From Religion Foundation, Inc.

Historians and Law Scholars

Religious Scholars and Theologians

Seattle Atheists et al.

United Fathers of America et al.

On March 24, 2004, Newdow was granted 30 minutes to argue his case before the Supreme Court. A goodly number of observers expected him to flounder in his exchanges with the eight justices. However, the outcome was quite the opposite. Witnesses called his performance a "virtuoso" display of "passion and flair." Kenneth Starr, the attorney representing Ms. Banning, told reporters that Newdow had been "superb." Linda Greenhouse, who covered the case for the *New York Times*, wrote that Newdow "managed a trick that far more experienced lawyers rarely accomplish: to bring the argument to a symmetrical and seemingly unhurried ending just as the red light comes on." Columnist William Safire observed in the *New York Times* that "the only thing this time-wasting pest Newdow has going for him is that he's right" (Block, 2004).

The Supreme Court decision in *Elk Grove v. Newdow* was announced on Flag Day, June 14, 2004. All eight justices concurred in the judgment. They had found in favor of Elk Grove and against Newdow. (The ninth justice, Antonin Scalia, had withdrawn earlier from the case because, prior to the oral arguments, he had spoken publicly in favor of the "under God" version of the pledge.) However, to the disappointment of many on both sides of the "under God" issue, the jurists had dodged the real question that was at stake. They had based their rejection of Newdow's case solely on the first of the two charges in the Elk Grove petition—the claim that Newdow lacked proper standing to bring his complaint to court. The justices ruled that he did not have the decision-making custody of his daughter, so he was not qualified to represent her welfare in a lawsuit. So it was that the central issue in the whole proceedings had been left untouched. The members of the Court were either unwilling or unable to reach a conclusion about whether "under God" in the pledge violated the establishment clause of the Constitution.

The confusion among the justices seemed to reflect the confusion within the U.S. public as a whole. Consider, for example, the different explanations that three of the justices offered in support of their vote. Chief Justice William Rehnquist said there was nothing really religious in the pledge. Justice Clarence Thomas proposed throwing out all laws bearing on the Constitution's establishment clause. And Justice Sandra Day O'Conner reasoned that the under-God version of the pledge was an acceptable form of "ceremonial deism" that was not a truly religious expression because it was very brief, recited by rote, did not refer to any particular religion, and did not assume the form of true worship or prayer (Pew Forum, 2004). All three justices thought that children being led by teachers to repeat the pledge was not a violation of the Constitution's first amendment.

Resolving the Issue

Public response to the Supreme Court's action varied. Many people thought the Court had done nothing to settle the issue of whether the "under God" form of the pledge was unconstitutional. Others appeared to believe that the Court ruling had resolved the issue. For example, Jay Sekulow, who had filed a friend-of-the-court brief on behalf of members of Congress and the Committee to Protect the Pledge, said,

By dismissing this case and removing the appeals court decision, the Supreme Court has removed a dark cloud that has been hanging over one of the nation's most important and cherished traditions—the ability of students across the nation to acknowledge the fact that our freedoms in this country come from God, not government. (Pew Forum, 2004)

In contrast, Doug Laycock, who had filed a brief for thirty-two Christian and Jewish clergy in support of the Ninth Circuit Court's original ruling, was not delighted with the justices' ducking the case's true issue. But he did concede that from the viewpoint of the justices' personal welfare, the Court's decision was "an entirely sensible resolution to a difficult question. For most justices, this result avoided a very difficult problem: it was politically impossible to strike down the pledge, and legally impossible to uphold it" (Pew Forum, 2004). Here again was the American dilemma. In the Constitution, government was portrayed as a secular institution whose domain did not overlap religion's domain. At the same time, a large majority of the citizens believed in an omnipotent God whose power competed with and dominated the power of government so that "under God," "in God we trust," and "I swear on the Bible" were appropriate expressions to include in public ceremonies.

As a result of the Supreme Court's failing to render a judgment about the substantive issue in *Elk Grove v. Newdow*, the advocates of "under God" won a victory. By default, God remained in the oath. But that victory was bound to be short-lived, for Newdow and his compatriots soon geared up for a renewed assault on the pledge. On January 3, 2005, Newdow, along with eight other plaintiffs who were either custodial parents or children in California public schools, filed a new lawsuit in the Sacramento federal court (*Newdow v. Congress*), averring that

atheistic (and other non-monotheistic) Americans have had their religious free-exercise rights abridged, since they cannot attend government meetings, attend public schools, or participate in other activities without being given the message that their religious beliefs are wrong. (Marus, 2005).

Newdow included codefendants in his suit to ensure that the plaintiffs had proper standing. Hence, the ploy the Supreme Court had used in 2004 to dismiss Newdow's earlier case would no longer be applicable.

At the same time, the emergency-room physician was not confining his legal efforts to the pledge of allegiance in schools. His campaign to insulate church from state had prompted him on December 17, 2004, to file a complaint in a Washington, DC, court, seeking to prevent the inclusion of Christian religious elements in President George W. Bush's inauguration ceremony in January—such elements as the president swearing his oath of office ("so help me God") with his hand on a Bible and a minister offering a prayer. The complaint charged that "It is an offense of the highest magnitude that the leader of our nation—while swearing to uphold the Constitution—publicly violates that very document upon taking his oath of office" (Ward, 2005). The judge in the case dismissed Newdow's complaint on the ground that Newdow had no legal basis for his claim because he could not prove that he would suffer any legal injury from a prayer offered at the ceremony (ADF attorneys, 2005).

Subsequent Events

The following incidents illustrate five types of reaction that appeared in the aftermath of the U.S. Supreme Court's rejecting Newdow's appeal: (a) readjusted pledge, (b) student refusal, (c) other reasons to object, (d) Congress shackling the courts, and (e) Newdow revisited.

Readjusted Pledge

Some educators have taken the initiative to revise the pledge in a manner intended to upset no one and satisfy all. Such was the aim of a guidance counselor at Everitt Middle School in Wheatridge (Colorado) when she recited the pledge over the school's intercommunication system and substituted "One nation, under your belief system" for "One nation, under God." Students and teachers alike were dismayed. The astonished school principal sent a letter of apology to parents, while the superintendent of schools said, "It was completely inappropriate. We completely believe any teacher or student has the right to follow their individual conscience; however, when leading children, you adhere to the Pledge of Allegiance" (Miller, 2005).

The apologetic counselor, noting that this particular April day was the sixth anniversary of the much-publicized shooting spree at nearby Columbine High School, said, "It was a spur-of-the-moment choice that I made, intended to acknowledge differences that lie in our society. It's not a reflection of the district, and it was not my intention to offend anyone, [but] rather to include everyone" (Miller, 2005).

Recalcitrant Students

The problem of students refusing to recite the pledge was the focus of a lawsuit filed against the Boynton Beach (Florida) school district in early 2006. When a 17-year-old boy twice refused to stand during the recitation of the pledge, his teacher publicly accused him of being "so ungrateful and so un-American." The American Civil Liberties Union then filed the suit on the student's behalf. As a result, the Boynton school district was obliged to pay the youth $32,500 and send a written reprimand to the teacher. The school board then issued a statement explaining that students did not have to recite the pledge or stand for it, and a letter from a parent was no longer needed to excuse a student from the pledge (School board, student, 2006).

Other Reasons to Object

Edward R. Myers, the father of two pupils in a Louden County (Virginia) elementary school, filed a lawsuit in which he challenged the school system's requiring children to recite the pledge of allegiance. Myers was a member of the Anabaptist Mennonite faith, a Christian sect, which condemns the mixture of church and state. In the late seventeenth-century, Mennonites emigrated from Central Europe to America to escape religious persecution for believing in the separation of church and state. The sect's Confession of Faith asserts that "the primary allegiance of all Christians is to Christ's kingdom, not the state or society.

Because their citizenship is in heaven, Christians are called to resist the idolatrous temptation to give to the state the devotion that is owed to God" (Williams, 2005).

Like other school districts throughout America, Louden County's public schools required

the daily recitation of the Pledge of Allegiance in each classroom . . . During such Pledge of Allegiance, students shall stand and recite the Pledge while facing the flag with their right hands over their hearts or in an appropriate salute if in uniform; however, no student shall be compelled to recite the Pledge if he, his parent, or legal guardian objects on religious, philosophical, or other grounds to his participating in this exercise. Students who are thus exempt from reciting the Pledge shall remain quietly standing or sitting at their desks while others recite the Pledge and shall make no display that disrupts or distracts others who are reciting the Pledge. School boards shall provide appropriate accommodations for students who are unable to comply with the procedures described herein due to disability. (Williams, 2005)

After the case of *Myers v. Louden County Public Schools* was argued in the U.S. Fourth District Court of Appeals, the three judges ruled in August 2005 that the pledge requirement did not violate the separation of church and state because it passed the Lemon test. In the jurists' opinion, asking children to recite the pledge "did not have a religious purpose or effect and did not create an excessive governmental entanglement with religion" and thereby was "not a religious exercise and did not threaten an establishment of religion" (Williams, 2005).

In announcing their decision, the judges were careful to point out the difference between *Myers v. Louden* and an earlier case, *West Virginia v. Barnette.* By permitting students to opt-out of reciting the pledge, the Louden requirement avoided the constitutional problems at issue in *West Virginia v. Barnette,* where a court struck down

a statute that mandated daily recitation of the pledge by school children and required expulsion of students who refused to participate. The court, explaining that 'no official, high or petty, can prescribe what shall be orthodox in politics, nationalism, religion, or other matters of opinion,' struck the statute as violating the free-speech clause of the [U.S. Constitution's] First Amendment. . . . Because the [Louden schools'] recitation statute permits students to opt-out, no concern regarding free speech arises. (Williams, 2005)

Congressional Effort to Shackle the Courts

During three congressional sessions—2002, 2004, 2005—a Republican congressman, Todd Akin of Missouri, sponsored a bill in the House of Representatives called the Pledge Protection Act. The purpose of the act was to prevent federal courts from issuing judgments about the constitutional status of the pledge of allegiance, particularly about the suitability of the "under God" phrase that had been added in 1954. Akin's bill required that "no court created by Act of Congress shall have any jurisdiction, and the Supreme Court shall have no appellate jurisdiction, to hear or decide any question pertaining to the interpretation of, or the validity under the Constitution of, the Pledge of Allegiance ... or its recitation" (U.S. House of Representatives, 2005).

Akin defended his proposed legislation by saying,

The words "under God" are not just there for window dressing, but they address a central aspect of what America is all about: We believe there is a God, even though we don't agree on exactly what his name is. God grants basic rights to people and government's job is to protect those rights. That's why that phrase in our pledge is in need of defense. (Tammeus, 2006).

In 2004, the Pledge Protection Act passed in the House of Representatives by a 247-to-173 margin and was sent to the Senate, where it quietly died. In 2005 Akin's bill was renewed in the House and again sent to the Senate, unlikely ever to come out of committee to face a Senate vote.

Members of the nation's legal community were appalled at the Pledge Protection Act, predicting that it would lead to chaos if put into effect. Legal experts did not deny that Article III of the U.S. Constitution did give Congress the right to limit the jurisdiction of the federal courts. However, the experts also warned that if the act passed, each of the states would need to settle pledge issues separately, potentially resulting in fifty different interpretations about whether God could remain in the pledge and under what circumstances. Furthermore, if anyone wished to appeal a state-court decision to a higher court, they would be stymied, because Akin's act would prevent the U.S. Supreme Court from hearing an appeal. Observers' also noted that the intended separation of the three branches of government—legislative, executive, and judicial—would be compromised if the Pledge Protection Act was voted into law. If Congress could ban federal courts from trying pledge cases, would that not encourage Congress to ban courts also from trying other types of cases whose outcome legislative-branch politicians wished to control?

In advocating passage of the protection bill, William J. Murray, chairman of the Religion Freedom Coalition that sought to keep "under God" in the pledge, said, "The courts don't interpret law anymore, they simply make law—that's the broad issue." Hence, according to Murray, the bill would "tell the federal courts that this [under God] issue is none of your business" (Tammeus, 2006).

In contrast, one legal analyst, Marci Hamilton, predicted that the Pledge Protection Act

is doomed to fail in the courts (for federal courts—least of all the Supreme Court—cannot be stripped of jurisdiction this way). Yet it also signals a larger failure on the part of institutions and persons [such as members of Congress] who should be upholding our system, not trying to undermine it. This is not the time to abandon liberty. (Hamilton, 2004)

Newdow Revisited

In September 2005, a decision was rendered in Michael Newdow's new attempt (*Newdow v. Congress*) to have "under God" removed from the pledge of allegiance. Lawrence K. Karlton, senior judge of the federal court of the eastern district of California, ruled that the words "under God" in the pledge as recited by pupils in Elk Grove (California) public schools did, indeed, violate the establishment clause of the U.S. Constitution. Karlton assumed that he was bound to follow the earlier Ninth District Court judgment that had been sidestepped by the U.S. Supreme Court in 2004 when the justices dismissed Newdow's plea on the ground that Newdow did not have the proper standing to represent his daughter in the case. In effect, since the Supreme Court had not ruled on the central issue in the earlier Newdow suit—the controversial phrase "under God"—Karlton felt obligated to honor the Ninth Court's original decision. Thus, the Elk Grove schools were again enjoined to cease using the "under God" version of the pledge (Karlton, 2005).

Observers hoped that Elk Grove officials would now appeal the ruling so the matter could again reach the U.S. Supreme Court where both sides in the debate hoped that this time the issue of "under God" would actually be resolved.

Conclusion

The event that established the pledge of allegiance as a lasting tradition in American public schools was the publication of an initial version of the oath in the September 8, 1892, issue of a magazine for young people, *The Youth's Companion*. On several occasions over the next century, minor revisions were wrought in the wording of the oath until, in 1954, the U.S. Congress voted to follow the words "one nation" with "under God." Prior to that event, the domains of *state* and *religion* had been kept separate. But with the addition of "under God," religion intruded into *state* and *public schools*.

God in public schools' pledge of allegiance

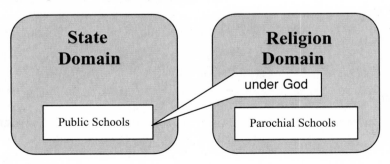

Across the ensuing half-century, questions were raised about whether the "under God" rendition of the oath violated the nation's constitution. The most publicized of the challenges to "under God" appeared in 2002–2004 as an atheist physician/lawyer took the matter to court.

The progress of the Newdow case from a federal district court, through an appeals court, and to the U.S. Supreme Court in 2004 illustrated the importance of power—and particularly the power of authority—in settling disputes over religion in the schools. The district court had rejected the atheist plaintiff's claim that "under God" violated the establishement clause of the U.S. Constitution's first amendment. But that decision was overturned by the appeals court, which enjoyed greater authority. Then, when the case arrived at the Supreme Court, with its highest level of official power, the appeals-court decision was essentially side-stepped.

In ruling on *Elk Grove v. Newdow,* justices of the Supreme Court faced a daunting, dangerous political task. Each justice appeared to be a religious person, and each was also an agent of the secular U.S. government, so their allegiance was divided between their religious faith and the Constitution, with its traditional separation of church and state. Furthermore, the constituencies lined up in support of "under God" were greater in membership and authority (Congress, the U.S. president) than those arrayed behind the atheist defendant, Newdow. There was also evidence that the majority of Americans saw themselves as Christians. Most of them would likely be affronted by attempts to oust God from the pledge, so that if the Court found in favor of Newdow, unwelcome political consequences could result. Census data showed that 85 percent of Americans identified themselves as Christians. In a 1998 survey, 53 percent of Americans considered religion very important in their lives, even though only about 20 percent actually went to church one or more times a week (How many people, 2004).

Thus, when the Supreme Court took the easy way out by charging that Newdow lacked standing rather than by issuing a judgment about whether "under God" was a religious expression, the justices were offering what Laycock had described as "an entirely sensible resolution to a difficult question. For most justices, this result avoided a very difficult problem: it was politically impossible to strike down the pledge, and legally impossible to uphold it" (Pew Forum, 2004).

In effect, the pledge controversy highlighted once again the conflict in American society between the citizenry's dominantly Christian tradition and people's commitment to a secular government that honors non-Christians' right to subscribe to other belief systems.

In a footnote to his ruling in *Newdow v. Congress,* District Judge Karlton drew attention to the difficult position that jurists in courts below the federal Supreme Court face as a result of the curious (some would call it "ridiculous") reasoning displayed by the Supreme Court justices—reasoning which contended that church and state should be separate but which, at the same time, allowed government bodies (such as Congress) to include Christian prayer and oaths in which office holders swore "by God." In his self-confessed confusion, Karlton wrote,

This court would be less than candid if it did not acknowledge that it is relieved that, by virtue of the disposition above [which depended on the Ninth Court's earlier decision], it need not attempt to apply the Supreme Court's recently articulated distinction between those governmental activities which endorse religion, and are thus prohibited, and those which acknowledge the Nation's asserted religious heritage, and thus are permitted. As last term's cases—McCreary County v. ACLU, 125 S.Ct. 2722, 2005 WL 1498988 (2005) and Van Orden v. Perry, 125 S.Ct. 2854, 2005 WL 1500276 (2005)—demonstrate, the distinction [that the Supreme Court offered] is utterly standardless, and ultimate resolution depends on the shifting, subjective sensibilities of any five members of the High Court, leaving those of us who work in the vineyard without guidance. Moreover, because the doctrine is inherently a boundaryless slippery slope, any conclusion might pass muster. It might be remembered that it was only a little more than one hundred ago that the Supreme Court of this nation declared without hesitation, after reviewing the history of religion in this country, that "this is a Christian nation." Church of the Holy Trinity v. United States, 143 U.S. 457, 471 (1892). As preposterous as it might seem, given the lack of boundaries, a case could be made for substituting "under Christ" for "under God" in the pledge, thus marginalizing not only atheists and agnostics, as the present form of the Pledge does, but also Jews, Muslims, Buddhists, Confucians, Sikhs, Hindus, and other religious adherents who not only are citizens of this nation, but in fact reside in this [Eastern California] judicial district. (Karlton, 2005)

GUIDELINES FOR EDUCATORS

As explained earlier, the Supreme Court justices in the 2004 case of *Elk Grove v. Newdow* avoided issuing a decision about whether or not the words "under God" could remain in the pledge of allegiance without violating the Constitution's establishment clause. That avoidance left school personnel in the awkward position of not knowing if students should include "under God" when they recited the pledge. As a result, school officials appeared to face three main options from which to choose.

• Schools in all sections of the nation could continue using the "under God" version that had been the standard form over the past half century, thereby ignoring the Ninth District Circuit Court's ruling that the words "under God" offended the Constitution, or

• Schools in all sections of the nation could honor the Ninth District Circuit Court's ruling and, therefore, revert to the original form of the pledge before "under God" was inserted during President Dwight D. Eisenhower's term of office, or

• Schools within the jurisdiction of the Ninth District Circuit Court could omit "under God" whereas schools in the rest of the nation could retain "under God."

So it was that educators were compelled to tolerate this currently indeterminate condition until a new case—perhaps *Newdow v. Congress*—reached the U.S. Supreme Court and the justices were actually willing to rule on the legality of "under God" in the pledge.

Chapter 9

Released Time and Clubs

The expression *released time* refers to a school's permitting students to use a portion of the school day for religious instruction. That portion may be spent either within the school or at a location away from the school.

A religious club is a student organization that conducts activities intended to promote a particular religious faith and to foster the welfare of the faith's adherents. The club's aims usually include the goal of attracting converts to the faith. Formal or informal instruction in the religion's doctrine and rituals is typically part of club activities.

The purpose of this chapter is to inspect issues relating to released time and religious clubs in order to answer two sets of questions:

- Can a school release students for part of the school day in order to receive instruction in a particular religion? If so, under what circumstances?
- Can public schools include religious clubs? If so, under what conditions?

HOW THE CONTROVERSY DEVELOPED

As noted in Chapter 2, from colonial times through the nineteenth century, public schools bore a strong Protestant-Christian cast. In school, students were obliged to pray, read, and recite passages of the Bible, and use textbooks that continually alluded to Judeo-Christian history and culture. Schools were also often used for separate Bible-study and prayer-meeting sessions. However, the great upsurge of immigration during the final decades of the nineteenth century and into the twentieth brought to America large numbers of non-Protestants and diverse Protestant denominations. As a result, the traditional religious features of public schools were questioned at an increasing rate by non-Protestant church groups, public-education officials, and advocates of the separation of church and state.

In 1914, a school superintendent in Gary (Indiana) introduced a released-time plan to cope with complaints that public schools taught the beliefs of a single religion. Under the plan, a period during the school day was set aside for students to study their own family's chosen faith under the tutelage of an expert in that faith who would visit the school. Thus, in schools that enrolled students from various religious denominations, different classrooms would be used by either clergy or lay persons to instruct pupils of the different faiths. As the decades advanced, a growing number of schools throughout the nation established those programs. In some schools, released-time sessions assumed the form of religious-club meetings.

Such programs continued without legal restrictions until the middle of the twentieth century when concerned citizens began filing lawsuits charging that released time for religious instruction and club activities violated the Constitution's ban on promoting religion in public schools. This chapter identifies those legal intrusions' effect on released time and religious clubs.

Released Time for Religious Instruction

When the initial released-time policy was introduced in the Gary (Indiana) public schools, 619 students received religious instruction during school hours. By 1947, nearly two million students in 2,200 communities were in released-time programs (Long, 2006). Thus, the released-time option rapidly became a popular method for engaging public-school students in religious instruction during school hours. How that method was defined during the mid-1900s can be explained by two court decisions—*McCollum v. Board of Education* and *Zorach v. Clauson*.

McCollum v. Board of Education

In the mid-1940s the program conducted by the Champaign County (Illinois) school system was challenged in a state court by a parent, Vashti McCollum, as a violation of the constitutional separation of church and state. In the Champaign schools, pupils received once-a-week religious instruction in school during class hours by teachers selected by church denominations and approved by local school officials.

After state courts decided in favor of the Champaign program, McCollum in 1948 appealed the ruling to the U.S. Supreme Court where the justices, in an 8-to-1 vote, reversed the lower courts' decision by declaring the policy unconstitutional. Justice Hugo Black, who penned the majority decision, wrote that "this is beyond all questions a utilization of the tax-established and tax-supported public school system to aid religious groups to spread their faith" because the religious instruction was offered in public-school classrooms, and secular teachers were assigned to keep track of which students attended. Furthermore, students who did not choose to receive religious instruction might suffer the potential shame of being cast as "heathens" or "outsiders" as they were sent to another place in the school building for "secular" studies (Long, 2006).

So the McCollum ruling established that released-time religious classes were not to be conducted on school premises, and secular teachers were not to be used as attendance monitors.

Zorach v. Clauson

In 1952, four years after the McCollum decision, the U.S. Supreme Court was called on to rule in *Zorach v. Clauson*. The issue at stake was a New York City law permitting public schools to release students during school hours, on written requests of their parents, to receive religious instruction taught by private groups at sites away from the school.

The Court's justices, by a 6-to-3 vote, defended New York's released-time statute. Justice William O. Douglas, writing for the majority, declared,

We [Americans] are a religious people whose institutions presuppose a Supreme Being. When the state encourages religious instruction or cooperates with religious authorities by adjusting the schedule of public events to sectarian needs, it follows the best of our traditions. For it then respects the religious nature of our people and accommodates the public service to their spiritual needs. To hold that it may not would be to find in the Constitution a requirement that the government show a callous indifference to religious groups. That would be preferring those who believe in no religion over those who do believe. (Douglas, 1952)

However, the three dissenting judges believed the New York law tended to "establish" religion by using the state's coercive power to promote a religious cause. Justice Robert H. Jackson, despite the fact that his own children attended private religious schools, wrote,

Stripped to its essentials, the [New York] plan has two stages: first, that the State compel each student to yield a large part of his time [that is intended] for public secular education; and, second, that some of [that time] be "released" to him on condition that he devote it to sectarian religious purposes. No one suggests that the Constitution would permit the State directly to require this "released" time to be spent "under the control of a duly constituted religious body." [But] this program accomplishes that forbidden result by indirection. The greater effectiveness of this system over voluntary attendance [at religious studies] after school hours is due to the truant officer who, if the youngster fails to go to the Church school, dogs him back to the public schoolroom. Here schooling is more or less suspended during the "released time" so the nonreligious attendants will not forge ahead of the churchgoing absentees. But it serves as a temporary jail for a pupil who will not go to Church . . . It is as unconstitutional, in my view, when exerted by indirection as when exercised forthrightly (Douglas, 1952)

Three features distinguished the Illinois case from the New York case. In Illinois, *McCollum v. Board of Education* had involved (a) state-approved religious instruction (b) in school (c) upon parental *consent*. On the other hand, New York's *Zorach v. Clauson* concerned students participating in (a) privately conducted religious instruction (2) off campus (3) upon parental *request*.

As a result of the 6-to-3 decision in *Zorach v. Clauson*, released time for religious instruction was accorded the U.S. Supreme Court's blessing, with the practice followed in numerous communities since that time.

Variations of released-time programs have appeared periodically. For instance, in mid-2006 the South Carolina legislature passed a law making classes in religion part of the public-school curriculum by awarding credit for off-campus Bible study. In effect, the new law went beyond the schools' existing released-time provision by giving high-school students credit toward graduation for church-sponsored religious classes that are not conducted on school property and not financed with tax dollars. The law specifies that participation in religious study must be voluntary, requested by a student's parents, not take more than 45 minutes each week away from school, and not be at a time that removes a student from a core academic course. The likelihood that such an option might be popular is suggested by attendance in existing released-time programs, such as one for elementary-school pupils in Clover (South Carolina), where 90 percent of children in grades 3 through 6 at Griggs Road and Bethany schools have participated in once-a-week Bible-study classes (Hirsch, 2006).

Religious Clubs

During the early 1980s, numbers of lower-level courts supported the right of school districts to prohibit student-led religious clubs on campus. School administrators then interpreted those decisions as meaning that if schools rejected religious clubs, they were simply enforcing the Constitution's separation of church and state. However, such perceptions would change when, in 1984, the U.S. Congress passed the Equal Access Act (EAA), primarily as a result of conservative Christians pressing for legislation that would permit the establishment of Bible-study, fellowship, and prayer clubs in public high schools. As a result of the act, the number of Christian Bible clubs rose from around 100 in 1980 to an estimated 15,000 by 1995 (Robinson, 2003b).

The act specified conditions under which religious clubs could be formed. First, a qualifying school must

- be a public secondary school,
- receive federal financial assistance, and
- have designated certain facilities as a limited open forum.

The phrase *limited open forum* refers to a school's allowing noncurriculum (outside the normal course of study) student groups to meet on school premises during noninstructional time. That time could be either after school or during a free-activity period within the school day.

Second, permission to conduct club activities on school property could be granted only if

- meetings were voluntary and student-initiated
- meetings were not sponsored by the school, government, or employees
- school employees attended meetings only as observers, not as participants
- group activities did not interfere with the orderly conduct of the school's educational program
- people from outside the school staff did not direct or regularly attend club activities

A school is providing a "limited open forum" if it permits such noncurriculum clubs as ones focusing on chess, skiing, stamp-collecting, folk-dancing, scuba-diving, environment-protection, and the like. If those sorts of groups are accepted, then religious clubs must be accepted as well. Schools are free to decide whether or not they will provide a "limited open forum." If they feel that having religious clubs use school facilities is undesirable, then no other kinds of clubs can meet on school property either. In effect, there will be no limited open forum.

In recent years, a growing number of gay and lesbian students have taken advantage of the Equal Access Act to organize their own clubs, a development that has distressed conservative religious groups that had originally urged Congress to pass the act.

Representative Club Programs

A variety of religious denominations—mainly Christian—have promoted high-school clubs both nationwide and internationally. The following are examples of four large-scale club efforts.

Student Venture is the senior- and junior-high-school outreach program of Campus Crusade for Christ, headquartered in Orlando (Florida). The endeavor is advertised as "a ministry of tens of thousands of students and 900 full-time staff and volunteers." *Student Venture* offers resources for students to conduct weekly meetings, discussion groups, focused one-to-one counseling, leadership training, conferences and retreats. In all these activities, students are encouraged to develop their Christian life. (Student *venture*, 2006)

Young Life operates out of Colorado Springs (Colorado) as "a non-profit, non-denominational Christian organization reaching out to teens with programs in more than 800 communities in the United States and Canada and more than forty-five countries overseas. More than 100,000 kids are involved in Young Life weekly, with more than 1 million kids participating in Young Life throughout the year." (About Young Life, 2006)

The aim of *Youth for Christ*, based in Denver (Colorado), is "to share the Good News about Jesus in a way that is relevant to [youth]." The organization lists "ministries in over

200 cities throughout the USA and over 100 countries around the world. The young people in every city and every country have needs that are somewhat unique to them. For that reason, local YFC ministries vary from location to location." *Youth for Christ* conducts two sets of programs titled *Campus Life* (for high-school students) and *Campus Life-M* (for middle-school and junior-high students). The high school version is designed "to help senior-high young people make good choices, establish a solid foundation for life, and positively impact their schools. Like every ministry of YFC, *Campus Life* seeks to engage these young people wherever they are found as life-long followers of Jesus Christ . . . A *Campus Life* club generally meets in various homes each week, hosted by students. In some cities, *Campus Life* may own a building they use to host club meetings, or have access to a school gym, cafeteria or classroom, or, less frequently, churches. (Youth for Christ, 2006)

The purpose of the Kansas-City-based *Fellowship of Christian Athletes* is advertised as that of "challenging coaches and athletes on the professional, college, high school, junior high, and youth levels to use the powerful medium of athletics to impact the world for Jesus Christ. FCA is the largest Christian sports organization in America. FCA focuses on serving local communities by equipping, empowering and encouraging people to make a difference for Christ." (About FCA, 2006)

Refining the Equal Access Act

Occasionally over the past two decades, the Equal Access Act's provisions have been challenged in courts, thereby yielding rulings that have not altered the act but have tested and refined ways the act can properly be applied under various circumstances. How this process has developed can be illustrated with a trio of court decisions.

Good News Club v. Milford Central School, 2001. After the U.S. Supreme Court outlawed mandatory prayer, Bible reading, and displays of the Ten Commandments in public schools, many people thought religious instruction had been entirely eliminated from schools. However, that view changed when the Court's ruling in *Good News Club v. Milford Central School* gave constitutional approval to religiously oriented clubs on public-school campuses.

A policy adopted by Milford (New York) Central School allowed community groups to use the school building during after-school hours for "(1) instruction in education, learning, or the arts and (2) social, civic, recreational, and entertainment uses pertaining to the community welfare" (Thomas, 2001). In 1996, the Rev. Stephen and Darleen Fournier, as sponsors of a Good News Club, applied to hold weekly after-school club meetings at the school. Their request was denied by school officials on the ground that permitting a religious club in a public school would violate the U.S. Constitution's establishment clause. The organizers of the national Good News Clubs responded to the denial by filing a lawsuit against the school, claiming that the Fourniers' free-speech rights had been breached.

Good News Clubs are a nationwide outreach program for children aged 5 to 12, developed by the Missouri-based Child Evangelism Fellowship to "evangelize boys and girls with the Gospel of the Lord Jesus Christ and establish... them in the Word of God and in a local church for Christian living." According to a vice president of the Fellowship, "The main thrust of the Good News Club is to help children understand that God loves them and cares about them" (Vaznis, 2005). The Child Evangelism Fellowship was reported to have had contact with 4.9 million children in 2004 (Abolish the U.S. Department, 2005).

In the Milford case, school officials decided that the proposed use of the school facilities (to sing songs, hear Bible lessons, memorize scripture, and pray) was religious worship prohibited by the school's community-use policy. Critics of Good News Clubs complained that "At weekly meetings, children are divided into groups of 'saved' and 'unsaved.' Children labeled 'unsaved,' who may be as young as 5 or 6, are pressured to make faith professions" (Supreme Court approves, 2001).

The district court that tried the case found in favor of the school district by ruling that "the Club's subject matter is religious in nature, not merely a discussion of secular matters from a religious perspective that [the Milford policy] otherwise permits" (Thomas, 2001). However, when the case was appealed to the U.S. Supreme Court, the justices, by a 6-to-3 margin, reversed the district court's judgment and decided, instead, that the Good News Club could meet in school because (a) club meetings would be held after the end of the school day, (b) the instructors were not the schools' regular teachers, (c) the children ranged in age from 5 to 12, and (d) the children had signed permission from their parents. Justice Clarence Thomas, who wrote the majority opinion, also used the freedom-of-speech clause of the Constitution's first amendment to defend the ruling. He declared,

[S]peech discussing otherwise permissible subjects cannot be excluded from a limited public forum on the ground that the subject is discussed from a religious viewpoint. Thus, we conclude that Milford's exclusion of the Club from use of the school... constitutes impermissible viewpoint discrimination. (Supreme Court approves, 2001)

In its decision, the Supreme Court thus established the principle that public schools may not exclude private religious groups from using classrooms for meetings immediately after the school day if those facilities are open to other community groups. But the majority decision did not go unchallenged. Justice William Souter, expressing the position of the three dissenting judges, wrote,

It is beyond question that Good News intends to use the public school premises not for mere discussion of a subject from a particular, Christian point of view, but for an evangelical service of worship, calling children to commit themselves in an act of Christian conversion. The majority avoids this reality only by resorting to the bland and general characterization of Good News's activity as "teaching of morals and character, from a religious standpoint." If the majority's statement ignores reality, as it surely does, then today's holding may be understood only in equally generic terms. Otherwise, indeed, this case would stand for the remarkable proposition that any public school opened for civic meetings must be opened for use as church, synagogue, or mosque. (Supreme Court approves, 2001)

While the high court's ruling encouraged religious clubs to use school facilities, it did not require all public schools to permit evangelistic groups to meet on school premises. School authorities could still ban all outside organizations from holding club activities in school settings.

The announcement of the Court's ruling was followed by a surge of religious groups applying to conduct club activities in schools. Over the four years following the 2001 decision, Good News Clubs in public schools had quintupled to 2,330 (Vaznis, 2005).

Prince v. Jacoby, 2003. After a court issues a judgment, new cases frequently arise to test or refine that judgment. An example of such an event is *Prince v. Jacoby.*

In 1997, Tausha Prince sought permission from the Bethel (Washington) School District to form a World Changers Bible Club at Spanaway Lake High School where Tausha was enrolled as a student. World Changers club members would be required to "Evangelize our campus for Jesus Christ" and to "teach students that Jesus Christ is the Answer to the confusion, pain and uncertainty this world offers" (Robinson, 2003b). Her request was rejected because officials said accepting the application would violate the U.S. Constitution's establishment clause that banned public school from promoting a religious cause.

When attorneys from evangelist Pat Robertson's American Center for Law and Justice took the issue to court on Tausha Prince's behalf, they argued that Bethel District officials, by refusing to accept World Changers, violated Tausha's constitutional free-speech rights and also breached provisions of the Equal Access Act. The district court that heard the case decided that the school district was correct in turning down the World Changers application. However, when that judgment was taken to the U.S. Ninth Circuit Court of Appeals, the ruling was overturned in a 2-to-1 decision that supported Tausha's cause.

The appeals-court majority opinion written Judge Kim M. Wardlaw stated that the Equal Access Act obligates schools to allow religious clubs to form and meet under the same terms as other noncurriculum-related clubs. Those terms included equal access to the school newspaper, bulletin boards, the public address system, and school-wide activities for clubs, such as an annual extracurricular group fair.

However, as the jurists' 2-to-1 vote shows, *Prince v. Jacoby* did not pass without opposition. Whereas Judge Marsha S. Berzon agreed with the majority decision that World Changers had the right to meet in the school, she disagreed about the Changers' right to use school supplies, audiovisual equipment, and school vehicles paid for out of public funds. Berzon acknowledged that the U.S. Supreme Court had earlier ruled that public funds could be used to pay secular expenses of private religious schools, and religious clubs at public universities had a right to use money raised from student fees. But she believed Wardlow stretched the law beyond those decisions by giving "religious clubs the right to use public money to fund religious activities—a violation that goes to the very heart of the Establishment Clause" (Dowling-Sendor, 2003).

A legal expert, Benjamin Dowling-Sendor, in his analysis of the appeals-court decision, wrote,

I agree with Judge Berzon's dissent about the right of World Changers to use school supplies, audiovisual equipment, and school vehicles. While the Free Speech Clause certainly gives religious clubs the right to meet on school grounds under the same terms and conditions as other noncurriculum-related clubs, I believe that free speech rights end, and Establishment Clause prohibitions begin, when it comes to spending public money to pay for religious activity. That's regardless of whether that activity comes in the classic form of church worship or in the more modern form of student evangelical activities in a high school. (Dowling-Sendor, 2003)

When the Bethel School District in 2003 asked the U.S. Supreme Court to review the circuit court's judgment, the Supreme Court justices declined to accept the case, thereby leaving the appeals-court decision to stand as a precedent for future religious-club cases.

Wigg v. Sioux Falls School District, 2004. Like *Prince v. Jacoby,* the Wigg case challenged jurists to interpret how the Equal Access Act and U.S. Constitution should apply to the conditions in a particular religious-club case.

Barbara Wigg, a teacher in Sioux Falls (South Dakota), requested permission to lead an after-school Good News Club at Anderson Elementary School where she taught during the school day. School-district officials rejected her request as a violation of the Constitution's establishment clause.

Wigg reacted to the school district's refusal by soliciting the aid of Liberty Counsel, a Florida-based conservative religious organization that sued the Sioux Falls School District on her behalf. In July 2003, the federal district court for South Dakota denied Wigg's motion that the school district allow her to participate in Good News Club meetings at Anderson Elementary. However, the court did order the school district to allow her to join Good News Club meetings at other schools in the district as a way of granting her free-speech rights. In addition, the court applied the Lemon test to determine if the school district had a legitimate fear of an establishment-clause violation. The jurists reasoned that when a teacher goes from teaching her class in a school to teaching religious doctrine to students in that same school, "[it] would appear to a reasonable adult observer that a child would view this as just another class at the end of the school day taught by a teacher that was there all day. A reasonable observer would consider this excessive government entanglement with religion. However, the court reached the opposite conclusion under the Lemon analysis when the teacher travels to another school to teach the Good News Club's religious message. Under those circumstances, the teacher— trading her teacher's badge for a visitor's badge—would avoid impermissible entanglement. As a result, the district court ruled that Ms. Wigg could participate in Good News Club activities at a school where she is not currently teaching" (Hutton, 2003).

When the school district objected to the ruling at the federal Eighth District Circuit Court of Appeals, the panel of three judges not only supported the lower court's allowing Wigg to conduct club meetings in other schools in Sioux Falls but also allowed her to direct meetings in her own school, Anderson Elementary. In the appeals court's opinion, Judge Lavinski R. Smith wrote,

[No] reasonable observer would perceive Wigg's private speech as a state endorsement of religion by Sioux Falls School District. SFSD's desire to avoid the appearance of endorsing religion does not transform Wigg's private religious speech into a state action in violation of the Establishment Clause. Even private speech occurring at school-related functions is constitutionally protected. . . .

Wigg seeks nothing more than to be treated like other private citizens who are allowed access to Club meetings. SFSD's policy permitting participation by all interested parties— so long as they are not district employees—in after-school, religious-based, non-school related activities violates that mandate of neutrality. As such, we affirm the district court's order allowing Wigg to participate in the Club at other SFSD school locations, but we reverse the court's decision prohibiting Wigg from participating at Anderson Elementary. (Smith, 2004)

A curious feature of the *Wigg v. Sioux Falls School District* appeals-court decision is that it conflicts with the ruling in *Good News Club v. Milford Central School* by permitting a public-school teacher to lead an after-school religious club, whether or not the club meets in the teacher's own school. That privilege was not allowed under the Supreme Court's opinion in *Milford*. Thus, school officials will continue to be confused by that discrepancy until a case focusing precisely on a teacher's acceptable role reaches the U.S. Supreme Court.

Illustrative Cases

The nature of religious-club issues that often arise in schools is suggested by the following three examples.

The Grand-County incident. Nuances of the issue of teachers leading religious clubs in their own schools confronted administrators of the Grand County (Utah) School District in 2006. The school board agreed that a Good News Club had a right to hold after-school meetings on the campus of Helen M. Knight Inter- mediate School. However, officials estimated that they would run afoul the U.S. Constitution's establishment clause if they allowed two regular teachers to serve as club instructors. The pair of sticking points in this case were (a) meetings of the district's thirty-two after-school clubs started at 3:30 PM, but the school's regular teachers remained on contract until 3:45 and (b) all club leaders received a $15 stipend per club meeting, with the stipends partly funded through public moneys.

The school board, for fear of violating the first amendment's separation of church and state, turned down the two teachers' request. The board president explained that if permission were granted, "we would be paying these teachers to teach religion. We cannot, under any circumstances, allow teachers to teach religion in the schools when public funds are involved" (Church, 2006).

In rebuttal, the teachers argued that their free-speech rights had been violated by the board decision. To press their claim, they contemplated filing a lawsuit with the help of evangelist Pat Robertson's Washington-based American Center for Law and Justice.

The Schenectady incident. Since 2003, a group of students at Schenectady (New York) High School had sought official recognition for their Christian Alliance club—recognition that would provide access to such facilities as the public address system, bulletin boards, and classroom space. However, the school's administrators continually denied the club's request, even though official recognition had been accorded other noncurricular clubs—Spectrum Gay/Straight Alliance, Amnesty International, and SOS (Save Our Sphere). To support their cause, members of the club in 2006 enlisted the aid of the Alliance Defense Fund's chief legal counsel who wrote to Schenectady High's administrators, stating that

Christian students on campus should not be treated as second-class citizens. The Supreme Court has affirmed in no uncertain terms the right of religious clubs to meet on public school campuses to the same extent as other kinds of clubs. The requirement of equal access means just that—equal. School officials do not have the prerogative to open up their facilities to any and every extra-curricular group and at the same time deny access to a Christian student group. (Alliance Defense Fund, 2006)

The Colleyville incident. In 2004, a mother in Grapevine (Texas), who wanted her middle-school children to find "like-minded" Christian friends, founded the Students Standing Strong club. However, she was frustrated by the Grapevine-Colleyville School District's unwillingness to afford SSS the same privileges as those accorded other noncurricular clubs. In April 2006, when SSS leaders were told they would have to rent the Colleyville Heritage High School gymnasium in order to hold an evening rally and would need to show $1 million insurance coverage, they solicited the help of Liberty Legal Institute, an organization that represents people in legal battles over religious freedom and first-amendment issues. As a result of a letter from Liberty Legal threatening the school district with litigation for charging a rental fee that was not assessed to other student-led clubs, the district permitted the rally without the fee or evidence of insurance.

A representative of Liberty Legal said he believed school officials had been influenced by complaints from parents who did not want a Christian club at the school. He added, "It's an ongoing malfunction of the school district. Under the law, [not wanting a Christian club] is not a legal justification. That's the whole point about equal access—it stands for all groups" (Brock, 2006).

Conclusion

As demonstrated in previous chapters and reinforced in Chapter 9, the judicial branch of the government has been more important than the legislative and executive branches in determining the role of religion in public schools. True, the legislators in Congress, by passing the Equal Access Act, established the basic rules for permitting religious clubs in schools, and those rules were endorsed by the executive branch when the nation's president signed the act into law. But how the act is actually applied in schools has been decided in federal courts—most significantly in the U.S. Supreme Court.

It is evident that not everyone has been happy about the way the Equal Access Act and the First Amendment's establishment and free-speech clauses have been interpreted in court decisions. U.S. Supreme Court rulings about released time and about clubs have exposed sharp—sometimes acerbic—differences of opinion among the justices. In both *Zorach v. Clauson* and *Good News Club v. Milford Central School* the vote was 6-to-3. And in both cases the Supreme Court overturned judgments of lower courts, thereby revealing additional disagreements among jurists.

Furthermore, conflicts of interpretation continue to appear as new episodes arise, as shown in (a) *Wigg v. Sioux Falls School District*, where an appeals court approved of teachers leading religious clubs in their own school (apparently contrary to the Supreme Court's *Milford* ruling), and (b) the Grand-County, Schenectady, and Colleyville incidents.

The constituencies—that is, the kinds of people—actively engaged in released-time and religious-club disputes appear to belong in three categories—(a) strong advocates of released time and clubs, (b) moderate advocates, and (c) strong opponents of released time and clubs.

- *Strong advocates.* The dominant proponents of religious clubs are evangelical Christian sects that sponsor clubs. Their intent is to recruit children and youths to the faith, with public schools regarded as fertile territory in that effort. They favor increasing the benefits allowed religious clubs, including the greater use of public moneys and facilities in support of club activities. Smaller in number, but with the same aims as evangelical Christians, are the organizers of Jewish and Islamic clubs (Vaznis, 2005).

- *Moderate advocates.* Less aggressive in their support of religious clubs are people who honor the Equal Access Act and thereby choose to allow the religious activities the act permits. Moderates prefer to abide by the rules and funding restrictions set by the U.S. Supreme Court in *Good News Club v. Milford Central School.* Members of traditional mainline Christian denominations—Episcopal, Presbyterian, Lutheran, Methodist, and the like—are apt to hold moderate views.

- *Strong opponents.* Groups that intensely object to released time and religious clubs include such fervent church/state separationists as secular humanists, agnostics, atheists, school officials who dread trouble over the Constitution's establishment clause, and members of mainline sects who fear that beliefs contrary to their own convictions will be spread through the public-school population via clubs operated by opposing sects.

In summary, the controversial, complex nature of released-time, as reviewed in this chapter. suggests that conflicts about religious clubs in public schools are far from over. More can be expected in the years ahead.

Religion in schools via clubs and released time

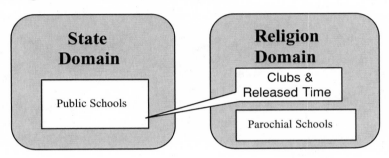

GUIDELINES FOR EDUCATORS

As the result of legislation and court decisions, advice about the legality of some aspects of released time and clubs can be offered with great confidence. However, advice about other aspects needs to be tentative and cautious.

First is the question of released time. It is clear that school districts can release students during school hours for religious instruction away from the campus, although districts are not required to do so. If a school does provide a released-time program, teachers and other staff members cannot encourage or force students to participate. School funds can never be used in any way to support a released-time program, nor can a religious group rent school facilities for instructional sessions.

Two disadvantages of released-time plans are that (a) students who choose not to attend sessions may feel isolated and ostracized, particularly if schoolmates taunt or criticize them, and (b) such programs remove study time from the school day and can disrupt classroom activities. In order to avoid such problems, school officials may decide not to institute released-time programs at all.

As a means of advertising either released-time programs or religious clubs,

students have the right to distribute religious literature to their schoolmates, subject to those reasonable time, place, and manner or other constitutionally-acceptable restrictions imposed on the distribution of all non-school literature. Thus, a school may confine distribution of all literature to a particular table at particular times. It may not single out religious literature for burdensome regulation. Outsiders may not be given access to the classroom to distribute religious or anti-religious literature. No court has yet considered whether, if all other community groups are permitted to distribute literature in common areas of public schools, religious groups must be allowed to do so on equal terms subject to reasonable time, place, and manner restrictions. (Religion in the public, 1995)

Because courts have declared that distributing free religious literature is a form of religious expression that should not be curtailed, students may pass out religious materials during non-instructional time. Expressing religious convictions may be restricted only when it disrupts the smooth conduct of the school's instructional program, not just because the content of the material may offend some members of the school community.

Next, consider the matter of religious clubs. Any school that permits noncurricular clubs (ones not associated with the school's regular study program) must accord religious groups the same privileges available to secular clubs. For example, in 2003 a federal appeals court ruled that the Punxsutawney (Pennsylvania) School District had erred in requiring a student religious club to meet before the regular school day rather than being allowed to meet during the period within the school day that was set aside for extracurricular activities (Slobodzian, 2003). In short, all clubs must be treated equally.

Each club must have equal access to meeting spaces, the PA system, school periodicals, bulletin board space, etc. School officials have the right to monitor meetings. Officials can require all clubs to follow a set of rules, including non-discrimination policies. However, a court has ruled that religious clubs can discriminate against persons of other faiths in their selection of officers. The school may limit meeting times and locations, but must apply rules equally to all groups. The school may prohibit people from the community from attending student clubs. However, they must apply this rule equally to all groups. (Robinson, 2003b)

Most rules governing the conduct of religious clubs in public schools seem clear. However, other rules can be confusing because (a) the majority opinion of one court may conflict with the majority opinion of another and (b) the dissenting opinions in nearly all court cases demonstrate that there remain serious questions about the logic employed by the jurists who have endorsed the majority views. By way of illustration, consider two instances mentioned earlier in this chapter. First, after the U.S. Supreme Court ruled in *Good News Clubs v. Milford* that a school's regular teachers should not serve as religious-club instructors, the Eighth District Court of Appeals allowed teachers to do so in *Wigg v. Sioux Falls School District*. Second, although the Equal Access Act requires that clubs be entirely financed by the religious groups themselves, the Ninth District Court of Appeals in *Prince v. Jacoby* allowed church clubs to fund religious activities out of tax funds. Such inconsistent rulings leave school officials in the uneasy position of not knowing the exact circumstances under which they may be violating the federal Constitution's establishment clause, freedom of religious choice, or freedom of speech.

Chapter 10

Symbols and Maxims

Religious symbols are visual or auditory representations associated with a religion.

Examples of visual symbols are the Judaic six-pointed Star of David, Christianity's Latin cross, the Islamic crescent moon and star, the Buddhist eight-spoked dharma wheel, the Cheyenne morning-star glyph, and Taoism's pictograph. A color can also serve as a religious symbol, as with Buddhism's saffron (yellow-orange) and Islam's green.

Auditory symbols are typically melodies or rhythm patterns associated with a faith, often as played on bells, chimes, drums, or stringed instruments. Frequently the symbol is a song or chant that may accompany a dance, as with the Hopi snake dance and Navajo arrow dance.

Religious maxims are sayings that proponents of a belief system revere as important, eternal truths. For instance, the following are maxims treasured by adherents of six major faiths.

The Hebrew Ten Commandments, as summarized in Chapter 1, enjoin the faithful to (1) Worship only the one true God, (2) respect one's parents, and (3) respect the Sabbath day by not working. In addition, people should not (4) use God's name in an insulting fashion, (5) worship idols, (6) kill, (7) steal, (8) commit adultery, (9) tell lies about others, or (10) yearn for anyone else's property or spouse.

The eight Christian beatitudes (Matthew 5, 1611) declare,

• Blessed are the poor in spirit: for theirs is the kingdom of heaven.

• Blessed are they that mourn: for they shall be comforted.

• Blessed are the meek: for they shall inherit the earth.

• Blessed are they which do hunger and thirst after righteousness: for they shall be filled.

- Blessed are the merciful: for they shall obtain mercy.
- Blessed are the pure in heart: for they shall see God.
- Blessed are the peacemakers: for they shall be called the children of God.
- Blessed are they which are persecuted for righteousness' sake: for theirs is the kingdom of heaven.
- Blessed are ye, when men shall revile you, and persecute you, and say all manner of evil against you falsely, for my sake. Rejoice, and be exceeding glad: for great is your rewarded in heaven.

From Islam's *Quran*, a verse about the world's final judgment day prophesies:

On that day [the unbelievers] shall be sternly thrown into the fire of Hell. But in fair gardens the righteous shall dwell in bliss, rejoicing in what their Lord will give them. Their Lord will shield them from the scourge of Hell. He will say: Eat and drink to your heart's content. This is the reward of your labors.

A Confucian analect says,

To put the world right in order, we must first put the nation in order. To put the nation in order, we must first put the family in order. To put the family in order, we must first cultivate our personal life—we must first set our hearts right.

A Taoist proverb advises,

There is no greater sin than yielding to desire; no greater misery than discontentment; no greater calamity than the propensity to acquire.

A Buddhist adage informs adherents,

Hatred never ceases in this world by hating, but by love. Overcome anger by love. Overcome evil by good. Overcome the miser by giving. Overcome the liar by truth.

The purpose of this chapter is to answer a pair of questions about symbols and maxims:

Can a particular faith's symbols or maxims be displayed in schools and in students' learning materials? If so, under what circumstances?

HOW THE CONTROVERSY DEVELOPED

Public schools during the nineteenth and early twentieth centuries, in keeping with their colonial Christian tradition often had Christian symbols or maxims on permanent display. Especially in a community of staunch, cohesive Christians, the ubiquitous picture of George Washington or Abraham Lincoln above the blackboard at the front of the classroom might be matched at the back of the room with a portrait of Jesus. The Savior would be depicted as a white man with a neatly trimmed mustache and beard, shoulder-length hair, and white robe—as some artist in the distant past envisioned the Christ's appearance and thus set the lasting stereotypical image of Jesus. A Christian cross might also be displayed on a wall beside such a passage from the Bible as the Ten Commandments, the Lord's Prayer, or the Apostles' Creed. And we might have seen reproductions of religious paintings, perhaps Da Vinci's *Last Supper* or Durer's *Praying Hands*.

But as the decades of the twentieth century advanced, pressure on school officials to abide by the constitutional separation of church and state encouraged them to eliminate enduring exhibits of Christian symbols and sayings from classrooms and corridors. Yet those Christian relics of the past did not entirely disappear from public schools. Rather, they assumed a different role. Christian regalia were no longer permanent fixtures, nor were they the only religious objects in classrooms. Instead, Christian symbols and maxims took their place beside those of other faiths in social-studies lessons designed to teach children about cultural diversity. Today, that remains the legitimate use of religious symbols and sayings in a public school. No religious symbols or adages can legally be on permanent display. Instead, they need to serve as temporary exhibits contributing their part to the study of comparative cultures.

However, this transition of Judeo-Christian symbols and adages—from their traditional place in public schools to their newly assigned role—has not gone uncontested. Nor has the expected place of other faiths' symbols and sayings been amicably accepted by all religious sects and all critics of public schools. To illustrate this somewhat uneasy state of affairs, we turn to a series of controversies about such matters, first addressing the issue of symbols and then considering maxims.

Conflicts over Religious Symbols

Present-day dilemmas over symbols in public schools can be illustrated with eight recent incidents.

Jesus in the Kindergarten

In 1999, a kindergartener in Baldwinsville (New York) Central School District submitted a poster he had created—with considerable help from his mother—to fulfill an assignment about ways to save the environment. His poster showed children holding hands around the world, people picking up garbage and recycling trash, and Jesus kneeling with hands stretched toward the sky. School administrators rejected the poster on the ground that it violated a district rule against depicting recognizable religious personalities, a rule designed to avoid violating the Constitution's ban on religion in public schools. In response to the rejection, the boy's parents filed a lawsuit against the school system, claiming that (a) the child's right to free expression had been breached and (b) school officials had displayed official discrimination against religion.

Over the next 7 years, the suit crawled through the court system. After a federal district court dismissed the case as without merit, the parents took it to the Second Circuit Court of Appeals where the judges ruled that (a) the school district's censoring the poster suggested an antireligious "viewpoint discrimination" on the part of school officials and (b) such a viewpoint could only be justified if officials showed that their censorship served an "overriding" government interest. Thus, the appeals court sent the case back to the district court "for further examination of whether there was discrimination and, if so, whether it might be justified, for example by the need to avoid the appearance of religious endorsement" (Greenhouse, 2006).

School district representatives were dissatisfied with the ruling and sought to have the U.S. Supreme Court settle the conflict between individuals' rights of religious expression and church/state separation in public schools. However, the Court in April 2006 refused to consider the case, thereby leaving the appeals-court ruling in place. Some observers interpreted the appeals-court decision to mean that "public schools cannot censor the religious viewpoints of students in class assignments" (U.S. Supreme Court, 2006). However, other observers disagreed, charging that (a) the matter had not been settled and (b) the Supreme Court's refusal was simply a way for the justices to dodge the knotty issue of church/state separation versus individuals' right of religious expression.

In the court hearings, the kindergartner's parents had been represented by Liberty Counsel, a conservative Christian legal organization that described itself on its Internet website as committed to "restoring the culture one case at a time" (Greenhouse, 2006).

Jesus in the Corridor

A lawyer for the American Civil Liberties Union (ACLU) in March 2006 asked the Harrison County (West Virginia) School Board to remove the picture of Jesus which, for the past 40 years, had been displayed in a hallway next to the main office in Bridgeport High School. The lawyer said, "I have absolute respect for anyone who looks at the painting for comfort. This is just a pure constitutional issue" of the separation of church and state. In support of his request, the attorney cited a 1994 Michigan case in which a court had ruled that a picture of Jesus hanging in the hallway of a Michigan school violated the U.S. Constitution's first amendment.

As a potential solution to the problem, the superintendent of schools suggested that the high school could start an "inspirational wall" on which pictures of other influential historical figures could be displayed, with the picture of Jesus moved to that wall. Christ's portrait would then not appear to be favoring Christianity over other faiths. However, an ACLU representative questioned the feasibility of such an attempt: "Will they allow Wiccans to put up their displays? Jews, Muslims, Buddhists, Hindus? I think they would run into some problems" (Anderson, 2006).

Rosary Beads and Crosses

During a violence-control training session for staff members of Chelan (Washington) High School, a police officer warned that Latino street-gang members often wore rosary beads around their neck. Thus, in an effort to curb gang activities, school officials altered the student dress code to prohibit the wearing of rosary beads. Immediately students, parents, and members of the clergy challenged the new rule, claiming that it violated students' religious rights. As a result of the furor, high-school officials not only rescinded the rosary rule but also dropped the existing ban on other symbols, including an owl, the numbers 13, 14, and 18, and several sports jerseys of famous players (Washington school, 2005).

Similar issues were at stake in an Alabama case that involved a sixth-grade girl being warned by the principal at Curry Middle School in Jasper that she could not wear an exposed Christian cross. Doing so would violate the Walker Country Schools' dress code that forbade students to wear any jewelry on the outside of their clothing. The American Center for Law and Justice heard of the incident and filed a lawsuit against the county school board, claiming that the ban on crosses offended both the federal and state constitutions by infringing on students' religious liberties. The attorney defending the school board said that he was not convinced that the American Center was correct in declaring that the dress code violated the constitutions, but he said the board would settle out of court in order to avoid the costs that a lengthy trial could entail. The board agreed to award the sixth-grader $30,000 for attorney and court fees, and the Center agreed to drop the federal suit against the board. School officials then announced that the district would not prevent any Walker County students from wearing jewelry with religious symbols or emblems outside their clothing (Leaming, 2000).

Head Scarves

In France in 2003, parliament passed a secularity law prohibiting students from wearing ostentatious religious symbols in public schools. The ban was aimed at preventing Muslim girls from dressing in an Islamic headscarf (*hijab*) in public schools. The law reflected the French populace's fear of the cultural and political influence of the nation's 5 million Muslims. But the law also necessarily prevented Christian students from continuing to wear large crosses and Jewish boys from donning a skull cap (*yarmulke*) (Thomas, 2006).

Recent years have also witnessed problems of Muslim headscarves in other European nations (Britain, Germany, Italy), but rarely have such problems risen in American schools. And the few that have occurred appeared only after the terrorist attacks on the New York Trade Center and Pentagon Building in 2003.

The following case illustrates how the United States government has responded to such incidents.

A sixth-grade girl at Benjamin Franklin Science Academy in Muskogee (Oklahoma) was suspended from school twice in 2004 for violating the school dress code by wearing a headscarf in class. The code prohibited the wearing of hats, bandanas, or jacket hoods inside the building. But the girl's parents contended that the headscarf was part of the Muslim dress code, so their child was obligated to wear it all of the time, both inside and outside the school. As a lawsuit was in the offing, the U.S. Department of Justice sent the school both an official complaint and a motion to intervene on the girl's behalf in the upcoming litigation. Federal officials cited the case as a violation of the 14th Amendment to the Constitution, which guarantees citizens equal protection under the law.

U.S. Assistant Attorney General Alexander Acosta said, "We certainly respect local school systems' authority to set dress standards, and otherwise regulate their students, but such rules cannot come at the cost of constitutional liberties. Religious discrimination has no place in American schools" (Iqbal, 2004).

Islamic leaders in the United States applauded the government's intervention and publicly chided France President Jacques Chirac for having sponsored the secularity law that banned Muslim head coverings in France's public schools.

Kirpans

School safety regulations collided with students' rights of religious expression at Woodlands High School in Greenburg (New York) when a ninth-grade honor student, Amandeep Singh, was suspended for eight days for carrying a knife in violation of the school's no-weapons policy. According to Sikh religious doctrine, all Sikh males, after their baptism in later childhood, are duty-bound to carry a ceremonial knife (*kirpan*) at all times. Amandeep, now age 15, had carried his kirpan since age 8 but had not been cited for a violation until ninth grade. The Washington-based Becket Fund for Religious Liberty sent lawyers to work out an agreement between the family and school. During negotiations, a member of the Singh family pointed out that (a) the boy's kirpan was hardly 3-inches long and no sharper than a butter knife and (b) "several other classroom items, including a steel ruler and a compass, were sharper and more lethal than the kirpan" (New York school, 2005).

The controversy was resolved when school officials allowed the student to carry a smaller kirpan that he could keep "securely fastened into a cloth pouch . . . worn under Amandeep's clothing so that it would not be visible" (New York school, 2005).

A similar case in Canada ended in March 2006 with the Canadian Supreme Court, in an 8-to-0 decision, striking down a Montreal school board's ban on Sikh students wearing ceremonial daggers. For the sake of public safety, the Court allowed some restrictions on kirpans worn in public, such as limiting their length and requiring that they be sheathed and worn underneath clothes. Justice Louise

Charron wrote in the judgment that "Religious tolerance is a very important value of Canadian society. A total prohibition against wearing kirpans to school undermines the value of this religious symbol and sends the message that some religious practices do not merit the same protection as others" (Brown, 2006). However, parents who had campaigned for heightened school safety measures were distressed. One mother asked, "As a parent, is the life and safety of a child more important than religious freedom? I think so" (Canada backs Sikh, 2006).

Wicca Pentagrams

The American Civil Liberties Union (ACLU) filed a lawsuit against Lincoln Park High School in Chicago on behalf of a senior honor student who had been disciplined for wearing a pentagram to school. The pentagram—a five-pointed star whose points touch a surrounding circle—is a Wicca symbol. The incident occurred after school authorities adopted a new dress code that not only outlawed pentagrams but also witches, white supremacists, Satanists, black nail polish, and vampire-style makeup. Under the ban, the accessories associated with such practices would be confiscated if worn to school, and the wearer would be suspended indefinitely. As a result of the lawsuit, the school agreed to permit pentagrams, recognizing them as symbols of Wicca, a neopagan religion based on the symbols, seasonal days of celebration, beliefs, and deities of ancient Celtic society. However, the school continued to ban white supremacists and Satanists, along with accessories associated with those belief systems.

Dreadlocks

When a family moved from California to Louisiana and the parents attempted to enroll their eight children in school, the children were turned away because their hairstyles—dreadlocks—and head coverings were not permitted under the Lafayette Parish schools' dress code. The parents, followers of the Rastafari[1] religion, were affronted by the decision, charging that the ban violated their religious rights. Rastafarians typically wear their hair long and plaited, frequently covered with a cap (called a *crown*) when in public.

An attorney from the American Civil Liberties Union who took the issue to federal court said, "If this were a Catholic child wanting to bring rosary beads to school, this never would have happened. In light of the many unfortunate incidents [of violence] that have happened in schools recently, many school officials have rushed to these sort of measures to prevent further misfortunes, but this is a clear case of the school and the superintendent going overboard" (Mack, 2000).

A stalemate over the conflict continued for eight months until a compromise was worked out between the family and the Lafayette school board. The children could keep their dreadlocks and head coverings so long as the hair and coverings could be inspected. A board member said, "It's foolish to try to fight it. The law

says they have the right to wear it. They told us there's no chance we can win"
(Mack, 2000).

Sacred American-Indian Cultures

Recent decades have found increasing public attention to controversies over
schools' use of American-Indian names and religious paraphernalia. The most
publicized conflict has focused on sports teams adopting nicknames, mascots,
logos, and symbols ostensibly drawn from Indian cultures. The practice of asso-
ciating athletic teams with Indian traditions began in the 1920s and continued to
expand into the 1950s when an estimated 3,000 schools throughout the country
identified their teams as Indians, Chiefs, Warriors, Braves, Seminoles, Apaches,
Savages, Redskins, and the like. Beginning in the 1960s, groups of Native Americans became more vocal in protesting that such practices denigrated Indians and
distorted Native Americans' real characteristics and life styles. The growing collection of Indian activists was particularly offended by the label *Redskins*, a term
that originated in the practice of some early white settlers stripping off the skin
of Indians they had slain and keeping the bloody skin as a trophy. Efforts to rid
schools of Indian symbols became particularly brisk after 1978 when Congress
passed the American Indian Religious Freedom Act.

Consider these examples of the growing trend during the 1980s and 1990s:

* The Minnesota State Board of Education declared "[t]he use of mascots, emblems, or
symbols depicting American Indian culture or race (is) unacceptable" and encouraged
all school districts to immediately remove such mascots and symbols.
* Public Schools in Wisconsin began changing their American-Indian-related sports team
logos, mascots, and nicknames.
* Siena College in New York dropped its "Indians" nickname to become the "Saints";
Saint Mary's College in Minnesota changed from "Red Men" to "Cardinals"; and Eastern
Michigan University moved from "Huron" to "Eagles."
* The Nebraska Commission on Indian Affairs asked twenty-seven public schools to stop
using American Indian mascots and nicknames.
* The Portland Oregonian newspaper no longer printed the word "Redskins" or similar
terms. Radio stations WASH and WTOP in Washington, DC, adopted similar policies.
* The National Congress of American Indians issued a resolution denouncing "the use of
any American Indian name or artifice associated with team mascots."
* The National Education Association passed a resolution denouncing ethnic related mascots, nicknames and symbols.
* St. John's University dropped "Redmen" in favor of "Redstorm."
* The American Jewish Committee announced that it deplored and opposed "the use of
racial or ethnic stereotypes in the names or titles of business, professional, sport, or their
public entitles when the affected group has not chosen the name itself." (*Chronology*,
2004)

The movement to eliminate Indian-related nicknames and symbols from school's athletic teams accelerated further in the early years of the twenty-first century, with more than 600 of the nation's schools replacing Indian imagery by 2002 (Coleman, 2002).

Among the Indians' complaints was the charge that their religious traditions were being ridiculed, such traditions as their venerating feathers, especially eagle feathers.

Both Bald and Golden Eagles (and their feathers) are highly revered and considered sacred within American Indian traditions, culture and religion. They are honored with great care and shown the deepest respect. They represent honesty, truth, majesty, strength, courage, wisdom, power, and freedom. As [eagles] roam the sky, they are believed to have a special connection to God. According to traditional American Indian beliefs, the Creator made all the birds of the sky when the World was new. Of all the birds, the Creator chose the Eagle to be the leader . . . the Master of the Sky. (Harris, 2006)

A Lakota Indian remarked that when "you sit down on Saturday afternoon and watch a Florida State [football] game, you see this Seminole come riding out with his blue eyes and his feathers. He charges across the field and throws a spear down. I'm thinking, 'That spear is sacred.' To see your culture and religion disrespected like that is not good" (Fightin' whites, 2002).

Although the debate over Indian imagery associated with school athletics has been the most publicized of the conflicts over Native American symbols, it has not been the only one. Another less frequent controversy has involved members of Christian faiths complaining that Indian symbols are permitted in public schools at the same time that the courts have banned the display of Christian imagery. For example, the creator of one Internet website complained that

Native American religious symbols such as the images of eagle feathers, symbols of clothing, song, dance and nicknames that refer to "Indians" are religious symbols . . . Native American religious images are permanently placed in 32 Kansas high schools and 33 middle schools. In many of these schools, Native American consultants, advisors, and spiritual people who believe in the sacredness of Native American cultural and religious traditions have been invited into classrooms . . . to teach about their cultural and religious beliefs and to guide students in their permanent use. Are Christians being given the opportunity to permanently display their religious symbols and teach students about Christianity? No, they are not. This is a violation of the fourteenth amendment providing equal protection under the law. Non-Indian religious symbols do not receive equal protection. (American Comments, 2006).

In sum, recent years have seen American Indians' religious rights being promoted as never before, with pressure from both private and government bodies urging respect for Native American belief systems and permitting permanent exhibits of Indian religious relics in public schools.

Conflicts over Religious Maxims

The most publicized debate over displays of religious sayings in public schools has concerned the biblical Ten Commandments as found in the Jewish Torah, which also serves as the first five books of the Christian Old Testament.

There are four versions of the Commandments—two in the book of Exodus (20:2–17, 34:12–26), one in Leviticus (19: 3–36), and one in Deuteronomy (5:6–21). The Chapter-20 rendition in Exodus is the one most commonly used. According to the Bible, the Commandments were cast by God onto a pair of stone tablets that Moses was ordered to take to the tribes of Israel during their escape from Egypt en route to the "promised land." The Commandments would thereafter serve as the primary guides to moral behavior for faithful Jews and Christians until the present day (but later supplemented—and in some Christians' minds *supplanted*—by Jesus' directive to treat other people as we ourselves wish to be treated).

Since slightly before the middle of the twentieth century, increasing debate has ensued over what role, if any, the Ten Commandments should assume in public schools. Two questions that have attracted particular attention are: Should any of the commandments affect school policies? Should the commandments be posted in schools as a moral compass for students and staff?

Commandments' Influence on School Policies

As explained earlier, the version of the commandments in Exodus, Chapter 20, includes three ways people should act and seven ways they should not act. People should (1) worship only the one true God, (2) respect one's parents, and (3) respect the Sabbath day by not working. People should not (4) use God's name in an insulting fashion, (5) worship idols, (6) kill, (7) steal, (8) commit adultery, (9) tell lies about others, or (10) yearn for anyone else's property or spouse. Four of these directives are specific to the Judeo-Christian religious tradition (worship the one true God, respect the Sabbath, never use God's name in vain, and avoid worshiping idols or "graven images"). The remaining six are precepts common to many other of the world's belief systems, both religious and secular. Thus, using the four specifically Judeo-Christian rules to influence public-school policies could be interpreted as violating the Constitution's establishment clause, whereas using the six general rules would not. Following this line of logic, we could understand why public prayer to "the one true God" would be judged an offense to the Constitution's separation of church and state. However, instances other than the prayer issue have posed knottier problems of church/state separation. Consider, for example, a case that came before the U.S. Supreme Court more than six decades ago. The question was not whether a religious symbol or maxim should be tolerated in a school but, rather, whether pupils' religious commitments could legally excuse them from a patriotic duty, that of expressing devotion for the United States government by saluting the American flag.

In 1935, 10-year-old Billy Gobitas and his sister, Lillian, were expelled from school in Minersville (Pennsylvania) for refusing to salute the flag. The children's parents, as dedicated Jehovah's Witnesses, approved of their children's act on the ground that the flag, in their view, was equivalent to a "graven image" so that saluting it would be the same as worshiping an idol and thus violate of one of the Ten Commandments. In response to his expulsion, Billy had written to school authorities:

Dear sirs, I do not salute the flag [not] because I do not love my country but [because] I love my country and I love God more and I must abide by His commandments. Your pupil, Billy Gobitas. (Herndon, 2004)

The Gobitas family filed a lawsuit—*Minersville School District v. Gobitis* (sic). When the case reached the U.S. Supreme Court in 1940, the justices ruled, in an 8-to-1 decision, that school authorities had acted properly in ousting the rebellious pair.

The Court held that the state's interest in "national cohesion" was "inferior to none in the hierarchy of legal values" and that national unity was "the basis of national security." The flag, the Court found, was an important symbol of national unity and could be a part of legislative initiatives designed "to promote in the minds of children who attend the common schools an attachment to the institutions of their country." (Goldman, 1940)

However, the single dissenting judge, Harlan Fiske Stone, warned that it was constitutionally dangerous to deny religious liberties to citizens, even if they were children: "The state cannot compel belief or the expression of it where the expression violates religious convictions" (Herndon, 2004).

Three years later the Court revisited the Gobitas case and overturned the earlier opinion. Justice Robert Jackson, who wrote the majority view, declared, "If there is any fixed star in our constitutional constellation, it is that no official, high or petty, can prescribe what will be orthodox in politics, nationalism, religion, or other matters of opinion or force citizens to confess by word or act of faith therein . . . Free public education, if faithful to the ideal of secular instruction and political neutrality, will not be partisan or enemy of any class, creed, party, or faction" (Herndon, 2004).

Therefore, under the revised judgment, school children could not be compelled to salute the flag if doing so conflicted with their religious or philosophical convictions. In short, the Ten Commandments ultimately trumped the Minersville schools' patriotism policy.

Posting the Commandments in Schools

The question of displaying the Ten Commandments (the Decalogue) on government property illustrates once again the courts' vacillating between a dedication to Christian tradition and the secular demands of the Constitution's establishment clause. This wavering from one side to the other can be illustrated with the following succession of events.

Stone v. Graham. In 1980 the U.S. Supreme Court entertained a case referred from the Kentucky Supreme Court where state judges had upheld a 1978 Kentucky statute requiring that the Ten Commandments be posted in every public-school classroom. Kentucky legislators, when voting for the bill, had asserted that the statute's purpose was secular—that of encouraging pupils to behave properly. In addition, the legislators buttressed their secularity claim by contending that the ten biblical precepts formed the foundation of American jurisprudence: "The secular application of the Ten Commandments is clearly seen in its adoption as the fundamental legal code of Western Civilization and the Common Law of the United States" (*Stone v. Graham*, 1980).

However, the U.S. Supreme Court, in a 5-to-4 vote, reversed the lower court's judgment by declaring that the statute failed all three of the Lemon-test criteria because it (a) had a religious—not a secular—purpose (b) promoted the Judeo-Christian tradition, and (c) unduly entangled the government with religion. Kentucky's attorneys argued that the postings did not violate the Constitution's establishment clause because the cost of the classroom plaques had been paid by voluntary contributions. Furthermore, students were not required to read the plaques, so reading the commandments would be a voluntary act at each individual's discretion. In reply, the Court deemed those reasons insufficient to overcome the appearance that schools were promoting a sacred religious text.

Congressional action. The year 1999 marked continuing efforts to display the commandments in schools in the wake of the Columbine High School shooting spree. The Jackson County (Kentucky) School Board allowed volunteers to post the Ten Commandments in all public-school classrooms in "an effort to start having good morals in school . . . because of all the violent issues that have been showing up." Protestant ministers in Adams County (Ohio) placed tablets containing the commandments in front of four high schools in an attempt to reverse "moral decline." The Glynn County (Georgia) School Board assigned their attorney to "come up with a display of non-religious documents" that would include the Ten Commandments, with the "non-religious" label intended as a ploy to circumvent the Constitution's establishment clause. In Val Verde (California), the school board initially approved the school superintendent's request to post the commandments in the district office, but the board withdrew its permission after being threatened with a lawsuit by the American Civil Liberties Union (Robinson, 1999).

In the nation's capital, the House of Representatives in 1999 appended a *Ten Commandments Defense Act* to a *Juvenile Justice Bill*. The act was passed by the House but died in the Senate. It suffered the same fate the next two years. When reintroduced in 2003, the act was endorsed by the House in a 248-180 roll call vote but again failed in the Senate. The intent of the act was to give states the option of deciding whether or not to permit displays of the Decalogue on public property, including schools.

The Alabama judiciary-building case. While occasional skirmishes over exhibiting the Ten Commandments in schools continued into the early years of the twenty-first century, those scuffles were dwarfed by battles over posting the Decalogue in other public places, such as courthouses and state capital buildings. The most widely publicized of those events was the Alabama judiciary-building case. In 2001, the chief justice of the Alabama Supreme Court, Roy Moore, installed in the state judiciary building's rotunda a 2.6-ton granite monument that featured the Ten Commandments. Critics charged that the exhibit violated the U.S. Constitution's establishment clause by supporting a key symbol of the Judeo-Christian tradition, and they filed a lawsuit to have the monument removed. In 2003 the case was tried at a federal district court, which ruled that the granite carving was an unconstitutional endorsement of religion and ordered Moore to take it out of the building. Moore refused and pled for his eight fellow state-supreme-court judges to support him, but the eight overruled his plea. A judicial ethics panel reviewed the matter and concluded that Moore had put himself above the law by "willfully and publicly" flouting the court order. The panel removed him from his position on the Alabama Supreme Court. When Moore appealed to the U.S. Supreme Court, the justices there refused to hear the case, thereby allowing his dismissal to stand (Ten Commandments judge, 2003).

Critics of the Court's refusal noted that a portrayal of "Moses the Lawgiver" holding the Ten Commandments appeared above the justices' bench in the U. S. Supreme Court, and a similar image of Moses was embossed on the bronze doors leading into the Court's main chamber. Moses' portrait was also one of twenty-three marble relief images of lawgivers above the gallery doors of the House of Representatives.

The Texas capital-grounds case. In contrast to court decisions in the Alabama judicial-building episode was the outcome of *Orden v. Perry*, a case in which a resident of Austin (Texas) filed a lawsuit to remove from the Texas capital-building grounds a 6-feet-high monolith containing the Ten Commandments. The monument was one of thirty-eight historical markers and stoneworks surrounding the building. It had been a gift from the Fraternal Order of Eagles as part of that organization's effort to reduce juvenile delinquency. The district court that heard the suit decided that the Eagles' monument did not contravene the Constitution's establishment clause and thereby the state, in exhibiting the Commandments, had a valid secular purpose—that of combating teenage misconduct: "A reasonable observer, mindful of history, purpose, and context, would not conclude that this passive monument conveyed the message that the State endorsed religion" (Rehnquist, 2005). An appeals court sustained the district court's ruling as did the U.S. Supreme Court, in a 5-to-4 decision. Surprisingly, on the day the Supreme Court announced the Texas judgment, it also issued a ruling in a Kentucky case, *McCreary County v. ACLU,* that struck down Ten Commandments displays inside two courthouses (Full 8th Circuit, 2005). The Supreme Court justices' main rationale was that a display was illegal if there was a religious purpose behind it. However, a Ten-Commandment exhibit would be acceptable if its primary purpose was to honor the nation's legal, rather than religious, traditions. And the justices added a second rather curious consideration—the location of a posting would also be significant, with wide open spaces more acceptable than schoolhouses filled with young students (Full 8th Circuit, 2005).

The Texas decision soon affected judgments in other parts of the nation. For example, in 2004 the American Civil Liberties Union had filed a lawsuit to have a Ten-Commandments tombstone-like monument taken out of Memorial Park in Plattsmouth (Nebraska). The stone plaque's Commandments were accompanied by two Jewish stars of David. A federal district court agreed with the ACLU and ordered the five-foot granite slab removed. Subsequently a three-judge panel of the U.S. Eighth Circuit Court of Appeals sustained the district court's ruling. However, following the U.S. Supreme Court judgment in the Texas case, the full membership of the Eighth Appeals Court, in an 11-to-2 decision, reversed their panel's earlier ruling and allowed the monument to stay put. To reach such a decision, the judges abandoned the Lemon test and, instead, based their ruling on historical precedent. In the Court's decision, Judge Pasco Bowman wrote,

The Plattsmouth monument makes passive and permissible use of the text of the Ten Commandments to acknowledge the role of religion in our nation's heritage. Similar references to and representations of the Ten Commandments on government property are replete throughout our country. Buildings housing the Library of Congress, the National Archives, the Department of Justice, the Court of Appeals and District Court for the District of Columbia, and the United States House of Representatives all include depictions of the Ten Commandments. (Full 8th Circuit, 2005)

Perhaps emboldened by the U.S. Supreme Court's Texas decision, Georgia lawmakers in April 2006 passed a law—by a 236-to-4 margin—permitting the posting of the Ten Commandments in such public places as courthouses. To give Commandment displays a secular cast, the law stipulated that courthouse exhibits of the ten moral directives would need to be accompanied by copies of the Mayflower Compact, Declaration of Independence, Magna Carta, lyrics of the national anthem, preamble to the state constitution, the Bill of Rights, and an image of Lady Justice (Full 8th Circuit, 2005). How that legislation might fare in the courts and how it might affect school officials' decisions about posting the Commandments would be unclear until someone filed a lawsuit that could end up in the U.S. Supreme Court.

Conclusion

This chapter's description of events suggests that judicial decisions about students and teachers' personal right to exhibit religious symbols and maxims have been clear and consistent. Students do have a right to wear religious regalia and include religious allusions in their assignments. Teachers do have a right to wear symbols of their faith—a Catholic cross, a Jewish *yarmulke*, a Muslim headscarf.

However, schools' official display of religious symbols and maxims has become a very confusing matter. Can a cross or a plaque containing the Ten Commandments be permanently displayed by itself in a school—or if not in the school building, at least on the campus? Or does the cross or plaque need to be exhibited along with other faiths' symbols, or perhaps accompanied by secular symbols or documents, in order to be acceptable? Or are only temporary displays permitted, and then only in connection with particular holidays or social-studies units? Are the rules governing symbols in schools the same as those governing symbols in other government-controlled settings? Well, we really don't know for sure.

Such puzzlements bring to the fore the question of what principles and lines of reasoning jurists and legislators have been using to guide their decisions about religious symbols and maxims in government institutions, and particularly in schools. Consider, for example, four competing principles on which such officials might base their decisions: (a) the strict separation of church and state as inferred from the Constitution's establishment clause, (b) the jurist's or legislator's own personal worldview—either religious or nonreligious, (c) what the majority of the American public seems to prefer, or (d) what the particular jurist's or legislator's political compatriots favor.

Religious symbols and maxims in schools

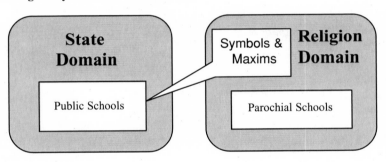

We might now use those four options to speculate about why such cases as the Texas capital grounds and the Nebraska park turned out as they did. If the judges who endorsed the majority opinion in those cases had based their decisions on the Jeffersonian "wall of separation" between church and state, then they would have ruled that the Ten Commandment displays were unconstitutional and should be removed, because the Commandments obviously valorize Judeo-Christian tradition. However, the judges discarded the Lemon test and argued that the exhibits simply reflected the nation's historical religious foundation. (However, the justices did not reach farther back in America's religious history to authorize the display of Indians' sacred relics.) Therefore, the principle on which the Texas and Nebraska majority decisions were founded was not the Constitution's establishment clause but something else—perhaps the jurists' own religious commitments, or what they thought the American public preferred, or what their own political pals favored, or a combination of all three. (Public preference was reflected in the Alabama case of the Ten Commandments monument in the rotunda of the state court building;

77 percent of the respondents in a public-opinion poll wanted the monument to remain in the building [Ten Commandments judge, 2003].)

Understanding the reasoning behind recent court decisions has been further complicated by justices' proposing that the location of a symbol or maxim is significant in determining if the display is constitutionally acceptable. They contended that placing the Commandments in an outdoor open space would be allowed, but not in a school building or courthouse.

In summary, supporters of the American court system often boast that the system ensures the "rule of law" in contrast to the rule of individuals' opinions and special interests. However, events chronicled in this chapter suggest that "rule-of-law" is an ideal, which, at least on some occasions, yields to legislators', government executives', or jurists' own religious values and their desire to be popular among their constituents and political comrades.

GUIDELINES FOR EDUCATORS

As noted above, laws about students' and teachers' rights to wear religious attire are far clearer than those bearing on schools displaying religious symbols and maxims.

Where schools have dress codes, students may still wear religious items such as pins and badges so long as those items represent sincere religious convictions. Schools may not discipline students for religious messages printed on tee shirts, nor may officials force a student to wear gym clothes that the youth's faith considers immodest.

Teachers may also wear religious symbols and attire, but they may not urge students to follow their example.

Schools cannot prohibit students from wearing religious symbols—beads, crosses, crescents—that ostensibly are associated with gang activities when there is no evidence that doing so disrupts the peaceful conduct of the learning program.

In contrast to the unambiguous statutes governing individuals' rights to display their religious affiliation, laws bearing on what government institutions—including public schools—can do about exhibiting religious symbols and maxims are often vague and contradictory. As noted above, the rationales on which jurists have based decisions in recent years have often seemed arbitrary and divorced from constitutional principles. Thus, school officials are left wondering about what religious displays they can legally permit. From a constitutional perspective, the safest practice would be to forbid all exhibits of a religious nature. But from a political perspective, such a practice could prove risky. In communities whose dominant political power is held by a vocal, widely supported religious sect, school officials may be subjected to strong social pressure to display a cross, a picture of Jesus or God, or the Ten Commandments. And by basing their rationale for their policy on such arguments as "the nation's religious heritage" rather than the Constitution, officials may successfully defend such practice—as did the justices in the Texas and Nebraska lawsuits.

Chapter 11

Sexual Matters

In the realm of church/state/school relationships, two of the most divisive issues in recent times have concerned the nature of sex education and the recognition of gay/lesbian life styles. Thus, the two sets of questions on which this chapter focuses are:

What should be the purpose and content of sex education in public schools? From what sources should the goals and substance of sex education be drawn? Who should do the teaching?

What, if anything, should be taught in public schools about types of sexual preferences (heterosexual, homosexual, bisexual, transsexual, asexual)? What should be the purpose of such instruction? Who should do the teaching?

HOW THE CONTROVERSY DEVELOPED

Prior to the twentieth century, teaching the young about sexual matters had no place in public schools. Instructing youths in "the facts of life" was a family responsibility, assigned primarily to parents, sometimes with the aid and advice of the clergy—a minister, priest, or rabbi. In practice, however, parents often avoided the topic of sex out of their embarrassment or lack of knowing how and when to approach the topic. Therefore, much of youngsters' sexual knowledge came from siblings, peers, or older youths and adults who sought to engage the young in sexual activities. Pornography and bawdy songs also contributed to youths' views of what sex was all about. The result was often a distorted understanding of the biological, social, moral, and emotional features of human sexuality. Or, for children who were shielded from such sources, the result was simply a void—little or no knowledge about sexual behavior and its potential consequences.

Jeffrey Moran, in his chronicle of formal sex education in public schools (*Teaching Sex: The Shaping of Adolescence in the 20th Century*), traces the beginning of planned sex education to Chicago, the site of the nation's first formal sex hygiene program that was

compelled in part by the city's rampant venereal disease problem, thriving red light districts, and an increasingly permissive sexual culture. When Superintendent Ella Flagg Young led the effort to implement this program in 1913, she encountered breathtaking resistance among local politicians—in a battle that would presage many others to come. (Blount, 2003)

As more schools adopted sex education programs over the next four decades, they sought to sanitize the erotic aspects of sex behavior by giving instruction a "scientific" flavor. Biological processes were described in technical terms accompanied by depersonalized diagrams, resulting in lessons "too boring to be suggestive" (Moran, 2000, p. 49).

Soon public willingness to openly discuss sexual issues was expanded by the publication of such studies as Alfred Kinsey's *Sexual Behavior in the Human male* in 1948 and *Sexual Behavior in the Human Female* in 1953. As sexual mores grew more open, high schools in their life-adjustment classes increasingly added topics about dating, choosing a mate, parenting, and avoiding delinquent behavior.

The social revolution in youth culture during the 1960s further liberalized sexual behavior and its discussion. One indicator of this change was the founding of the Sexuality Information and Education Council of the United States (SIECUS) by Dr. Mary Calderone. SIECUS advocated a scientific approach to such topics as reproduction, responsible sex, and "sexuality as a healthy entity" (Moran, 2000, p. 162). However, a variety of conservative church groups—representing the Religious Right—were appalled by SIECUS and succeeded in preventing the introduction of its program into many conservative communities. But such events as the appearance and rapid spread of AIDS (acquired immune deficiency syndrome) in the final decades of the twentieth century would heighten popular support for comprehensive sex education in schools.

During the early years of the twenty-first century, the level of conflict over sex instruction increased, particularly as a result of conservative religious groups strongly influencing the policies of the Republican administration of President George W. Bush. "One could argue that activists—with an interest in sexual morality—fight over the public schools because they know that is where they can seem to make an impact on society's sexual standards" (Moran, 2000).

The nature of current conflicts over the sex education in schools is described in the following pages under the headings: (a) types of sex-education programs, (b) the contending constituencies, and (c) sexual orientation and preference.

Types of Sex-Education Programs

For convenience of discussion, sex-education programs can be divided into three general types—abstinence, abstinence-plus, and comprehensive. Each type can subsume subtypes.

Abstinence-Only

The typical chastity or abstinence sex-education program urges students to wait until they are married before they engage in sexual intercourse. Some advocates of abstinence include self-stimulation (masturbation) among the sexual activities to be avoided, whereas others would permit it.

In Catholic moral theology, there are two degrees of sin, with *mortal sin* more serious than *venial sin*. Mortal sin is an offense against God that meets three conditions: the offense must be about a "grave matter," must be committed with full knowledge that it is a sin, and must be committed intentionally. "Grave matters" include such acts as murder, perjury, adultery, rape, slander, and idolatry. Venial sin is an offense that meets at least one of three conditions: it concerns only a minor matter, is committed without full knowledge that it is a sin, or is not committed deliberately. Examples of venial sin are idle gossip and momentary jealousy. When a priest, Father Mateo, was asked if masturbation is a mortal or venial sin, he replied that it is "a mortal sin because it negates the whole purpose of one of our most sacred powers, the power to fashion family and procreate human life" (Mateo, 1992). Hence, Catholic youths who accept such an interpretation have reason to feel they will pay a heavy penalty for self-stimulation.

During the past quarter century, the abstinence movement has profited from laws that furnish federal funds for such programs. In 1981, Congress passed the Adolescent Family Life Act, also known as the "chastity law," which paid for school sex education that promoted student "self-discipline and other prudent approaches" to adolescent sex. Applications to create such programs poured in, and federal dollars poured out to churches and religious conservatives nationwide.

However, programs sponsored by church groups suffered a minor setback in 1991 when the U.S. Supreme Court declared unconstitutional any programs that included evidence of religious involvement, such evidence as the mention of God or "the suggestion that students take Christ on a date as chaperone" (Planned Parenthood, 2005).

In 1996, Congress attached a rider to a welfare bill that increased chastity programs by providing funds for abstinence sex education. "Since the inception of the abstinence-only movement, approximately $135 million a year, totaling nearly $1 billion, has been spent on programs whose only purpose is to teach the social, psychological, and health benefits that might be gained by abstaining from sexual activity" (Planned Parenthood, 2005).

Abstinence-only sex education spread rapidly between 1999 and 2005, reaching several million children ages 9–18 in 100 federal chastity programs. There has been no controversy about whether chastity is the safest way to avoid pregnancy, sexually transmitted diseases (STD), and the human immunodeficiency virus (HIV). Even the fiercest opponents of abstinence-only agree that chastity works. However, they also cite a host of evidence showing that many youths engage in a variety of sexual behaviors in spite of being told to abstain until marriage. Thus, according to critics, what sex education programs also need is information about ways teenagers can protect themselves if they do have sexual encounters.

Two features of chastity-only programs that have come under fire are (a) their effectiveness in preventing students from intimate sexual acts until marriage and (b) the accuracy of the information youths are given.

Effectiveness of Abstinence-only. In chastity programs, teenagers are often pressed to pledge that they will remain virgins until wed. However, research has shown that as many as 88 percent who pledged virginity in middle school and high school will still engage in premarital sex. The students who break this pledge are less likely to use contraception at first intercourse, and they have similar rates of sexually transmitted infections as nonpledgers. Evidence suggests that students in comprehensive sex-education classes do not engage in sexual activity more often or earlier than those in abstinence-only classes, but those in comprehensive programs use contraception and practice safer sex more consistently when they do become sexually active (Bearman & Brueckner, 2001; Walters, 2005).

Even when youths avoid genital intercourse, they still may try other sorts of sexual activity. For example, a study published in 2005 revealed that slightly over half of Americans ages 15–19 had engaged in oral sex, with females and males reporting similar levels of experience. The incidence rose to 70 percent by age 19. Nearly 25 percent of virgin teens reported having tried oral sex, apparently unaware that oral sex has been associated in clinical studies with gonorrhea, syphilis, herpes, and the human papillomavirus that is linked to cervical cancer.

A pediatric professor explained that

many teenagers have fully accepted the idea that postponing intercourse is a good thing to do. When they weigh the advantages and disadvantages of intercourse versus other forms of sex, they decide that they are far more at risk with intercourse, because of possible pregnancy and the greater risk of infection. Teens also consider oral sex more acceptable in their peer group than vaginal sex ... Maybe we need to do a better job of showing them they need to use condoms. (Stepp, 2005)

Accuracy of information. In 2004, Congressman Henry Waxman issued a report showing that two-thirds government-funded abstinence-only programs offered misleading or inaccurate information about abortion, contraception, genetics, and sexually transmitted infections. The researchers analyzed the thirteen most popular abstinence curricula and concluded that eleven of them—which were used by sixty-nine organizations in twenty-five states—included unproved claims, subjective conclusions, or outright falsehoods regarding reproductive health, gender traits, and when life begins. For example, one program was wrong in stating that "Tubal and cervical pregnancies are increased following abortions." Another taught that among couples who used condoms, 14 percent of the women became pregnant within a year, whereas the correct figure was 2 percent. A third program asserted that that HIV could be transmitted through tears and sweat, but the U.S. Centers for Disease Control and Prevention reported that HIV is only transmissible through blood, semen, and vaginal secretions (Connolly, 2004; Planned Parenthood, 2005).

The Waxman views were contested by such groups as the National Heritage Foundation—a Washington, DC, think tank whose mission has been to "formulate and promote conservative public policies based on the principles of free enterprise, limited government, individual freedom, traditional American values, and a strong national defense." The Heritage reaction to Waxman charged that his report contained errors and failed to recognize that a higher percentage of sexually active teens were more prone to depression and suicide than were sexually inactive adolescents (Pardue, 2004).

Abstinence-Plus

Sex-education curricula that stress abstinence, but also give minor attention to other preventive measures, are known as *abstinence-plus* programs.

In 2006, Wisconsin Governor Jim Doyle signed into law the requirement that sex-education teachers in the state's public schools emphasize abstinence as the best way for students to foster their own and others' welfare. Thereby, Wisconsin joined twenty-one other states in stressing the desirability of chastity, yet allowing some mention of contraceptive devices. A legislator who had sponsored the Wisconsin bill praised the governor's action and added, "Rather than teaching that condoms and birth-control pills are acceptable modes of behavior, students will be taught they're not safe, acceptable or healthy, and what is acceptable is abstinence" (Foley, 2006b).

A critic of the Wisconsin bill charged that the statute was a "really incomplete and shortsighted look at a problem, but the blame falls squarely on the Republicans in the legislature. They ignored the overwhelming public testimony, support, and expert information about the importance of comprehensive sex education that talks about abstinence as well as contraceptive use. Abstinence is an important part but it is not the only part" (Foley, 2006b).

Comprehensive

The label *comprehensive* is applied to sex-education programs that inspect many facets of sexual behavior that affect individuals' well-being and the interests of society in general. The following line of reasoning from the Planned Parenthood organization is typical of the arguments that proponents of comprehensive sex education adduce in support of their cause.

The U.S. has the highest rate of teen pregnancy in the developed world, and American adolescents are contracting HIV faster than almost any other demographic group. The teen pregnancy rate in the U.S. is at least twice that in Canada, England, France, and Sweden, and 10 times that in the Netherlands. Experts cite restrictions on teens' access to comprehensive sexuality education, contraception, and condoms in the U.S., along with the widespread American attitude that a healthy adolescence should exclude sex. By contrast, the "European approach to teenage sexual activity, expressed in the form of widespread provision of confidential and accessible contraceptive services to adolescents, is . . . a central factor in explaining the more rapid declines in teenage childbearing in northern and western European countries." California, the only state that has not accepted federal abstinence-only money, has seen declines in teenage pregnancy similar to those seen in European countries. Over the last decade, the teenage pregnancy rate in California has dropped more than 40%. (Planned Parenthood, 2005)

Sex-education programs that subscribe to a comprehensive approach are not all alike. Their components can differ from one school system to another. What they do share in common is their attention to a variety of safe-sex practices beyond abstinence. For an impression of the diversity of topics that comprehensive programs may include, consider the following sampling of items from the SIECUS plan.

SIECUS guidelines. The Sexuality Information and Education Council of the United States (SIECUS) has distributed the organization's set of *Guidelines for Comprehensive Sexuality Education* to more than 100,000 individuals and groups throughout the nation. The guidelines' third edition provides thirty-nine topics that include around 800 *developmental messages* for four age groups—middle childhood (ages 5–8), preadolescence (9–12), early adolescence (12–15), adolescence (15–18). The messages are "brief statements that contain the specific information young people need to learn about each topic" (Guidelines, 2004, p. 17).

The SIECUS plan was originally developed by a task force of twenty professionals in the fields of medicine, education, sexuality, and youth services representing such organizations as the American Medical Association, the March of Dimes Birth Defects Foundation, the Planned Parenthood Federation of America, the National Education Association, the American Social Health Association, the U.S. Centers for Disease Control, and the National School Boards Association.

The guidelines' thirty-nine topics are arranged in groups of six or seven under six *concepts*—human development, relationships, personal skills, sexual behavior, sexual health, and society-and-culture. The diversity of topics can be suggested by these ten examples[1]:

- Reproduction and sexual anatomy and physiology
- Sexual orientation [heterosexual, homosexual, bisexual]
- Love
- Romantic relationships and dating
- Sexual abstinence
- Decision making

- Sexuality and the Law
- Abortion
- Sexual dysfunction
- HIV and AIDS

The nature of the developmental messages subsumed under topics is illustrated by the following eight from among the guidelines' 800. Messages define the focus of sex-education lessons.
For ages 9–12:

- Children dealing with [their parents'] separation or divorce may need to talk with an adult about their feelings.
- [The term] *sexual orientation* refers to a person's physical and/or romantic attraction to an individual of the same and/or different gender.
- To make a good decision one must consider all of the possible consequences, good and bad, and choose the action that one believes will have the best outcome.
- Masturbation does not cause physical or mental harm.
- Pregnancy can happen anytime a girl/woman has unprotected vaginal intercourse with a boy/man.
- Some religions and cultures teach that contraception is acceptable while others do not approve of using contraception.
- STDs (sexually transmitted diseases) include such diseases as gonorrhea, syphilis, HIV infection, Chlamydia, genital warts, and herpes.
- Families might need outside help to deal with problems involving alcohol, drugs, money, violence, health, and abuse.

The SIECUS topics and messages are founded on a set of nineteen convictions about values, such as

- Sexuality is a natural and healthy part of living.
- Families should provide children's first education about sexuality.
- Young people explore their sexuality as a natural process in achieving sexual maturity.
- Abstaining from sexual intercourse is the most effective way of preventing pregnancy and STD/HIV.
- Individuals can express their sexuality in varied ways.

The SIECUS guidelines are intended to serve as a resource on which curriculum planners can draw in fashioning a comprehensive sex-education program suited to their particular school's student population, time allotment for sexual matters, teachers' talents, and attitudes of the surrounding community.

Ideally, all sexuality education programs would cover all of the concepts, topics, and developmental messages included in the *Guidelines*. SIECUS realizes, however, that due to constraints on time, staff, and other resources, many programs will not be able to tackle every topic in the *Guidelines* . . . Educators can use the key concepts and topics as a jumping off point and then work with staff, parents, and/or young people to narrow down and prioritize this list. Many educators prioritize topics based on their personal observations of the needs of the young people they work with. For example, after hearing young people spread misinformation about reproduction or demonstrate a lack of information about anatomy, an educator may choose to focus a program or lesson on *Key Concept 1: Human Development*. It can also be helpful to ask young people directly for their input in determining which topics will be covered. (*Guidelines*, 2004, p. 81)

In summary, comprehensive sex-education programs are designed provide a many-sided view of sexual relationships—physical, emotional, intellectual, societal—as adjusted to the maturity level of children at different age stages.

Sex-Education Program Preferences

Proponents of different forms of sex education offer their favorite arguments in support of the types of programs they prefer. For instance, advocates of abstinence-only programs may cite passages from religious writings, such as St. Augustine's (354-430 CE) *On Marriage and Concupiscence* in which he asserts—as did St. Paul—that the only permissible reason for sexual intercourse is to produce offspring in a marriage. Hence, sexual relations should never be for enjoyment or "the gratification of lust." And while St. Augustine held that sexual intercourse outside of marriage was entirely unacceptable, he did concede that

a certain degree of intemperance is to be tolerated in the case of married persons; the use of matrimony for the mere pleasure of lust is not without sin, but because of the nuptial relation the sin is venial. (Augustine, 1893)

Proponents of comprehensive sex education (information about various contraception methods, different sexual orientations [hetero, homo, bi, trans], sex practices in diverse cultures, and more) are prone to buttress their preference with results of public-opinion polls. For example, a SIECUS announcement states that

a 2004 national poll of parents found that 93% of parents of junior high school students and 91% of parents of high school students believe it is very or somewhat important to have sexuality education as part of the school curriculum. 72% of parents of junior high school students and 65% of parents of high school students stated that federal government funding "should be used to fund more comprehensive sex education programs that include information on how to obtain and use condoms and other contraceptives" instead of funding sex education programs that have "abstaining from sexual activity" as their only purpose. More than 6 in 10 voters would be more likely to vote for a candidate that supported comprehensive sexuality education. (SIECUS, 2005)

The Contending Constituencies

A convenient way to classify the groups that support different approaches to sex education is to place them in three categories—(a) conservatives, (b) centrists and liberals, and (c) parents in general.

Conservatives

In the main, people who qualify as conservatives favor sex education that teaches abstinence. Stricter conservatives advocate abstinence-only programs. More lenient conservatives accept abstinence-plus alternatives that stress the desirability of abstinence over the "plus" options that are included in the curriculum (condoms, birth-control pills, masturbation, and the like).

Two influential Christian groups that qualify as sex-education conservatives are Right-wing Protestants and Roman Catholics. Furthermore, an important political body that has promoted conservatives' interests is President George W. Bush's administration as supported by the Republican majority in both houses of Congress.

Right-wing Protestants. Perhaps the most influential Christian Protestant group is the Southern Baptist Convention because of its size—16.3 million members—and vigorous political activity. At the organization's 2005 annual conference, delegates urged parents to "demand discontinuation" of public school programs that were morally offensive. One vocal branch of the membership recommended withdrawing children from public schools in order to home-school pupils or enroll them in private schools. However, the public statement that the conference issued did not go that far. It only advised parents to "fully embrace their responsibility to make prayerful and informed decisions regarding where and how they educate their children, whether they choose public, private, or home schooling ... [and] hold accountable schools, institutions, and industries for their moral influence on our children" (Vara, 2005).

Officially, Southern Baptists subscribe to abstinence-only sex-education. As a means of judging the success of that policy, a researcher at Baptist-affiliated Baylor University in Texas interviewed young married couples from Baptist churches in order to learn about their premarital sexual experience. The results showed that

The majority [64%] of the couples surveyed admitted to having sexual intercourse prior to marriage. However, the study was consistent with previous findings in its suggestion that Baptist couples were more likely to save sex for their wedding night if they took a formal abstinence pledge ... Six out of ten who made purity commitments did not have sexual intercourse until marriage, while only three of ten who did not pledge purity remained abstinent ... Only 27% of the young people surveyed entered marriage "chaste," having refrained not only from intercourse but also from other sexual practices such as oral sex. (Apparently true love, 2006)

Thus, a religious denomination's official endorsement of a sex-education policy does not mean that all congregates agree with the policy, so that a substantial number of Baptists could be expected to hold a view different from the church's position, preferring instead some version of abstinence-plus or comprehensive sex instruction.

It is also the case that a faith identified by a broad label—Baptist, Presbyterian, Methodist—can actually be divided into more than one branch, with each branch advocating a different sort of sex education. For instance, American Lutherans in the mid-1970s split into two factions—the Lutheran Church Missouri Synod (LCMS) with a nation-wide membership of 2.6 million members (tenth-largest Christian denomination in the United States) and the Evangelical Lutheran Church of America (ELCA) with 5.1 million members. Usually the word *evangelical* is associated with faiths that are dedicated to a literal interpretation of the Bible and conservative social policies, such as abstinence-only sex education. But in the case of Lutherans, the two groups' titles are misleading. The Missouri-Synod branch is the conservative wing that approves of abstinence-only instruction (Lutheran church, 2006). In contrast, the Evangelical branch is liberal, endorsing an expanded version of sex education.

Roman Catholics. The official position of the Vatican in Rome is that abstinence-only should be taught in sex-education programs. As Pope John Paul II wrote in his 1981 apostolic exhortation (*The Role of the Christian Family in the Modern World*), sex education is "education in love as self-giving" that is not "solely with the body and with selfish pleasure" but must be "education for chastity, for it is a virtue which develops a person's authentic maturity and makes him or her capable of respecting and fostering the 'nuptial meaning' of the body" (Whitehead, 1993). Hence, like popes before and after him, John Paul II agreed with St. Augustine's conviction that sexual behavior should be solely for the purpose of producing offspring in a marriage.

As is true in other Christian faiths, Catholics—including Catholic educators—are not all of one mind about what should be included in sex education. This point has been illustrated in Walter Feinberg's book *For Goodness Sake* (2006) in which he describes religious-education classes in four Catholic schools he visited, classes that revealed the extent of pedagogical variation that can be found within a single faith. Feinberg applied the label *traditionalist* to a class in which the instructor taught students "the fixed nature of doctrine as defined by the authorities in Rome" (p. 47). He called two other classes *modernist*, because the teachers presented traditional doctrine but modified its application as they tried to protect the self-esteem of individual students, such as homosexuals, children of divorced parents, and ones who were sexually active. Feinberg dubbed a fourth class *postmodernist*, because its teacher (a nun in an all-girls school) subscribed to feminism and liberation theology. She used historical analysis to show how church doctrine changed over the centuries from what she viewed as a gender-equality position in Jesus' time to a present-day male-dominated church, a patriarchy that she believed could be reversed in the future. Thus, in Catholic schools, "teachers will differ from one another in their view of the moral authority of the Church hierarchy and the emphasis they place on critical thinking" (Feinberg, 2006, p. 47).

Not only do some priests and nuns who teach in parochial schools deviate in practice from the strict abstinence policy of the church, but there are also splinter groups, such as Catholics for a Free Choice, that openly advocate comprehensive sex education.

In a modern-day American society that increasingly strays from traditional Christian sexual values, orthodox Catholics and like-minded conservatives face a daunting challenge in promoting abstinence among the young. Christian educators' appeal to youths frequently involves recommending intensive religious study in order to reap the reward of self-fulfillment that is earned by chastity. Consider, for example, Stafford's (1993) advice about what Catholic teens need to know about sex.

Parents, catechists, and parish youth leaders should stress the importance of Bible reading, prayer, and frequent reception of the sacraments of Reconciliation and the Eucharist in forming a close relationship with Christ. As God becomes increasingly important in their lives, teens will find it much easier to say no to illicit sex. Today's Catholic teens also need to know about the lives of saints such as Maria Goretti, who died a martyr's death to preserve her purity, and Augustine, who turned from a life of immorality to become one of the greatest bishops and saints in the Church's history. Teens should be encouraged to read about the lives of these saints and other famous saints who overcame sexual temptations so that they will realize chastity is a realistic and attainable goal.

One outstanding Catholic who has high expectations for today's teens is Mother Teresa of Calcutta, whom many consider a living saint. In a speech she gave in Assisi, Italy, on June 6, 1982 she said: "It is very beautiful for a young man to love a young woman and for a young woman to love a young man, but make sure that on the day you get married you have a pure heart, a virgin heart, a heart full of love; purity, and virginity." (Stafford, 1993)

Federal and state governments. During the presidency of George W. Bush (2001–2008), the executive branch of the federal government distributed millions of dollars in tax money to organizations that promoted abstinence-only sex education. Most recipients of such funds were church-related groups. By 2005, more than $1 billion had been granted to faith-based abstinence programs.

Tax money from individual states has also been given to churches' abstinence efforts. For instance, the Catholic diocese of Helena (Montana) received $14,000 from that state's Department of Health & Human Services to conduct "Assets for Abstinence" classes. The Louisiana Governor's "Program on Abstinence" furnished money for the same purpose to such religious groups as the Baptist Collegiate Ministries, Diocese of Lafayette, Revolution Ministries, All Saints Crusade Foundation, Concerned Christian Women of Livingston, and Catholic Charities (Planned Parenthood, 2005).

The most widely publicized Christian just-say-no program has been the Silver Ring Thing (SRT), created in 1995 by Denny Pattyn, executive director of the

John Guest Evangelistic Team in Sewickley (Pennsylvania). The aim of the SRT has been to convince young people to avoid sexual contacts until they are wed. Each youth who pledges abstinence is entitled to wear a silver ring. The way the SRT sponsors recruit teenagers is by conducting performances in cities around the nation, often in convention halls or on college campuses. The typical performance is a 3-hour show in which the first 90 minutes consist of live music, skits, and lectures informing the audience about the dangers of HIV/AIDS and the emotional distress that accompanies risky sexual behavior. During the second 90 minutes, youths choose which of two discussion groups they wish to join—one religious (a strong Christian theme) and the other secular (no religious content). Members of both groups are pressed to make an abstinence pledge and publicly attest to the pledge by wearing a silver ring. The actual number of young people who have accepted rings over the past decade is unclear. However, in 2003 Pattyn said his goal was to have rings on the fingers of 2 million youths by 2010 (Saltzman, 2005).

Initially, the SRT was funded entirely by private sources, but in 2003 the organization began receiving funds from the federal government's faith-based-initiatives program.

In May 2005, the American Civil Liberties Union (ACLU) filed a lawsuit against the U.S. Department of Health and Human Services, charging that the Department had granted the SRT over $1 million, a violation of the U.S. Constitution's establishment clause. The ACLU, to support its claim that the SRT promoted religion, noted that the typical show featured passages from the Bible and included testimonials about accepting Jesus Christ. In addition, the silver rings youths bought for $15 were inscribed with a reference to a New Testament verse: "God wants you to be holy, so you should keep clear of all sexual sin." Teenagers who bought a ring also received a Bible (Saltzman, 2005).

In response to the ACLU lawsuit, the government suspended further grants to SRT, and SRT officials immediately altered their public performances, removing all religious matter from the first 90 minutes, thereby limiting Christian content to the faith-related discussion section, which officials said was financed from private sources. The ACLU then dropped the suit after being assured that tax money would no longer be used to fund any faith-related SRT activities. In effect, the federal government could give money to faith-based groups that performed social services, but it could not bankroll activities that explicitly promoted a religion.

During the first decade of the twenty-first century, the U.S. government not only funded abstinence programs, but in 2002—at the urging of conservative church groups—members of the Bush administration pressed the United Nations to adopt a just-say-no approach to family-planning efforts around the world. The United Nations rejected the abstinence-only proposal on the ground that a wide range of birth-control measures was required to cope with the world's health and population-growth problems.

[W]omen's health experts, inside and outside the United Nations ... say Washington's campaign can only hurt girls in the poorest nations ... [More than] 82 million girls between the ages of 10 and 17 living in developing countries will be married before their 18th birthdays. Young women ages 15 to 19 are twice as likely to die in childbirth than are women in their 20s, and those under 15 are five times as likely not to survive pregnancy ... Sex education is not a moral question but often a matter of life or death, especially now that AIDS has begun to affect girls and women in sharply rising numbers in Africa and Asia, outstripping the spread of the disease among men. (Crossette, 2002)

Centrists and Liberals

The word *centrist* refers to people who favor sex education that features abstinence but also includes a substantial amount of information about other health-protection and birth-control methods. Thus, centrists advocate abstinence-plus programs.

The label *liberal* identifies proponents of comprehensive sex education that includes a wide diversity of topics, such as the array of subject matter found in the SIECUS guidelines.

Two types of centrist and liberal constituencies are non-evangelical mainline religious denominations and secular organizations that subscribe to the separation of church and state.

Mainline religious denominations. Religious groups with policies supporting comprehensive sex education in public schools include the Central Conference of American Rabbis, Church of the Brethren, Episcopal Church, Evangelical Lutheran Church of America, Presbyterian Church (USA), Unitarian Universalist Association, United Church of Christ, and United Methodist Church. In addition, more than 2,400 religious leaders signed a Religious Declaration on Sexual Morality, Justice, and Healing, which advocates lifelong, age-appropriate sexuality education in schools, seminaries, and community settings. And a statement by Planned Parenthood Federation of America, calling for comprehensive sexuality education in schools and opposing abstinence-only education, was endorsed by more than 1,600 members of the clergy.

Secular organizations. The website for the National Coalition to Support Sexuality Education lists 140 national, nonprofit organizations and associations that advocate comprehensive sex education in schools. The groups on the list range from (a) *Advocates for Youth* and the *AIDS Alliance* to (b) *YAI/National Institute for People with Disabilities* and *The Young Women's Project.*

A typical sex-education policy of such organizations can be illustrated with a resolution of the National Education Association, the country's largest teachers union with 2.8 million members.

The Association urges its affiliates and members to support appropriately established sex-education programs, including information on sexual abstinence, birth control and family planning, diversity of culture, diversity of sexual orientation, parenting skills, prenatal care, sexually transmitted diseases, incest, sexual abuse, sexual harassment. To facilitate the realization of human potential, it is the right of every individual to live in an environment of freely available information, knowledge, and wisdom about sexuality. (Sex education, 1995).

Parents in General

Obviously such a category as *parents nationwide* overlaps with *conservatives* and *centrists and liberals*. But I include it here to show how general public opinion compares with the positions of specific religious and secular organizations that have issued sex-education policies.

A Planned Parenthood analysis of national sex-education polls reported that 81% of Americans and 75% of parents wanted school children to receive a range of information about sexual behavior, including "contraception and condom use, sexually transmitted infection, sexual orientation, safer sex practices, abortion, communications and coping skills, and the emotional aspects of sexual relationships." Fifty-six percent of survey respondents did not believe that abstinence-only programs would prevent sexually transmitted infections or unintended pregnancies (Planned Parenthood, 2005).

Sexual Orientation and Preference

Beginning primarily in the 1960s, American youths faced a widening range of sex-behavior choices. Premarital sex, casual sex, group sex, and couples living together out of wedlock became more open and more acceptable. The decade also launched "the gay revolution," a social movement that would accelerate into the twenty-first century. More homosexual, bisexual, and transsexual individuals publicly announced their love-making orientation and pressed for what they envisioned as respect and rights equal to those accorded heterosexuals. The result was a bitter clash between tradition and the evolving new sexual standards, with the clash reflected in vitriolic debate over how—or even *if*—non-heterosexual life styles should be portrayed in schools' sex-education programs. A typical conservative opinion about the issue is reflected in a resolution passed unanimously by the 12,000 delegates at the 2005 Southern Baptist national convention. The resolution was preceded by a series of "whereas" statements that furnished the rationale supporting the decree. The following were among those preparatory statements:

Whereas:
The Bible clearly teaches that homosexual behavior is sin;
Homosexual activists are devoting substantial resources and are using their political influence to shape the curricula and institutional rules of public schools to promote acceptance of homosexuality among schoolchildren as a morally legitimate lifestyle;
Thousands of public middle and high schools have officially sanctioned homosexual clubs;

Homosexual activists and their allies, such as the National Education Association and its affiliates, are pressuring state legislatures and bureaucrats to transform public school sex education curricula to promote acceptance of homosexuality as a legitimate lifestyle in grades k-12;

Many public schools are promoting acceptance of homosexuality as a legitimate lifestyle through programs that use such deceptive labels as "Safe Sex," "Diversity Training," "Multicultural Education," "Anti-Bullying," and "Safe Schools";

Any school district that recognizes homosexual clubs or treats homosexuality as an acceptable lifestyle is a clear and present danger to all of its children and is violating the community's trust. (Baucham & Shortt, 2005)

Prefaced by such introductory statements, the resolution then

- Urged Baptists to "pray for the salvation of homosexuals and their deliverance from their same-sex attraction."
- Rebuked "homosexual activists for slandering minorities by claiming that homosexual behavior has any authentic connection with the civil rights movement."
- Instructed every Baptist church to "investigate diligently whether the school district in which the church is located has either one or more homosexual clubs or curricula or programs in any of their schools that present homosexuality as an acceptable 'lifestyle'."
- Recommended that every Baptist church "located in a school district with either (1) curricula or programs that treat homosexuality as an acceptable lifestyle or (2) one or more homosexual clubs inform the parents of this fact and encourage them to remove their children from the school district's schools immediately." (Baucham & Shortt, 2005)

In contrast to the Southern Baptist conservative position, a typical liberal view was voiced in a National Education Association resolution.

[The NEA] recognizes the importance of raising the awareness and increasing the sensitivity of staff, students, parents, and the community to sexual orientation in our society. The Association therefore supports the development of positive plans that lead to effective ongoing training programs for education employees for the purpose of identifying and eliminating sexual orientation stereotyping in the educational setting. Such programs should attend to but not be limited to:

a. Accurate portrayal of the roles and contributions of gay, lesbian, and bisexual people throughout history, with acknowledgment of their sexual orientation,

b. The acceptance of diverse sexual orientations and the awareness of sexual stereotyping whenever sexuality and/or tolerance of diversity is taught,

c. Elimination of sexual-orientation name-calling and jokes in the classroom,

d. Support for the celebration of a Lesbian and Gay History Month as a means of acknowledging the contributions of lesbians, gays, and bisexuals throughout history. (Sex education, 1995)

Some observers have despaired of achieving an amicable solution to the conflict over homosexuality in schools because people on both sides of the debate hold diametrically opposite, unyielding opinions. But as an effort to resolve the impasse, a group of concerned individuals representing both camps issued a 2006 publication titled *Public Schools and Sexual Orientation—A First Amendment framework for finding common ground.* The purpose of the document was not to offer a "proper solution" to the conflict but, rather, to describe a series of steps participants in the debate could adopt in each community to work out a plan that would be at least minimally acceptable to nearly everyone. Such negotiations, according to the publication's guidelines, should be based on principles from the first amendment of the U.S. Constitution.

The rights and responsibilities of the First Amendment provide the civic framework within which we are able to debate our differences, to understand one another, and to forge public policies that serve the common good in public education. (First Amendment Center, 2006)

Conclusion

By the beginning of the twenty-first century, two thirds of American public-school districts had policies about teaching sex education, with most of the policies developed during the 1990s' intense debate over abstinence versus comprehensive approaches. The great majority of policies required that abstinence be promoted. Few districts stipulated that abstinence be presented as only one option among a variety of sex-behavior choices.

In the 1990s, most districts that switched from one policy to another had moved away from comprehensive programs toward abstinence-plus approaches, but not to extreme abstinence-only plans. Thus, two-thirds of all districts that had sex-education policies espoused abstinence-plus that allowed contraception methods to be discussed as effective means of protecting against pregnancy and disease. Around one third of districts had policies requiring that abstinence be taught as the only option outside of marriage, with contraception discussed in a way to highlight its shortcomings. A small percentage of districts prohibited any mention of contraception.

The research team that had conducted the survey of 1990 practices concluded that

The exclusive focus on abstinence promotion in [many schools'] policies is troubling, in light of the dearth of research demonstrating that the abstinence-only approach is effective in delaying young people's sexual initiation. This lack of documentation stands in sharp contrast to the growing weight of evidence showing that broader educational approaches appear to delay sexual initiation ... By emphasizing the failure rates of contraceptive methods or by permitting no discussion about contraception at all, abstinence-only efforts might discourage effective contraceptive use and thereby put individuals at greater risk of unintended pregnancy when they become sexually active. (Landry, Kaeser, & Richards, 1999)

The opening decade of the twenty-first century was marked by continuing conflict over sex education in public schools, particularly over sexual orientation—homosexuality, bisexuality, and transsexuality.

During the presidency of George W. Bush, the federal government increased its efforts to foster abstinence by means of providing funds (primarily to religious groups) to conduct such abstinence programs, although with a ban on including religious doctrine in program presentations. Apparently that ban is not honored in all classrooms, as teachers insert their own views and explain the religious sources of those views. Such practices continue unless someone files a lawsuit, thereby exposing the matter in court. However, in communities in which the great majority of citizens are members of a particular faith, religion-tinged sex education is likely to continue unchallenged.

Religious influence in schools' sex education

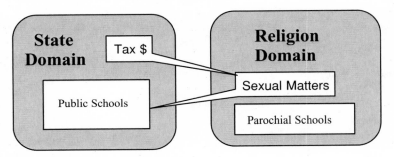

GUIDELINES FOR EDUCATORS

The permissible content of sex education in public schools depends on each school district's policy. The only restriction courts have placed on content is that programs cannot include a particular faith's religious doctrine, such as mottos reflecting biblical passages or instructions to follow Jesus', Moses', or Mohammad's teachings.

Thus, for guidance about what sexual matters can be discussed in public-school classrooms, teachers and administrators are obliged to discover their own school district's sex-education policy.

Chapter 12

State/Church/Secularists/Schools

Chapters 3 through 11 were filled with cases of controversy about interactions among four operatives in American society—the state, the church, secularists, and public schools. However, the nature of those operatives was depicted in no more than a fragmentary fashion through separate cases rather than comprehensively. Thus, the purpose of this final chapter is to draw together separate strands from earlier chapters in order to reveal the overall pattern of the operatives' relationships.

Throughout this book the term *state* has been used in two ways: first, in its generic sense to mean *government* at national, provincial, and local levels; second, to identify the fifty provinces that comprise the United States, such as Massachusetts, Florida, Texas, and Oregon.

The term *church* has referred to religious belief systems as represented by such denominations as Baptist, Roman Catholic, Anglican, Judaic, Islamic, Hindu, and Wiccan.

The labels *secularists* and *the concerned secular public* have been applied to individuals who are neither (a) government employees, such as legislators, judges, school principles, or teachers, nor (a) highly dedicated adherents of a religious body, such as ministers, priests, rabbis, imams, or doctrinaire parishioners. Instead, the secular public consists of humanists, materialists, naturalists, agnostics, and atheists as well as people who identify themselves with a religious faith—at least nominally—but assign secular considerations a higher priority than religious doctrine. Such people are called *concerned* because they are particularly interested in supporting the U.S. Constitution's separation of church and state as implied in the first amendment's establishment clause.

Finally, *public schools* are state institutions governed by elected school boards and funded by tax moneys.

These four kinds of participants in controversies over religion in schools provide the structure for Chapter 12, which opens with *the state* and continues with *the church*, *the concerned secular public*, and *the public schools*.

THE STATE

Since the founding of the American republic in the late 1700s, each of the three divisions of government—legislative, executive, and judicial—has played a particular role in determining the nature of religion in public schools. Legislators, at national, provincial, and local levels have issued laws affecting how religion is to be represented in schools. The executive branch of government has been responsible for implementing those laws, and the judicial branch has judged whether the laws and their implementation have conformed to the nation's basic values and operating principles as defined in the U.S. Constitution.

The following discussion of the three branches begins with the judicial, because I believe jurists have been more important than either legislators or administrators in affecting the place of religion in public schools. Courts have not only decided if laws passed by legislatures are permissible under either the U.S. Constitution or state constitutions, but they have also decided the legality of how laws have been implemented by the executive branch. In effect, the power of the judicial branch has often trumped the power of the legislative and executive branches.

Jurists—The American Court System

For convenience of discussion, the nation's courts can be divided into two broad categories—provincial (the fifty states) and federal. The courts under each category are arranged in tiers, with the power and duties differing from one tier to another. Although the court systems of the fifty states are not all alike, in general they can be thought of as having three tiers, as does the federal system. Lawsuits are filled in the lowest-level court. If litigants are dissatisfied with the decision at that level, they can have their case reviewed at the next higher level, that is, at a court of appeals. If unhappy with the judgment rendered by the appeals-court judges, litigants can attempt to take their grievance to the top level—the supreme court.

All of the cases reviewed in this book have been ones in which the constitutionality of a law or of some individual's or group's behavior was at stake. For instance, the Florida school-voucher law in Chapter 7 was legislation judged by the Florida Supreme Court to be in violation of the state constitution. The cases involving school-sponsored prayer in Chapter 5 were deemed by the U.S. Supreme Court to offend the U.S. Constitution's establishment clause.

An important feature of a court is the breadth of its jurisdiction, that is, the range of people and places to which that court's decisions apply. A county court's judgments directly bear only on cases of the same kind within that county. A state supreme court's rulings apply only to cases of the same kind within that state. Likewise, a federal court's decisions—while applicable in a broader range of places than are state-court rulings—still directly bear only on the people and places within its jurisdiction.

Throughout this book, most cases have been adjudicated in federal courts, so the federal court system has been of particular importance for issues of religion in schools. The three tiers of federal courts are called, in ascending order, *district courts, circuit courts of appeals,* and the *United States Supreme Court.* The nation is divided into ninety-four judicial districts that are organized within eleven regional circuits (plus a federal district that handles special kinds of cases, such as ones involving other nations). Each regional circuit has its own court of appeals. The circuits vary significantly in the number of states within their jurisdiction. For example, the first circuit includes Maine, Massachusetts, New Hampshire, Puerto Rico, and Rhode Island. The ninth circuit encompasses Alaska, Arizona, California, Idaho, Montana, Nevada, Oregon, Washington, Guam, and Hawaii. Some states, such as Montana, form a single district, whereas other more populous states contain several districts, such as California with four.

Two advantages of filing a lawsuit in a federal district court rather than in a state court are that (a) the constitutionality of the case will be judged in terms of the U.S. Constitution rather than of a state constitution and (b) the effect of the judgment will extend to a broader population if the case advances to the circuit court of appeals and is ruled upon there. For instance, in *Elk Grove v. Newdow* (Chapter 8), which concerned the inclusion of "under God" in the pledge of allegiance, the California eastern-district court found against the plaintiff, Newdow. Then Newdow appealed the ruling to the Ninth Circuit Court of Appeals, where the judges reversed the district-court decision and found in Newdow's favor. Whereas the district court's judgment applied only to schools in the eastern sector of California, the appeals' court's ruling applied to schools in all nine states within the Ninth Circuit's bailiwick.

The court whose decisions have the broadest influence is the U.S. Supreme Court, whose rulings affect the entire United States and its territories. The usual way a case arrives at the Supreme Court is by its having started in a federal district court, then moved to a circuit appeals court, and finally to the Supreme Court. However, cases can also be appealed to the Supreme Court from state courts.

Justices in either state supreme courts or the U.S. Supreme Court are not obligated to accept all submitted cases, but are free to choose which ones they will hear. Most appeals are denied. For example, the Wisconsin Supreme Court has typically accepted only 100 to 120 of the 1,000 or so cases submitted to it during a given year. The U.S. Supreme Court holds full hearings for approximately 170 appeals each year.

Hopes and Assumptions

A hope is someone's desire that a potential event or condition will prove to be true—a desire that it will come to pass. An assumption is someone's belief that an anticipated event or condition actually is true—it already has happened or certainly will happen. In the realm of court decisions about religion in schools, some people's hopes are other people's assumptions. Understanding how religion-in-schools cases turn out the way they do can be furthered by our recognizing four common hopes or assumptions about the nation's court system—that (a) higher is wiser, (b) judges are politically neutral, (c) lifelong tenure encourages impartiality, and (d) rulings are just and stable.

Higher is wiser. The fact that jurists in an appeals court can overturn rulings made at the district level, and that supreme-court justices can reverse decisions issued in an appeals court, implies that judges higher in the three-tiered system are wiser than those lower in the hierarchy. Some people apparently assume that's true. Other people hope it might become true, but they suspect that rulings by lower courts are often more justified than decisions of a higher court that overturns a lower-court's judgment, and so a higher court's reversal of a lower-court's ruling can produce injustice.

Judges are politically neutral. When judges are in the courtroom, they are expected to base their decisions solely on objective logic and a sound knowledge of the law that is unaffected by personal values and biases. But people who assume that judges make entirely objective decisions—basing their rulings solely on careful analysis of facts in a case—may need to sustain that conviction more by wishes than evidence. As illustrated in cases throughout this book, jurists' judgments seem influenced by considerations beyond their knowledge of the law and the facts in cases. Those additional considerations include personal values, self-interest, political ties, and religious affiliation. On the assumption that the issues at stake in some cases will impinge more on jurists' personal concerns than in other cases, I would speculate that the degree to which a judge will arrive at an objective opinion will be a function of how closely issues in a given case are linked to the judge's self-interests, with closer issues decided more by personal concerns than are issues remote from the jurist's own life.

The suspicion that jurists' decisions will be prejudiced by personal beliefs is the reason so much political-party combat in the U.S. Senate accompanies the U.S. president's submission of candidates for federal judgeships. In the checks-and-balances arrangement among the three branches of government, the legislative branch—in the form of the U.S. Senate—is assigned the task of consenting to the appointments of federal-judgeship candidates that are proposed by the executive branch. Senators realize that the president will probably submit candidates who share the values favored by the president and the president's political party. Senators who disagree with the president's values typically grill judgeship candidates at length to learn how closely the candidates' values match the senators' own convictions.

The rigor and fuss of the Senate's judge-confirmation process varies with the different tiers of the federal court system. Whereas the process of confirming district-court judges is usually amicable, prompt, and routine, the process of vetting appointments to the U.S. Supreme Court is typically time-consuming and conflict-ridden. A principal reason that senators express more concern for Supreme Court appointees than for district- and appeals-court candidates is that decisions of the U.S. Supreme court will apply to the entire nation, not just to the limited jurisdiction of a lower court.

Lifelong tenure encourages impartiality. Although members of Congress and the U.S. president must come before the public periodically to seek re-election, federal judges need not face that risk, since they are appointed to their posts for life. They serve as long as they choose and— as the U.S. Constitution says— "hold their offices during good behavior." They can forcibly be removed only through "impeachment for, and conviction of, treason, bribery, or other high crimes and misdemeanors." The Constitution's provision of life-long appointments was intended by the founding fathers to remove—or at least reduce—political pressures on the federal judiciary. In effect, if justices need not fear the political whims of the populace that so often accompany public elections, they should be able to base their decisions entirely on the Constitution, their knowledge of similar cases in the past, and the facts of the case at hand.

However, the suspicion that jurists' rulings are affected by extraneous factors—including their belief systems (religious or otherwise) and political commitments—is supported by analyses of voting patterns in court rulings. For instance, close observers of the U.S. Supreme Court are usually able to predict rather accurately how votes on such matters as religion in schools will turn out. The predictions derive from records of the justices' rulings in the past that reveal individuals' political and social values. Particularly enlightening are the ratio-nales justices adduce in support of their votes. Among the Supreme Court judges on the bench in 2005 (Breyer, Ginsburg, Kennedy, O'Connor, Rehnquist, Scalia, Souter, Stevens, Thomas), pundits could usually predict that Rehnquist, Scalia, Thomas, and Kennedy would favor more religious influence in public schools while Souter, Ginsburg, Breyer, and Stevens would favor less. O'Connor would serve as a "swing vote," tipping the scale one way or the other in 5-to-4 or 6-to-3 decisions—sometimes supporting a strict division of church and state and other times favoring a more porous church/state relationship.

Although Republicans have generally been expected to advocate a larger role for religion in schools than Democrats, justices appointed by Republican presidents have not always fit the religious-conservatives model in their votes on religion-in-schools issues. David H. Souter, perhaps the strongest current advocate of separating church and state in public-school matters, was a 1990 appointee of Republican President George H. W. Bush.

In the 2005 Court, Stephen G. Breyer was the only judge who had been selected by a Democratic president (Clinton). Although Breyer usually adopted a strong church/state-separation position, he strayed in the Texas Ten-Commandments case by suggesting that the Commandments monument on the Texas state capital grounds be left standing (Chapter 10).

After the death of Chief Justice William H. Rehnquist in late 2005, President George W. Bush proposed John Roberts Jr., a Roman Catholic, as Rehnquist's replacement. When senators questioned Roberts during confirmation hearings, they asked his opinion of past Court decisions bearing on religion and schools. Roberts said, "First Amendment issues were not where his emphasis has been or his expertise lies, [but] he admitted that the Court's religion jurisprudence really was not consistent and that he hoped to be the means of forging a greater consensus" (Long, 2005). When Sandra Day O'Connor retired from the bench in 2006, she was replaced by a second Catholic, Samuel Alito Jr. (making the Court 58% Catholic). Thus, as 2007 arrived, Court observers waited to learn what the presence of these two newest Republican justices would mean for future religion-in-schools cases, such as Newdow's revised version of "under God" in the pledge of allegiance that was apparently in the offing.

A hint of what the future might hold for religion-in-schools cases could perhaps be inferred from the voting pattern of justices on a different issue in mid-2006. That case involved a question about public employees' right to openly express opinions about their job situations. Specifically, can administrators of public institutions or government departments legally punish employees for their job-related remarks that the administrators dislike? Or is such public-employee speech protected by the freedom-of-speech guarantee of the U.S. Constitution's first amendment? In a 5-to-4 vote, the Court's justices ruled that such speech was not protected, so administrators could punish employees whose comments relating to their jobs were deemed unacceptable by the administrators. The potential relevance of this vote for later religion-in-schools cases is implied in the composition of the Court's majority and minority groups, because the justices on each side of the issue were the same as the ones in typical 5-to-4 votes on religion-in-school issues of the recent past. The five who voted to curtail employees' free-speech protection were the traditional proreligion judges—Kennedy, Scalia, and Thomas—plus the two new justices, Alito and Roberts. The four dissenters were the ones who usually favored the separation of church and state in the conduct of public schools—Souter, Breyer, Ginsburg, and Stevens. Hence, if the voting pattern in the public-employees case can be interpreted as a harbinger of things to come, advocates of the separation of church and state in public schools could expect hard days ahead as Jefferson's wall of separation between church and state sprang more leaks.

Because teachers in public schools and colleges are public employees, educators who watched the protected-speech case feared that the ruling put teachers in jeopardy for what they might say in their classrooms or at educational conventions. As a possible move to quell such fears, Justice Kennedy wrote in the majority opinion,

We need not, and for that reason do not, decide whether the analysis we conduct today would apply in the same manner to a case involving speech related to scholarship or teaching. (Trotter, 2006).

However, such vague assurance left educators concerned about what retaliation they could expect from school administers who might not like what teachers say in public, including what they might say about religion in public schools.

In summary, the notion that life-time appointments promote impartiality in court decisions apparently can far more easily be accepted as a hope than as an assumption.

Just and stable verdicts. A *just ruling* is one that people believe was warranted, meaning that people feel the judges made the right decision. A *stable ruling* is one that people believe will remain in effect in the future, one unlikely to be altered. I expect that nearly everyone wants court judgments to be both just and stable. Therefore, we might ask how just and stable the court decisions described in this book have been.

I believe public confidence in the American court system is strengthened whenever all jurists who rule on a case agree on the verdict. In other words, unanimous decisions are apt to convince the public that justice prevailed. In the U.S. Supreme Court, unanimity requires a 9-to-0 vote. On the other hand, when cases result in a split vote—with some judges agreeing and others dissenting—the public may well doubt that the final decision was either just or stable.

To estimate how well Americans' hopes and assumptions have been fulfilled about just and stable religion-in-schools judgments, consider the voting patterns in the following examples.

First are seven U.S. Supreme Court cases in which the vote was 5-to-4.

- *Lee v. Weisman* (prayer)
- *Zelman v. Simmons-Harris* (vouchers)
- *Everson v. Ewing Township* (busing)
- *Regan v. Committee for Public Education* (parochial-school tests)
- *Stone v. Graham* (Ten Commandments)
- *Orden v. Perry* (Ten Commandments)
- *Minnesota law* (tax credit)

Next are five Supreme Court cases that ended in a 6-to-3 split.

- *Good News Club v. Milford Central School* (religious clubs)
- *Wallace v. Jaffree* (prayer)
- *Santa Fe Independent School District v. Doe* (prayer)
- *Committee for Public Education v. Nyquis* (parochial-school repair)
- *Zorach v. Clauson* (released time)

Rulings in other cases, either in the U.S. Supreme Court or appeals courts, also resulted in divided decisions.

- *Engel v. Vitale* (prayer) 5-to-2
- *Elk Grove v. Newdow* (pledge) 2-to-1
- *Prince v. Jacoby* (religious clubs) 2-to-1

Only one case described in Chapters 1 through 11 ended in a unanimous ruling. That happened when the U.S. Supreme Court justices avoided making a decision about the constitutionality of "under God" in the pledge of allegiance. The judges took the easy way out of a potentially explosive ruling by dismissing the case on the ground that the appellant, Dr. Newdow, lacked proper standing to represent his daughter's interests.

In all of the above examples, one or two judges determined the outcome of the cases. If one or two judges had voted the opposite way, all of those laws would have turned out differently. So how much confidence can the public place in the assumption that laws are just and stable when the fate of legislation depends on one or two jurists' inclinations?

Summary

By issuing decisions about which religious practices are constitutionally permissible in government institutions, the nation's courts have played a critical role in determining how religion is represented in America's public schools. The highly controversial nature of courts' opinions has been reflected in split votes among jurists in nearly all cases, with most judgments in the U.S. Supreme Court passed by 5-to-4 or 6-to-3 margins. Furthermore, judgments have been inconsistent between tiers of the court system, with lower-court rulings frequently overturned on appeal. Contradictory decisions have even been issued within the U.S. Supreme Court itself. Consequently, educators are often puzzled about which religious practices should be allowed in schools and which should not.

Lawmakers—The American Legislative System

State legislatures and the U.S. Congress have affected the role of religion in public schools, but each in different ways.

The influence of state legislatures has resulted mainly from state laws being challenged in courts on the charge that they offended the establishment clause of the U.S. Constitution. When the lawsuits reached federal courts, the resulting judgments defined what is, and what is not, constitutionally permissible. Examples of state laws that have precipitated such judgments include

- The New York Regents' prayer
- Pennsylvania funding parochial-school teachers' salaries
- Michigan allowing tax deductions for parochial-school parents
- New York supplying textbooks to parochial schools
- Kentucky posting the Ten Commandments
- Illinois releasing students for religious instruction

In contrast, two kinds of attempts by the U.S. Congress to influence the place of religion in schools have been those of (a) passing laws enabling schools to expand their religious content and (b) seeking to limit the jurisdiction of the courts in matters of religion. Examples of enabling laws are

- The Equal Access Act that permitted the establishment of Bible-study, fellowship, and prayer clubs in public high schools.
- Special-education provisions that extended tax-supported services to physically and mentally disadvantaged students in parochial schools.
- The District of Columbia voucher plan that gave tax funds to parents to pay their children's fees in religious schools.
- The No-Child-Left-Behind Act that furnished federal money to pay for private organizations—including religious groups—to tutor children who experienced academic difficulties in public schools.
- Legislation authorizing the use of tax money to fund abstinence-only sex-education programs conducted by religious groups.

The second congressional effort to affect the religious nature of public schools has been the attempt in the House of Representatives to limit the authority of federal courts in matters of religion. The most notable example has been the Pledge Protection Act, designed to prevent federal courts from issuing judgments about the constitutional status of the pledge of allegiance, particularly about the legality of the "under God" phrase that was added to the pledge in 1954. In recent years, each time the act was submitted in the House—and actually passed in 2004—it subsequently died in the Senate. If such legislation actually were passed in both houses of Congress and signed by the nation's president, it would probably end up in the U.S. Supreme Court where it likely would be deemed unconstitutional—a violation of the independent status of the legislative, executive, and judicial branches of the government.

Administrators—The American Executive System

At the national level, the executive branch of government is headed by the U.S. president and includes all of the departments responsible for carrying out the nation's business. At the state level, the executive branch is headed by the state governor and includes all departments assigned to manage the state's affairs.

When the founding fathers designed the U.S. Constitution, they left matters of educating the American populace to each state rather than to the federal government. Therefore, the authority to create and conduct public schools is held by the states and assigned to local school districts that are governed by locally elected school boards. School districts are free to design their own curricula, constrained only by state laws that may define what subject matter can be—or must be—taught. An example of a state law that bears on religion is the 2006 Georgia statute authorizing high schools to teach a two-semester course in the Bible. After the legislature adopted the statute, the executive branch of the government was instructed to produce two courses of study by February 2007—one specifying the content of a first-semester class titled "History and Literature of the Old Testament Era" and the other describing the content of a second-semester class titled "History and Literature of the New Testament Era."

Although the federal government has no constitutional authority over education, during the past half century Washington has launched forays into the nation's schools at an accelerating pace. Money has served as the incentive for states and school districts to accept federal initiatives—such as the 2001 No-Child-Left-Behind program. States that adopt federal education programs receive millions in support funds. As a result, states and school districts nearly always accede to the national government's demands. An example of a federal plan that has affected the religious component of public schools' curricula is the abstinence-only sex-education initiative promoted by the federal government's Republican administration during the early years of the twenty-first century.

At the national level, advocates of increasing Christianity's presence in public schools profited during President George W. Bush's first 6 years in office (2001–2006) by the Republican Party controlling not only the executive branch but also both houses of Congress. A strong religious influence on Republican policies was exerted by the Religious Right, a movement dominated by evangelical, fundamentalist, and pentecostal Protestant Christians. During this same period, the Democratic Party—prone in the past to favor less religion in schools—was in disarray, lacking both commanding leadership and a program of convincing solutions to the nation's woes. Therefore, there seemed little likelihood that Democrats and like-minded church/state separatists would be able to stem the trend toward more religious influence in the nation's public-education system.

School districts, as units of the executive branch of state governments, decide what will be taught in their schools. But ultimately, it is the classroom teachers who determine what pupils study, including what they learn about religion. While it is true that schools are subject to constitutional' restrictions on religious content, they can ignore the restrictions so long as no one files a lawsuit, with the case then settled in court. Thus, religious content and practices (prayer, reading scripture, proselytizing, displaying maxims) that are forbidden by court rulings can continue unless openly challenged. The continuation of banned religious practices is likely to occur in smaller communities whose active residents subscribe to a particular religious denomination.

Summary

Understanding the religious features of America's public schools is fostered by study of the interaction among the three branches of federal and state governments—legislative, executive, and judicial. In the above discussion, the judiciary has been portrayed as the most influential of the three branches in determining the role of religion in the nation's public education system.

Table 12.1
Ten Largest Denominational Families in the United States

	2001	% Change (1990–2001)
Catholic	24.5%	+11
Baptist	16.3%	0
Methodist/Wesleyan	6.8%	0
Lutheran	4.6%	+5
Presbyterian	2.7%	+12
Pentecostal/Charismatic	2.1%	+38
Episcopalian/Anglican	1.7%	+13
Judaism	1.3%	−10
Latter-Day Saints/Mormon	1.3%	+8
Churches of Christ	1.2%	+47
Congregational/United Church of Christ	0.7%	
Jehovah's Witnesses	0.6%	−4
Assemblies of God	0.5%	+68

Source: Kosmin & Lachman, 2002.

THE CHURCH

In the 2000 U.S. census, over 85 percent of Americans identified themselves as affiliated with a religious faith, a 5 percent increase over 1990. Only 14 percent of respondents said they held a secular or nonreligious worldview, which was a 110 percent increase since 1990. Thus, the overwhelming majority of Americans were religious, at least nominally. Nearly 77 percent of the population was Christian. The 10 largest Christian denominations are displayed in Table 12.1, along with the percentage of the population that each represented and the percentage change between 1990 and 2001.

One way to simplify the analysis of the influence of Christian faiths on religion in public schools is to divide churches into two general categories—evangelical and mainline. Granted, such a division is an over-simplification that may do injustice to faiths that fail to fit comfortably into such a pair of groupings. Nevertheless, the scheme can be useful for identifying major religious trends in present-day America and thus will be used throughout the following discussion.

Evangelical Churches

Evangelical faiths are versions of Christian Protestantism distinguished by their subscribing to (a) the literal (rather than figurative or symbolic) meaning of the Bible, (b) evangelism (proclaiming the gospel), (c) a personal, born-again experience of conversion to Christianity, (d) faith in the truth of the Bible, and (e) activism, in the sense of believing Christian faith is relevant to the cultural issues of the day and acting to influence society's affairs. In Table 12.1, denominations that would qualify as evangelistic include Baptist, Pentecostal/Charismatic, Jehovah's Witnesses, Assemblies of God, and the Missouri Synod branch of Lutheranism. There are also evangelical churches that are not part of a national denomination and thus operate independently.

Evangelical churches in America and abroad—particularly in Africa and Latin America—have been expanding rapidly. An impressive phenomenon of the past three decades has been the growth of U.S. megachurches. The Hartford Institute of Religious Research defines megachurches as evangelical Protestant religious centers that have

2,000 or more persons in attendance at weekly worship, a charismatic, authoritative senior minister, a very active 7-day-a-week congregational community, a multitude of social and outreach ministries, and a complex differentiated organizational structure. Most megachurches are located in suburban areas of rapidly growing sprawl cities such as Los Angeles, Dallas, Atlanta, Houston, Orlando, Phoenix and Seattle. These large churches often occupy prominent land tracts of 50 to 100 acres near major traffic thoroughfares. Nearly all megachurch pastors are male, and are viewed as having considerable personal charisma. The senior minister often has an authoritative style of preaching and administration and is nearly always the singular dominant leader of the church. Supporting these senior pastors are teams of 5 to 25 associate ministers, and often hundreds of full-time staff. (Hartford Institute, 2006).

America's megachurches increased from 350 in 1990 to more than 600 in 2000 and over 1,200 by 2006. The majority are located in southern states, with the highest concentration in Florida, Georgia, Texas, and Southern California. An average of 3,857 people attend a megachurch each week (Hartford Institute, 2006).

Megachurches, along with increasing numbers of smaller evangelical bodies, are often politically aggressive, voicing opinions from the pulpit about public affairs (including religion in schools) and urging congregates to write and phone those opinions to the White House, Congress, state governors, and state legislatures. Evangelical groups in recent decades have achieved notable success in electing their candidates to both local and state school boards, as in Kansas and Ohio. Evangelicals were highly effective in supporting George W. Bush's successful run for the U.S. presidency in 2000 and his re-election in 2004. In turn, the Religious Right's efforts were rewarded by the Bush administration's providing tax money to advance the Right's school agenda (school vouchers, abstinence-only sex education). As a consequence, the presence of conservative Christian Protestantism in public schools and in the funding of religious schools was stronger by 2007 than it had been at any time in recent decades.

Liberal Mainline Churches

Mainline churches are chiefly the present-day descendents of the major Christian faiths that the colonists from Western Europe brought to the Americas in the seventeenth and eighteenth centuries—Anglicans, Presbyterians, Baptists, Methodists, Lutherans, Quakers, Catholics, and the like. Since the early days, most of those original faiths have evolved into both conservative and liberal (modernist) variants. Conservatives hold steadfast to long-established church doctrine, including a literal interpretation of the Bible. Conservatism's virtue lies in its providing doctrinal permanence—trustworthy convictions unshaken by the vagaries of changing times. In contrast, liberals or modernists adjust their beliefs to accommodate social and technological change in order to "keep up with the times." They do not interpret the Bible as representing God's literal word. The virtue of liberalism or modernism lies in its flexibility that enables it to cope with new conditions. Conservatives call liberals "flighty" and "deviant." Liberals call conservatives "archaic" and "unrealistic."

Particularly during the past half century, conservatives and liberals within a given denomination have formally split into separate groups. In the mid-1970s, Lutherans divided into a conservative branch (the Missouri Synod) and a liberal branch that adopted a curiously misleading title—Evangelical Lutheran Church of America. Although the division of Baptists into northern and southern associations predates the Civil War, the Southern Baptist Convention's exit from the World Baptist Alliance did not come until 2004, when the increasingly evangelical Southern Baptists departed from the World Alliance for the Alliance's "liberal, dangerous, and aberrant" theological teachings (*Southern Baptists v. World Baptists*, 2004).

Mainline Christian Protestant denominations that today qualify as liberals/modernists include the Episcopal Church, Evangelical Lutheran Church of America, Presbyterian Church (USA), Unitarian/Universalist Association, United Church of Christ, United Methodist Church, American Baptist Convention (known as the Northern Baptist Convention before 1950 and formally re-titled the American Baptist Churches in the USA in 1973), the Religious Society of Friends (Quakers), and a substantial portion of the United Church of Christ (Congregationalists). Such groups tend to favor a ban on religion in schools, except for the comparative study of religions that does not permit proselytizing.

The Roman Catholic Church is officially conservative and joins evangelical Protestants in promoting abstinence-only sex education, anti-homosexual policies, the use of tax funds to support religious schools, and the right of students and teachers to wear religious symbols. At the same time, Catholic schools teach Darwinism and do not favor traditional public-school prayers and readings from a Protestant Bible.

THE CONCERNED SECULAR PUBLIC

As noted earlier, throughout this book the expressions *secularists* and *concerned secular public* have been applied to individuals who are neither (a) government employees, such as legislators, judges, school principles, or teachers, nor (a) highly dedicated adherents of a religious body, such as ministers, priests, rabbis, imams, or doctrinaire parishioners. Instead, the secular public consists of humanists, materialists, naturalists, agnostics, and atheists as well as people who identify themselves with a religious faith—at least nominally—but assign secular considerations a higher priority than religious doctrine. Those individuals who continue to maintain an affiliation with a religious faith but favor strictly secular public schools are from liberal denominations—Protestant, Catholic, or Jewish.

The size of the concerned secular public is difficult to estimate. Although recent polls have suggested that perhaps 15 percent of adult Americans are nonreligious, it is unknown how many people list themselves as religious but adopt a secular position on questions of religion in public schools. However, it is clear that members of this public have assumed a very active role in controversies over church/state relationships, primarily by means of lawsuits filed through such organizations and the *American Civil Liberties Union* and *Americans United for the Separation of Church and State* (a group headed by a Christian minister).

THE PUBLIC SCHOOLS

In the religion-and-schools skirmishes, America's 105,000 public elementary and secondary schools have played several roles.

- First, schools have been the source of lawsuits challenging the place of religion in school practice (creationism in science classes, prayer, Bible readings, sacred symbols and maxims, the celebration of holy days, released time for religious instruction, religious clubs, sex education, and tax moneys paid to private religious schools).
- Court decisions resulting from the lawsuits have helped define permissible roles for religion in public schools and the permissible financing of religious schools with tax dollars.
- Schools have served as key targets in the nation's "cultural wars" over which values and belief systems will dominate American society as influenced by (a) laws passed by legislatures, (b) policies of government administrators, and (c) the endorsement or rejection of laws by the courts.
- The belief systems that students acquire can be influenced by the amount and kind of religious doctrine and practices they experience in school. I expect that the more religion of a particular variety that students meet in school, the more aspects of that faith that students are prone to adopt.
- Some schools have been able to adopt whatever religious elements they wished, so long as they were willing to risk a lawsuit. In effect, schools can "get away with" inserting religion into their programs until a suit requires that they defend their practice in court. Consequently, there are always school boards, teachers, and administrators who are able to violate the law with impunity because they are never required to account for their practices before a judge. However, in many cases, school personnel who might be tempted to go beyond the law are apparently deterred by the specter of enormous attorney fees and court costs incurred in defending a lawsuit.

CONCLUSION

The dominant theme linking together all of this book's chapters—1 through 11—is the continuing confrontation between two strong American traditions.

The older tradition, extending back two millennia, is the commitment of most Americans to Christian religion as erected on a Judaic foundation. The newer tradition, beginning two centuries ago at the outset of the republic, is the U.S. Constitution's ban on the government subscribing to any religion, a ban interpreted to mean keeping church and state separate. However, the question of how strict that separation should be is answered differently by different segments of the American population—legislators, government executives, jurists, and advocates of different religious and secular belief systems. A key purpose of this book has been to illustrate how conflicts over answers to the church-state-separation question have been negotiated over the decades.

A final question can be asked about the likelihood that controversies over religion-in-schools will soon be resolved. My estimate is that they will never be resolved to everyone's satisfaction because the adversaries in the encounters base their attitudes on very different belief systems. The foundations of the nation's religious tradition are too different from the foundations of the secular tradition to yield any easy compromise.

The people most successful in reconciling a religious commitment with the separation of church and state in matters of schooling are perhaps members of mainstream religions (a) who do not interpret the Bible literally but view it as an estimate of what perhaps occurred in the past, along with some helpful moral precepts and the vision of a power in the universe that might be called *God, Yaweh,* or *Allah,* and (b) who believe in keeping public schools free from religion except as a subject of study—that is, the study of comparative religions, in which different faiths are described as social phenomena without teachers attempting to convince learners that one faith is superior to the others.

In brief, the controversies inspected throughout this book will, I believe, wax and wane indefinitely.

Notes

CHAPTER 2

1. Citations throughout this volume that refer to the Christian Bible are cast in the following sequence: (a) the name of the "book" within the Bible, (b) the number of the chapter within that "book," followed by a colon (:), (c) the number of the verse or verses in the quoted passage, and (d) the Bible's original year of publication. All quotations are drawn from the most popular English translation of the past four centuries, the version authorized by King James I of England in 1611. Here are two examples of such citations— (Genesis 1:1, 1611), (Mark 16:15, 1611)

2. The conflicts alluded to in this section are limited to ones that concerned theology, that is, ones that concerned the belief systems of the contending faiths. However, it is also true that conflicts between religious groups often are power struggles in which one individual or faction is seeking to be in charge—to gain control over the group's activities or resources; in such cases, the competing individuals or factions have no differences over their denomination's worldview.

CHAPTER 4

1. The quotations are from Schippe, C., & Stetson, C. (2005). *The Bible and Its Influence.* New York & Fairfax: Bible Literacy Project. By permission of the publisher.

2. The quotations are from Bible Literacy Project. (2006). *The Bible and Its Influence Teacher's Edition,* Chapter 3. Fort Royal, VA: Bible Literacy Project. By permission of the publisher.

CHAPTER 7

1. The expression *Blaine amendment* refers to a proposed addition to the U.S. Constitution offered by a United States congressman, James G. Blaine, in 1875 when he served

as the speaker of the U.S. House of Representatives. "Pushed along by a wave of anti-immigrant (and largely anti-Catholic) bigotry, [the amendment} passed overwhelmingly in the House but fell short in the Senate. Afterwards, nativists shifted tactics and began pushing for adoption of such amendments to state constitutions, and were particularly successful in requiring them as a condition of admission to the Union. Such was the case with the Enabling Act that admitted South Dakota (as well as North Dakota, Montana, and Washington) as a state in 1889" (Becket Fund, 2006).

CHAPTER 10

1. The Rastafari religious movement originated in Jamaica during the early 1930s among poor working-class and peasant black people. The religion's title derived from *Ras (Duke) Tafari Makonnen*, the precoronation name of Ethiopia's King Haile Selassie I, whom Rastafari followers revere as God incarnate. The faith "has spread throughout much of the world, largely through immigration and interest generated by Nyahbinghi and reggae music—most notably, that of Bob Marley, who was baptised *Berhane Selassie* (Light of the Trinity) by the Ethiopian Orthodox Church before his death . . . By 2000, there were more than one million Rastafari worldwide . . . Most Rastafarians are vegetarian, or only eat limited types of meat, living by the dietary laws of Leviticus and Deuteronomy in the Old Testament" (Psych Central, 2006).

CHAPTER 11

1. The quotations are from *Guidelines for comprehensive sexuality education*, 3rd ed. (2004). New York: SIECUS. By permission of the publisher.

References

AAUW. (2004, April). *School vouchers.* Available online: http://www.aauw.org/issue_advocacy/actionpages/positionpapers/vouchers.cfm.

Abolish the U.S. Department of Education? (2005). *Theocracy watch.* Available online: http://www.theocracywatch.org/schools2.htm.

About FCA. (2006). *Fellowship of Christian athletes.* Available online: http://www.fca.org/AboutFCA/.

About Young Life. (2006). *Young life.* Available online: http://www.younglife.org/pages/AboutYL.htm.

ADF attorneys available to comment on Newdow loss. (2005, January 14). *Alliance defense fund.* Available online: http://www.alliancedefensefund.org/news/story.aspx?cid=3294.

Adherents.com. (2005, December). *Religious affiliation of the founding fathers of the United States of America.* Available online: http://www.adherents.com/gov/Founding_Fathers_Religion.html.

Adkins, R. (2004, August 24). Arkansas school loses prayer appeal. *Jurist.* Available online: http://jurist.law.pitt.edu/paperchase/2004/ 08/arkansas-school-loses-prayer-appeal.htm.

Age of enlightenment. (2005). *Wikipedia.* Available online: http://en. wikipedia.org/wiki/The_Enlightenment.

Alliance Defense Fund. (2006, January 5). *Schenectady school denies recognition to student Christian club.* Available online: http://www.alliancedefensefund.org/news/story.aspx?cid=3651.

American Association for the Advancement of Science. (2005, April 12). *AAAS 'respectfully declines' invitation to controversial Kansas evolution hearing.* http://www.eurekalert.org/pubreleases/2005-04/plos-ad041 205.php.

American Civil Liberties Union. (2000). *The "high school football prayer" decision.* Available online: http://www.civilrightsunion.org/aclu watch/football.htm.

————. (2002, March 11). *Constitutional amendment on school prayer or moment of silence.* Available online: http://www.aclu.org/religion/gen/16039res20020311. html.

American Civil Liberties Union of Florida. (2006, February 7). *2nd Circuit upholds NYC policy on school.* Available online: http://www.aclufl.org/news_events/alert_ archive/Index.cfm?action=viewRelease&emailAlertID=1646.

American Comments. (2006). *Denied access: Unequal treatment of non-Indian religious symbols.* Available online: http://www.iwchildren.org/eagle1.htm.

American Indian religious freedom act. (1978). Available online: http:// www.cr.nps.gov/ local-law/FHPL_IndianRelFreAct.pdf.

Americans United for Separation of Church and State. (2006). *Prayer and the public schools.* Available online: http://www.au.org/site/Page Server?pagename= resources_brochure_schoolprayer.

Anderson, J. D. (2006, April 21). ACLU enters Jesus picture dispute. *Wren's Nest News.* Available online: http://www.witchvox.com/wren/wn_detaila.html?id=15354.

Anderson, L. (2005a, May 22). Darwin's theory evolves into culture war. *Chicago Tribune.* Available online: http://www.chicagotribune.com/business/content/education/chi-0505220366may22,1,6112119.story?coll=chi-education-hed&ctrack=2&cset= true.

————. (2005b, October 30). Evolution of intelligent design. *Chicago Tribune.* Available online:http://www.chicagotribune.com/business/content/education/chi-0510300281oct30,1,1065836.story?coll=chi-education-hed.

Anglican leader opposes creationism in schools. (2006, March 21). *New York Times.* Available online: http://www.nytimes.com/reuters/news/news-religion-creationism-britain.html.

Anti-Defamation League. (2004a). *Evolution and creationism.* Available online: http://www.adl.org/religion_ ps_2004/evolution.asp.

————. (2004b). *Prayer in public school.* Available online: http://www.adl.org/religion_ ps_2004/prayer.asp.

————. (2004c). *Teaching About Religious Holidays.* Available online: http://www. adl.org/religion_ps_2004/teaching.asp.

Apparently true love doesn't always wait. (2006, March 29). *Agape Press.* Available online: http://headlines.agapepress.org/archive/3/292006 d.asp.

Augustine. (1893). On marriage and concupiscence. *St. Augustine: Anti-Pelagian Writings.* In *Select Library of Nicene and Post-Nicene Fathers,* Ser. 1, Vol. V. Available online: http://www.fordham.edu/halsall/source/aug-marr.html.

Ave, M. (2005a, October 7). Schools may drop religious holidays. *St. Petersburg Times.* Available online: http://www.sptimes.com/2005/ 10/07/Hillsborough/Schools_ may_drop_reli.shtmlß.

————. (2005b, October 26). School calendar will be strictly secular. *St. Petersburg Times.* Available online: http://www.sptimes.com/2005/ 10/26/Hillsborough/School_ calendar_will_.shtml.

Avril, T. (2005, October 11). Few scientists doubt evolution. *Philadelphia Inquirer.* Available online: http://www.philly.com/mld/inquirer/12870915.htm.

Azimov, N. (2004, June 9). Scientology link to public schools. *San Francisco Chronicle.* Available online: http://www.sfgate.com/cgi-bin/article.cgi?file=/c/a/ 2004/06/09/MNGO572ISD1.DTL.

Badertscher, N., & Gutierrez, B. (2006, March 21). Ga. poised to OK Bible studies bill. *Atlanta Journal-Constitution*. Available online: http: //www.ajc.com/metro/content/metro/stories/0321biblestudies.html

Baer, J. W. (1992). *The pledge of allegiance*. Available online: http:// history.vineyard.net/pledge.htm.

Baldauf, S. (2006, January 24). India history spat hits US. *Christian Science Monitor*. Available online: http://www.csmonitor.com/2006/0124/p01s03-wosc.html.

Baucham, V., & Shortt, B. N. (2005, April 29). *Resolution on homosexuality in public schools*. Available online: http://www.exodusmandate.org/20050503-resolution/20050503-resolution-homosexuals-in-public-schools.doc.

Bauchman v. West High School. (1997). *About—Agnosticism/atheism*. Available online: http://atheism.about.com/library/decisions/ religion/bl_l_BauchmanWestHigh.htm.

Bayer, P. B. (2003, October 16). The right call on 'under God.' *Philadelphia Inquirer*. Available online: http://www.philly.com.mld/inquier_er/news/editorial/7023821.htm.

Bearman, P. S., & Brueckner, H. (2001). Promising the future: Virginity pledges and first intercourse. *American Journal of Sociology*, 106(4), 859–912.

Becket Fund for Religious Liberty. (2006). *Pucket v. Rounds*. Available online: http://www.becketfund.org/index.php/case/13.html?PHP SESSID=098140c6162cd10ffcd5a7c8c3e418f4.

Behe, M. J. (1996). *Darwin's black box: The biochemical challenge to evolution*. New York: Free Press.

Bender, M. L. (2004, June 28). *Owens v. Colorado Congress of Parents, Teachers, and Students*. Available online via: http://www.nea.org/vouchers/colosupremecourt.html.

Bible Literacy Project. (2006). *The Bible and its influence, teacher's edition*, Chapter 3. Fort Royal, VA: Bible Literacy Project.

Black, H. (1947, February 10). *Everson v. Board of Education of Ewing Township*. Available online: http://caselaw.lp.findlaw.com/scripts/ getcase.pl?court=us&vol=330&invol=1.

———. (1962, June 25). *Engel v. Vitale (No. 468) 10 N.Y.2d 174, 176 N.E.2d 579, reversed*. Available online: http://supct.law.cornell.edu/ supct/html/historics/USSC_CR_0370_0421_ZO.html.

Block, Z. (2004, May/June). Mr. Newdow goes to Washington. *Brown Alumni Magazine*. Available online: http://www.brownalumnimaga zine.com/storydetail.cfm?ID=2345.

Blount, J. (2003). The history of teaching and talking about sex in schools. *History of Education Quarterly*, 4(4). Available online: http://www.historycooperative.org/journals/heq/43.4/ess_1.html.

Boccella, K. (2005, October 31). Obscure biology textbook evolves as focus of 'intelligent design' trial. *Philadelphia Inquirer*, p. B01.

Brians, P. (2000, May 18). *The enlightenment*. Available online: http://www.wsu.edu:8080/~brians/hum_303/enlightenment.html.

Broadway, B. (2001, March 13). Faith communities in the United States today. *Washington Post*. Available online: http://washingtonpost. com/wp-dyn/articles/A944-2001Mar13.html.

Brock, K. C. (2006, April 10). Christian club allowed to rally at school. *Star-Telegram*. Available online: http://www.dfw.com/mld/dfw/news/14310551.htm.

Brorby, W. (1997). *Bauchman v. West High School.* Available online: http://caselaw.lp.
findlaw.com/scripts/getcase.pl?court=10th&navby=case&no=954084.

Brown, J. (2006, March 3). Top court quashes Sikh dagger ban. *Canadian Press.* Available
online: http://cnews.canoe.ca/CNEWS/Law/2006/ 03/01/1468573-cp.html.

Brown v. Board of Education. (1954). *United States Supreme Court.* Available online:
http://www.Google.com/search?hl=en&ie=ISO-88591&q=Brown+versus+
Board+of+Education&btnG=Google+Search.

Brown v. Board of Education. (2004). Available online: http://brownv board.org/summary/.

Burger, W. (1971). *Lemon v. Kurtzman.* Available online: http://www.oyez.org/oyez/
resource/case/207/.

————. (1973). *Levitt v. Committee for Public Education.* Available online: http://
caselaw.lp.findlaw.com/cgi-bin/getcase.pl?navby= case&court=us&vol=413&
invol=472.

Burress, C. (2006, March 17). Lawsuit challenges how Hinduism is taught. *San
Franciso Chronicle.* Available online: http://www.sfgate.com/cgi-bin/article.cgi?
file=/c/a/2006/03/17/BAGM0HPET01.DTL.

California quick facts. (2002). U.S. Bureau of the Census. Available online: http://
quickfacts.census.gov/qfd/states/06000.htm.

Calvert, J. (2002, December 11). Ohio state board adopts science standards that permit
the discussion of intelligent design. *Intelligent design network.* Available online:
http://www.intelligentdesign_network.org/PressRelease121102.htm.

Canada backs Sikh dagger rights. (2006, March 3). *BBC News.* Available online:
http://news.bbc.co.uk/2/hi/americas/4770744.stm.

Caputo, M. (2005, October 9). Gov. Bush oddly evasive on evolution. *Miami Herald.*
Available online: http://www.miami.com/mld/miamiherald/12855555.htm.

Cassidy, T. J. (2004, March 24). *Elk Grove Unified School District v. Michael
A. Newdow.* Available online: http://www.supremecourtus.gov/oral_arguments/
argument_transcripts/02-1624.pdf.

Cavanagh, S. (2005a, September 7). Views on life's origins. *Education Week,* p. 5.

————. (2005b, September 30). Outside courtroom, intelligent-design beliefs at odds
with scientists. *Education Week.* Available online: http://www.edweek.org/ew/
articles/2005/09/30/06dover4_web.h25.html?

————. (2005c, December 20). U.S. judge rules intelligent design has no place in
science classrooms. *Education Week.* Available online: http://www.edweek.org/
ew/articles/2005/12/20/16dover_web.h25.html.

————. (2006, April 3). Legislators debate bills on the teaching of evolution.
Eduction Week. Available online: http://www.edweek.org/ew/articles/2006/04/03/
30evolve.h25.html.

Christian group alleges New Age beliefs taught in public school. (2005, September 26). *Raleigh News & Observer.* Available online: http://www.newsobserver.
com/news/ncwire_news/story/2804450p-9248436c.html.

Christian Legal Society. (2006). *Religious holidays & public schools: Questions
and answers.* Available online: http://www.clsnet.org/clrf Pages/pubs/pubs_
holida5.php.

Chronology of the American Indian sports team issue. (2004). Available online:
http://www.aistm.org/1chronologypage.html.

Church, L. J. (2006, January 16). Grand County: Two teachers want to lead an after-
school Christian group; district says no. *Salt Lake Tribune.* http://www.sltrib.
com/utah/ci_3514278.

Clark, T. (1963, June). *Abington School District v. Schempp, 374 U.S. 2003*. Available online: http://www.justia.us/us/374/203/case.html.

Cline, A. (2004a). Southern Baptists. *About*. Available online: http://atheism.about.com/od/baptistssouthernbaptists/a/southernbaptist. htm.

———. (2004b). Evolution and creationism: Balanced presentation? *About*. Available online: http://atheism.about.com/library/FAQs/ evolution/blfaq_evolution_jw.htm.

Clyne, M. (2005, November 14). School vouchers taking hold in Washington. *New York Sun*. Available online: http://www.nysun.com/article/22972.

Cockrell, C. (2005, November 3). The 'soul-satisfying' work of repatriation. *UC Berkeley News*. Available online: http://www.berkeley.edu/news/berkeleyan/2005/11/03_repatriation.shtml.

Cohn, R. L. (2001). *Immigration to the United States*. Available online: http://www.eh.net/encyclopedia/article/cohn.immigration.us.

Coleman, C. (2002, March 17). Mascot spotlights Indian grievances. *Denver Post*. Available online: http://www.uwm.edu/~gjay/Whiteness/whitiesarticles.htm.

Colonial population estimates. (2006). Available online: http://www.infoplease.com/ipa/A0004979.html.

Colonial-era immigration. (2006). *Historical immigration*. Available online: http://en.wikipedia.org/wiki/Immigration_to_the_United_States.

Colorado Constitution. (1876). Available online: http://www.colorado.gov/dpa/doit/archives/constitution/index.html.

Compulsory school attendance laws. (2006). *Infoplease*. Available on-line: http://www.infoplease.com/ipa/A0112617.html.

Connolly, C. (2004, December 2). Some abstinence programs mislead teens, report says. *Washington Post*, A01. Available online: http://www.washingtonpost.com/wp-dyn/articles/A26623-2004Dec1.html.

Constitutional amendment on school prayer or moment of silence. (2002, March 11). *American Civil Liberties Union*. Available online: http://www.aclu.org/religion/gen/16039res20020311.html.

Constitution of the Commonwealth of Massachusetts. (1788). Available online: http://www.mass.gov/legis/const.htm.

Constitution of the state of Kansas. (1861). Available online: http:// skyways.lib.ks.us/KSL/ref/constitution/preamble.html.

Constitution of the state of New Mexico. (1911). Available online: http://www.harbornet.com/rights/newmexio.txt.

Constitution of the state of Utah. (1895). Available online: http://www.archives.state.ut.us/exhibits/Statehood/1896text.htm.

Constitution of Virginia. (1788). Available online: http://legis.state.va.us/ Laws/search/Constitution.htm#1S1.

Corbett, C. L. (1995, June 26). Abington Township School District v. Schempp: The day God was kicked out of school. *Secular Web*. Available online: http://www.infidels.org/library/modern/cale_corbett/abington.html.

Council of Indian Nations. (2006). *Indian Self-Determination and Education Assistance Act-1975*. Available online:http://www.cinprograms.org/history_selfdeterminationact.cfm?ep=9&ec=6.

Court rejects "intelligent design" in science class. (2005, December 20). *CNN*. Available online: http://www.cnn.com/2005/LAW/12/20/intelligent.design.ap/index.html.

Crampton, S. (2005). *Why the Bible is the best textbook for a Bible curriculum*. Available online: http://www.bibleinschools.net/sdm.asp?pg=curriculum.

Cremin, L. A. (1970). *American education: The colonial experience.* New York: Harper & Row.

————. (1980). *American education: The national experience.* New York: Harper & Row.

————. (1988). *American education: The metropolitan experience.* New York: Harper & Row.

Crossette, B. (2002, May 20). U.S. tells teen girls worldwide to just say no. *WomensENews.* Available online: http://www.womensenews.org/article.cfm/dyn/aid/914/context/archive.

Dao, J. (2005, May 17). Sleepy election is jolted by evolution. *New York Times.* Available online: http://www.nytimes.com/2005/05/17/ national/17evolve.html?

Darwin, C. (1859). *The origin of species.* London: John Murray.

————. (1887). *Darwin's Views on Religion.* Available online: http://www.origins.tv/darwin/religion.htm.

Davis, P., & Kenyon, D. H. (1993). *Of pandas and people: The central question of biological origins.* Dallas, TX: Haughton.

Davy, L. E. (2005, November 2). *List of religious holidays permitting pupil absence from school.* Available online: http://www.nj.gov/njded/genfo/holidays.htm.

Dean, C. (2004, October 26). Creationism and science clash at grand canyon bookstores. *New York Times.* Available online: httpz://www.nytimes.com/2004/10/26/science/26cany.html?ex=1100581200&en= 6fa918c90f114388&ei=5070.

Discovery Institute staff. (2004, October 6). Pennsylvania school district considers supplemental textbook supportive of intelligent design. *Discovery Institute.* Available online: http://www.discovery.org/scripts/viewDB/index.php?command= view&id=2231.

Douglas, W. O. (1952, April 28). *Zorach v. Clauson.* Available online: http://caselaw.lp.findlaw.com/scripts/getcase.pl?court=us&vol=343&invol=306.

Dowling-Sendor, B. (2003, February). A question of equality. *American School Board Journal,* 190(2). Available online: http://www.asbj.com/2003/02/0203schoollaw.html.

Draper, P. (2005). *The Secular Web.* Available online: http://www. infidels.org/.

Eastman, C. A. (1911). *The soul of the Indian.* Available online: http://www.mountainman.com.au/eastman5.html.

Education group blasts Kansas' evolution view. (2005, December 8). *Kansas City Star.* Available online: http://www.kansascity.com/mld/kansascity/news/13354636.htm.

Egelko, B. (2005, October 20). Lessons on Muslims called indoctrination. *San Francisco Chronicle.* Available online: http://sfgate.com/cgi-bin/article.cgi?f=/c/a/2005/10/20/BAGDCFB50T1.DTL.

————. (2006, October 3). Appeal on school's lesson in Muslim culture is rejected. *San Francisco Chronicle.* Available online: http://www.sfgate.com/cgi-bin/article.cgi?file=/c/a/2006/10/03/MNG4ILH1201.DTL.

Evolution and creationism. (1982). *United Presbyterian Church in the USA.* Available online: http://www.don-lindsay-archive.org/creation/voices/RELIGIOU/PRESS82.htm.

Exodus. (1611). *Holy Bible.* New York: American Bible Society, 1925 edition.

Federal appeals court says Arkansas district flouted order on prayer. (2006, April 19). *Education Week,* p. 13.

Feinberg, W. (2006). *For goodness sake.* New York: Routledge.

Fergusson, E. (1931). *Dancing gods.* New York: Knopf.

Fightin' whites' team mascot has rural town seeing red. (2002, March 17). *Atlanta Journal-Constitution*. Available online: http://www.uwm.edu/~gjay/Whiteness/whitiesarticles.htm.

Filiatreau, J. (2000, June 29). Presbyterian science-and-religion group naturally selects a defender of evolution. *Presbyterian Church (USA) News*. Available online: http://horeb.pcusa.org/ga212/News/ga 00125.htm.

FindLaw. (1985). *Wallace v. Jaffree 472 U.S. 38 (1985)*. Available online: http://caselaw.lp.findlaw.com/scripts/getcase.pl?court=US&vol=472&invol=38.

First Amendment Center. (2006). *Public schools and sexual orientation: A first amendment framework for finding common ground*. Available online: www.firstamendmentcenter.org/PDF/sexual.orientation.guidelines.PDF.

Fisher, I., & Dean, C. (2006, January 19). Vatican article backs judge on intelligent design. *San Francisco Chronicle*. Available online: http:// sfgate.com/cgi-bin/article.cgi?f=/c/a/2006/01/19/MNG6VGPCIB1. DTL.

Fly, C. (2005, December 9). Wisconsin schools facing lawsuits over 'holiday' programs. *Minneapolis Star-Tribune*. Available online: http://www.startribune.com/stories/614/5772991.html.

Foley, R. J. (2006a, February 8). Science teaching gains attention. *Pioneer Press*. Available online: http://www.twincities.com/mld/twin cities/news/local/13816458.htm.

———. (2006b, May 24). Sex ed classes must promote abstinence. *Pioneer Press*. Available online: http://www.twincities.com/ mld/twincities/news/local/14651409.htm.

Fonte, J. D. (2000, January 1). *Anti-Americanization*. Available online: http://www.aei.org/publications/pubID.6842/pub_detail.asp.

Ford, J. (2006). *Course: Comparative religion*. Available online: http://www.rsu.edu/faculty/jford/Comparative%20Religion.htm.

Foundation for Thought and Ethics. (2006). *About FTE*. Available online: http://www.fteonline.com/about.htm.

Fredrix, E. (2006, April 15). City expands school voucher program. *Pioneer Press*. Available online: http://www.twincities.com/mld/twincities/news/local/states/wisconsin/14347376.htm.

Frieden, T. (2002, June 27). Supreme Court affirms school voucher program. *CNN*. Available online: http://archives.cnn.com/2002/ LAW/06/27/scotus.school.vouchers/.

Full 8th Circuit OKs Nebraska commandments display. (2005, August 19). *Associated Press*. Available online: http://www.firstamendmentcenter.org/news.aspx?id=15685.

Fusarelli, L. D. (2004). Will vouchers arrive in Colorado? *Education Next*. Available online: http://educationnext.org/20044/51.html.

Genetics Society of America. (2003, June). *Statement on evolution and creationism*. Available online: http://genetics.faseb.org/genetics/g-gsa/statement_on_evolution.shtml.

Gillam, C. (1999, August 11). Kansas board votes to bar evolution from classroom. *Reuters*. Available online: http://www.holysmoke.org/ kansas03.htm.

Goldman, J. (1940). *Minersville School District v. Gobitis*, 310 U.S. 586. Available online: http://www.oyez.org/oyez/resource/case/249/.d

Good, A. G. (1962). *A history of American education*, 2nd ed. New York: Macmillan.

Goodwin, A. T. (2002, December 40. *Newdow v. U.S. Congress, G. W. Bush, State of California, Elk Grove Unified School District, and Sacramento Unified School District*. Ninth Federal Circuit Court of Appeal, No. 00-16423, D.C. No. CV-00-00495.

Greenhouse, L. (2004, June 14). Eight justices block effort to excise phrase in pledge. *New York Times*. Available online: http://www.nytimes.com/2004/06/14/politics/14CNDSCOT.html?ex=1116820800&en= 8bcf8d3faa6d20de&ei=5070&hp.

———. (2006, April 25). Justices decline church-state case involving a kindergarten poster of Jesus. *New York Times*. Available online: http://www.nytimes.com/2006/04/25/washington/25 scotus.html?ex=1147233600&en= 43289c39f09297ef&ei=5070.

Group defends The Bible and Its Influence textbook. (2006, March 3). *Spero News*. Available online: http://www.speroforum.com/site/article.asp?id=2780.

Growth of the nation. (2004). *Encyclopaedia Britannica* (CD). Chicago: Encyclopaedia Britannica.

Guidelines for comprehensive sexuality education, 3rd ed. (2004). New York: SIECUS. Available online: www.siecus.org/pubs/guidelines/guidelines.pdf.

Hall of Heroes. (2005). *The pledge of allegiance*. Available online: http://www.homeofheroes.com/hallofheroes/1st_floor/flag/1bfc_pledge.htmls.

Hamilton, M. A. (2004, September 23). Lunacy of Pledge Protection Act. *FindLaw*. Available online: http://www.cnn.com/2004.LAW/09/23/ hamilton.pledge/index.html.

Hanna, J. (2005a, October 5). Corkins agrees with board conservatives on evolution, sex ed. *Kansas City Star*. Available online: http://www.kansascity.com/mld/kansascity/news/local/12826580.htm.

———. (2005b, November 14). Abrams: Evolutionists engaged in character assassination. *Kansas City Star*. Available online: http:// www.kansascity.com/mld/kansascity/news/local/13167359.htm.

Harris, S. (2006). *American eagle and Native American Indian*. American Eagle Foundation. Available online: http: //www.eagles.org/native_american.htm.

Hart, A. (2005, January 14). Judge in Georgia orders anti-evolution stickers removed from textbooks. *New York Times*. Available online: http: //www.nytimes.com/2005/01/14/national/14sticker.html.

Hartford Institute for Religion Research. (2006). *Megachurch definition*. Available online: http://hirr.hartsem.edu/org/megachurchesdefinition.html.

Heaney, R. (1980, April 22). *Florey v. Sioux Falls School District*. Available online: http://www.belcherfoundation.org/florey_v_sioux_falls_ scho ol_district.htm.

Hentoff, N. (2002, May 31). Your taxes for church schools? *Village Voice*. Available online: http://www.villagevoice.com/news/0223,hentoff,35348,6.html.

Herndon, P. N. (2004, January 4). In God we trust: Public schools and religious freedom. *Yale-New Haven Teachers Institute*. Available online: http://www.yale.edu/ynhti/curriculum/units/2004/1/04.01.03.x.html.

Hirsch, A. (2005, November 27). Science, faith clash in class. *Baltimore Sun*. Available online: http://www.baltimoresun.com/news/nationworld/bal-te.evolution27nov27,1,3890042.story?coll=bal-pe-asection.

Hirsch, D. (2006, June 1). S.C. clears way for religion courses. *Kansas City Star*. Available online: http://www.kansascity.com/mld/kansascity/news/nation/14715444.htm.

Historical immigrant admission data: 1821–2002. (2006). *Federation for American immigration reform*. Available online: http://www.fairus.org/site/PageServer?pagename=research_research9c29.

How many people go regularly to weekly religious services? (2004, November 22). *Religious Tolerance*. Available online: http://www.re-ligious tolerance.org/rel_rate.htm.

HUAC, McCarthy, and the reds. (2005). *Tripod.* Available online: http://huac.tripod.com/.

Hughes, K. (2005, December 22). Berkner High School clarifies student worship policy. *Dallas Morning News.* Available online: http://www.dallasnews.com/ sharedcontent/dws/news/localnews/stories/DN-muslimprayer_22met.ART.North. Edition2.102ca3ad.html.

Huntington, S. P. (2004). One nation, out of many. *One America.* Available online: http://www.taemag.com/issues/articleid.18144/article_detail.asp.

Hutton, T. (2003, August). *Wigg v. Sioux Falls School District. Legal Clips.* Available online: https://secure.nsba.org/site/doc_cosa.asp? TRACKID=&DID=31873&CID= 164.

Iqbal, A. (2004, April 1). DOJ allows hijab in school. *Washington Times.* Available online: http://washingtontimes.com/upi-breaking/20040 401-051342-5704r.htm.

Is US becoming hostile to science? (2005, October 28). *New York Times.* http://www. nytimes.com/reuters/news/news-science-usa.html.

Jackson, A. (1830, December 8). *First annual message to Congress.* Available online: http://www.mtholyoke.edu/acad/intrel/andrew.htm.

Jackson, S. M. (Ed.). (1953). *New Schaff-Herzog encyclopedia of religious knowledge, Vol. VIII: Morality.* Grand Rapids, MI: Baker Book House. Available online: http://www.ccel.org/s/schaff/encyc/encyc08/ htm/ii.iii.htm.

Johnson, K. (2006a, February 5). Evolution measure splits state legislators in Utah. *New York Times.* Available online: http://www.nytimes.com/2006/02/05/national/ 05evolution.html.

————. (2006b, February 28). Anti-Darwin bill fails in Utah. *New York Times.* Available online: http://www.nytimes.com/2006/02/28/ national/28utah.html?_r= 2&oref=slogin&oref=slogin.

Johnson, P. E. (1993). *Darwin on trial.* Downers Grove, IL: Intervarsity Press.

Joliet Catholic High School. (2004, September 6). *Football prayer.* Available online: http://joliet.faithsite.com/content.asp?SID=1105& CID=85782.

Jonsson, P. (2005, October 31). Banned at the schoolhouse door: Pint-size ghosts and goblins. *Christian Science Monitor.* Available online: http://www.csmonitor. com/2005/1031/p02s01-ussc.html.

Karlton, L. K. (2005, September 23). *Newdow v. Congress.* United States District Court, Eastern District of California, No. Civ. S-05-17 LKK/ DAD.

Kennedy, A. (1992, June 24). *Lee v. Weisman, 505 U.S. 577.* Available online: http:// caselaw.lp.findlaw.com/scripts/getcase.pl?court=US &vol=505&invol=577.

Kennedy, S. S. (2001, February). Privatizing education: The politics of vouchers. *Phi Delta Kappan.* Available online. http://dbproxy.lasalle. edu:2056/pqdweb/ index=143&did=000000067497850&SrchMode.

Kentucky school district defies constitution, posts Ten Commandments in public school classrooms. (1999, August 16). *American Atheists.* Available online: http://www. atheists.org/flash.line/tenco6.htm.

King, D. S. (2000). *Making Americans: Immigration, race, and the origins of the diverse democracy.* Cambridge, MA: Harvard University Press, 2000.

Kober, N. (2000). School vouchers: What we know and don't know ... and how we could learn more. *Center on Education Policy Report.* Available online: http://www.ctredpol.org/vouchers/schoolvouchers.pdf.

Kosmin, B. A., & Lachman, S. P. (2002). *American Religious Identity Survey.* Available online: http://www.adherents.com/rel_USA.Html #Pew_branches.

Krieger, L. M. (2006, March 9). Vote on textbooks upsets some Hindus. *San Jose Mercury Herald*. Available online: http://www.mercurynews.com/mld/mercurynews/living/education/14055497.htm.

Landry, D. J., Kaeser, L., & Richards, C. L. (1999, November/December). Abstinence promotion and the provision of information about contraception in public school district sexuality education policies. *Family Planning Perspectives*, 31(6). Available online: http://www.guttmacher.org/pubs/journals/3128099.html.

Largen, K. J. (2006). *Relg 110: Introduction to religious studies*. Available online: http://www.cas.sc.edu/relg/syllabi/relg110kl.html.

Lawmakers blast pledge ruling. (2002, June 27). *CNN.com*. Available online:www.cnn.com/2002/LAW/06/26/pledge.allegiance/.

Leaming, J. (2000, March 1). Alabama school district settles dispute over cross necklace. *First Amendment Center*. Available online: http://www.firstamendmentcenter.org/news.aspx?id=7530.

Lee, D. J. (2005, December 21). Board chooses Bible course. *Odessa American*. Available online: http://www.oaoa.com/news/nw122105 a.htm.

Leland, C. G. (1884). *The Algonquin legends of New England*. Boston: Houghton, Mifflin.

Lester, W. (2005, September 1). 64% want creationism taught with evolution. *Chicago Sun-Times*. Available online: http://www.sun times.com/output/education/cst-nws-teach01.html.

Levy, R. (2004, November 10). Wisconsin school district is focus of evolution debate. *Minneapolis Star-Tribune*. Available online: http://www.edweek.org/clips/news/us/2004/11/10/index.html.

Lewis, R. (2006). *Up from slavery: A documentary history of Negro education*. Available online: http://www.nathanielturner.com/education historynegro17.htm.

Litigant explains why he brought pledge suit. (2002, June 26). *CNN*. Available online: http://archives.cnn.com/2002/LAW/06/26/Newdow.cnna/.

Lively, T. (2006, February 1). Study urges restructuring of D.C. school vouchers. *Washington Times*. Available online: http://www.wash times.com/metro/20060131-110150-3090r.htm.

Long, G. (2006). *McCollum v. Board of Education*. Available online: http://www.drbilllong.com/ReligionandLaw/McCollum.html.

Long, W. R. (2005, September 17). Establishment clause jurisprudence. *Religion and Law*. Available online: http://www.drbilllong.com/ ReligionandLaw/ReligionandLaw.html.

Look at Berkeley UC freshman admissions. (2004, June 1). *Associated Press*. Available online:www.gjsentinel.com/news/content/shared-gen/ap/National/Berkeley_Black_Admissions_Glance.

Lutheran Church Missouri Synod. (2006). *Abortion and the gospel*. Available online: http://www.lcms.org/pages/internal.asp?NavID= 8174.

Lynn, B. (1999, November 3). *House vote on football prayer is 'shameless political posturing,' says Americans United*. Available online: http://www.au.orgsite/News2?JServSessionIdr010=cctftw3f41.app13a&abbr=pr&page=NewsArticle&id=6166&news_iv_ctrl=1474.

MacDonald, G. J. (2005, May 3). Now evolving in biology classes: A testier climate. *Christian Science Monitor*. Available online: http://www.csmonitor.com/2005/0503/p01s04-legn.html.

Mack, A. (2000). Louisiana school district relents, allows Rastafarian students' dreadlocks, caps. *Freedom Forum*. Available online: http://www.firstamendmentcenter.
org/news.aspx?id=5845.

MacLeod, L. (2000, September 1). School prayer and religious liberaty: A constitutional perspective. *Women for America*. Available online: http://www.cwfa.org/
articledisplay.asp?id=1266&department=CWA&categoryid=freedom.

Mann, C. C. (2005). *1491*. New York: Knopf.

Marus, R. (2005, January). Newdow refiles "under God" case. *Associated Baptist Press*. Available online: http://www.nfbnet.org/pipermail/ faith-talk/2005-
January/004782.html.

Mason, M. (2004, January 20). *Religious education: Could we do better?* Available
online: www.ippr.org.uk/research/files/team23/project 164/Marylin%20Mason%
20Paper_doc1.PDF.

Mateo, F. (1992, July 29). Masturbation a venial or mortal sin? *Catholic Information
Network*. Available online: http://www.cin.org/mateo/m 920729e.html.

Matthew. (1611). *Holy Bible*. New York: American Bible Society, 1925 edition.

Matus, R. (2005, December 30). Florida gets an F in science. *St. Petersburg Times*. Available
online: http://www.sptimes.com/2005/12/30/State/Florida_gets_an_F_in_.shtml.

Mauro, T. (2000, June 19). Supreme Court bans student-led prayer at football games. *Freedom Forum*. Available online: http://www.freedomforum.org/
templates/document.asp?documentID=12727.

McGuffey's readers. (2006). Available online: http://www.howtotutor.com/guffy.htm.

Messerli, J. (2006, February 21). Should government vouchers be given to pay for private
schools, even if they are religious schools? *Balanced Politics*. Available online:
http://www.balancedpolitics.org/school_vouchers.htm.

Miller, J. (2005, April 22). 'Fix' in pledge raises concern. *Rocky Mountain
News*: http://www.rockymountainnews.com/drmn/local/article/0,1299,DRMN_15_
3720499,00.html.

Miller, K. M., & Dáte, S. V. (2006, April 19). Senate committees move along
voucher proposals. *Palm Beach Post*. Available online: http://www.palmbeachpost.
com/politics/content/state/epaper/2006/04/19/a8a_xgr_vouchers_0419.html.

Miller, K. R. (1966). Review of *Darwin's Black Box*. *Creation/Evolution, 16*, 36-40. Available online: http://biomed.brown.edu/Faculty/M/ Miller/Behe.html.

Moon, J. (2005, October 31). Pupils get to have costume fun, but it's kept
within guidelines at area schools. *St. Louis Post-Dispatch*. Available online:
http://www.stltoday.com/stltoday/news/stories.nsf/educa tion/story/
C73026EBF27CF815862570AB00032FC0?OpenDocument.

Moran, J. P. (2000). *Teaching Sex: The Shaping of Adolescence in the 20th Century*.
Cambridge, MA: Harvard University Press.

More quotes in evolution debate. (2005, November 14). *Kansas City Star*. Available online:
http://www.kansascity.com/mld/kansascity/news/local/13167402.htm.

Morello, C. (2005, January 23). Bible breaks at public schools face challenges in rural
Virginia. *Washington Post*. Available online: http://www.washingtonpost.com/wp-
dyn/articles/A29266-2005Jan2 2.html.

Morison, S. E. (1936). *The Puritan pronaos*. New York: New York University Press.

Muslim holidays urged in Baltimore County schools. (2005, May 10) *Washington Times*. Available online: http://www.washingtontimes.com/metro/20050510-
101931-1313r.htm.

National Center for Health Statistics. (1997). *Vital statistics of the United States, 1997, Vol. I: Natality.* Available online: http://www.cdc.gov/nchs/datawh/statab/unpubd/natality/natab97.htm.

National School Boards Association. (2006). *Cleveland voucher program.* Available online: http://www.nsba.org/site/page.asp?TRACKID=& CID=1315&DID=32344.

NCBCPS—National Council on Bible Curriculum in Public Schools. (2005, August). *Textbook—Curriculum.* Available online: http://www.bibleinschools.net/sdm.asp?pg=curriculum.

NCES—National Center for Education Statistics. (2006, April 17). *Characteristics of private schools.* Available online: http://nces.ed.gov/ pubsearch/pubsinfo.asp?pubid=2006319.

New England primer: Or an easy and pleasant guide to the art of reading. (1836). Boston: Massachusetts Sabbath School Society.

New York school allows kirpan. (2005, March 24). *Times of India.* Available online: http://www.wwrn.org/article.php?idd=16080&sec=67&con=4.

Non-Christian religious adherents in the United States. (1995). Available online: www.infoplease.com/ipa/A0193644.html.

Novak, P. (1991). *The world's wisdom: Sacred texts of the world's religions.* San Francisco: Harper.

Nussbaum, P. (2005a, October 2). The divide over Darwin. *Philadelphia Inquirer.* Available online: http://www.philly.com/mld/inquirer/living/education/12797106.htm

———. (2005b, October 10). Intelligent design's big ambitions. *Philadelphia Inquirer,* p. A01.

Paine, T. (1794). *Age of reason.* Available online: http://libertyonline. hypermall.com/Paine/AOR-Frame.html

———. (1776). *Common sense.* Philadelphia: W. & T. Bradford. Available online: http://www.bartleby.com/133/.

Panikkar, K. N. (2005). History textbooks in India: Narratives of religious nationalism. *International Congress of Historical Societies.* Available online: http://www.cishsydney2005.org/images/HISTO RY%.

Pardue, M. G. (2004, December 2). Waxman report is riddled with errors and accuracies. *Heritage Foundation.* Available online: http://www.heritage.org/Research/Welfare/wm615.cfm.

Pariente, B. J. (2006, January 5). *Bush v. Holmes.* Florida Supreme Court No. SC04-2323.

People for the American Way. (1998). *Case in Bible study: Lee County, Florida.* Available online: http://www.pfaw.org/pfaw/general/default.aspx?oid=1357.

———. (2000). *Tuition tax credit referenda.* Available online: http://www.pfaw.org/pfaw/general/default.aspx?oid=2970.

Pennsylvania Code. (2006). *Religious holidays and religious instruction.* Available online: http://www.pacode.com/secure/data/022/chap ter11/s11.21.html.

Pew Forum on Religion and Public Life. (2004). *Pledge of allegiance resources.* Available online: http://pewforum.org/religion-schools/ pledge/.

Pinzur, M. I., & Waller, N. (2005, December 1). Florida's school evolution showdown delayed at least a year. *Lexington Herald-Leader.* Available online: http://www.kentucky.com/mld/kentucky/news/nation/13301851.htm.

Pittman, S. (2005, October 27). Evolution of Darwin vs. design. *Washington Times.* Available online: http://www.washtimes.com/culture/20051026-105745-1173r.htm.

Planned Parenthood. (2005). *Abstinence-only "sex" education.* Available online: http://www.plannedparenthood.org/pp2/portal/files/portal /medicalinfo/teensexualhealth/fact-abstinence-education.xml.

Population Resource Center. (2006). *A demographic profile of Hispanics in the U.S.* Available online: http://www.prcdc.org/summaries/hispanics/hispanics.html.

Porterfield, K. (2006) *Brainwashing and boarding schools.* Available online: http://www.kporterfield.com/aicttw/articles/boardingschool.html.

Postman, D. (2006, April 26). Seattle's Discovery Institute scrambling to rebound after intelligent-design ruling. *Seattle Times.* Available online: http://seattletimes.nwsource.com/html/education/2002953668_id26m.html.

Powell, L. F. (1973). *Committee for Public Education v. Nyquist.* Avaliable online: http://caselaw.lp.findlaw.com/cgi-bin/getcase.pl?navby=case   &court=us&vol=413&page=780.

Powell, M. (2005, October 20). No easy victory ensues in legal battle over evolution. *Washington Times.* Available online:http://www.washingtonpost.com/wp-dyn/content/article/2005/10/20/AR20050 20 01986_2.html.

Problems with the Bible Literacy Project. (2006, March 6). *Christian communications network.* Available online: http://www.earnedmedia.org/cuddy0306.htm.

Psych Central. (2006). *Rastafari movement.* Available online:psych central.com/psypsych/Rastafarian.

Radin, P. (1945). *The road of life and death.* New York: Pantheon.

Ramesh, R. (2004, June 26). Another rewrite for India's history books. *The Guardian.* Available online: http://education.guardian.co.uk/schoolsworldwide/story/0,14062,1247860,00.html.

Ranganathan, D. (2006, January 26). Hindu history ignites brawl over textbooks. *Sacramento Bee.* Available online: http://www.sacbee.com/content/news/story/14116804p-14946146c.html.

Rastafari. (2006). *Psych Central.* Available online: psychcentral.com/ psypsych/Rastafarian.

Reaves, J. (2002, June 28). Person of the week: Michael Newdow. *Time.* Available online:http://www.time.com/time/pow/article/0,8599,266658,00.html.

Rehnquist, W. H. (1983). *Mueller v. Allen.* Available online: http://case law.lp.findlaw.com/cgi-bin/getcase.pl?court=us&vol=463&invol=388.

———. (2002). *Zelman v. Simmons-Harris.* Available online: http://caselaw.lp.findlaw.com/scripts/getcase.pl?court=US&vol=000&invol=00-1751.

———. (2005, June 27). *Orden v. Perry.* Available online: http://caselaw.lp.findlaw.com/scripts/getcase.pl?court=US&vol=000&invol=03-1500.

Religion in the public schools: A joint statement of current law. (1995, April). Available online: http://www.ed.gov/Speeches/04-1995/prayer.Html.

Religious Freedom. (1992). *Lee v. Weisman.* Available online: http:// religiousfreedom.lib.virginia.edu/court/lee_v_weis.html.

Religious freedom amendment. (1995). Available online: http://www.concentric.net/%7EDannemyr/rfa.htm.

Reluctant Messenger. (2006). *The gospel of St. Thomas.* Available online: http://reluctantmessenger.com/gospel-of-thomas.htm.

Riley, R. W. (1995). *Religious expression in public schools.* Available online: http://www.ed.gov/Speeches/08-1995/religion.html.

Risinger, C. F. (1993, August). Religion in the social studies curriculum. *ERIC Digest.* Available online: http://www.ericdigests.org/1994/religion.htm.

Robinson, B. A. (1999, July). Ten Commandments legal developments 1999. *Religious Tolerance.* Available online: http://www.religioustoler ance.org/equ_acce.htm.

Robinson, B. A. (2001, February 21). History of Wicca—Partly real; partly imaginary. *Religious Tolerance.* Available online: http://www.religioustolerance.org/wic_hist. htm.

————. (2002a, October 19). How to have prayers in public classrooms . . . legally. *Religious Tolerance.* Available online: http://www.religioustolerance.org/ps_pra2.htm.

————. (2002b, June 25). Religion and prayer in U.S. public schools. *Religious Tolerance.* Available online: http://www.religious.

————. (2003a, February 21). Court decisions on prayers during graduation ceremonies at U.S. public schools. *Religious Tolerance.* Available online: http://www. religioustolerance.org/ps_prae.htm.

————. (2003b, April 18). The federal Equal Access Act. *Religious Tolerance.* Available online: http://www.religioustolerance.org/equ_acce.htm.

————. (2004, October 13). Overcoming opposition to student religious clubs in public schools. *Religious Tolerance.* Available online: http://www.religioustolerance. org/chr_club.htm.

Rubin, J. (2005, October 1). District scrables to ensure human rights event is religion-free. *Los Angeles Times.* Available online: http://www.latimes.com/news/education/la-me-jordan1oct01,1,7585100. story ?coll=la-news-learning.

Rudy, D., & Lattimer, R. (2004). Science Excellence for All Ohians (SEAO) applauds state board adoption of science model curriculum. *Science Excellence for All Ohians.* Available online: http://www.sciohio.org/start.htm.

Ryman, A. (2005, December 7). Schools wrestling with holiday concerts. *Arizona Republic.* Available online: http://www.azcentral.com/arizonarepublic/news/articles/ 1207nocarols.html.

Saltzman, J. (2005, May 17). ACLU suit sees religious content in abstinence plan. *Boston Globe.* Available online: http://www.boston.com/news/education/k_12/articles/ 2005/05/17/aclu_suit_sees_religious_content_in_abstinence_plan?pg=2.

Samuel, I. (1611). *Holy Bible,* chapter 17. New York: American Bible Society, 1925 edition.

Sarfati, J. (1999). *Refuting evolution.* Green Forest, AZ: Master Books.

Schippe, C., & Stetson, C. (2005). *The Bible and its influence.* New York: Bible Literacy Project.

School board sent wrong message. (2005, November 10). *St. Petersburg Times.* Available online: http://www.sptimes.com/2005/11/10/Opinion/School_Board_sent_wro. shtml.

School board, student settle suit over Pledge of Allegiance. (2006, February 3). *Miami Herald.* Available online: http://www.miami com/mld/miamiherald/news/ state/13778745.htm.

School Matters. (2006). *United States public schools and districts.* Available online: http://www.schoolmatters.com/App/SES/SPSServlet/MenuLinksRequest?StateID =1036196&LocLevelID=162&StateLocLevelID=676&LocationID=1036195& Site=pes.

School prayer decision. (1988, July). *American Atheist.* Available online: http:// www.atheists.org/courthouse/prayer.html.

Science Excellence for All Ohians. (2006, February). *The Ohio firestorm of 2006: State board of education rejects critical analysis.* Available online: http://www.sciohio. org/start.htm.

Science standards articulated by grade level-high school. (2005). Available online: http://www.ade.state.az.us/standards/science/articulated.Asp.

Sex education in the public schools. (1995, November). *The Message,* 20(5), 28–29. Available online: http://www.missionislam.com/homed/sexeducation.htm.

Should schools have organized classroom prayers? (2003, March 1). *School prayer and debate poll.* Available online: http://www.youdebate.com/DEBATES/SCHOOL_PRAYER.HTM.

SIECUS. (2005, May). *In good company: Who supports comprehensive sexuality education?* Available online: http://www.siecus.org/ policy/in_good_company. pdf.

Slevin, P. (2005a, March 14). Battle on teaching evolution sharpens. *Washington Post,* p. A01.

———. (2005b, November 9). Kansas education board first to back 'intelligent design'. *Washington Post,* p. A01.

Slobodzian, J. A. (2003, July 16). Court: Religious clubs can meet during school day. *Philadelphia Inquirer.* Available online: http://pew forum.org/news/display. php?NewsID=2423.

Smith, H. (1991). *The world's religions: Our great wisdom traditions.* San Francisco: Harper.

Smith, L. R. (2004, September 3). *Wigg v. Sioux Falls School District,* Nos. 03-2956/3107. United States Court of Appeals for the Eighth District.

Southern Baptists v. World Baptists. (2004, June 15). *World Views.* Available online: http://www.worldmagblog.com/blog/archives/ 005592.html.

Sparks, J. K. (2004). Religion. *Britannica 2004 book of the year.* Chicago, IL. Encyclopaedia Britannica, pp. 499–737, 767–769.

St. Mark. (1611). *Holy Bible,* chapter 16, verse 11. New York: American Bible Society, 1925 edition.

Stack, P. F. (2005, June 12). Teaching humanity's origins: Evolved or designed? *Salt Lake Tribune.* http://www.sltrib.com/utah/ci_2797617.

Stafford, G. (1993, October). What Catholic teens need to know about sex. *The Homiletic and Pastoral Review.* Available online: http://mafg.home.isp-direct.com/ sexedu01.htm.

State v. John Scopes (the monkey trial). (2004). *University of Missouri-Kansas City School of Law.* Available online:http://www.law.umkc.edu/faculty/projects/ftrials/ scopes/evolut.htm.

Steel, D. W. (1996–1997). "Religious freedom" or hypocrisy? *The Oxford Eagle.* Available online: http://www.mcsr.olemiss.edu/~mudws/ prayer.html.

Steinmetz, J. (2004). *Here is a Roman Catholic prayer to say for graduations.* Available online: http://catholicism.about.com/od/childrensprayers/qt/gradpr04.htm.

Stephens, S. (2005, November 28). Intelligent-design ruling could affect Ohio schools. *Cleveland Plain Dealer.* Available online: http://www.cleveland.com/news/ plaindealer/index.ssf?/base/news/1133170215316170.xml&coll=2.

Stepp, L. S. (2005, September 16). Study: Half of all teens have had oral sex. *Washington Post,* p. A07. Available online: http://www.washingtonpost.com/wpdyn/ content/article/2005/09/15/AR2005091500915.html.

Stevens, J. P. (2000, June 19). *Santa Fe Independent School District v. Doe (99-62) 530 U.S. 290 (2000).* Available online: http://www.law.cornell.edu/supct/html/99-62.ZO.html.

Stone v. Graham. (1980, November 17). Available online: http://caselaw.lp.findlaw. com/cgibin/getcase.pl?court=US&vol=449&invol=39.

Student venture. (2006). Available online: www.studentventure.com.

Supreme Court approves after-school religious clubs in public schools. (2001, July/August). *Church & State.* Available online: http:// www.findarticles.com/ p/articles/mi_qa3944/is_200107/ai_n8989323/pg_2.

Supreme Court will not reconsider prayer at graduation case. (2002, December 10). *Fox News.* Available online: http://www.foxnews.com/story/0,2933,40490,00. html.

Szasz, M. C. (2006). Education. *Encyclopedia of North American Indians.* Available online: http://college.hmco.com/history/readerscomp/ naind/html/na_010900_ education.htm.

Szucs, L. D., & Luebking, S. H. (1997). *The source: A guidebook of American geneology.* Orem, UT: Ancestry. Available online: http://en.wiki pedia.org/ wiki/Immigration_to_the_United_States.

Talev, M. (2005, September 22). Secular bid to teach the Bible. *Sacramento Bee.* Available online: http://www.sacbee.com/content/news/educa tion/story/13602875p-14443606c.html.

Tammeus, B. (2006, April 3). Attorney renews his fight against 'under God' in allegiance pledge. *Kansas City Star.* Available online: http://www.kansascity.com/ mld/kansascity/14249232.htm.

Tanner, L. (2005, July 5). Pediatricians decry abstinence-only ed. *Hartford Courant.* Available online: http://www.courant.com/news/ nationworld/wire/sns-ap-teen-pregnancy,0,763943.story.

Tapper, J., & Sandell, C. (2005, June 9). In Louisiana, a school prayer showdown. *WNT News.* Available online: http://abcnews.go.com/ WNT/story?id=834908&page=2

Teachers get choice on 'intelligent design.' (2005, January 8). *San Diego Union-Tribune.* Available online: http://www.signonsandiego.com/ uniontrib/20050108/news_ 1n8nation.html.

The teaching of evolution. (2004). *National Science Teachers Association.* Available online: http://www.nsta.org/159&psid=10.

Ten Commandments judge removed from office. (2003, November 13). *CNN.* Available online: http://www.cnn.com/2003/LAW/11/13/moore.tencommandments/.

Ten Commandments monument in Nebraska park to stay put. (2005, August 19). *Foundation for Moral Law.* Available online:

Tenets of scientific creationism. (1985). *Graduate School Catalog 1985-1987.* Santee, CA: Institute for Creation Research.

Thapar, R., & Witzel, M. (2006, March 6). How does California teach about Hinduism? *San Francisco Chronicle.* Available online: http:// sfgate.com/cgibin/article. cgi?f=/c/a/2006/03/06/EDGGGHI9881.DTL.

Thomas, C. (2001, June 11). *Good News Club v. Milford Central School.* Available online: http://www.law.cornell.edu/supct/html/99-2036.ZS.html.

Thomas, R. M. (2006). *Religion in schools: Controversies around the world.* Westport, CT: Praeger.

Texas Constitution. (1845). Available online: http://www.capitol.state.tx.us/txconst/toc. html.

Townsend, T. (2006, February 4). Some public schools offer courses on the Bible. *St. Louis Post-Dispatch.* Available online: http://www.stl today.com/stltoday/

news/stories.nsf/religion/story/E6C572FB98BCA4EB8625710B006D9AB7? OpenDocument.

Tropiano, D. (2005, November 14). Drama reflects evolution debate. *Arizona Republic*. Available online: http://www.azcentral.com/ arizona republic/local/articles/1114monkeytrial14.html.

Trotter, A. (2006, June 7). Public employees' speech rights curtailed. *Education Week*, 25(39), 27, 29.

United Nations. (1948, December 10). *Universal Declaration of Human Rights*. Available online: http://www.un.org/Overview/rights.html.

USCCB—United States Conference of Catholic Bishops. (2003). *The Catholic Church*. Available online: http://www.usccb.org/comm/cip.shtml.

U.S. Department of Education. (1995, April). *Religious holidays*. Available online: http://www.ed.gov/Speeches/04-1995/prayer.html.

———. (2003, February 7). *Guidance on constitutionally protected prayer in public elementary and secondary schools*. Available online: http://www.ed.gov/policy/gen/guid/religionand schools/prayer_guidance.html.

U.S. House of Representatives. (2005). *Pledge protection act*, H.R. 2389. Available online: http://www.theorator.com/bills109/hr2389.html.

U.S. Supreme Court: Public schools can't censor religious views of students in class assignments. (2006, April 24). *Charleston Gazette*: Available online: http://wvgazettemail.com/forums/viewtopic. php?t=7525&sid=52f5bb44f34a9e1515f0d05d5f73d168.

Vara. R. (2005, June 22). Baptists agree to hold schools accountable. *Houston Chronicle*. Available online: http://www.chron.com/cs/ CDA/ssistory.mpl/nation/3237327.

Varian, B., & Ave, M. (2005, November 3). Hillsborough commission urges schools to keep holidays. *St. Petersburg Times*. Available online: http://www.sptimes.com/2005/11/03/Hillsborough/Hillsborough_commissi.shtml.

Vaughn, A. T. (1972). *The Puritan tradition in America, 1620-1730*. Columbia, SC: University of South Carolina.

Vaznis, J. (2005, November 15). When classes are out, religious clubs increasingly are in. *Boston Globe*. Available online: http://www.boston.com/news/education/k_12/articles/2005/11/15/when_classes_are_out_religious_clubs_increasingly_are_in/.

Walters, J. (2005, January 2). No sex is safe sex for teens in America. *The Observer*. Please provide the page number, if possible.

Ward, J. (2005, January 8). Atheist sues to ban hand on Bible. *Washington Times*. Available online: http://www.washingtontimes.com/metro/20050108-120519-9586r.htm.

Washington school rescinds ban on rosary beads. (2005, November 12). *Boston Herald*. Available online: http://news.bostonherald.com/ national/view.bg?articleid=111813.

Washington State Constitution. (1889). Available online: http://www.courts.wa.gov/education/constitution/index.cfm.

Weinstein, H. (2006, January 11). 1st suit in state to attack 'intelligent design' filed. *Los Angeles Times*. Available online: http://www.latimes.com/news/local/la-me-design11jan11,0,7737779.story?coll=la-home-headlines.

West, J. (2005, December 22). Decision 'totally misrepresents intelligent design'. *Atlanta Journal-Constitution*. Available online: http://www.ajc.com/opinion/content/opinion/1205/22edequal.html.

West Texas schools adding Bible class. (2005, April 27). *Houston Chronicle*. Available online: http://www.chron.com/cs/CDA/ssist ory.mpl/metropolitan/3156223.

Wherry, J. H. (1969). *Indian masks and myths of the west*. New York: Funk & Wagnalls.

White, B. (1968). *Board of Education v. Allen*. Available online: http://caselaw.lp. findlaw.com/cgi-bin/getcase.pl?court=US&vol=392 &invol=236.

————. (1980). *Committee for Public Education v. Regan*. Available online: http:// caselaw.lp.findlaw.com/cgi-bin/getcase.pl?court=US &vol=444&invol=646.

Whitehead, M. M. (1993, May). Sex education: The Catholic scene. *Voices*. Available online: http://www.wf-f.org/Whitehead-SexEdin tro.Html.

Williams, K. (2005, August 10). *Myers v. Loudoun County Public Schools*. U.S. Fourth District Court of Appeals, No. 03-1364.

Worden, A. (2004, December 15). Civil liberties groups file lawsuit over teaching 'intelligent design.' *San Luis Obispo County Tribune*, p. A7.

Wyatt, K. (2004, November 9). Textbook disclaimer on evolution in Ga. Court. *Boston Globe*. Available online: http://www.boston.com/news/nation/articles/2004/11/ 09/textbook_disclaimer_on_evolution_in_ga_court/.

Young, C. (2005, November 14). Fact and fiction on evolution. *Boston Globe*. Available online: http://www.boston.com/news/globe/ editorial_opinion/oped/articles/ 2005/11/14/fact_and_fiction_on_evolution?mode=PF.

Youth for Christ. (2006). Available online: http://www.yfc.net/Brix?pageID=6552.

Zindler, F. R. (1992). The wild, wild world of creationism. *American Atheists*. Available online: htt://www.atheists.org/evolution/wild.html.

Name Index

Subject Index

About the Author

R. MURRAY THOMAS is Emeritus Professor at the University of California, Santa Barbara, where he taught educational psychology and headed the program in international education for three decades. His professional publications over a 56-year period exceed 370, including such books as *Moral Development Theories: Secular and Religious*, *What Wrongdoers Deserve: The Moral Reasoning Behind Responses to Misconduct*, and *Religion in Schools: Controversies around the World*.